Because You Bear This Name

Biblical Interpretation Series

EDITORS
R. ALAN CULPEPPER
ELLEN VAN WOLDE

ASSISTANT EDITORS
DAVID E. ORTON
ROLF RENDTORFF

EDITORIAL ADVISORY BOARD
JANICE CAPEL ANDERSON
MIEKE BAL
PHYLLIS A. BIRD
ERHARD BLUM
WERNER H. KELBER
EKKEHARD STEGEMANN
VINCENT L. WIMBUSH
JEAN ZUMSTEIN

VOLUME 81

BECAUSE YOU BEAR THIS NAME

Because You Bear This Name

Conceptual Metaphor and the Moral Meaning of 1 Peter

BY

Bonnie Howe

Society of Biblical Literature
Atlanta

Copyright © 2005 by Koninklijke Brill NV, Leiden,
The Netherlands

This edition published under license from Koninklijke Brill NV,
Leiden, The Netherlands by the Society of Biblical Literature.

All rights reserved. No part of this work may be reproduced or transmitted in any form or by any means, electronic or mechanical, including photocopying and recording, or by any means of any information storage or retrieval system, except as may be expressly permitted by the 1976 Copyright Act or in writing from the Publisher. Requests for permission should be addressed in writing to the Rights and Permissions Department, Koninklijke Brill NV, Leiden, The Netherlands.

Authorization to photocopy items for internal or personal use is granted by Brill provided that the appropriate fees are paid directly to The Copyright Clearance Center, 222 Rosewood Drive, Suite 910, Danvers, MA 01923, USA. Fees are subject to change.

Library of Congress Cataloging-in-Publication Data

Howe, Bonnie.
  Because you bear this name : conceptual metaphor and the moral meaning of 1 Peter / by Bonnnie Howe.
    p. cm. –(Biblical interpretation series ; v. 81)
  Originally published: Boston : Brill, 2006
  Includes bibliographical references (p.) and indexes.
  ISBN 978-1-58983-383-8 (paper binding : alk. paper)
  1. Bible. N. T. Peter, 1st–Criticism, interpretation, etc. 2. Ethics in the Bible. 3. Metaphor in the Bible. I. Title.
  BS2795.6.E8H69   2008
  227'.9206–dc22   2008040681

CONTENTS

List of Illustrations xv
Foreword xvii
Preface xxi

Introduction 1
   Overview 5

PART A

HISTORICAL AND CONTEMPORARY METAPHOR THEORIES:
IMPLICATIONS FOR BIBLICAL HERMENEUTICS AND ETHICS

Chapter One. Metaphor and Hermeneutics: A History 11
   Metaphor: Traditional Western View(s) 13
   Plato and Neoplatonism—Smoke and Mirrors: Metaphor as
      Shadow Talk 14
      Platonic Psychology: Passion and Poetry 15
      The Politics of Platonic Metaphor 16
      Good and Bad and Metaphor 17
      Neoplatonism 18
      Plato on Metaphor: Summary 20
   Aristotle on Metaphor 21
      Transfer of Names 22
      Similarity in Dissimilars 22
      Deviance from the Ordinary 22
      Notion of the 'Fitting' 23
      Intuitive Perception 23
      Metaphor and Aristotelian Philosophical Categories 24
      Metaphor's Place in the Aristotelian Worldview 24
      Metaphor and Analogy 25
      Metaphor and Aristotelian Ethics 26
   Recap: Aristotle v. Plato on Metaphor 27
   Metaphor in Medieval Rhetoric and Christian Theology 28

Augustine: Drinking in Eternal Light 30
   Augustine and Christian Neoplatonism: Language, Signs,
     and Theology 30
   World, Words, and "Signs" 31
   Metaphor and Augustinian Interpretation of Scripture 31
   The Literal / Figurative Split 32
   Core Characteristics of Augustine's Approach to Metaphor .. 33
   Metaphor, Figure, and Ethics 34
   Re-Cap: Augustine, Metaphor, and Biblical Interpretation.... 36
Thomas Aquinas... 37
   Essences and God Language: The Problem 38
   Theory of Language 39
   Analogy of Being, Proportion, Participation: The Solution.... 41
   Scriptural Metaphor: Aquinas the Aristotelian Exegete 43
Sidebar: Scripture Study in the Middle Ages...................... 45
   The Four Senses of Scripture................................... 45
Thomas on the Four Senses of Scripture 46
Re-Cap: Thomas on Metaphor, Analogy, and Scripture 47
Enlightenment Views of Metaphor 48
   Hobbes and the Literal-Truth Paradigm 49
   Immanuel Kant and Friedrich Nietzsche: Exceptions to the
     Rule.. 50
Views of Metaphor in Western Tradition: Summary 53
Metaphor and Ethics 54
Why the Need for a New Theory?.................................. 55
   Patterns in usage of metaphors and clusters of metaphors..... 55
   Ordinary, everyday usage of metaphorical language 56
   Conventional and Stock Metaphors 56
   Asymmetric metaphors 56
   Semantic change 57
   Inconsistent inferences and usages 57

Chapter Two. A Contemporary Theory of Metaphor................ 59
Conceptual and Experiential Grounding.......................... 60
Category Structure Concepts 62
   Prototype Theory 62
   Radial Categories 63
   Frame and Schema Semantics 64
   Mental Spaces... 66
   Domains 66

The Structure of Metaphor 69
  Mapping.. 69
  Notation and Naming Metaphors.............................. 70
  Directionality... 71
  Image Metaphors: Distinguishing Image from Conceptual
    Metaphor Mappings 72
  Image Schema Mappings.. 75
  Novel Metaphors, Alternative Mappings, and Interpretation   77
  The Invariance Principle 78
  Inference Structure 79
  Primary Metaphors 81
  Complex Metaphors and Blends................................ 84
  Idiomatic Metaphors 88
Metonymy... 90
Cultural Models and Beliefs, Choices and Ethos................. 92
Reading as Mental Space Blending................................ 94
Responses to Traditional Views 95
Literal Meaning Theory.. 96
  The use of the same words across conceptual domains 97
  The use of the same inference patterns across conceptual
    domains... 97
  The use of conceptual frameworks............................. 97
Methodology that Fails to Generalize Properly 98
The Dead Metaphor Theory 98
The Interaction Theory or Bi-Directionality Mistake 99
The "Linguistics Expressions Only" Position..................... 99
The "It's All Metaphor" Position 99
The 'It's All (or Mostly) Analogy' Position...................... 100
Conclusion: Why Metaphor?.. 106

Chapter Three. Two 'Analogical Imagination' Approaches to
  Metaphor and NT Ethics 109
  Scripture & the Analogical Imagination: William Spohn's Go
    and Do Likewise 110
  Spohn's Strengths 112
  Spohn's Approach to the New Testament 114
  Analogical and Moral Imagination 115
  Metaphor in the Analogical Mix................................ 119
  Back to the Story, Forward to Appropriation.................. 120
  Conclusion: Cognitivist Responses and Questions 121

Unified Moral Vision: Richard Hays' Approach to NT Ethics ... 127
    Section Overview 128
    The 'Problem(s)' and Hays' Goals 128
    Definition(s) of Metaphor 129
    Hays on Analogy Versus Metaphor 130
Hays' Analytical Model and Methods 132
The Descriptive Task 132
The Daunting Ditch and Other Matters 133
    Descriptive Evidence—Images and Metaphors 135
    Summary: Cognitive Perspectives on Hays' Descriptive
        Methods 139
The Synthetic Task 140
    Kelsey's 'Single Synoptic' Model 141
    Focal Images As Singular Synoptics 142
    Summary: Tri-focal Vision as Synthetic Model 146
The Hermeneutical Task: Reading Other People's Mail 146
    'Using' the Texts; Moral Judgment as 'Metaphor-Making' 148
    Modes of Appeal to Scripture: Rules, Principles, Paradigms,
        Symbolic World 150
Diagnostic Review of Five Approaches 151
The Pragmatic Task 152
Conclusion: Hay's Moral Vision 153
Questions and Issues Raised by 'AI' Approaches 156
Concluding Question: Interdisciplinarity? 158
    Alternative Model of Interdisciplinarity for Biblical Ethics:
        Scripture as Exemplar 158

PART B

CONCEPTUAL METAPHOR IN I PETER:
METHODOLOGICAL DEMONSTRATION

Introduction 165

Chapter Four. Before Reading 1 Peter 167
    Excursus on Discourse 168
    Reading and Writing as Acts of the Human Mind 169
    Who is Reading? Conventions and Communities: Conceptual,
        Linguistic, Literary 173
    Is Nothing Sacred? The Role of Belief in Reading 1 Peter 176

Reading 1 Peter *As* a Letter 178
Linguistic Community and Convention 179
Blended Spaces, Multiple Reading Communities 181
So What? Moral Politics and Why Reading 1 Peter Matters 182
Conclusion: Disposition Before Reading Matters 184

Chapter Five. Metamoral Metaphors: Moral Accounting and
  Authority 185
  About Metaphors for Morality 185
  The Experiential Basis of Metaphors in Moral Discourse 188
  Moral Language and Moral Logic 189
  Moral Accounting: The General Metaphor 191
    Linguistic Evidence: The General Moral Accounting
      Metaphor in 1 Peter 193
    Sub-Categories: Moral Accounting Schemes in 1 Peter 196
    Reciprocation and Retribution 197
    Restitution 199
    Altruism 199
    Related 1st-century Schemes: Debt Slavery and Ransom 201
    Debt Slavery Frame 201
    Variation on the Scheme of Debt Slavery: Ransom or
      Deliverance 204
    λυτρόωμαι—Ransom Reconsidered 206
  Judgment and Moral Bookkeeping 208
  Slots and Relations: Alternate Method 213
  Variations on the Themes of Moral Accounting 216
    The Books and the Account Holders 216
    The Day or Time of Judgment 217
    The Offenses: Shame versus Guilt 218
    The Account Judges 219
  Significance of Accounting and Judgment 219
  Summary: Moral Accounting Schemes and 1 Peter 220
  Moral Authority and the Great Chain of Being 222
    Literal Authority 223
    Moral Authority 225
    Κύριος and Authority in Households 225
  The Great Chain of Being 227
    The Basic Great Chain 228
    Moral Implications: Macrocosm and Microcosm 230

Peter's Point 231
Summary... 231

Chapter Six. Living in Christ 233
   Good Behavior 'in Christ'... 234
   Various NT Uses of ἐν... 235
   Ἐν in 1 Peter.. 237
   Characters as Conceptual Landmarks............................. 239
   Metonymy 'in Christ'... 239
   Usage of ἐν in Reference to Conduct or Behavior 240
   Coordinated Spatial Metaphors: In and Out, Into and Out of .. 246
   Summary: 'in Christ' Demonstrated; Four Coordinated
      Domains... 248

Chapter Seven. Time and Events: Structured Space for Moral
   Living... 249
   Events and Time: About the Domains 250
   Method: How to Read for Time Concepts......................... 250
   Metonymy and Definitions of Time 251
   The Metaphorization of Time 251
   Spatial Time 252
   Past Time as Place: Behavior *then* 253
   Beyond the Present Here and Now: Life *in* Eternal Spatial
      Time... 254
   Καιρός: Blending *Divine* and Human Time....................... 255
   Spatial Time: Summary 256
   The Moving Time Metaphor 257
   The Time-Substance Variation 258
   Timely Metonymies 259
      Days for Era or Lifespan: Metonymic Definitions of Time 259
      Blended Metaphors and Metonymies 261
      Summary: Time and Morality in 1 Peter 262

Chapter Eight. Living in the Nation, in the Household, and in
   the Body... 265
   Ἐν τοῖς ἔθνεσιν: Christian Morality In Social-Political Reality ... 265
      People Who Belong *As* A People 266
      People who are Exiles.. 269
      Jesus Christ as Prototypical Stranger............................. 276

Ἐν τοῖς ἔθνεσιν As Site of Moral Interplay; Court of Moral
  Judgment 276
 Summary: Moral Conduct & Moral Accounting ἐν τοῖς
  ἔθνεσιν   278
Οἴκου τοῦ Θεοῦ—Living In God's Household 279
 Household Frame 280
 What Is and Is Not Metaphorical 283
 The House For Household Metonymy 284
 The Church Is God's Household 285
 The Brotherhood 287
 Brothers (and Daughters) Are Heirs 288
 God as Paterfamilias: Honor and Holiness 289
 Traditional Israelite Household: Blessing and Honor 290
 Ἐν ὀνόματι Χριστοῦ—The Family Name 290
 The *Cognitive* Power of Household Conventions 291
 Nested Houses or Spheres 292
Ἐν τῷ σώματι, ἐν σαρκὶ βιῶσαι: Good Living In the Body 292
 Methodology and Reading Process Issues 294
 Body, Ψυχή and Βίος: Sites for Display of Good and Evil 294
 The FORCE of Bodily Desire 298
 Good Desire / Bodily Goodness 302
 Misreading Desire 304
 Body, Desire and Holiness: What Does Peter Teach? 306
Conclusion: Metaphors Christians Live In and By 307

Chapter Nine. After Reading 1 Peter........................... 309
 Moral Accounting and Authority in 1 Peter 311
  Individual and Collective Accountability 312
  Moral Accounting and Deontology 313
  Justice Models: Blame and Guilt Versus Shame and Honor ... 313
  Deliverance or Release and Suffering as Payment of Moral
   Debt 314
  Well-Being, 1st-Century Style 315
  Rejection of Retaliation and Retribution 315
  Moral Authority Structures 317
  Conclusion: Exemplary Response to Moral Accounting in
   1 Peter 319
 Timely Good Behavior 'in Christ' 319
  Exclusive Christianity 320
  Χρόνος and Καιρός: Time and Time Again 320

Apocalyptic Now? 322
Lifespans (Individual, National) and History are Morally
    Meaningful 322
Moral Development 323
Christ as Paradigm 323
Christian Living In Social-Political Reality 324
Exiles 324
Questions 326
Good Living 'in the Household' 327
Household Code 328
Slavery 328
Wives 330
Obedience 330
'In the Body': Body as Site for Moral Struggle 331
Ethics Review 333
Starting Point 333
Loyalties 334
Values 334
Normative Modes: Duty vs. Teleology vs. Character 335
Authorities 336
Autonomy and Agency 336
Motivation 336
Model of Justice 337
Freedom 337
Virtue and Character 338
Some Implications for NT hermeneutics 338
Changing minds: Translating versus understanding 338
Framing the Moral Discourse: Epistle, Exhortation,
    Exemplar 338
Reading Communities 339
Blended Spaces 339
Conclusion: Responsive Reading of 1 Peter 340

Conclusion. Because You Bear this Name 341
Implications for Cognitive Linguistics 342
Interdisciplinarity Required and Revised 344
Scripture and Ethics 345
The 'Problem(s)' 346
Exemplar, not Source 347

Metaphorical Moral Imagination versus Analogical
    Imagination 348
Paradigm Shift 349
Universal Foundations 349
Grounding Cross-cultural Ethical Critique 350
Lively Moral Discourse 352
Required Reading 353
Hard Reading 354
Coda: Why go to all this trouble? 355

Appendices 357
  Appendix to Chapter Two. Variations of the Literal Truth
      Theory 357
  Appendix to Chapter Five. The Moral Bookkeeping Schema.
      Instantiation in 1 Peter 359
  Appendix to Chapter Six. "Living in Christ" 365
  Appendix to Chapter Eight. Time and Events: Structured
      Spaces for Moral Living 366
  Appendix to Chapter Nine 367

Bibliography 371
  Primary Sources 371
  History of Metaphor and Hermeneutics; Traditional
      Approaches to Metaphor 372
  Conceptual Metaphor Theory and Method 373
  Reading Theory 374
  Biblical Hermeneutics and Theological Approaches to the
      Figurative 375
  1 Peter 377
  New Testament—Cultural Background 378
  Biblical Reference Works 379
  Miscellaneous Works 379

Author Index 381
Subject Index 383

LIST OF ILLUSTRATIONS

Blend Diagram 1: Standard Blend 86
Blend Diagram 2: Roaring Lion Adversary 87
Blend Diagram 3: Reading Moral Discourse as Blending 94
Moral Debt Trial Blend 212
Moral Debt Trial Megablend 214
Container Schematic Logic 237
The "in Christ" Container Schema 238
Concept: Move Out of One Space Into Another 247
Chart: Exile Source Domain Frame 270
Chart: Christians in Asia Minor are Exiles from their Native
 Lands 273
Chart: Christians in Asia Minor are Exiles from Heaven 274
Chart: 1st-Century Οἶκος Frame 280

FOREWORD

> *Metaphor is not a mere matter of words, not based on similarity, not just a feature of poetic or rhetorical language, and not deviant. Rather, metaphor is conceptual, not merely linguistic. A metaphor is a systematic conceptual mapping from one conceptual domain (the source) onto another (the target). It may introduce conceptual structure. And metaphor functions primarily to allow sensory-motor reasoning to apply to subjective judgements.*[1]

Tightly packed as it is, this claim, if taken seriously, changes everything about the way we understand language, the way we think about thinking. From the pioneering work in neurobiology in the 17th century to advances in the neurosciences in the past two decades, it has become irrefutably clear that thought is largely unconscious, the mind is embodied, and our thinking is metaphorical. Accordingly, "metaphor" cannot be relegated to the margins of literary window-dressing or examined as merely poetic phenomenon or rhetorical device. Metaphor is not a literary technique but a sensory phenomenon, a cross-activation whereby seemingly unrelated things, like "sharp" and "cheese," are linked in the brain[2]

The world of biblical studies has gone about its business quietly, unaffected by these tectonic shifts, largely unaware of the quiet revolution gathering around the work of George Lakoff, Mark Johnson, Eve Sweetser, Mark Turner, and other cognitive linguists. Content with an old-world understanding of symbols and ideas, disembodied and abstract, biblical scholars have recognized the importance of metaphor, but have usually treated it as evidence of a writer's cultural conditioning or as flowery decoration. In either case, we learned that, like peeling off

---

[1] George Lakoff, "How the Body Shapes Thought: Thinking with an All-Too-Human Brain," in *The Nature and Limits of Human Understanding* (ed. Anthony Sanford; The 2001 Gifford Lectures at the University of Glasgow; London: T. & T. Clark, 2003), 49–74 (62).

[2] See the accessible discussion in V.S. Ramachandran, *A Brief Tour of Human Consciousness: From Imposter Poodles to Purple Numbers* (New York: Pi, 2004), esp. pp. 60–82.

the wrapping paper of a birthday present, utterances in biblical texts could be stripped of their metaphorical garments so as to get at the real message. Indeed, this was a necessary first step for those desiring to enclothe the biblical message in the metaphorical world of contemporary audiences. The challenge would center here: how to negotiate the gaps between then and now, or span the chasms from that world to this one. With the help of the work of cognitive linguists, we now see that even our way of stating the problem contributed to the problem.

To Bonnie Howe belongs the distinction of being one of the first, if not the first, to press the question how cognitive linguistics might reshape how we read the Bible, and particularly how we read the Bible as Scripture in moral discourse. Of course, she is not the first to recognize the importance of metaphor in discussions about the role of Scripture in ethics. This is well-worn territory, on display most recently, and perhaps best, in the work of a New Testament scholar like Richard Hays or a moral theologian like Bill Spohn. Spohn and Hays were working with an old-world notion of "metaphor," however, which located the hermeneutical quandary in the wrong place and, therefore, whose utility was limited.

Attempts to relate Scripture and ethics have been plagued with yet another malady. Since the late 1700s, when Johann Philipp Gabler taught us to distinguish pointedly the descriptive and prescriptive modes of the theological enterprise, the search for historical meaning has been sundered from the articulation of transcendent meaning. The hermeneutical model that ensued posited the linear movement from "what it meant" to "what it means," requiring a kind of scholarly baton-passing from the exegete to the theologian to the ethicist. This all but ensured that the biblical materials would be sidelined in serious ethical inquiry. After all, that was then and this is now. What is more, what are we to make of the diversity of the biblical materials? If they cannot agree to speak with a common ethical voice, how might biblical texts provide the foundation needed for contemporary moral discourse?

Howe refocuses then redirects the conversation in ways that hold genuine promise. Rather than discover and retrieve ancient truth from the biblical materials for those contemporary communities that look to the Bible as authoritative Scripture in theology and ethics, rather than setting down yet another pair of supports for building a bridge across the ugly ditch separating ancient and contemporary worlds, she insists that Scripture is already engaging, and engaging us, in moral discourse. She uses the tools of conceptual metaphor for reading 1 Peter as an exemplar of Christian moral discourse. As her work demonstrates, this is not an exercise in descriptive ethics serving as prerequisite to the real work of ethical inquiry; rather, it is itself already ethical engagement in the service of human formation.

Bonnie Howe sets before us a proposal for Scripture As Exemplar. In doing so, she issues an invitation for others to engage in this important work and underscores how much work there is yet to do. It is a good thing, then, that her proposal is itself exemplary in showing the way.

Joel B. Green

PREFACE

ὅν οὐκ ἰδόντες ἀγαπᾶτε

Ἀγαπητοί, *beloved*, this work could not have been brought to completion without the support of many. Special thanks to my husband Alan and sons Jonathan and Andrew for persevering to the end of "the big, fat book." Jon and Drew, your tech support was indispensable, but even more moving is your deep affirmation. You honor me. Thank you.

I was well supported by the community of scholars that is the Graduate Theological Union, and especially by my dissertation committee's gentle, adept midwifery. Judith Berling, Joel Green, Martha Stortz and Eve Sweetser: What an amazing gift your mentorship is. Thank you.

Thanks, too, to the New College Berkeley and RUMC communities. I recall especially the Rockridge 1 Peter study group and the NCB seminar and workshop students. Your kindness and courage as we tried out some of these ideas and methods was most gratifying.

So many friends in Christ—'αγαπητοί, *beloved*—have stood with me, have walked with me on this journey. I cannot name them all here, but I thank especially the Ramos-Thompson family, the GTU "Colleagues", and Therese DesCamp. Without you, the book simply could not have been done. Thanks to all of those who have lovingly encouraged me to recognize the metaphors I live by—especially those who have a shared vision of the life of the beloved on this leg of the journey, East of Eden.

INTRODUCTION

For we all of us, grave or light, get our thoughts entangled in metaphors, and act fatally on the strength of them.

—George Eliot[1]

Metaphors entangle thoughts and thereby engender ill-considered actions. This is a standard view of the relationship between metaphors and morals. If it is correct, it would be prudent to excise metaphor from thought and, by extension, from moral discourse and ethical analysis altogether. Right choices, good moral actions, would follow from cool, untangled, syllogistic reason.

No wonder, then, that ethics, including Christian ethics, has relied principally on cool, Cartesian reason, wedded—at least in liberal American ethics—to a pragmatic consequentialism. There is in the field of ethics an occasional flurry of interest in the imaginative. Kant comes to mind, as does Hume, and now Martha Nussbaum. But on the whole, we are schooled to eschew entanglement with metaphors and other emotive devices. Morality is about patterns and standards in human behavior in relation to some notion of the good versus the bad. If ethics is about noticing how people think about those patterns and standards, and analyzing decision-making processes to make normative judgments and recommendations, then the ethicist ought to begin by clearing out the metaphorical underbrush in any given case or dilemma. The metaphorical is associated with the emotive, and in the formal garden of cool reason, emotive metaphors are "mere" metaphors. But they are not merely exotics; they are, in many final analyses, treated as noxious plants. They have to be weeded out in order to reveal the operative argument, so that its merits may be assayed: this is standard procedure.

There has been, then, a metaphor-thought split in ethics. This split also underlies a perennial problem Christian ethicists wrestle with, the "problem" of Scripture and ethics. How can a cogent, universal ethic

---

[1] George Eliot, *Middlemarch* (London: Penguin Classics, 1994 [1871–1872]), 85.

be founded upon such a set of wildly diverse documents as the Christian Scriptures—or even upon the sayings of such a sage as Jesus, who "spake in parables"? This traditional model, the "metaphors tangle thoughts" model, has generally held sway in the post-Enlightenment biblical scholarly guild, as well. Metaphor has been treated mostly as a poetic phenomenon and rhetorical device.

Scholarly readers interested in the ethical and moral aspects of the biblical texts have generally been of two minds with regard to this situation. One tendency has been to evaluate the tangled-in-metaphor-and-parable character of the texts as evidence of their cultural embeddedness; the metaphors belong to ancient symbol systems. In the scholarly discussion, this perception of cultural contextual features of the texts has been collapsed into talk about different 'worlds'. The 'world' of the text, the 'world' behind the text, and the 'world' of the reader are taken to be separate worlds or even different 'universes'. Moreover, the old 'world' way (apocalyptic or Hellenized Judaic or pre-Enlightenment) of approaching moral issues hardly holds up to modern standards of rational rigor. There is said to be an unbridgeable *gap* between these 'worlds.'

In *this* world, the world of contemporary constructive Christian ethics, we need normative, cogent, pragmatically applicable input. If the metaphorical-parabolic character of the texts frustrates attempts to gain direct access to the definitive solutions to moral problems we seek, extrication from such entanglements is a worthy goal. Extrication (or avoidance) then, is one mode by which biblical scholars and Christian ethicists respond to biblical metaphors for morality. We find we must found our arguments on other grounds, look to other sources of authority. But the cost of radical extrication is the effective loss of Scripture as the 'norming norm' among sources of authority in Christian ethics. "It becomes not a challenge but an echo."[2] This is a price many in the Christian faith community—and some Christian ethicists and biblical scholars—find too high to pay.

Recovery or retrieval is a second *modus operandus*. Retrieval has behind it a worthy goal: preservation of functional authoritative status for Scripture in Christian theology and ethics. When readings focus

---

[2] William C. Spohn. *What Are They Saying About Scripture and Ethics?* Rev. ed. (New York and Mahwah, N.J.: Paulist Press, 1995), 9. Spohn said, in this context, that "if the reader merely seeks to find biblical support for moral positions arrived at on other grounds, Scripture no longer functions as an authoritative source."

on retrieval from metaphor-and-parable- entangled texts something of theological and ethical value for modern Christians, the task becomes to decipher the parabolic code. Sometimes this is accomplished by filtering out foreign and culture-bound material, to produce elements of a timeless theological-ethical distillate. Each extract appears in the form of a certain unifying theme or focal point. The core biblical ethical message is said to be "the love command," or liberation, or the life of Christ.

Extraction of a reified distillate is arduous and the product of all that effort has been of limited value for Christian ethics. When all is said and done, although some express gratitude to Scripture for the provision of general thematic motifs and motivational messages, many contemporary Christian ethicists mostly avoid Scripture in their constructive ethical work. No consensus has been reached; no one distillate or set of ethical-thematic extracts seems to suffice for all situations. Christian ethical arguments and recommendations rely for their heft and logic on other sources. The biblical texts retain some motivational value, or provide support for arguments actually founded elsewhere. Again, Scripture seems to offer insufficient source material on which to found a cogent, applicable, universal ethic.

A third way looks to metaphor itself to bridge the chasms between the worlds, to be the spark that arcs the gaps. Just how that might work, though, remains something of a mystery, since the metaphors of the text belong, inherently, to *that* 'world'. And if (logic-tangling) metaphors function analogically, how are we to understand and evaluate this function? Approaches in this category hold some promise but have been hampered by incomplete and incoherent metaphor theories and inadequate methods of metaphor analysis.[3]

Most Christian ethicists today still profess commitment to Scripture as a source of ethical authority, but just how it can and ought to function authoritatively remains a difficult issue. Thus we confront the current 'problem' of Scripture and ethics: the effective loss of Scripture as reliable, authoritative source in Christian ethics.[4]

---

[3] Theologian David Tracy, whose articulation of an analogical imagination model has been so influential, has pointed to the need for a more complete metaphor analysis method for Christian hermeneutics. David Tracy, *Blessed Rage for Order: The New Pluralism in Theology* (Chicago: Chicago University Press, 1975, 1996), 50.

[4] Regarding the Scripture and ethics "problem," see Spohn, *What Are They Saying About Scripture and Ethics?* A helpful historical overview and interdisciplinary approach

But the "thoughts entangled in metaphors" speaker is George Eliot (Mary Ann Evans, 1819–1880), novelist and master metaphor maker. Metaphor- entangled thought was her *forte*. Social morality was one of her vital interests. By "act *fatally*," she probably meant *inevitably* or "with *unfortunate*" (rather than "deadly") "results."[5] George Eliot may well have intuited what contemporary linguist George Lakoff and philosopher Mark Johnson—and a growing company of scholars across many disciplines—believe can be empirically demonstrated: *thoughts are inextricably metaphor-tangled*. In this alternative view, the metaphor-thought-morality linkage is not always an entanglement of the confusing, obfuscating variety. Our thoughts are often engendered and expressed metaphorically and we cannot help but act upon them. We *get* our thoughts via metaphor, and we inevitably—"fatally," in Eliot's vocabulary—act upon them. If this is so, then it would be prudent to notice how metaphors operate, not only in formal ethical argument but also in everyday thought and interchange. For, as Eliot observes, "we *all* of us, grave or light"—scholar or lay reader, dispositionally attracted to the figurative and imaginative or not—act upon the metaphors we think with. If the cognitivists are right, metaphors have enormous potential to shape human behavior at individual, interpersonal, and communal levels. The metaphors we talk with reveal and shape the values we live by, and uncovering a community's habitual metaphor usage can reveal its operative value system.[6]

This book confronts the tangle, our sense of entanglement and obstruction, between metaphor and thought, focusing on the part of the tangle that is about the role of metaphor in moral discourse.[7] It uses cognitive (conceptual) metaphor study to analyze and untangle the tangle, to find the rhyme and reason between thought and metaphor and moral concepts. The aim is to see if cognitive metaphor analysis can help explain how modern readers make sense out of Scripture and

---

is offered in J.I.H. McDonald, *Biblical Interpretation and Christian Ethics* (Cambridge: Cambridge University Press, 1993).

[5] Moreover, the most coolly rational *Middlemarch* characters make the direst, most fatal (in the deadly sense) choices.

[6] George Lakoff and Mark Johnson, *Metaphors We Live By* (Chicago and London: University of Chicago Press, 1980).

[7] I use the term *moral discourse* to mean naturally occurring connected speech and written discourse that contains material pertaining to how people in various social contexts conceptualize and explain how they *should* live. See the Excursus on Discourse in Chapter 4.

are able to enter into a kind of moral discourse with it. If that can be achieved, a new perspective on the church's claim that Scripture's moral authority and relevance persists might be attained. The thesis is that conceptual metaphor, grounded in basic embodied human experience, makes possible a shared moral language and discourse between the New Testament writers and readers of the New Testament today. To test that claim, I use conceptual metaphor tools in a analysis of 1 Peter, reading it as an exemplar of Christian moral discourse.

Overview

Metaphor theories, and methods of studying figurative language, do not drop out of the sky or arise by spontaneous generation. Cognitive theories and methods are no exception; they arise from a long history of study and thought in Western tradition, in response to specific inadequacies and inconsistencies of those traditional approaches. Section A presents a history of metaphor in Western hermeneutics and demonstrates the persistence of traditional approaches while arguing that we need to find another way to deal with the issues of meaning generation, of the status of figurative language, and of the role of imagination in Christian moral discourse.

Chapter 1 is an historical overview of approaches to metaphor, targeting figures and trends that have special relevance to the conversation between biblical hermeneutics and constructive Christian ethics. As this survey proceeds, the inconsistencies and inadequacies of traditional approaches become clear, and an argument builds: a new theory and new analytical methods for metaphor study in biblical and theological hermeneutics are needed.

Chapter 2 introduces cognitive metaphor theory and methods. It focuses on concepts and terminology that will help New Testament scholars and Christian ethicists employ and adapt this approach for their own purposes.

In Chapter 3, two contemporary scholars' attempts to address the Scripture-and-ethics problem are presented and critiqued. Richard Hays (*The Moral Vision of the New Testament*) and William Spohn (*Go and Do Likewise*) employ a hermeneutics of analogy that values the metaphorical and symbolic in Scripture. I argue that while their work is careful and helpful in many ways, it falters at the brink of the Two Worlds Gap.

Section B is a methodological demonstration, designed to employ and test conceptual metaphor analysis methods and to demonstrate what can be learned about 1) some of the ways in which morality is conceived in the New Testament, and 2) how those concepts can be understood and used for constructive Christian ethics today. I have chosen 1 Peter as the test text for several reasons. Metaphor has figured into recent scholarly work on the letter, and some have argued that the social-ethical message of the letter hinges on the 'literal' (versus the metaphorical) status of certain expressions in the letter. 1 Peter is richly metaphorical; there is plenty of material with which to work. The letter also includes a household code whose moral advice many contemporary Christian ethicists and other readers find problematical. A further goal of this demonstration is to identify some of the ways metaphors operate in the moral argument of 1 Peter. I ask how metaphors are conventionalized in the text, and how they systematically are used to express the conceptual, cultural logic at work in the moral discourse of 1 Peter.

The section begins with Chapter 4, Before Reading, which provides a theoretical grounding, connecting conceptual metaphor study with cognitive understandings of the reading process. The following three chapters present some findings of a conceptual metaphor analysis of 1 Peter. Chapter 5 presents the Moral Accounting system and discusses the metaphorical grounding of the construal of moral authority in the text.

The following three chapters present five image schemas that serve as 'living spaces' for moral conduct in 1 Peter. Chapter 6 is concerned with living 'in Christ,' and Chapter 7 with living "in time." I discuss in some detail how these image schemas lend coherence and grounding to the moral discourse of 1 Peter. Chapter 8 concerns three additional metaphor clusters within which metaphors for morality in 1 Peter cohere: living as a people; living in the household; and living in the body. Via examination of this image schematic structure, one can see how the moral discourse of 1 Peter is rooted in basic bodily and primary social experiences that enable 21st-century readers to understand and respond to its message.

Section B concludes with a responsive review of the findings, Chapter 9: After Reading. As I reflect on my own reading of 1 Peter, I consider how its metamoral concepts blend and clash with my own, and ask what might happen if I allowed the text to 'read' me and my reading communities. The moral politics of 1 Peter are both familiar and foreign, but they are understandable enough. In conversation with 1 Peter, I find that its moral value, its ethical weight, as moral discourse is not restricted to a set of opinions, instructions or bits of advice that can reflexively be accepted or rejected as inapplicable. I find myself both resisting and being challenged to revise my thinking, and perhaps even my actions.

Why study the role of metaphor in the creation of meaning in Christian moral discourse? For Christian ethicists and biblical scholars who belong to the community that holds the New Testament texts as Scripture, avoidance or radical extrication from the Scriptural texts is not an acceptable option. Retrieval methods deliver us such thin, vague, or coolly distilled abstractions that we thirst for something more substantial. We need a model that describes how lively moral discourse can and does happen when modern readers encounter the New Testament, a model that is culturally aware and intellectually sound. Conceptual metaphor, rooted in basic human bodily and primary social experience might point the way to a transcultural conversation about how to live in Christ.

PART A

HISTORICAL AND CONTEMPORARY
METAPHOR THEORIES: IMPLICATIONS FOR
BIBLICAL HERMENEUTICS AND ETHICS

CHAPTER ONE

METAPHOR AND HERMENEUTICS: A HISTORY

> *For his talk is of pack-asses and smiths and cobblers and curriers, and he is always repeating the same things in the same words, so that any ignorant or inexperienced person might feel disposed to laugh at him; but he who opens the bust and sees what is within will find that they are the only words which have a meaning in them, and also the most divine, abounding in fair images of virtue, and of the widest comprehension, or rather extending to the whole duty of a good and honorable man. This, friends is my praise of Socrates ... as concerning justice, what is it?*
>
> —Plato, *Symposium* 1.331

Metaphor and meaning, "fair images of virtue" and words "most divine," have been thought to work in concert from the beginning of Western thought. Plato suggests that Socrates used "fair images of virtue" to help people understand their "whole duty," the shape of a good and honorable life. But also from the beginning, metaphorical, image-laden talk has evoked laughter—and perhaps boredom—from some ("the ignorant or inexperienced") but engendered awe, wonder in others. The question is, how would "fair images" work in the evocation or construction of moral meaning, of "widest comprehension"? What do metaphors and images have to do with complex, deep philosophical concepts like justice and the good? And what does the divine—God or the gods—have to do with all of this? Western philosophy and ethics arose in part from a desire to understand concepts like 'justice' and 'the good' and to appreciate how these operate in everyday life and yet are connected to the transcendent. As Plato suggests, the bond between metaphor and questions concerning the nature of virtue and divine communication could not be tighter. But are we laughing or are we mystified or are we curious?

Plato praises Socrates' talk of pack-asses, smiths and cobblers and pokes fun at those who fail to get the point. What does this have to do with how we read the Bible? Think Greek. Moral discourse like the New Testament letter we call 1 Peter, for example, may not be formal philosophical dialog, but the vocabulary of Greek philosophical ethics is both evident in and important to its moral purpose. Terms of classical philosophy—the good, honor, virtue, and justice (καλός, τιμή, ἀρετή, ἀγαθός, δικαιοσύνη)—pepper 1 Peter and reinforce the judgment that it should be read as moral discourse. Furthermore, debates over whether these and other terms should be understood metaphorically or literally have taken centerstage in contemporary scholarly arguments about the ethical and moral message of 1 Peter. Scholars still struggle to interpret its vocabulary of the 'stranger' or 'resident alien' or 'sojourner' (πάροικος, παρεπίδημος), for example. Whether these words are to be taken metaphorically or not, and what metaphors can be said to "control" the discourse of 1 Peter—these are lively questions batted around among 1 Peter scholars.

The controversy indicates how important detection and interpretation of metaphors can be for descriptive and constructive Christian ethics, as well. But 1 Peter experts have been confused about the nature of metaphor. What biblical scholars and Christian ethicists have thought metaphor was has shaped the functions to which it has been consigned both at the microcosmic level, in direct interpretation of specific texts and arguments, and at a macrocosmic level, in the philosophy of text interpretation and hermeneutics. One core question I want to address, then, is this: What is metaphor, and how does it work in biblical moral discourse?

Classical philosophers, medieval theologians and biblical scholars realized that *how* words were used was as critical as *what* words were used. Some of them tried to categorize types of language use and sought to understand how language functioned in philosophical and religious discourse. One mode of language use they noticed and named was μεταφέρειν ("to transfer, carry over"). But they were confused about what metaphor is and about its role in human cognition and expression. Recent interdisciplinary research on metaphor is beginning to yield a much clearer picture of metaphor's role in language and in human cognition.[1] This clearer picture of the role of metaphor in everyday language, in philosophical discourse, and in sacred texts can

---

[1] See Chapter Two regarding cognitive linguistic research. The following works summarize and interpret findings in the field, and include bibliographies: George Lakoff and Mark Johnson, *Philosophy in the Flesh* (New York: Basic Books, 1999); Gilles Fauconnier and Mark Turner, *The Way We Think: Conceptual Blending and the Mind's Hidden Complexities* (New York: Basic Books, 2002).

give those of us working in the fields of Christian ethics and biblical study valuable descriptive and analytical tools. But its value, its particular merits, cannot be assessed or the need for it appreciated absent an understanding of the history from which it arises. Most current work in biblical hermeneutics and ethics that touches on metaphor relies on classical or medieval understandings of metaphor. I will argue that those traditional approaches are inadequate and that biblical scholarship will be better served by cognitive linguistic theories and methods.

Metaphor: Traditional Western View(s)

It is important at the outset of this survey to post a cautionary note: It cannot strictly be claimed that there is "a" traditional Western theory of metaphor or of language as a whole, for that matter. The classical philosophers and writers expressed various views regarding metaphor, the nature of language, and the place of imagination in human thinking and knowledge. Medieval writers adapted and appropriated various aspects of the classical tradition, but there is no monolithic metaphor theory, no one take on metaphor that could be correctly called "the" medieval position. Moreover, none of the early figures—not even Aristotle—set out to build and present a theory of metaphor or of language. To suggest that such was the case would be anachronistic. Classical theoretical frameworks related to metaphor must be recovered deductively from evidence found in texts whose arguments are focused elsewhere, on other issues.

This is a caution light, not a stop sign, however. In the course of arguments regarding the nature of the good and of virtue, and in their deliberations on the definition of justice, the earliest philosophers found it necessary and helpful to consider the nature of language and its relationship to processes of human thought and to reality. There is no unified classical or traditional theory of metaphor. But from ancient times in the West, metaphor, analogy, and imagination have been important aspects of discussions of the nature and role of language in philosophical, rhetorical, and artistic discourse. This is not a new line of inquiry, nor is it an especially esoteric or ancillary line of inquiry.

There is no unified classical theory of metaphor, but Aristotle comes closest to articulating a coherent position on the matter. His view won, since it predominated in olden times and persists in Western philosophy. But because I want to focus on how metaphor theory relates to Christian ethical thought and to biblical hermeneutics, it will be important to back up—to begin, not with Aristotle, but with Plato and the Neoplatonists, for this strand of the tradition historically has been highly influential in Christian thinking on these matters.

Plato and Neoplatonism—Smoke and Mirrors: Metaphor as Shadow Talk

Plato is commonly taken to be the progenitor of an *anti*-metaphorical, anti-imagination strand in the Western philosophical tradition.[2] He is known as a master of *suspicion* of metaphor. How did Plato acquire this reputation? He got the reputation chiefly, it seems, because of certain remarks he makes in the *Republic*, especially in Book Ten, where he banishes philosophically uneducated mimetic poets from the Republic. He gives two reasons why poets should be expelled. The first is grounded in his epistemology. In Plato's view, poets are imitators who have no direct or genuine knowledge of that which they imitate. They are working not with Idea or Form or Essence, but with shadow and reflection: "They produce imitations of imitations of the real and are thus 'three removes from the king and the truth as are all other imitators.'"[3] When it comes to language use in the search for truth, Plato asserts, the "real" must be distinguished from mere "imitation." Real talk, or reality-talk—philosophical discourse—is qualitatively different from imitative talk, poetry. This great divide—Real v. Imitation or shadow—is the prominent feature in Plato's epistemological topography. Features that show up in language use—in rhetoric, dialog, and poetry—are only the surface manifestations of deeper structures.

Essence, Idea and Form: these fundamental, formal Platonic notions are keys to unlocking not only Plato's own understanding of metaphor, but also those that will follow. Together they comprise the master key to metaphor theory in Western tradition. This is because Essence, Idea and Form work in concert as Plato formulates his construal of

---

[2] Mark Johnson observes the irony that Plato, who uses analogy, parable and conceptual metaphor so adeptly in his philosophical argumentation, has this reputation; "Introduction: Metaphor in the Philosophical Tradition," in *Philosophical Perspectives on Metaphor*, ed. Mark Johnson (Minneapolis, Minn.: University of Minnesota Press, 1981), 4. And see Martha Nussbaum's assessment of the "ancient quarrel" between poets and philosophers: Martha C. Nussbaum, *Poetic Justice: The Literary Imagination and Public Life* (Boston: Beacon Press, 1995), 53–60, 69.

[3] Ibid. Johnson is quoting Plato *Republic* 10.597c.

categories and his explanation of how categories function in human thought and language. Platonic Essence functions prototypically; that is, the array of properties that members of a category share is taken as definitive, *essential*. Add to this Plato's assumption that the categories of being are hierarchical, and you have the outline of the philosophical underpinnings of his approach to metaphor. But to see even the basics of how all of that works, a bit more must be said about metaphor's relationship to Platonic Essence and Idea.

Platonic categorization of ways of knowing—its epistemology—is framed along a continuum—a graded hierarchy—of beings. Ideas are at the top of the hierarchy because ideas are the most real entities. Physical objects come next, and representations or images of those objects come last. What does this have to do with metaphor? Metaphor works with images, shadowy reflections of the objects that themselves are less real than the Ideas or Forms that "are directly present in the mind." Metaphor, then, is at least two major gradients removed from Idea, essential Form.[4] That is why metaphor, in this construal, is said to be an imitation of an imitation.

Platonic Psychology: Passion and Poetry

The second reason why Plato thinks poets and poetry are dangerous is psychological—it rests on his view of the human person, on his 'faculty' psychology. Poetry, he warns, tends to be generated out of the poet's passion—emotions—and then to inflame readers' (or hearers') emotions. Emotions are forces that threaten to disrupt and dethrone reason.[5] Poetry and fiction pose a danger to the inner harmony of the individual as a rational being whose passions and appetites must be kept under control if he (sic) is to flourish. But such de-stabilized persons also lack the social strength and circumspection that might allow them to contribute to the strength and balance of the collective, of the πόλις. So the perceived danger of poetry is internal, psychological, but with a social twist or spin.

---

[4] Lakoff and Johnson, *Philosophy in the Flesh*, 367. They define Essence and Form helpfully: "An essence for Plato is an *eidos*, a form, that is, the 'look' of a thing that makes it what it is." (Ibid., 374).

[5] Poetry "feeds and waters the passions, instead of drying them up; she lets them rule instead of ruling them as they ought to be ruled, with a view to the happiness and virtue of mankind." Plato *Republic* 10.606d.

The Politics of Platonic Metaphor

> Then must we not infer that all these poetical individuals, beginning with Homer, are only imitators; they copy images of virtue and the like, but the truth they never reach?[6]

Poems and heroic myths, the drama of tragedy and comedy—and the metaphors with which these work—are dangerous because they stir the emotions and give rise to "thoughts that attach importance to unstable external things." Passion, emotion, is "destabilizing" and gives rise to false judgments.[7] Thus, the dangerous influence of emotion-charged language does not stop at the level of the individual. Poetry has collective, politically charged potential as well.

There are other clues to Plato's concerns about certain dangers metaphor poses. In Books 1–5 of the *Republic*, Plato puts in question the role of literature in society and challenges the social-political value of much of the received tradition. The Homeric literature, which expresses moral imperatives and norms via poetic portrayals of conflicts among the gods, is in a sense the sacred canon of his day.[8] Plato thought it destructive. In Plato's view, only that which contributes to the universal (to peace, order, and harmony) is good. By focusing on conflicting heroic individuals instead of on harmony and society as a whole,[9] poets like Homer undermine the good of the Republic. Plato concludes that "the first thing will be to establish a censorship of the

---

[6] Plato *Republic* 2.383a–c. See the context of these remarks regarding the inadequacy of poetic treatment of virtue: "Then must we not infer that all these poetical individuals, beginning with Homer, are only imitators; they copy images of virtue and the like, but the truth they never reach? The poet is like a painter who, as we have already observed, will make a likeness of a cobbler though he understands nothing of cobbling, and his picture is good enough for those who know no more than he does, and judge only by colors and figures ... The imitator or maker of the image knows nothing of true existence; he knows appearances only ... Thus far then we are pretty well agreed that the imitator has no knowledge worth mentioning of what he imitates. Imitation is only a kind of play or sport, and the tragic poets whether they write in Iambic or Heroic verse, are imitators in the highest degree?" (*Republic* 10.601).

[7] M. Nussbaum, *Poetic Justice*, 56–57. Nussbaum observes that in the classical view, emotionally charged judgments are "false because they ascribe a very high value to external persons and events that are not fully controlled by the person's virtue or rational will. They are acknowledgments, then of the person's own incompleteness and vulnerability."

[8] Plato *Republic* 2.383a–c.

[9] Plato *Republic* 2.378b–c.

writers of fiction, and let the censors receive any tale of fiction which is good, and reject the bad ... but most of those which are now in use must be discarded."[10]

Good and Bad and Metaphor

Good, order and harmony—these are key ideas and ideals, formal concepts, for Plato. Keep in mind that Plato's approach to ethics and metaethics is of a piece with his metaphysics—with his understandings of Essence and Causation, of Categories, Ideas and Ideals. The Platonic idea of the Good as the most excellent Essence, the greatest good, the Ideal, permeates the Neoplatonic thought that will turn out to be highly influential, especially in the Augustinian stream of Christian theology and ethics. *Summum bonum* is the later, Latin, permutation of this Platonic ideal.

So too, the Platonic wedding of Essence and *causation* in the realm of the Good will persist in Western thought. The core causal construct in play here is an informal cultural assumption that the essential properties of any substance or object determine, *cause*, its behavior. In Platonic thought that essence-cause dyadic connection is held to be true in the physical realm of water and of stones just as it is assumed to be true of people. It is true first of all because the cosmos is so constructed, in a formal sense. This is why he can jump so quickly from (or lump together in the same sentence) talking about the Real versus imitation in an abstract sense to a particular socio-political structure (philosopher kings, and their obvious right to rule) to the assertion that poets do not belong in the Republic. Poets and philosopher-kings are essentially distinct kinds of people; their essential characters cause them to behave in certain ways and to be fit for certain societal roles. Philosophers are disposed to discourse at the level of the Form, and this causes them to be fit to rule. Poets, on the other hand, use their passionate faculties to deal with words, and their preferred method of discourse is as unreliable—destabilizing—as their characteristic behavior is erratic, intemperate.

Let us, however, not descend into caricature—Poet pitted against Philosopher—or be satisfied to caricature Plato himself. His understanding of the nature of metaphor, of the role of image and imagination in thought, has deep, persistent power to shape his overall philoso-

---

[10] Plato *Republic* 2.377b–c.

phy and his social ethical vision. What is at stake for Plato is illustrated in the *Gorgias*, where a dialog about the goal of rhetoric, speech and discussion takes place. One of Socrates' most challenging dialog partners is Callicles, who articulates the position that dialog is a weapon, a set of rhetorical techniques for overpowering one's opponent. For Callicles, life is a struggle in the pursuit of power with which to realize one's passions. But (in Socrates' voice) Plato presents another way of construing the nature, power, and purpose of human discourse. In this alternative view, the goal of dialog is the pursuit of truth, with the aim of building a harmonious society. What is most real for Plato is truth-seeking and the relational structures this pursuit builds and entails. Deep discourse, careful listening and speaking, are core community-building activities. Plato mistrusts passionate, power-wielding uses of language—and the metaphor-making he associates with such power plays—because he believes that they elevate passion above reason and subvert legitimate exercise of power, disrupting and destroying harmonious community.

Neoplatonism

> For the poet is a light and winged and holy thing, and there is no invention in him until he has been inspired and is out of his senses, and the mind is no longer in him ... for not by art does the poet sing, but by power divine.[11]

It is with Platonism, or more precisely Neoplatonism—the later movement inspired by the tradition of Plato and his school—that both the suspicion of metaphor and of imagination and, conversely, its valorization as a mode of knowledge and expression comes fully into play. If for no other reason than that Philo and Augustine were influenced by Neoplatonism, it has deeply influenced (I might even say, "infiltrated") Christian theology and hermeneutics. Accordingly, at least a cursory survey of the Neoplatonist attitudes toward metaphor is in order.

Philosopher Mark Johnson, a cognitivist, discerns that the Neoplatonist suspicion of metaphor (or more precisely, of imagination) arises from the school's appropriation and interpretation of Plato's metaphor of the Divided Line.[12] The Neoplatonist reading of this extended met-

---

[11] Plato *Ion* Great Books of the Western World Edition [Chicago and London: Encyclopedia Britannica, Inc., 1952] 534c.
[12] Mark Johnson, *The Body in the Mind: The Bodily Basis of Meaning, Imagination, and Reason* (Chicago: University of Chicago Press, 1987), 142. The metaphor of the Divided Line is found in Plato *Republic* 4.509c.

aphor moves beyond the distinctions Plato made in his hierarchical schematization of human perception and thought. The Neo's push the model further, to emphasize that imagination is the *lowest* form of cognition. Plato said that imagination was the form of cognition connected with that which is secondary, reflected, and shadowy. To arrive at truth, knowledge, one would need to grasp the unchangeable Essence of a thing, to move beyond mere imagination. The Neoplatonists decided that nothing in the physical world could directly yield real knowledge.[13] Their interpretation of Plato's epistemology was combined with a faculty psychology model to create a picture in which imagination was a sub-rational or even anti-rational faculty.[14] Poetic power was attributed to possession by the *daimon* (the muse),[15] which donated images with which to stir up the passions, the emotions, of an audience.[16] Later,

---

[13] *"Nothing* in the physical world gives us real knowledge, since all perceptible objects are constantly changing, while their essences are fixed. To grasp such essences, therefore, it is necessary to jump to the 'intelligible' realm beyond the senses—to transcend all sensuous and imaginative cognition. Only in this way are we able to find out the 'essence' of an object, that is, to find out what properties all objects of *that same kind* have. In the Platonic tradition, then, the Divided Line is interpreted as a scale of ascending levels of cognition, from the lowest, imagining, to the highest, intellection;" Johnson, *Body in the Mind*, 142–143.

[14] The faculty psychology model is an informal theory of how the human mind and human nature work; see Mark Johnson, *Moral Imagination: Implications of Cognitive Science for Ethics* (Chicago and London: University of Chicago Press, 1993), 15–16, 68, 227, 245.

[15] In classical mythology, the muses were sister goddesses whose powers were felt in the human sphere in certain functions: Aoede (song), Melete (meditation), and Mneme (memory). Later, and more commonly, the term "muse" came to refer to any of the nine daughters of Zeus and Mnemosyne who presided over various arts: Calliope (epic poetry), Clio (history), Erato (lyric poetry), Euterpe (music), Melpomene (tragedy), Polyhymnia (religious music), Terpsichore (dance), Thalia (comedy), and Urania (astronomy). Some time later the "muse" was simply the goddess or the power inspiring poets.

[16] Such Neoplatonic notions are rooted in Plato's own position. For example, consider this saying: "For the poet is a light and winged and holy thing, and there is no invention in him until he has been inspired and is out of his senses, and the mind is no longer in him ... for not by art does the poet sing, but by power divine ... God takes away the minds of poets, and uses them as his ministers ... in order that we who hear them may know them to be speaking not of themselves who utter these priceless words in a state of unconsciousness, but that God himself is the speaker, and that through them he is conversing with us." (Plato *Ion* 534c). Johnson further remarks that, "Plato's expulsion of the imitative poets must not ... be read as a condemnation of figurative language per se. But it does show his awareness of the power of metaphor and myth to influence conviction, and it reveals his fear of their potential for misuse. This vulnerability to abuse seems to be the reason for his claim that the poet, 'knowing nothing but

Augustine and others in the Christian tradition will reject the—to them—pagan notion of the *daimon* but will develop a related idea, the divine dispensation of image-making. For the Neoplatonists, imagination is a specialized mode of expression, divinely-inspired, and therefore of interest and even charged with a transcendental aura.

In this view, then, imagination—and the metaphorical images with which it works—is non-rational, even anti-rational. Those sentiments, too, will persist in Western tradition. In some hands, the imaginative / rational split will be construed in such a way that the imaginative is supra-rational in a positive sense. The basic notion of the split is rooted in Platonic formal idealism; the positive valorization of the imaginative as a mode of connection with the divine is a Neoplatonic legacy. Idealism is the distinctive feature of Platonic and Neoplatonic construals of the figurative, of the metaphorical. Reality is formal, above and beyond the sensory, bodily realm; metaphor, poetry and allegory are methods for transcending the visible, bodily plane to contact the divine. Metaphor, then, is spiritualized.

Plato on Metaphor: Summary

Though Plato theorized that metaphor belonged to a stratum or type of language use far removed from the formal realm of (real) Good, his own discourse demonstrates his (necessary) reliance on metaphorical concepts even to attempt to describe and conceptualize his cosmology, his metaphysic, his ethical philosophy.[17] What Plato says he believes about imagination and metaphor, then, must be read with awareness that he himself was a master of metaphor, and that his remarks about poets and poetry were motivated by his specific epistemology, metaphysic, and social-political agenda.

The larger questions about language and thought that Plato grappled with are still good questions. In addition, his theories raise important issues for anyone interested in the function of metaphor: Where does human metaphorizing capacity come from? Is it a manifestation of human passion and emotion or of human rationality? Does

---

how to imitate, lays on with words and phrases the colors of the several arts in such fashion that other equally ignorant men, who see things only through words, will deem his words most excellent;'" Johnson, *Body in the Mind*, 4; he quotes Plato *Republic* 10.601.

[17] Lakoff and Johnson, *Philosophy in the Flesh*, 364–372.

metaphor have the capacity to connect us with the spiritual, the divine and transcendent? What functions does metaphorizing have in human discourse, particularly in political and moral discourse? Does it have power to shape (and to distort) human community? Can people choose how they will use their metaphorizing capacity? If so, what responsibilities toward society does metaphor-making entail? These are no small matters. They are matters at the core of this study, and I will return to them repeatedly.

Aristotle on Metaphor

> But the greatest thing by far is to be a master of metaphor. It is the one thing that cannot be learnt from others; and it is also a sign of genius, since a good metaphor implies an intuitive perception of the similarity in dissimilars.[18]

These words from the end of Aristotle's *Poetics* signal a significant shift in appraisal and understanding of the role of the poet and of imaginative writing. With Aristotle, we encounter the first sustained reflection on the nature of metaphor and its role in human cognition. And it is Aristotle's understanding of metaphor that has been most influential in the West, even down to the present day. Here is his most succinct and revealing statement regarding metaphor:

> Metaphor consists in giving the thing a name that belongs to something else; the transference being either from genus to species, or from species to genus, or from species to species, or on grounds of analogy.[19]

If we hold these two statements together—the one with which we began, and this definitional sentence—we have before us six key features of Aristotle's understanding of metaphor: 1) transfer of names, 2) based on similarities, 3) involving deviance from ordinary usage, 4) in which "fittingness" or appropriateness it at issue. 5) All of this is taken to be a matter of intuition and perception. 6) In addition, a connection between metaphor and analogy is posited. Since the Aristotelian approach has been so highly influential, it is worth considering each of these features in turn.

---

[18] Aristotle *Poetics* Ann Arbor Paperbacks Edition, tr. Gerald F. Else (Ann Arbor: University of Michigan Press, 1967, 1970) 1459a 5–8.
[19] Aristotle *Poetics* 1457b 6–9.

Transfer of Names

Aristotle was interested in thinking about how metaphor worked, and he concluded that what was happening occurred at the level of individual words (nouns/names). In a sentence like "My love is a rose," the *name* "rose" was *transferred* to "my love." It was, thought Aristotle, a transfer (ἐπιφόρα) of names, a movement between categories of nouns, so that a word belonging in one category was used in another. The process of transfer might occur at any of several levels: from genus to species, from species to genus, across species, or "on grounds of analogy."

Similarity in Dissimilars

It seemed to Aristotle that what enabled such transfers was some quality of perceived similarity between the two words or names. That is, there was always some underlying resemblance that made the transfer work. Aristotle thought it a work of genius to notice such similarities and to make the connections, hence his valorization of poetic genius. This is important: while he saw metaphor as language that embellished, as decorative, he also saw that an underlying quality of cognition was at work. He valorizes metaphor-makers (and perceivers) because he believes that the connections made in metaphorizing are only possible (and apt) when they point to similarities that are actually present in the world of substances and objects. To perceive such similarities among essential properties, then, is a scientific enterprise, and apt metaphors are to be applauded.

Deviance from the Ordinary

Since metaphor involved the transfer of a name to some object that was not ordinarily known by that name, metaphor was understood as linguistic *deviance*. "Diction becomes distinguished and non-prosaic by the use of unfamiliar terms, i.e., strange words, metaphors, lengthened forms, and everything that deviates from ordinary modes of speech."[20] Metaphor, then, belongs to the specialized language of poets and not to the sphere of ordinary, everyday speech and language. Note that at

---

[20] Aristotle *Poetics* 148a.

this point a critical separation has been signaled: the literal (everyday) vs. figurative (poetic). A related split between poetic discourse and philosophical or argumentative discourse is also entailed.

Notion of the 'Fitting'

A good metaphor, according to Aristotle, corresponds rightly to the thing signified. The potential for misuse of metaphor bothered Aristotle, and he gives much attention to the problem in the *Poetics*, but also in both the *Rhetoric* and the *Topics*. A metaphor that is misleading or too obscure is not 'fitting.' In the *Rhetoric*, Aristotle lists his criteria for good metaphors: not too ridiculous, too grand or theatrical,[21] nor too far-fetched.[22] A good metaphor ought to "set the scene before our eyes in a way that allows us to get hold of new ideas."[23] The key seems to be the appropriateness of the similarities the metaphor reveals or suggests. Like a good riddle, a good metaphor should not be too obvious, and when we catch it, our response should be surprise and delight.[24]

Intuitive Perception

"Metaphors," says Aristotle, "must be drawn, ... from things that are related to the original things, and yet not obviously so related—just as in philosophy also an acute mind will perceive resemblance even in things far apart."[25] It takes an acute mind to perceive resemblances even in "things far apart"—and that, again, is why for Aristotle metaphor is, paradoxically, the provenance of both poets and philosophers. The elitism in Aristotle's conclusion here is noteworthy, but laying that aside for the moment, note also the perspicacity with which he sees the intimate connection between metaphor-making, perception, and a kind of cognition that is intuitive.

Aristotle's view of metaphor—the focus on single *words* (especially nouns, naming words) that *deviate* from ordinary, literal language use to evoke a change in meaning based on perceived *similarities* or resem-

---

[21] Aristotle *Rhetoric* Great Books of the Western World Edition (Chicago and London: Encyclopedia Britannica, Inc., 1952), 1406b.
[22] Ibid., 1410b.
[23] Ibid.
[24] Ibid., 1405b.
[25] Ibid., 1412a.

blances—became the standard understanding of metaphor. In Mark Johnson's evaluation, "Virtually every major treatment [of metaphor] up to the twentieth century is prefigured in Aristotle's account."[26]

Metaphor and Aristotelian Philosophical Categories

With these five features of Aristotle's understanding of metaphor before us, we have a rough map of the basic topography of the most dominant traditional Western view. But in order to grasp the significance of certain distinctive features of contemporary cognitivist conceptual metaphor theory, it is necessary to dig deeper, to get at the theoretical bedrock underneath the surface contours of Aristotle's remarks about metaphor and to touch on a sixth feature, the connection between metaphor and analogy.

Metaphor's Place in the Aristotelian Worldview

Metaphor theory does not stand alone or float above the surface of Aristotle's empirical, realistic world, as if it—or imagination, or even logic itself—were an abstraction. That would not be possible in Aristotle's view. For him, the human mind is a feature of reality and an organ of perception that senses or apprehends substances and motions—the essences and causalities of which are really there, literally in the world itself. The notion that categories and causal connections might be projected from the human mind onto a world that it might construct would be foreign—and anathema—to Aristotle. Over against Plato's idealism, then, Aristotle's realism stands out firmly, starkly.[27]

Let us touch on a few key features of Aristotle's worldview that continue to figure into discussions and debates about the nature of metaphor and analogy: the notions of essence and cause, category and being, substance, nature and τέλος.[28]

The first feature has already been mentioned: for Aristotle there is no fundamental, essential gulf between the human mind and the real,

---

[26] Johnson, *Philosophical Perspectives*, 8.
[27] Lakoff and Johnson make this point forcefully and clearly in their treatment of Plato and Aristotle in *Philosophy in the Flesh*, 364–390; see, especially, p. 364.
[28] See Lakoff and Johnson, "Aristotle," in *Philosophy in the Flesh*, 373–390, for a more complete discussion of Aristotle's distinctive understandings of essence, causation, category, and τέλος.

empirically observable and apprehendable world. And the second is like unto it: the features of the world that the human mind apprehends are really there, there in the world; they cannot be mere projections of the human mind. Additionally, each substance or object in the world has a unique essence.

In holding to a notion of essence, Aristotle is an heir of Plato, but his construal of essence is distinctive. Whereas for the idealist, Plato, essences are Forms or Ideas, Aristotle has it the other way around.[29] Essences are first *in the world*, they exist in the objects and substances in the world. It is the features of these essences that consign substances, various kinds of beings, matter, to their proper categories. Things naturally sort themselves out; there really are different categories of substances in the world, and they are arranged hierarchically. Again, this hierarchy and these categories exist in the world; they are not creations of human minds, not even of human minds working collectively to sort things out. Things belong to categories on the basis of essential features they hold in common, similarities that pertain in reality.

Categories, then, are real, empirically observable features of the world, comprised of various beings in the world. Aristotle thought he observed a natural hierarchy in place in the world, and he struggled to record accurately the actual taxonomy and to indicate the relationships between the categories of beings. He thought the causal connections he observed were actual, natural features of the world, particularly of the way motion effected changes in the world. The structure of his category model entailed that there be a super-category, one in which all the others fit and that functioned as the ultimate mover or cause of everything else, everything "below" it. This ultimate category was Being itself.

Metaphor and Analogy

Aristotle's doctrine of essences, wedded to his hierarchical category structure, constrains his account of how analogy and metaphor function. This in turn has deep significance for the struggle in the West satisfactorily to explain how metaphor and analogy might function in discourse about anything (or any being) transcendent or divine. For

---

[29] An insight from Lakoff and Johnson, Ibid.

if categories are apprehended—if they are real features of the world, comprised of entities bearing empirically observable similarities—and if words are the names of things, and if the names of things properly refer to things in the real world, then metaphors can in a sense only be matters of category mistake (though perhaps intentional mistake). To make a metaphor, μεταφέρειν, is to temporarily 'carry over' a feature from one category to another category, disrupting the ordinary ways of seeing how things fit in the given, immutable hierarchy. Metaphor-making is at base a matter of deviant, improper attribution or word usage even when it is an activity of genius and is done in a 'fitting' or approximately proper manner.

This brings us to the difficulty posed by discourse about the transcendent or about Being itself. Everything that is belongs to the category Being, and has the essence of Being. Since by definition, the category Being is above and beyond all other categories, there are no actual, literally shared attributes between Being and objects in the world. Metaphors, which attempt to pick out similarities between categories and temporarily transfer them across those genera, ultimately fail to make such a transfer work. That is, there are no literal similarities between the category Being and the other categories (other than the shared essential quality, Being itself). This is why under the Aristotelian framework metaphor and analogy are inadequate tools for analyzing or describing the ultimate, transcendent category, Being.

Metaphor and Aristotelian Ethics

For Aristotle, ethics belongs to the sphere of practical reason; it is 'prudential' reasoning. His focus is on the development of moral character and discernment over the course of an individual's (a male aristocrat's) lifetime. It is the role of ethical reasoning to help such a person know how a given general principle that has been articulated by the higher rational faculty, intelligence, applies in some certain situation. The goal is ethical behavior, action in accord with right reason, and there is a role for metaphor here. Metaphor can aid explicit and articulate grasp of principles that are, in turn, requisite to right action.[30] In addition,

---

[30] Alasdair MacIntyre concludes that both Plato and Aristotle suppose they can draw practical guidance from the elucidation of the necessary conceptual framework for human life (and he thinks they are mistaken); MacIntyre, *A Short History of Ethics* (New York: Macmillan, 1966), 95–96.

metaphor is deemed legitimate as rhetorical, poetic, and dramatic technique. It is a technique of persuasion in rhetoric and of evocation of emotion in tragedy and poetry. In the latter role, it contributes to catharsis, clearing the way for right action. The roles Aristotle assigns metaphor in ethics as an aid to prudential reasoning and as a persuasive technique are the roles to which metaphor is still largely consigned in Western philosophical and theological ethics.

Recap: Aristotle v. Plato on Metaphor

Plato recognized metaphor's persuasive and mimetic power and judged it a danger to the social order he had in mind. Mimetic poetry and the metaphor with which it was constructed was less than true; since it was indirect, it could be only imitative of the real. Metaphor, then, was inherently distorting. Perceiving danger in the passions metaphor evoked in people, he exercised his own sense of social responsibility by banning from the Republic the poets who wielded this weapon. It is the body politic that concerns Plato; that and the formal truth that might rightly order that politic, if only people would assume their appointed positions. Metaphor, he thought, mostly interfered with this project.

Like Plato, Aristotle also saw metaphor operating in political rhetoric, in poetry, and in drama, but his estimation of its social-political power differs fundamentally from Plato's. Aristotle's realistic empiricism allows him to notice the ways people use metaphor in prudential (ethical) reasoning, as they attempt to grasp and apply principles requisite to right action. Moreover, rather than lamenting the emotionally evocative potential of metaphor, Aristotle considers it potentially cathartic, and catharsis as opening the way for prudential action. The goal he has in mind is the development of moral character, of the Great Man, rather than of a great society, a republic. Of course he believed that a good and great society, a well-governed city, would be led by such great men. To the extent that metaphor functioned positively in the moral development that enabled great men to act rightly, it had a positive role in his ethical construction.

Metaphor in Medieval Rhetoric and Christian Theology

Just as there is no monolithic classical theory of metaphor, so also in the Middle Ages (spanning approximately the fifth through the fifteenth centuries) one encounters a diversity of practices and critical approaches to language, rhetoric, analogy, and metaphor. Three central themes appear repeatedly, and they have bearing on the status of metaphor in four basic areas: linguistics, metaphysics, logic, and theology.

1) The nature of discourse about reality is one of the central problems in medieval metaphysics. In particular, the concern was how both 'substances' (Socrates) and 'accidents' dependent on them (Socrates' beard) could be said to exist. Medieval thinkers explored the connections between lived experience, ultimate reality, and the nature of human language.
2) The truth status of words that seemed to have more than one meaning perplexed medieval logicians; they continued the discussions begun in the classical period on this matter.
3) The status and nature of religious language concerned medieval theologians. Polysemous or equivocal language perplexed them; they struggled to understand the nature of such language when the talk is about God and the divine.[31]

Over the course of this era, formal and informal theories were developed to address these problems. In general, the medieval approaches tend to create separate categories of word types and to look at words as individual units of signification operating independently of context. Medieval theories of analogy partake of that linguistic approach, and this, in turn, has deep consequences for work in logic and theology. Underneath it all lie particular doctrines about the nature of human concepts and their relationships—even their ontological relationships—to the divine. Cosmologies and ontologies that rely on notions of es-

---

[31] These questions concerned both Christian and Jewish scholars. For a cognitivist analysis of Maimonides' approach to metaphor and religious language, see Margaret A. Sandel, "Understanding Religious Language: An Integrated Approach to Meaning" (Ph.D. diss., Graduate Theological Union, 2002). Sandel notes (p. 107) that Aristotelian logic and empiricism influenced Maimonides, but that his approach departs from Aristotle's as Maimonides wrestles with the ubiquity of metaphor and equivocation in religious language.

sence and formal causation persist through this period and shape the expressed understandings, if not the uses, of metaphor and analogy in the Middle Ages.

Another major model in medieval textual interpretation and practical Christian ethics is allegory.[32] While metaphor and allegory are *not* identical phenomena, they are not unrelated. Both touch on attitudes towards biblical imagery, and both are concerned with reading and interpretive processes. Over the course of the Middle Ages, allegorical interpretation developed and shifted. It had its proponents and opponents. Even to this day, biblical interpreters often associate metaphor study with allegorical interpretation (or conflate the two). To this day, when ethicists query the manner in which scripture is appealed to as a source of authority, they express concern that when an argument has recourse to allegory, something of significance is lost. Focus on metaphor can be conflated with allegorizing. The fear is that in this allegorizing process, deep and difficult moral implications are distilled or dismissed in favor of a spiritualized 'meaning.'

Accordingly, I want to sketch the implications for the understanding of metaphor in approaches to these pivotal problems—linguistic, logical, metaphysical and theological—highlighting major lines of Neoplatonic and Aristotelian carry-over in two prominent medieval figures. Augustine and Aquinas could serve as bookends for the Middle Ages, Augustine standing at the beginning of the period and Aquinas at the end. I will argue that the Augustinian and Thomistic approaches to metaphor and analogy are distinctive and that these distinctions have significance for biblical hermeneutics and moral theology. This material is of more than historical interest, though that alone suffices to ground its significance. These two major modes of metaphor and analogy method and theory—Augustinian and Thomistic—persist and prevail in Christian theology and biblical hermeneutics today. An understanding of these strands, then, is a prerequisite to any analysis of current theory and practice with regard to metaphor in theology and hermeneutics.

---

[32] Regarding various attitudes towards allegorical interpretation, including a historical survey with an eye towards implications for post-modern interpretation, see Anthony C. Thistleton, *New Horizons in Hermeneutics* (Grand Rapids, Mich.: Zondervan, 1992), 142–178.

Augustine: Drinking in Eternal Light

> Now it is surely a miserable slavery of the soul to take signs for things, and to be unable to lift the eye of the mind above what is corporeal and created, that it may drink in eternal light.[33]

With Augustine, questions about the nature of metaphor and its role in the Christian Scriptures, theology and ethics come clearly to the foreground. Issues Plato raised about the deep significance of language in political discourse as it shapes the Republic now are applied to the City of God—to matters of state but also of church, to the role of rhetoric, but especially as it pertains to biblical interpretation and to Christian doctrine and ethics. What is perhaps most interesting in all of this is that here, so early on in church history, the three concerns—metaphor, scriptural hermeneutic, Christian social ethic—are so closely linked. It will be instructive to notice just how Augustine links these factors and functions, since he blazed the trail that so many Christians—particularly in the Protestant churches—have followed.

Augustine and Christian Neoplatonism: Language, Signs, and Theology

Augustine read Plotinus and was deeply influenced by Neoplatonism. In the *Confessions* and in *On Christian Doctrine*, it becomes clear that Augustine's epistemology is closely linked to the way he moves within a Neoplatonic philosophical model to speculate about the nature of language. How can one know and experience God, the ultimate reality? How are ineffable mysteries understood and articulated? They are articulated by human speech. In Augustine's worldview, there is an abyss between the transcendent realm of God and the contingent, finite, fallen world of everyday human life. But the Word—Christ, the Word made flesh, and the Word in Scripture—bridges that gap.[34] Thus Augustine gives a linguistic solution to the epistemological problem he has posed. Logos makes the divine, atemporal power of God at least partially intelligible in the finite, temporal world.[35]

---

[33] Augustine *On Christian Doctrine*, tr. J.F. Shaw, Great Books of the Western World Edition (Chicago and London: Encyclopedia Britannica, 1952), 3.5.

[34] Augustine *Confessions*, tr. Edward B. Pusey, Great Books of the Western World Edition (Chicago and London: Encyclopedia Britannica, 1952), 10.43, 11.29.

[35] Augustine did yearn for an afterlife in which humans could know God without needing the medium of language; *Confessions* 12.13.

World, Words, and "Signs"

On Christian Doctrine (De doctrina christiana) is a handbook demonstrating proper exegesis and hermeneutics. While Augustine counsels that 'charity'—Christian love—is the primary qualification or prerequisite for the biblical interpreter, it does not automatically render the meanings of Scripture transparent.[36] Evil has infected human minds, and confusion and ambiguity are postlapsarian givens in the Augustinian worldview. But damaged and darkened human intellect is not the only problem, in this construal. If Scripture is difficult to understand, its ambiguity results in part from the very nature of words as signs (*signa*) pointing to something beyond themselves, calling for interpretation. Augustine readily admits that Scripture is written by human beings, in human languages, but he believes these human authors are divinely inspired. So, via divine inspiration, the words are signs of 'light,' vehicles for the apprehension of the 'eternal.' This eternal light illumines 'corporeal,' earthly darkness, and Augustine pities people who live without it, those who live an unenlightened "slavery of the soul." This is Neoplatonic language, Neoplatonic thinking. It is here that metaphors, figurative signs, fit in Augustine's model. For by reading Scripture, and especially by attending to the figurative clues therein, the believing reader (full of 'charity') can cross that great chasm separating the spiritual and the material, the pure and the fallen, the eternal and the temporal, the worlds of words and of things.[37] No wonder then, that he is interested in the written word, in proper reading and interpretation of Scripture.

Metaphor and Augustinian Interpretation of Scripture

> It is a wretched slavery which takes the figurative expressions of Scripture in a literal sense. But the ambiguities of metaphorical words ... demand no ordinary care and diligence.[38]

---

[36] Augustine *On Christian Doctrine* 1.40.44; 2.7.10.

[37] Augustine *On the Trinity* 6.10.12. It is important to understand that this Augustinian approach to words, Word, and world is more than a theory about linguistic signification, or even sacred linguistic signification. All the things of this world—material objects and events, not only words—are signs that can lead to knowledge of God. John E. Rotelle, ed., *The Works of Saint Augustine: A Translation for the 21st Century*, tr. Edmund Hill (Brooklyn, N.Y.: New City Press, 1990–), v. 1:5.

[38] Ibid.

Augustine was keen on teaching Christians to think and read critically but also with spiritual acuity and heart. In *On Christian Doctrine*, he addresses these matters directly and at length. If Scripture is divinely inspired, it yet is cast in human language, and ought to be treated as such. Augustine's education as a rhetorician serves him here; he has been taught to recognize various forms of speech, to read and argue carefully—and he argues that Christian readers ought to use the critical, analytical tools available to them in order to unlock the (sometimes) hidden meanings of Scripture.[39] He points to particular kinds of interpretive difficulties: how to translate and interpret words that are used in more than one way; how to handle ambiguous passages; how to distinguish the kind of expression one is encountering—literal or figurative, ironic, parabolic, allegorical, and so on.

Augustine also follows standard understandings from the rhetoricians about the character and function of metaphor in discourse. So he says that metaphors, figures of speech, render truth or knowledge that elsewhere is given in plain language in a "more pleasant" or heartwarming manner or stimulating manner.[40] Figures of speech, then, are embellishments on arguments and goads or enticements to seek knowledge that is expressed elsewhere more plainly.

The Literal / Figurative Split

Augustine spends a lot of time (and ink) explaining how to tell a literal from a figurative expression—and explaining why this is so important.[41] He warns against two mistakes he says are twins—the error of taking a metaphorical form of speech as if it were literal, and the flip side: "we must also pay heed to that which tells us not to take a literal form of speech as if it were figurative."[42]

The litmus test of literal vs. figurative status is telling: "Whatever there is in the word of God that cannot, when taken literally, be referred either to purity of life or soundness of doctrine, you may set

---

[39] Augustine *On Christian Doctrine* 2.16.23; 3.10–29.
[40] Augustine, Ibid., 2.6.8. He says, for example: "[T]he Holy Spirit has, with admirable wisdom and care for our welfare, so arranged the Holy Scriptures as by the plainer passages to satisfy our hunger, and by the more obscure to stimulate our appetite. For almost nothing is dug out of those obscure passages which may not be found set forth in the plainest language elsewhere."
[41] Ibid., 3.10.14.
[42] Ibid.

down as figurative. Purity of life has reference to the love of God and one's neighbour; soundness of doctrine to the knowledge of God and one's neighbour."[43] One of his chief concerns in insisting upon attention to the literal / figurative split, is ethical. That is, he suspects that readers are apt to explain away passages that expose their sinfulness for what it is (the basic, primal, sin being lust, in his estimation).

Core Characteristics of Augustine's Approach to Metaphor

In keeping with his rhetorical training, Augustine understands metaphor to be a subset of the larger category, figurative speech. In one place he calls it one kind of 'trope.' In the same section he defines allegory and catachresis—distinguishing them as different types of 'trope'—and mentions enigma and parable.[44] The latter three are not only present in Scripture (examples abound), but Augustine finds that these 'names,' these terms, are present as well.

Augustine notices that "the same word does not always signify the same thing;" polysemy, then, points to the possibility that an expression is being used metaphorically.[45] He also recognizes that some kind of similarity or likeness between objects is being posited when words function metaphorically.[46] Again he counsels attention to context, noting that the meaning of a metaphor can only be ascertained by noticing its specific use *in situ*:

> But as there are many ways in which things show a likeness to each other, we are not to suppose that what a thing signifies by similitude in

---

[43] Ibid., 3.24.34. In the same place he says, "The chief thing to be inquired into, therefore, in regard to any expression that we are trying to understand is, whether it is literal or figurative. For when it is ascertained to be figurative, it is easy, by an application of the laws of things which we discussed in the first book, to turn it in every way until we arrive at a true interpretation, especially when we bring to our aid experience strengthened by the exercise of piety. Now we find out whether an expression is literal or figurative by attending to the considerations indicated above."

[44] Ibid., 3.29.40. Catachresis is misuse of words; mistaken definitions of words are often (wrongly) deduced via folk etymologies. Augustine's example here is the use of the name "fish pond" for "a pond in which there is no fish, which was not made for fish, and yet gets its name from fish."

[45] Ibid., 3.25.

[46] Ibid. "And when it is shown to be figurative, the words in which it is expressed will be found to be drawn either from like objects or from objects having some affinity."

> one place it is to be taken to signify in all other places. For our Lord used leaven both in a bad sense, as when He said, "Beware of the leaven of the Pharisees," and in a good sense, as when He said, "The kingdom of heaven is like unto leaven, which a woman took and hid in three measures of meal, till the whole was leavened."[47]

Augustine notices the conventionality and ubiquity of metaphor even in the speech of ordinary folks, sayings, "the speech of the vulgar makes use of [all sorts of figures of speech], even of those more curious figures which mean the very opposite of what they say, as for example, those called irony and antiphrasis."[48] He teaches that:

> the knowledge of these is necessary for clearing up the difficulties of Scripture; because when the words taken literally give an absurd meaning, we ought forthwith to inquire whether they may not be used in this or that figurative sense which we are unacquainted with; and in this way many obscure passages have had light thrown on them.[49]

In all of this he is especially concerned to explain how to read those Scriptural passages where the loving and just God seems to say or do something unloving, wrathful, or in any way out of character.

Metaphor, Figure, and Ethics

Augustine developed several key hermeneutic principles related to interpretation of moral discourse and they are linked to his understanding of metaphor and figurative language. First, there is the Love, Mercy and Justice rubric: No interpretation can be correct which attributes 'severity' or wickedness to God or to the saints.[50] Secondly, he offers a rule for interpreting figurative expressions:

> To carefully turn over in our minds and meditate upon what we read till an interpretation be found that tends to establish the reign of love. Now, if when taken literally it at once gives a meaning of this kind, the expression is not to be considered figurative.[51]

Between those two expressions of what is, essentially, the same rubric (the Golden Rule), Augustine inserts a piece on the "error of those who

---

[47] Ibid., 3.24.35.
[48] Ibid., 3.29.41. In Greek rhetoric, *antiphrasis* is the use of a word in a sense opposite to its proper meaning (ἀντί—"against" + φράζειν "to speak, explain, interpret").
[49] Ibid.
[50] Ibid., 3.11.17; 3.12.18.
[51] Ibid., 3.15.23.

think that there is no absolute right and wrong."[52] Are moral norms merely culturally constructed and hierarchically enforced? While admitting that mores vary culturally, he asserts that the core moral precept is universal and that this orders all other mores, in whatever culture:

> "Whatsoever ye would that men should do to you, do ye even so to them" cannot be altered by diversity of national customs. And this precept, when it is referred to the love of God, destroys all vices; when to the love of one's neighbour, puts an end to all crimes.[53]

Finally, recall that for Augustine, the core of the human problem, the primal human sin, is lust. By 'lust' he means not just sexual lust, but any drive or desire that wrests one's focus away from loving God and neighbor.[54]

The nexus of the literal versus figurative distinction—the deep significance of interpretive difficulties—is ethical. Augustine says this:

> But as men are prone to estimate sins, not by reference to their inherent sinfulness, but rather by reference to their own customs, it frequently happens that a man will think nothing blameable except what the men of his own country and time are accustomed to condemn, and nothing worth of praise or approval except what is sanctioned by the custom of his companions; and thus it comes to pass, that if Scripture either enjoins what is opposed to the customs of the hearers, or condemns what is not so opposed, and if at the same time the authority of the word has a hold upon their minds, they think that the expression is figurative. Now Scripture enjoins nothing except charity, and condemns nothing except lust, and that way fashions the lives of men. In the same way, if an erroneous opinion has taken possession of the mind, men think that whatever Scripture asserts contrary to this must be figurative. Now Scripture asserts nothing but the Catholic faith, in regard to things past, future, and present. It is a narrative of the past, a prophecy of the future, and a description of the present. But all these tend to nourish and strengthen charity, and to overcome and root out lust.[55]

---

[52] Ibid., 3.14.22.
[53] Ibid., 3.14.
[54] Ibid., 3.10. "I mean by charity that affection of the mind which aims at the enjoyment of God for His own sake, and the enjoyment of one's self and one's neighbour in subordination to God; by lust I mean that affection of the mind which aims at enjoying one's self and one's neighbour, and other corporeal things, without reference to God."
[55] Ibid., 3.10.15.

People being people, Augustine observes, they will tend to try to avoid blame and the hardship of moral reform—and they will interpret the literality or figurativeness of Scriptural passages accordingly. His hermeneutic principles are meant to circumvent this human tendency.

Re-Cap: Augustine, Metaphor, and Biblical Interpretation

Upon his conversion to Christianity, Augustine condemned secular writing, particularly poetry and drama, *fabula* (fictions).[56] In some places, he says that such fictions consist of falsehoods focused the immoral exploits of pagan gods, and Christians should have nothing to do with any of this. This notion that pagan or secular poetry and fiction contains dangerous 'falsehoods' was highly influential in Western Christian culture for the next thousand years; traces of it persist to this day. This is the attitude with which many scholars associate Augustine's name.

But Augustine also said that all truth is God's truth, and encouraged the learned to critically read the secular writings, mining from them the "gold and silver" that were there to be found. It is no wonder, then, that Augustine was interested in the interpretation of Scripture, and in the role of the reader in the process of rendering meanings.[57] For Augustine, reading figuratively does not stop with analysis of verbal tropes; it means seeing the connections between material realities and events and that to which they point, recognizing the symbolic significance of things. He has been identified (accused, some would put it) as the father of medieval allegorical hermeneutics. Since, however, for him meaning ultimately is not located in the words themselves, the allegory in which Augustine is interested happens not at the level of

---

[56] Augustine *Concerning the City of God against the Pagans*, tr. Henry Bettenson, Penguin Classics Edition (London: Penguin Books, 1972, 1984), 6.5.

[57] For Augustine, the Bible is actually the 'word' of God. Peter Brown observes: "[The Bible] was regarded as a single communication, a single message in an intricate code, and not as an exceedingly heterogeneous collection of separate books. Above all, it was a communication that was intrinsically so far above the pitch of human minds, that to be made available to our sense at all, the 'Word' had to be communicated by means of an intricate frame of 'signs.'" Peter Brown, *Augustine of Hippo* (Berkeley: University of California Press, 1967), 253. And see Brown's fairly extensive discussion of Augustine's exegetical method, his attitude toward allegory, and his biblical homiletics. Ibid., 252, 258.

texts or discourses, but in historical events. The goal of the interpreter is to draw out "the kernels from the husk,"[58] but not just as a verbal exercise. Medieval semiology is founded on this theory of signs, but it is also a major plank in the theoretical foundation for later monastic spiritual disciplines of reading and preaching, *lectio* and *praedicatio*.[59]

A nuanced understanding of Augustinian hermeneutics, then, will prevent us from caricaturing Augustine as the progenitor of a purely anti-rational, emotive transcendentalism. Augustine was not anti-philosophy; he was steeped in Neoplatonic thought. This brand of philosophy predisposed him to value the symbolic over the ordinary or empirically observable and to look for the deep (or the lofty) in holy writ. What can be fairly said is that for Augustine and his followers, the figurative and symbolic are desperately needed bridges across the gap between holy, transcendent truth and fallen, finite human perception. As the Middle Ages developed, Augustine's followers would devise elaborate methods for discerning transcendent, even mystical, meanings they assumed were hidden in the plain senses of Scripture. By the end of the medieval period, the great intellect and spirit of Thomas Aquinas will argue that in the process, in an allegorical shuffle that becomes sleight of hand, truth has been lost. The central question remains: How do words mean, and what is the role of the figurative, the metaphorical, and the analogical in the apprehension and expression of truth, especially transcendent truth?

Thomas Aquinas

> It is written (Hosea 12:10): "I have multiplied visions, and I have used similitudes by the ministry of the prophets." But to put forward anything by means of similitudes is to use metaphors. Therefore this sacred science may use metaphors.[60]

Turning now from the early to the later Middle Ages, we encounter Thomas Aquinas, the great doctor of the Church, whose work blends

---

[58] Augustine *On Christian Doctrine* 3.12.18.
[59] Augustinian theory also is a precursor to modern discussions of the nature of language and of semiotics.
[60] Aquinas *Summa Theologiae (ST)*, tr. Fathers of the English Dominican Province, revised by Daniel J. Sullivan, Great Books of the Western World Edition (Chicago and London: Encyclopedia Britannica, 1952), 1.1.9.

several of the major streams of medieval critical thought, and is heavily influenced by his study of Aristotelian texts.[61] Both Augustine and Aquinas understood metaphor to be helpful and necessary means for conveying that which is beyond the ordinary, particularly matters of faith, of the transcendent, and of religious understanding. But while Augustine was enthralled with Neoplatonic idealist models, Aquinas was attracted to Aristotle's empiricism. Having accepted fully the goodness and reality of the visible, empirically observable world, Thomas sought to understand that reality while at the same time holding to belief in a transcendent, utterly holy, qualitatively superior God.

Thomas found the issues around metaphor to be so important that he raised them in the very first section of the first book of his masterwork, the *Summa Theologiae*. He was fond of calling theology (*sacra doctrina*) *una scientia*, 'a science,' the 'sacred science'—as he does in the epigraph to this section. As soon as he established his position that theology was a science, he turned to the question of the status of metaphor in theology and in the study of the sacred texts, *sacra scriptura*. But to grasp the significance of the conclusions Aquinas reached concerning metaphor, it is necessary to understand what he thought was at stake in the discussion about metaphor and analogy. Why is metaphor such a matter of contention that Aquinas foregrounds it in the *Summa*? Beginning to answer that question can prepare the way for understanding how metaphor has become a matter of contention again today.

Essences and God Language: The Problem

It will be well, then, to attend to the basic problem Thomas was addressing. Aquinas and his contemporaries struggled to understand how human beings could even use human language to refer to God. The fear was that human language could not be used, trusted, to convey divine truth. Language in direct reference to God, language *naming* God, was particularly problematical.[62] The core of the problematic is ontological, the by-now familiar notion of essence that is keyed to a cosmology, a hierarchy of beings. Various versions of the essence doctrine (the basic form of it having, as we have seen, arisen

---

[61] Rita Copeland, "Medieval Theory and Criticism," in *Johns Hopkins Guide to Literary Theory and Criticism* (Baltimore: Johns Hopkins University Press, 1994), 500–507.

[62] Ricoeur concurs. See "Metaphor and *Analogia Entis*: Onto-theology" in *The Rule of*

in pre-Socratic and classical thought) permeated medieval Europe. By Thomas's time, this essentialism operated on more than one level. It operated, first of all, as an informal set of presuppositions constituting a kind of folk wisdom about the world, the truth of which seems simply to have been assumed. But on another, formal level, Aquinas and other philosopher-theologians struggled to define essence and related concepts more precisely. Its implications for the construal of causality were given particular attention. The key points are these: Each being has its own characteristic essence, constituting its 'nature.' The various kinds of being, the substances, have ontologically real differences. There is, then, a real and significant, ontological gap between the human and the divine—a vertical distinction between categories of being. There are ontological distinctions on the horizontal plane, as well. Category distinctions between various created beings are real, in this model. Thomas appreciates Aristotelian categories for their usefulness in providing a structured way to think about the transcendence, the otherness and superiority, of the Christian God in relation to his creatures. For God to be God, this essential, qualitative difference has to be maintained.

Theory of Language

A corollary to this core problem is that the theory of language with which Aquinas works defines what words do in such a way as to problematize religious language. Relationships between things in the world, concepts, and linguistic utterances are considered to be tight, natural. Concepts are thought to be objective, in the world, so that any human being would potentially hold the same concepts. They are there, in the world, to be perceived. While Aquinas recognizes that human concepts and ways of talking arise from human experience, from 'sensation,' he assumes that concepts are picked up as a matter of course, naturally, rather than constructed mentally.

Medieval semantics focuses on signs, signification, and the processes by which they function. Modern concern about 'meaning' and how meaning is created or constructed are foreign to Thomas's world.[63] To

---

Metaphor: Multi-disciplinary Studies of the Creation of Meaning in Language, tr. Robert Czerny (Toronto: University of Toronto Press, 1977), 272–280.

[63] That the pivotal semantic notion was signification rather than meaning is often obscured when translators render the Latin *significatio* as "meaning." Ashworth, E. Jen-

him, words are sign-bearers pointing to entities and properties existing outside the realm of human language and independent of human minds. Philosophers of language had struggled to understand the status and function of various kinds of words—nouns, and their predicates, verbs, and so on—and Thomas continues this discussion.

What is important here is the characteristic medieval understanding about words. Each word is assumed discretely to signify an entity in the real world and to have characteristic modes of signification (*modi significandi*) in and of itself, that is, independent of context. In some of these construals, words' significations were quite fixed and precise. Aristotle's categorical taxonomy (substance, quality, quantity, etc.) is taken to be empirically valid and words are keyed to it, so that they belong to one category or another. But some words, especially words used in theology and ordinary words used in reference to the divine, do not fit Aristotle's categorical framework. The linguistic problem was how to account for these kinds of words.

The compound problem (that is, the linguistic and epistemological issues raised by the ontological theory of essences), then, is how human beings—mere creatures—can claim to comprehend God, presume to speak of God, or to suggest that sacred writings can impart or carry divine truth with merely human words. Given this worldview, there is a potential problem in the transference or application of any concept or action that is divine, because it would belong to a category of being essentially superior, ontologically distinct from any creaturely category of being. How can a creature be said to share any attribute with God, while that essential, ontologically absolute, qualitative difference is maintained? Since the vertical divine / human gap is ontologically necessary and real in Thomas's worldview, linguistic expression seems bound to falter when it faces this gap. The dual danger is a radical (and, for Thomas, unacceptable) agnosticism, on the one hand, and the collapse of transcendence, on the other hand.[64]

---

nifer; "Medieval Theories of Analogy," in *The Stanford Encyclopedia of Philosophy* (Winter 1999 Edition), Edward N. Zalta (ed.), URL = http://plato.stanford.edu/archives/win1999/entries/analogy-medieval/.

[64] Paul Ricoeur explains this danger aptly: "[T]heological discourse encounters a ... choice: to impute a discourse common to God and to his creatures would be to destroy divine transcendence; on the other hand, assuming total incommunicability of meanings from one level to the other would condemn one to utter agnosticism." Paul Ricoeur, *The Rule of Metaphor*, 273.

Analogy of Being, Proportion, Participation: The Solution

In Aristotle's understanding of analogy, Aquinas discerned a key. It appeared to be the solution to the signification problem entailed in the vertical ontological gap, as well as the key to certain problems created by horizontal hierarchies (gradients of being within categories). By the analogy of being (*analogia entis*), human beings participated with God in God-given being; by logical analogy, human thought and language could bridge the gap with the divine, allowing transfer of attributes at the level of 'likenesses' without contaminating (and therefore negating the essential difference of) God.

Thomas found it necessary to specify the kind of analogy that could serve this function, and his thinking on this matter evolved during his lifetime. Divine-human comparison had to be a form of analogy that did not suggest equation of the terms, otherwise one would imply that God and a creaturely analogate were actually equal in some sense (an impossible—and heretical—notion, in this worldview). By the time of the composition of the *Summa*, Thomas had developed a model that divided words into three main kinds and created three basic kinds of analogy. First, consider the three kinds of words: 1) words whose sense remained constant were 'univocal;' 2) words that could be used in different senses, termed 'equivocal;' 3) words observed to be used in related senses, called 'analogical.' Again, recall that these features were thought to be a qualities of the words themselves, independently of context.

English examples of 'equivocal' words would be *match* (sporting event, something used to ignite a fire, a perceived connection between two or more objects) or *punt* (a kind of kick in American football, a kind of flat boat used on an English river—or the act of propelling such a boat). When words are used analogically, however, the meanings of the words are held to have some commonality, some aspect of similarity. The difficulty lies in determining with some precision what those common properties or qualities are, and how the relationship between those meanings operates.

Medieval scholars noticed that not all comparisons are alike in form or function and devised various models or typologies of analogy. Here we will focus on the three-part model (or typology) that Aquinas used in his later work.[65] In this model, the first kind of analogy compares

---

[65] Ricoeur summarizes the shifts in Thomas's thinking about analogy and analyzes

two proportions or relations. The Greek word translated 'healthy' was a commonly used example of this type of analogical term. The primary meaning of the term is something like 'hearty bodily functioning.' But the word can be used in other ways, in expressions that refer to *causes* of health ('healthy' diet) or to *signs* of health ('healthy' cheeks). The two things are thought to be related by a direct proportion of degree, distance, or measure; the healthiness of a diet is directly related to, and directly measured by, the health it produces. This kind of analogy is called 'analogy of proportion,' *proportio*.

Secondly, medieval scholars noticed that when 'healthy' was used to refer to food, the term 'healthy' was being used in a derived, or 'secondary' sense. 'Bodily health' is the *prime* or *principal analogate*, while the other ways of using the word are its secondary *analogates*. The term *analogia* or 'analogy of attribution' (*per prius et posterius*) referred to analogies like this. 'Analogies of attribution' point to relations between two things, one of which is clearly the primary entity, while the other is secondary, some kind of attribute of the first thing.

The third type of analogy highlights a relationship in which one entity imitates the other or somehow 'participates' in it, but without confusing the distinctive essences of the two entities—analogy of imitation or participation.[66] This type of analogy was useful to theologians when they wanted to understand (and explain) relations of likeness between God and God's creatures. Human beings, creatures, could truly be called 'good' or 'just,' but the quality of 'goodness' or 'justice' they enjoyed was qualitatively distinct from the goodness and justice of God. Only by an analogy of imitation or participation could be human beings and God both be said to be 'good.'

Medieval commentaries discussed the usefulness of Aristotle's teachings regarding the legitimate role of analogy in logic for the problematic of theological language. Rather than discussing these matters at length, Thomas simply uses these structures, assuming their validity.

---

their philosophical significance in *The Rule of Metaphor*, 272–280. David Tracy incisively evaluates the metaphysical grounding of Thomas's approach to analogy and metaphor, and indicates the core reasons for its inadequacy. David Tracy, *Blessed Rage for Order: The New Pluralism in Theology* (Chicago: Chicago University Press, 1975, 1996), 160–162.

[66] "To participate means, approximately, to have partially what another possesses or is fully"; Ricoeur correctly discerns that Thomas actually had to use (conceptual) metaphor even to frame and talk about analogy of "participation" and that this move has Neoplatonic undertones. Ibid., 274.

He employs the threefold division of word types—equivocal, univocal, and analogical—and the three distinctions about kinds of analogies in the course of his theological disputations.[67] Aquinas' account of the proper understanding of the relationships between the divine and the human displayed in metaphors and analogies—and of the truth status of such language—has been so highly influential. In his historical survey, Ricoeur, for example, finds it necessary to deal with Thomas's construal of the function of metaphor and analogy in philosophy and in Scripture, to explicate the Thomistic analogy typology, and then to point to its inadequacy. [It is worth looking at Aquinas' position on the function of metaphor in Scripture moral discourse before making claims about the inadequacies of his approach.]

Scriptural Metaphor: Aquinas the Aristotelian Exegete

Aquinas makes a statement in the *Summa* that sounds like it could have been taken directly from Aristotle:

> It is natural to man to attain to intellectual truths through sensible objects, because all our knowledge originates through sense.[68]

As I have said, Aristotelian empiricism and view of nature shapes Aquinas' epistemology, grounding "all our knowledge" in the experiential, in sensate apprehension. Aquinas carries this perspective over into his biblical hermeneutic. In fact, the very next sentence is this:

> Hence in holy Scripture spiritual truths are fittingly taught under the likeness of material things.[69]

Aquinas picks up a brand of Aristotelian empiricism and welds it to Christian traditional notions of the transcendent or 'spiritual' and 'spiritual truth.' It is in this arena of spiritual truth that metaphor, analogy, and figurative language come into play for Thomas. The supernatural realm consists in all that is beyond material sense, in that which human beings cannot know unless God reveals it. Thomas observes that Scripture itself uses 'likenesses' in order to teach 'spiritual truths.'

---

[67] Several further distinctions in Aquinas' construal of analogy are of interest but cannot be explicated here; for example, analogy of "proportionality" is not the same as analogy of "proportion." See Ricoeur, Ibid.
[68] Aquinas *ST* 1.1.9.
[69] Ibid.

If Holy Scripture uses likenesses, then it is also fitting that sacred doctrine "makes use of metaphors as both necessary and useful."[70] Aquinas recognizes that abstract or spiritual truths can sometimes be grasped via comparison with material objects. Consider, for example, Thomas's brief discussion of the biblical use of 'lion' to describe God:

> So it is that all names applied metaphorically to God are applied to creatures primarily rather than to God, because when said of God they mean only similitudes to such creatures. For as *smiling* applied to a field means only that the field in the beauty of its flowering is like to the beauty of the human smile by proportionate likeness, so the name *lion* applied to God means only that God manifests strength in His works, as a lion in his.[71]

Clearly, Aquinas is operating with an Aristotelian model of metaphor. He assumes that metaphor is based on 'similitudes,' similarities between two things (e.g., God and lion), and that it works by the transference ('application') of a name that does not properly belong to a second object.

Metaphor was thought to be a special type, a subset, of analogy of proportionality. Metaphoric proportionality relied, however, on an 'improper' use of words. If Scripture, for example, were to speak of "God's wrath," this would be metaphorical analogy. God cannot literally undergo human emotions, passions, but God can act so as to cause effects like anger. Thomas saw a parallel between this kind of language use in Scripture and 'poetic' metaphor. In Thomas's examples (God is *sun* and *lion* manifesting *strength*) of biblical metaphorical proportionality, he demonstrates that connection or parallel; biblical metaphor is poetic and functions symbolically. But he reserves a separate category for a kind of transcendental analogy that could handle speculative rational truth.[72] The distinction is significant.

Thomas attempts to understand and explain the *purpose* of metaphor and poetry in the sacred writings and moral theology. Poetry fits into Thomas's classification of the sciences, as part of 'inventive logic,' along with dialectic and rhetoric. As part of logic, poetry could also be identified with moral philosophy, especially as a heuristic tool. It was thought that sacred poetry, through the logical device of example,

---

[70] Ibid, 1.1.9.1.
[71] Ibid., 1.1.6.
[72] See Ricoeur for a discussion of these distinctions. Ibid., 279.

could become a form of moral logic, an instrument of moral philosophy complementary to rhetoric. There is a sense in Aquinas' treatment of metaphor, however, that it is usually a way of hiding truths, rather than revealing them. He will say that Scripture uses figurative language to teach important truths, but then suggest that in another part of Scripture the same truth is taught "more openly."[73]

It is this 'proper' and 'literal' or 'open' use of words that Aquinas uses to balance what he judges to have been undue weight accorded to the 'figurative' (read 'allegorical') in earlier exegesis. Aquinas' revision of the traditional 'four senses' methodology is intended as a corrective to the allegorical method that dominated biblical hermeneutics in the period preceding him.

Sidebar: Scripture Study in the Middle Ages

As we move out of the patristic period into the medieval era, a gradual but continuous trend develops. The Neoplatonic liking for symbolical interpretation comes into ascendancy and, by Thomas's time, the allegorical reading methods that are characteristic of, if not univocally adopted by, medieval scholars have full sway. Multiple meanings are sought in every text; in some versions of the method, seven levels of meaning are systematically delineated.[74] Perhaps the most famous of these medieval hermeneutical rubrics is the one outlining four 'senses' or levels of meaning, each 'sense' being referenced to a particular function or purpose that ensues from the reading process.

The Four Senses of Scripture

A little poem about how to read and interpret Scripture circulated during the Middle Ages, and would have been known in Thomas's time.[75] It goes like this:

---

[73] "Hence those things that are taught metaphorically in one part of Scripture, in other parts are taught more openly. The very hiding of truth in figures is useful for the exercise of thoughtful minds and as a defense against the ridicule of the impious, according to the words, 'Give not that which is holy to dogs.' (Mt. 7:6) ... thereby divine truths are the better hidden from the unworthy." (Ibid., 1.1.9.)

[74] This tendency is to be observed in Maimonides as well. See Sandel, "Understanding Religious Language: And Integrated Approach to Meaning."

[75] Robert M. Grant and David Tracy, *A Short History of the Interpretation of the Bible*,

Littera gesta docet, quid creda allegoria,
Moralis quid agas, quo tendas anagogia.

The letter shows us what God and our fathers did;
The allegory shows us where our faith is hid;
The moral meaning gives us rules of daily life;
The anagogy shows us where we end our strife.

The wedding of allegory with 'hidden' meaning tied to faith, *creda*, is transparent enough. But note the equation of 'letter' or 'literal' meaning with history and the assumption that moral meaning would be concerned with rules, while anagogical meaning—at least in this English version—is associated with the future, even the eschatological. It was Thomas Aquinas who, in the end of the medieval period, insisted that the *littera*, the 'literal' meaning, should be primary. He envisioned the *littera* governing, grounding and constraining the other three modes of meaning.[76]

Thomas on the Four Senses of Scripture

One does not have to guess what Thomas himself thought about the 'four senses' model; we have a summary of his position in the first book of the *Summa*. Here he quotes Gregory (*Moralia* 20:1), whose position is that "Holy Scripture, by the manner of its speech transcends every science, because in one and the same sentence, while it describes a fact, it reveals a mystery." Thomas replies:

> The author of holy Scripture is God, in whose power it is to signify his meaning, not by words only (as man can do) but by things themselves. So, whereas in every other science things are signified by words, this science has the property that the things signified by the words have themselves also a signification. Therefore that first signification whereby words signify things belongs to the *first sense, the historical or literal*. That signification whereby things signified by words have themselves also a signification is called the *spiritual sense*, which is based on the literal, and presupposes it. For as the apostle says (Heb. 10:1) the Old Law is a figure of the New Law and (Pseudo-) Dionysius says: 'The New Law

---

2d ed. (Philadelphia: Fortress, 1984), 85. Grant and Tracy say this verse circulated as late as the 16th century, but comes from the time of Augustine and John Cassian. Latin *agaso* < a driver, one who drives and takes care of horses; *credo* < to give as a loan, to make a loan; *tendo* < to stretch, make tense, spread out, extend.

[76] Underneath Thomas's model is a critique of the allegorical methods that had gained hegemony in his day.

itself is figure of future glory.' Again, in the New Law, whatever our Head has done is a type of what we ought to do. Therefore, so far as the things of the Old Law signify the things of the New Law, there is the *allegorical sense;* so far as the things done in Christ, or so far as the things which signify Christ, are types of what we ought to do, there is the *moral sense.* But so far as they signify what relates to eternal glory, there is the *anagogical sense.* Since the literal sense is that which the author intends, and since the author of holy Scripture is God, it is not unfitting, as Augustine says, if even according to the literal sense one word in holy Scripture should have several senses.[77]

Several features of this little piece are noteworthy: the assertion (assumption) that God is the author of Scripture; that the 'literal' sense and the author's intention are identical; that this 'literal' sense therefore has primacy over other senses; that the 'moral' sense of Scripture is keyed to "the things which signify Christ" and that these are 'types' of "what we ought to do."

Re-Cap: Thomas on Metaphor, Analogy, and Scripture

Thomas's understanding of metaphor and analogy is essence-driven and structured with Aristotelian categories and definitions. While he recognizes a key role for metaphorical language and for analogical thinking in theology and Scripture and interpretation of Scripture, his ontological and epistemological commitments force him to attempt to draw strict distinctions between the 'literal' and the 'imitative' or 'figurative.' Holding divine and creaturely beings in ontological distinction and tension, he understands metaphor to function in a back-room, back-door, indirect manner. It arises from sensate perception of reality, but when it comes to perception of the transcendent, it can only suggest in 'hidden,' 'veiled,' fashion truth that is elsewhere more literally and openly conveyed.

With reason, Thomas tries to rein in a biblical interpretive guild run amok, drunk with the infinite and mysterious possibilities of symbolic and 'fanciful' readings. He tethers the moralizing, spiritualizing, and allegorical modes of interpretation to what he calls the historical, literal sense, grounding it all, he hopes, in God's own intention to communicate naturally apprehendable truth. Since sacred Scripture is

---

[77] Aquinas *ST* 1.1.10.; emphasis mine.

full of similitudes and metaphors, Aquinas has to grant that they are good and must be useful. After all, God—the omniscient and Good—is their author: "Therefore this sacred science may use metaphors"!

The problems entailed in Thomas's essentialism, the questionable accuracy and validity of his account of analogy, and the literal / figurative split do not disappear, however.[78] The Scholastics would wrestle with these matters (and drop them, too), essentially deciding to denigrate the imaginative and metaphorical in favor of the so-called 'literal.' Thomists would come to be known for their rigorous insistence on a version of *recta ratio* that lost Thomas's own nuanced and genuine appreciation of metaphor. By the time the forces of "reason" come to their position of dominance, what came to be called the 'Enlightenment' (a metaphor of questionable aptness), the literal / figurative divide will come to center stage. We turn now, then, to a star performer on that stage, Thomas Hobbes.

Enlightenment Views of Metaphor

Modern philosophical and theological attitudes toward metaphor have their historical roots in the classical and medieval traditions, but they are filtered through an Enlightenment lens. That filter colors modernist hermeneutical approaches to biblical metaphor as well as certain attitudes towards metaphor, the role of the imagination and narrative of Christian ethicists trained in the liberal tradition.

In the course of the gradual but irreversible tectonic shift towards empiricism and rationalism in the sixteenth and seventeenth centuries, prevailing views of metaphor shifted as well. But the view expressed at the beginning of the period by Thomas Hobbes is representative of the basic orientation of would-be 'scientific' thinkers; his words put the matter starkly before us. Immanuel Kant takes a very different approach. His rigorous philosophical-theological ethic still is a benchmark for Christian ethics, but his approach to metaphor or imagination is perhaps mostly overlooked in current discussions and appropriations of his work. Friedrich Nietzsche represents the far end of the spectrum, the thorough-going, 'pro-metaphor' end.

---

[78] Regarding the core problems with Thomistic understandings of analogy and metaphor, and their persistence in current theology, see Tracy, *Blessed Rage for Order*, 160–162.

Hobbes and the Literal-Truth Paradigm

Thomas Hobbes (1588–1679) was interested in the role of speech in the formation and preservation of human society. In his view, one of the main purposes of speech is to communicate knowledge, and that purpose is thwarted by any use of metaphor, which is deceptive:

> Metaphors, and senslesse and ambiguous words, are like *ignes fatui;* and reasoning upon them is wandering amongst innumerable absurdities; and their end, contention and sedition, or contempt.[79]

Hobbes is employing an Aristotelian definition of metaphor as transfer of 'names' to assert that it inevitably leads to confusion and incorrect reasoning. Lost in the shuffle is Aristotle's notion of 'fitting' or proportionate metaphor; now confusion over a word's reference can only undermine rational argument. Hobbes made other pointed (and passionate) remarks about metaphor. He includes metaphor in his list of 'abuses' of speech and he assumed use of metaphor was inherently deceptive: "when they use words metaphorically; that is, in other sense than that they were ordained for; and thereby deceive others."[80] In Chapter 5 of *Leviathan*, the chapter entitled, "Reason and Science," Hobbes includes a list of errors in reasoning and use of language that lead to absurd conclusions. Metaphor is item number six on his list:

> The *sixth*, to the use of Metaphors, Tropes, and other Rhetoricall Figures, in stead of words proper. For though it be lawfull to say, (for example) in common speech, *the way goeth, or leadeth hither, or thither, The Proverb sayes this or that* (whereas wayes cannot go, nor Proverbs speak;) yet in reckoning, and seeking of truth, such speeches are not to be admitted.[81]

By 'reckoning,' Hobbes means reasoning, rational argument—the use of language in pursuit of truth. This statement expresses the core of the dominant attitude toward metaphor and figurative language in modern Western philosophy. Mark Johnson has outlined the key features of a Hobbesian-style view of metaphor, and it will be useful to outline them here for purposes of comparison with contemporary views, many of which inherit empiricist assumptions. Johnson calls the Hobbesian view 'the literal-truth paradigm.' It consists of three major points:

---

[79] Thomas Hobbes, *Leviathan*, Cambridge Texts in the History of Political Thought Edition (Cambridge: Cambridge University Press, 1991, 1994), 1.5.22.
[80] Ibid., 1.4.13.
[81] Ibid., 1.5.20.

(1) The human conceptual system is essentially literal—literal language ("words proper") is the *only* adequate vehicle of (a) expressing one's meaning precisely, and (b) making truth claims, which together make possible correct reasoning by the philosopher.
(2) Metaphor is a deviant use of words in other than their proper sense, which accounts for its tendency to confuse and deceive.
(3) The meaning and truth claims of a metaphor (if there are any) are just those of its literal paraphrase.[82]

In addition, Johnson notes that this literal-truth paradigm almost always has been accompanied by the association of metaphor with rhetoric:

> The alleged connection is simple: if truth can be formulated in literal terms, then figurative discourse can be, at best, an alternative form of expression, utilized merely for rhetorical purposes or stylistic embellishment.[83]

Johnson goes on to demonstrate adherence to the literal-truth paradigm in the writings of John Locke, Bishop Berkeley, Hegel, and John Stuart Mill.[84] Even many philosophers and theologians who want to recover or carve out a place in philosophical or theological discourse for figurative language actually adhere to the literal / figurative split entailed in the literal truth paradigm.

Immanuel Kant and Friedrich Nietzsche: Exceptions to the Rule

Kant (1724–1804) stands out from his contemporaries with regard to the attention he devotes to understanding the philosophical significance of metaphor and of imaginative thought.[85] He was interested in think-

---

[82] Johnson, *Philosophical Perspectives*, 12.
[83] Ibid.
[84] Ibid., 13. Hegel defines metaphor as an "abridged comparison," arguing that "metaphor cannot pretend to the value of an independent representation, but only to that of an accessory one. Even in its highest degree it can appear only as a simple ornament for a work of art." George Wilhelm Friedrich Hegel, *The Philosophy of Fine Art*, tr. William M. Bryant (New York: Appelton, 1879), 40–41. John Stuart Mill said, "A metaphor, then, is not to be considered an argument, but as an assertion that an argument exists; that a parity subsists between the case from which the metaphor is drawn and that to which it is applied." John Stuart Mill, *A System of Logic: Ratiocinative and Inductive*, ed. J.M. Robson (Toronto: University of Toronto Press, 1974), 5.5., ¶7).
[85] Rousseau and Nietzsche also departed from the Literal Truth Paradigm. See Johnson's discussion of their contributions. Ibid., 15–16.

ing about what imagination was, and how it might be involved in moral deliberation. Kant realized that metaphor is an important part of human creative capacity, and that it is not reducible to literal equivalents. He saw, therefore, that there was a need to give an account of metaphor within any account of human cognition.

It is in *The Critique of Practical Reason* that Kant most directly addresses the issues with which we are concerned here.[86] In his attempt to found a universalizable ethic while preserving human freedom and moral autonomy, Kant theorizes that moral law must abstract from all material content (i.e., any particular end arising from one's desires or from bodily contingencies). In his terms, the moral law must be 'pure' so that it can categorically (unconditionally and universally) command. A problem arises for Kant: How can such a 'pure' principle ever be applied to a given case, to actual human experience? Remember that he assumed the natural world was causally determined, but that he wished to uphold human freedom of will and moral autonomy. There seemed to be no way to apply pure moral rules (laws of freedom) to real-life cases. Kant found a way out of this impasse by suggesting that universal moral laws might be *indirectly* or *symbolically* presented. Here he sees a role for imagination and intuition. Mark Johnson explains how Kant tried to make his theory work:

> [For Kant], no pure moral rule can be applied directly to experience, because such a law of freedom cannot apply to our deterministic natural world. But the supreme moral law (the categorical imperative) involves only the *form* of all laws, that is, universality. Therefore, the universality of all moral law can actually be represented *figuratively* as the form of natural law (i.e., universality).[87]

So, while Kant attempted to found an ethical theory on purely rational grounds, in order for the theory to work in situational moral deliberation, it was necessary to include intuition and figurative and symbolic thought in the account.

Kant understood that figurative expressions, metaphors, might express and generate more conceptual work, thought, than could be represented if they were somehow distilled, reduced to propositional,

---

[86] Immanuel Kant, *Critique of Practical Reason*, tr. Werner S. Pluhar (Indianapolis: Hackett Publishing Co., 2002).

[87] Johnson, *Moral Imagination*, 71. And see his extended critique of Kant's moral theory, in which he convincingly argues that Kant's ethic is based on and expressed via conceptual metaphors; Ibid., 65–77. Johnson also treats Kant in *The Body in the Mind*, xxvii–xxix.

literal expressions. Finally, he realized that creative, figurative thought was an important component of human reason.[88]

Friedrich Nietzsche (1844–1900), represents romantic interplay and clash with the kinds of 'scientific' sensibilities that Hobbes expressed. The 'proper' versus 'improper: metaphorical' split that so convinced Hobbes of the dangerous character of 'tropes,' Nietzsche would not abide. He denied the divide's existence because he recognized the ubiquity of metaphor in human speech. Even more perspicaciously (from a cognitivist point-of-view), he recognized that metaphor was not "mere" metaphor, that it was a perceptive and cognitive process:

> What is a word? The expression of a nerve-stimulus in sounds ...
> A nerve stimulus, first transformed in a percept! First metaphor!
> The percept again copied into a sound! Second metaphor![89]

His view of metaphor fit—was part and parcel of—his critique of received, 'objective' and fixed cultural truths.

> What therefore is truth? A mobile army of metaphors, metonymies, anthropomorphisms: in short a sum of human relations which become poetically and rhetorically intensified, metamorphosed, adorned, and after long usage seem to a nation fixed, canonic, and binding; truths are illusions of which one has forgotten that they *are* illusions; worn-out metaphors which have become powerless to affect the senses ...[90]

The essay from which this quotation is taken, "Truth and Falsity in Their Ultramoral Sense," displays Nietzsche's interest in and attitude toward the classical rhetorical tradition. His project is to re-cast rhetoric. Classical idealist and metaphysical notions are rejected at the same time that rhetoric is essentially de-specialized. That is, Nietzsche notices that everyday language in use is rhetorical, and that it includes a conventionalized set of metaphors. But the deeper meaning of these metaphors and conventions is, essentially, socially constructed; it is not referenced to some transcendent, eternal structure of truth (and cer-

---

[88] Johnson surmises, however, that Kant would not have embraced the kind of cognitive status for metaphor that cognitive linguists propose: "since [for Kant] comprehending a metaphor is not a wholly rule-governed activity, it does not produce knowledge (through determinate concepts)." Johnson, *Philosophical Perspectives on Metaphor*, 14.

[89] Friedrich Nietzsche, "On Truth and Falsity in Their Ultramoral Sense," in *The Complete Works of Friedrich Nietzsche*, Vol. 2, ed. Oscar Levy, tr. Maximilian A. Mügge (New York: Russell and Russell, Inc., 1964), 177, 178. Nietzsche also says, in this essay, that "Every idea originates through equating the unequal." Ibid., 179.

[90] Ibid., 180.

tainly not to a Being, God). Nietzsche denied deep archetypical significance or transcendent power to metaphor, even while he celebrated its contingent power to shape society and to display the shape of societal values.

The inimitable and influential Nietzsche's views on metaphor failed to impress the philosophical community, and it was a long time until serious philosophical and scientific exploration of the dynamics of metaphor and thought he had so brilliantly (but imperfectly and incompletely) intuited began. The most interesting connections here are not, however, the possible affinities between cognitive metaphor approaches and Nietzsche's attitude toward metaphor, but the possible connections between his perceptions about metaphor and his distrust of traditional, conventional thought—and the potential implications of this connection for subsequent developments in biblical hermeneutics. If in Nietzsche's hands such an attitude toward metaphor was put in the service of cynical doubt and radical suspicion, does such an outcome prove inevitable? I suspect that Anthony Thistleton is correct when he suggests that in biblical hermeneutics the post-Nietzsche trend was toward focus on 'processes and variables' in texts.[91]

Views of Metaphor in Western Tradition: Summary

What, then, has been the thinking about metaphor and its role in philosophy and theology, especially in ethics? Aristotelian definitions and categories have been highly influential, to the point that generally they have been assumed to be true, rather than recognized for their theoretical status. Aristotle saw metaphor at work primarily in poetic and rhetorical persuasive discourse. As the tradition developed, those two streams—poetic and rhetorical—forked, so that the rhetorical and poetic functions of metaphor came to be regarded as fundamentally different. Further downstream, rhetoric split off from philosophy, with the result that metaphor comes to be seen as a 'mere' rhetorical, stylistic device, or as belonging to the realm of the 'imaginative' and poetic.

Two major strands—Aristotelian and Augustinian/Neoplatonic— persist in subsequent developments of the tradition. They can be traced

---

[91] Anthony C. Thistleton, *New Horizons in Hermeneutics*, 143.

through the later medieval and Enlightenment theologians and philosophers. A major shift occurs in the Enlightenment period, with the articulation of the Hobbesian 'literal-truth paradigm.' Defined as mere rhetorical device, metaphor is relegated to the sphere of the non-scientific, and therefore intellectually suspect. In the hands of Enlightenment empiricists, metaphor is devalued. But the Romantics lovingly, reverently pulled metaphor out of that trash-heap, and, by the time Nietzsche got hold of it, he declared it the foundation of all thought and language.

Metaphor and Ethics

Understandings of the relationship between metaphor and ethics have been diverse, as well. Plato pointed to the potential social-political power of metaphor, and attempted to wall off poetry from reason. Aristotle found a positive role for the imaginative faculty at the level of practical reasoning. Though his definition of metaphor itself underlay many thinkers' usages of the concept, the explicit role of metaphor in the kind of practical reasoning that was central to Aristotle's ethics did not persist. Later theorists continued to think of metaphor as rhetorical or cathartic-emotive device, but most did not continue along the path Aristotle began to clear for thinking about metaphor's conceptual, category-related roles. To the extent that ethics was thought to belong to a higher cognitive realm—variously conceived as 'intelligence,' 'rational faculty,' 'reason' or 'pure reason'—the role Aristotle outlined for metaphor in practical reasoning was denigrated or lost. The Neoplatonists, for example, relegated metaphor to the lowest level of cognition. Metaphor was spiritualized but dismissed from the arena of rational argument. Augustine and the medieval scholars who followed him held to a Neoplatonic-style view. Metaphor and imaginative expressions might have some heuristic value, might motivate ethical behavior, particularly for those unable to follow rational arguments, but the significant conceptual work of ethics—of argumentation and definition in areas like justice or virtue theory—belonged to the rational faculty.

Metaphor, then, is everything (Nietzsche) and it is (nearly) nothing, useless (Hobbes), in our ethical tradition. It is a (lesser) mode of practical reasoning and it is a conduit for the impartation of transcendent truth. But the dominant definitions of metaphor itself have been Aristotle's. Not until quite recently have these definitions come under close scrutiny. They have come under scrutiny for a number of reasons; the following section outlines the most prominent among those factors.

Why the Need for a New Theory?

The received tradition regarding metaphor is inadequate on at least three levels: 1) fundamental philosophical problems, 2) outdated and inaccurate understandings of human psychology and neurological makeup, 3) theoretical and pragmatic semantic and linguistic deficits. These three kinds of problems are not unrelated, and each area of concern is significant, but in keeping with the scope of this study, I will focus primarily on the linguistic evidence that points to the philosophical issues and touch briefly on the neuro-psychological issues.

Traditional approaches to metaphor fail to explain the following linguistic evidence:

Patterns in usage of metaphors and clusters of metaphors

If metaphor is merely deviant or improper usage of words, if metaphor is simply a phenomenon at the level of linguistic expressions—not thought patterns—then each metaphorical expression should be a different metaphor. But linguists have clear evidence that metaphorical expressions cluster and that the *concept* of a connection can precede any particular instantiation in a given expression.[92] Moreover, metaphors can create conceptual connections or extend conventional ones. They are not merely derivative.

---

[92] Lakoff and Johnson, *Philosophy in the Flesh*, 123. And see Antonio R. Damasio, *Descartes' Error: Emotion, Reason, and the Human Brain* (New York: G.P. Putnam's Sons, 1994; HarperCollins: 2000). Neurologist Damasio says that "both words and arbitrary symbols are based on topographically organized representations and can become images. Most of the words we use in our inner speech, before speaking or writing a sentence, exist as auditory or visual images in our consciousness. If they did not become images, however fleetingly, they would not be anything we could know." Ibid., 106. Damasio notes that this understanding of the value of neural images is new, and cites the research of Stephen Kosslyn and Roger Shepard. See Roger N. Shepard and L.A. Cooper, *Mental Images and Their Transformations* (Cambridge, Mass.: MIT Press, 1982). Also see the historical review in Howard Gardner, *The Mind's New Science* (New York: Basic Books, 1985).

Ordinary, everyday usage of metaphorical language

If metaphor is merely or mostly poetic and rhetorical, it should not be possible to demonstrate that metaphor is used in everyday conversation and in ordinary reasoning. The standard Aristotelian definition of metaphor makes room for its use in philosophical argument, persuasive oratory, and poetry, but it fails to account for the ubiquitous occurrence of metaphorical expressions in ordinary, everyday speech.[93]

Conventional and Stock Metaphors

If metaphor is 'deviant' usage of language, usage of words in improper senses, then it should be rare and difficult to understand, and we should not be able to find so many conventionalized, stock metaphors. Nor should we be able to discern how supposedly 'dead' metaphors are so useful—used in a quite lively manner—in reasoning and conversation.

Asymmetric metaphors

If metaphor were based on (objective) similarities, one should have no trouble finding preexisting similarities between the words or concepts used and there should be no metaphors that are not based on similarities. If they are based on similarity, then the transfer should operate bi-directionally, when in fact most metaphors are unidirectional.

What is 'similarity,' in the first place? The traditional view fails to account adequately for human ability to discern similarities and patterns before they are expressed in language.[94] It also cannot explain why so many metaphorical expressions seem to *create* similarities, to link domains that are not inherently related. Linguists have found that this happens in both novel and conventional metaphors.[95]

---

[93] Lakoff and Johnson, *Philosophy in the Flesh*, 123.
[94] Ibid., 126.
[95] Ibid.

Semantic change

Directionality of metaphorical transfer seems to persist even through the processes of semantic change, as does a trend to shift from concrete to more abstract domains.[96] "Words do not randomly acquire new senses," and metaphorical word usage is patterned over time.[97] The traditional views cannot adequately account for these patterns.

Inconsistent inferences and usages

If metaphor were based on essential properties, ontological similarities uncovered, then it should not be possible to find deep inconsistencies among multiple metaphors employed for describing the same entity or phenomenon.[98] But cognitive linguists are amassing evidence that clearly shows such inconsistencies are rampant. At the same time, they are finding that metaphorical expressions involve a transfer of inference patterns.

The traditional understandings of metaphor cannot account for these phenomena. When these kinds of patterns and issues are noticed, traditional models most often stop at the 'noticing' stage, without offering much in the way of explanation. It will be suggested that 'something' happens in the transfer that occurs in metaphor—something 'mysterious.' Can more be said, and more be understood, about how metaphor is structured and how it functions in discourse? Cognitive linguists have devised methods for understanding and articulating many aspects of the dynamics involved in metaphor that traditional models failed either to detect or to explain.

These linguistic issues, however, do not stand alone; they are not isolated phenomena of interest only to expert semanticists and pragmatic linguists. Traditional views of metaphor rely on outdated understandings of human reasoning and of the relationship between the world and the human mind. The 'faculty' psychology classical and medieval metaphor models rely on has long since been rejected as inadequate and inaccurate. The doctrine of Essences—or the various versions of the notion of essences—on which classical and medieval

---

[96] Ibid., 127. and see Eve Sweetser, *From Etymology to Pragmatics: Metaphorical and Cultural Aspects of Semantic Structure* (Cambridge; Cambridge University Press, 1990).
[97] Ibid., 9.
[98] Lakoff and Johnson, *Philosophy in the Flesh*, 127.

category structures were modeled has long since been discredited and discarded. But the traditional understandings of metaphor and analogy are based on these antiquated philosophical and psychological models. Cognitive metaphor theory does not rely on these antiquated and inadequate philosophical and psychological belief systems. It is grounded in cross-disciplinary empirical evidence concerning how human beings construct categories and display them in language. It is to that contemporary understanding of metaphor and thought that we now turn.

CHAPTER TWO

A CONTEMPORARY THEORY OF METAPHOR

The essence of metaphor is understanding and experiencing one kind of thing in terms of another.[1]

Many philosophers, linguists, cognitive scientists, and scholars in other fields recently have been working to understand metaphor in greater detail. There was divergence of opinion regarding metaphor among traditional thinkers, and contemporary scholars have carried on that part of the tradition—the tradition of disagreement.[2] But one major stream of contemporary theory of metaphor is gaining increasing support from scholars working in several disciplines. It is the metaphor theory whose major features were first worked out by linguist George Lakoff with philosopher Mark Johnson.[3] This chapter introduces that

---

[1] George Lakoff and Mark Johnson, *Metaphors We Live By* (Chicago: University of Chicago Press, 1980), 5.

[2] Lakoff names the major thinkers with whom he is arguing and briefly discusses key points of difference with Searle, Glucksberg and Keysar in George Lakoff, "The Contemporary Theory of Metaphor" in *Metaphor and Thought*, ed. Andrew Ortony, 2d ed. (Cambridge: Cambridge University Press, 1993), 202–251. Pointed critiques of the Lakoffian view are expressed by Virginia Held, "Whose Agenda? Ethics versus Cognitive Science" in *Mind and Morals: Essays on Ethics and Cognitive Science*, edited by Larry May, Marilyn Friedman, and Andy Clark (Cambridge, Mass: MIT Press, 1996), 68–87.

[3] Other linguists—notably Eve Sweetser, Joseph Grady, Christopher Johnson, Kevin Moore and Sarah Taub—have collaborated with Lakoff and Johnson and elaborated on the basic theory and methods. See Joseph E. Grady, "Foundations of Meaning: Primary Metaphors and Primary Scenes" (Ph.D. diss., University of California at Berkeley, 1997); Kevin E. Moore, "Spatial Experience and Temporal Metaphors in Wolof: Point of View, Conceptual Mapping, and Linguistic Practice" (Ph.D. diss, University of California at Berkeley, 2000); Sarah Taub, "Language in the Body: Iconicity and Metaphor in American Sign Language," (Ph.D. diss. University of California at Berkeley, 1997). These pioneering linguists have collaborated with cognitively-oriented scholars in other disciplines; I should note especially cognitive scientist Gilles Fauconnier and English literature scholar Mark Turner. See also the work of cognitive scientists Seana Coulson and Todd Oakley. Seana Coulson, *Semantic Leaps: Frame-shifting and Conceptual Blending in Meaning Construction* (Cambridge and New York; Cambridge University Press, 2001); Todd Oakley, "Presence: The Conceptual Basis of Rhetorical Effect," (Ph.D. diss., University of Maryland, 1995).

contemporary theoretical understanding of the nature, function, and structure of metaphor, and points to some of the ways it can be applied to the issues and questions biblical ethics addresses.

Conceptual and Experiential Grounding

The essence of metaphor is understanding and experiencing one kind of thing in terms of another.[4] This is the working definition George Lakoff and Mark Johnson offer in the ground-breaking book, *Metaphors We Live By*. According to this theory, metaphor is not merely a matter of words, it is the main way we comprehend abstract concepts and perform abstract reasoning. In fact, research data support the claim that metaphor is essentially conceptual, not linguistic, in nature, and that metaphorical expressions in language are 'surface manifestations' of conceptual metaphor.[5] Much that we need to think about and communicate can only be comprehended via metaphor, and this includes both highly difficult and complex matters (like scientific and philosophical theories) and ordinary, everyday matters. In fact, the linguistic data show that metaphor is ubiquitous in ordinary, everyday language, and that this is true not just in English or Indo-European languages, but cross-linguistically.

Metaphor is ubiquitous, but not omnipresent. A significant part of our conceptual system is *non*metaphorical. In fact, metaphorical understanding appears to be grounded in nonmetaphorical understanding. Much conceptual metaphor seems to have an experiential basis—particularly in bodily experience.[6] The author of 1 Peter, for instance, uses the word δοῦλος ('slave') metaphorically when he enjoins his

---

[4] Lakoff and Johnson, *Metaphors We Live By*, 5.
[5] The term "surface manifestations" is from Lakoff, "The Contemporary Theory of Metaphor." Five major types of evidence support the notion of a system of conventional conceptual metaphors: 1) generalizations governing polysemy [the use of words with a number of meanings]; 2) generalizations governing inference patterns; 3) generalizations governing novel metaphorical language; 4) generalizations governing patterns of semantic change; 5) psycholinguistic experiments. Bibliographic references for studies in each of these areas can be found in George Lakoff and Mark Johnson, *Philosophy in the Flesh: The Embodied Mind and its Challenge to Western Thought* (New York: Basic Books, 1999).
[6] Regarding the bodily experiential basis for metaphor, see Mark Johnson, *The Body in the Mind: The Bodily Basis of Meaning, Imagination, and Reason* (Chicago: University of Chicago Press, 1987). More concise treatments of the topic are found in the following: Lakoff, "The Contemporary Theory of Metaphor," 239–241; and Lakoff and Johnson, *Metaphors We Live By*, 56–60. See also section on Primary Metaphor, below.

readers to behave ὡς θεοῦ δοῦλοι ('as slaves of God'; 2.16), but that metaphor's power relies on readers' knowledge—perhaps even personal experience—of nonmetaphorical slavery, of primary cultural experience in which slavery entails low social status. When he counsels readers regarding their responses to masters who are less than divine, he uses the richly evocative adjective, σκολιός ('crooked'). The characteriological 'crookedness' of a bad slave master is being understood in terms of a physical property, crooked instead of straight.[7] In order for the more abstract evocation of this metaphor for bad masters to work, the reader must have the concept, based on experience, of actual crookedness in some physical object.

These cognitive theorists are not claiming that everything in thought and language is fundamentally metaphor-based, but they do theorize that metaphor facilitates understanding and communication, and that we typically use metaphor when we think and speak about abstract subject matter. Most often, metaphor works in such a way that relatively abstract or inherently unstructured subject matter is understood in terms of more concrete, or at least more highly structured, subject matter.[8]

In summary, then, a conceptual understanding of metaphor is distinguished from traditional understandings on a number of axes. From a cognitive linguistic point of view, metaphor is:

– conceptual before it is expressed in language
– grounded in human bodily and social experience
– ubiquitous and conventional
– systematic

These are the major points of departure from the traditional view. But they are only the starting points; much more can be said about

---

[7] Accordingly, Louw and Nida has two listings for σκολιός, "crooked" 79.90 and "unscrupulous" 88.268. Domain #79 is named "Features of Objects," and the subdomain, "Straight, Crooked." Domain #88 is named "Moral and Ethical Qualities and Related Behavior," while the subdomain to which they assign σκολιός is "Licentiousness, Perversion." They cite here another such usage of the word in the NT at Acts 2.40. Johannes P. Louw and Eugene A. Nida, eds., *Greek-English Lexicon of the New Testament Based on Semantic Domains*, 2d. ed. (New York: United Bible Societies, 1988, 1989), 702–703; 771. Cf. the complementary notion of goodness or righteousness in the Greek δίκαιος ("righteous, just").

[8] Lakoff, "Contemporary Theory", 245. But Grady and others have refined this aspect of the definition; see Grady, "Foundations of Meaning: Primary Metaphors and Primary Scenes."

how metaphor is structured and how it operates. To understand what cognitive linguists are doing with metaphor, however, it is helpful to understand the alternative ways they are approaching the notion of what a category is, in the first place.

Category Structure Concepts

Prototype Theory

Recall that Aristotle's understanding of metaphor was related to his theory of categories—categories of things and categories of kinds of cognition and expression. In brief, Aristotle thought that people categorized things according to perceived similarities, and that metaphor worked accordingly, by the perception of shared properties. Contemporary cognitive theorists still see connections between metaphor and categorization, but they have discovered that the way categorization works in human cognitive systems is better understood via a prototype model than under the classical model. Research data show that people tend to define categories (e.g., cat) by identifying certain prototypical members of the category (e.g., American shorthair housecat). We then recognize other nonprototypical category members (e.g., tiger, Manx, lion, Abyssinian, Persian) that differ in various ways from the prototypical ones. There is seldom any set of necessary and sufficient features possessed by all members of a category.[9] In ordinary human thought and language, this kind of categorization goes on constantly, automatically, and unconsciously.[10] This theory implies deep shifts in concepts of truth, of knowledge and meaning, and of rationality itself. Lakoff articulates the issues involved here clearly:

> To change the very concept of a category is to change not only our concept of the mind, but also our understanding of the world. Categories are categories *of* things. Since we understand the world not only in terms

---

[9] Mark Johnson, *Moral Imagination: Implications of Cognitive Science for Ethics* (Chicago: University of Chicago Press, 1993), 8.

[10] Lakoff's version of prototype theory builds on that of cognitive science pioneer Eleanor Rosch. He argues that "human categorization is essentially a matter of both human experience and imagination—of perception, motor activity, and culture on the one hand, and of metaphor, metonymy, and mental imagery on the other." George Lakoff, *Women, Fire, and Dangerous Things: What Categories Reveal about the Mind* (Chicago and London: University of Chicago Press, 1987), 8.

of individual things but also in terms of *categories* of things, we tend to attribute a real existence to those categories ... We have categories for everything we can think about. To change the concept of *category* itself is to change our understanding of the world.[11]

Aristotle was not wrong to point to the importance of categories, he simply did not understand how they work. Human conceptual categories are not so simply defined by a list of properties shared by all members of the category as Aristotle thought.

Radial Categories

Massive evidence suggests that cognitive categories are organized around central cases and variations on those core tendencies. Accordingly, Lakoff calls them 'radial' categories.[12] It will be important, in the work on 1 Peter in Chapter 4, to notice the operation of such radial categories in the text, as well as to become aware of specific contrasts between the typical (in itself a radial category—with perhaps various types of readers in the central place) 21st-century English Bible readers' conventional categories and those with which the text works. If, for example, an American reading the English Bible version of 1 Peter encounters the word 'slave,' the sort of slave the word evokes is likely to be the central case sort of slave from American experience—a chattel slave. This will happen automatically, unconsciously. But perhaps the word translated "slave" was δοῦλος in the Greek text. That sort of 'slave' might well have been a household servant, specifically often one who served at mealtimes, waited tables. His duties, as well as his economic and social status, differed markedly from that faced by an American chattel slave. Δοῦλος may or may not hold a place in its *koine* Greek semantic domain analogous to the central place that a chattel slave held in the English reader's conceptual and semantic category structure. English 'slave' and 'servant,' and Greek δοῦλος are, then, not simply two or three variations on one common category. The *koine* and English category structures differ; the social frames the words evoke differ. Such differences are masked when, for example, English translations of the *koine* text allow readers to assume that 'slave' or 'servant' is

---

[11] Ibid., 9.
[12] For a full explanation of radial categories, see Ibid., 91–114. For a brief introduction to radial categories and prototype structure, see George Lakoff, *Moral Politics: What Conservatives Know that Liberals Don't* (Chicago: Chicago University Press, 1996), 7–11.

equivalent to δοῦλος. These are the kinds of category structure issues that conceptual metaphor methods will tend to highlight. Semantic categories—and the concept of semantic 'domain'—are constructions dependent on cultural and social experience, and can therefore vary across or between languages.

Frame and Schema Semantics

Cognitive linguists have discovered the importance in human cognition and language use of idealized models and frameworks growing out of our experience. *Frames* are "structured understandings of the way aspects of the world function."[13] In order to understand new experiences we use terms and concepts from conventional frames or schemas. For example, the terms 'father,' 'mother,' 'son,' 'daughter,' 'aunt,' 'uncle,' 'grandfather' and 'grandmother,' 'stepfather,' and so forth, get their meanings in relation to a complex 'family' or 'household' frame. But each of these words can evoke quite different meanings in relation to other frames. A 'den mother' belongs to a Cub Scouting frame; her role bears some resemblance to the mother role in a biological/social family unit, but she is not the biological mother of each Cub Scout in the 'den.' Moreover, the specific social role the *paterfamilias* held in a Greco-Roman household differs from the role a 21st-century suburban American father plays; the Latin word *pater* and *familias* and the English words 'daddy' or 'father' and 'family' evoke distinctive frames. And each of these frames differs in some respects from the specific 'father' frame that Hebrew *'av* would evoke. So even though we translate Latin *pater* or Greek πατήρ with English 'father', and even though the men in each family frame (1st-century Greco-Roman; 21st-century suburban American) typically have the same biological relationship to the people in their households, the *cultural* frames the 'father' words evoke are different. These examples are nevertheless linked, in that each is an example of the central case in a (radial) category of biological familial relationships: each is the biological father.

---

[13] Gilles Fauconnier and Eve Sweetser, "Cognitive Links and Domains: Basic Aspects of Mental Space Theory" in *Spaces, Worlds, and Grammar*, ed. Gilles Fauconnier and Eve Sweetser (Chicago: University of Chicago Press, 1996), 5. They cite the research on frames of E. Goffman, *Frame Analysis* (New York: Harper and Row, 1974) and Charles Fillmore, "Frames and the Semantics of Understanding" in *Quaderni di Semantica* 6, no. 2 (1985): 222–254.

When a word or phrase triggers a frame, a stock scenario may be evoked. Such a scenario comes with roles for participants, certain properties and attributes conventionally assigned to participants, and even stock props.[14] When an American hears or reads the word 'father,' or 'daddy,' an entire family scenario can be evoked. Even if they are aware of variations on the stock frame, Americans immediately know what the traditional role of the father is. But those traditions are socio-culturally specific. A visitor from a different culture—from Taiwan, for example—would have to learn the features of the American suburban family frame in order for 'father' to evoke that frame, rather than conventional Taiwanese frames. Contextual clues could enable that kind of understanding to happen (and could signal cultural clash pointing to a need for different information, for interpretation). But neither the Taiwanese nor the American 'family' scenario would necessarily make sense to a 1st-century resident of a Roman province in Asia Minor. One can imagine some 21st-century Taiwanese and American fathers engaging in a cross-cultural exchange with a πατήρ from 1st-century Asia Minor. Each participant would need to describe in detail the scenario in which he functioned—properties, roles and attributes. If the exchange were to be a completely satisfying cross-cultural experience, however, perhaps the 1st-century person would offer to explain a stock frame from his own culture—one just as foreign to an American family man as the stock American frame was for the Roman provincial. Perhaps he would fill out the features of a wedding frame or—more helpful for a potential reader of 1 Peter—of marketing and accounting practices or of the Roman provincial governmental system. There would be points of connection, of similarity and there would be points of cultural clash.

The important point to remember is that different ways of reasoning about a situation—or a concept—will result from the way we frame or schematize it.[15] Again, if 21st-century readers unwittingly supply inappropriate frames to 1st-century texts, or fail to acquire the requisite socio-cultural knowledge with which to correctly identify source frames within the text, misunderstanding is bound to occur.[16]

---

[14] Regarding roles and slots in frames, see Fauconnier and Sweetser, *Spaces, Worlds, and Grammar*, 5–6.

[15] Johnson, *Moral Imagination*, 9. See Lakoff, *Women, Fire, and Dangerous Things*, for full explanation of prototype theory and idealized cognitive models.

[16] One further terminological note: While in the literature 'schema' is sometimes used synonymously with 'frame,' I will use the term 'schema mapping' to refer to

Mental Spaces

Cognitive metaphor theory is one aspect of a larger theoretical structure, cognitive linguistic theory. Metaphor theory does not stand alone; it works with, and is an aspect of, the more general theory of mental spaces and cognitive domains. At base, that is because metaphor is about thoughts, not just words. In this theoretical framework, it is understood that underneath linguistic, semantic domains, lie cognitive, mental domains or spaces.[17] Fauconnier and Turner define *mental spaces* as "small conceptual packets constructed as we think and talk, for purposes of local understanding and action. They are very partial assemblies containing elements, structured by frames and cognitive models."[18] Linguistic expressions and patterns (metaphors, frames and the roles they project, metonymies, schemas) are reflective and evocative of cognitive domains and connections between such mental spaces. In fact, one way to look at metaphor is to recognize it as a special one-sided blend of mental spaces.[19]

Domains

When in the early 1980s Lakoff and Johnson offered their simple definition of metaphor in *Metaphors We Live By*, they said it was about "understanding and experiencing *one kind of thing* in terms of *another kind of thing.*"[20] Often (but not always), metaphors work across semantic domains. Linguists use the term 'domain' for "kinds of things." A

---

the way a frame or model lends structure in a specific situation in context. Gilles Fauconnier, *Mappings in Thought and Language* (Cambridge: Cambridge University Press, 1997), 11.

[17] "Mental spaces are partial structures that proliferate when we think and talk, allowing a fine-grained partitioning of our discourse and knowledge structures." Ibid. For an overview of Mental Space theory, see Eve Sweetser and Gilles Fauconnier, "Cognitive Links and Domains," 1–28. The definitive work in this area is Gilles Fauconnier and Mark Turner, *The Way We Think: Conceptual Blending and the Mind's Hidden Complexities* (New York: Basic Books, 2002). For an introduction to the "wetware" neuroscientific research consonant with linguistic and other cognitive scientific work, see Antonio Damasio, *Descartes' Error: Emotion, Reason, and the Human Brain* (New York: G.P. Putnam's Sons, 1994; HarperCollins Quill, 2000).

[18] Fauconnier and Turner, *The Way We Think*, 102.

[19] Metaphor is one-sided in the sense that the structure of the input space (SD) is used to restructure or add structure to that of a target space (TD). The way metaphor works with mental spaces is described in more detail below.

[20] Lakoff and Johnson, *Metaphors We Live By*, 5.

domain is any coherent subset of human experience; each domain can have many subdomains. So, for example, when Louw and Nida based their organization of a Greek-English lexicon on semantic domains, they created a set of ninety-three major, over-arching domains, each of which then is divided into subdomains. Their first domain is labeled *Geographical Objects and Features*, and they identify sixteen subdomains within that category, ranging from A. "Universe, Creation," and B. "Regions Above the Earth" to P. "Thoroughfares: Roads, Streets, Paths, etc."[21]

Domains and subdomains are analytical tools human beings have created; the categories they delineate are human constructions, and their value is contingent on their usefulness for heuristic and analytical purposes.[22] Domains are separate from each other when people treat them as separate from each other. There will be overlap and cross-domain relationships in any comprehensive list of domains. If one consults the index to the Louw and Nida lexicon to find entries for the word ἀνάστασις, for example, one finds three listings, referring to three separate domains:

a) resurrection   23.93
b) rising up (status) 87.39
c) rising up (change) 13.60

Domain 23 is *Physiological Processes and States*. The editors explain what they have in mind with this domain label:

> The domain of *Physiological Processes and States* includes such events as eating, drinking, giving birth, sleeping, resting, living, dying, birthing, growing, being healthy or sick, and a number of physiological processes particularly characteristic of plants. As in the case of practically all domains, it is possible to classify some meanings in two or more different ways. This is particularly true of some of the physiological processes and states. For example, the meanings of 'banquet' and 'feast' could be classified under *Festival* (51). Similarly, certain meanings classified now under *Sensory Events and States* (24) could be regarded as examples of physiological states. These problems of classification simply emphasize the multi-dimensional character of semantic structures.[23]

---

[21] Louw and Nida, *Greek-English Lexicon*, V. 1, 1.
[22] While Louw and Nida's lexicon can serve as a useful tool, and their list of domains is fairly comprehensive, biblical scholars could ask whether the domains named in this lexicon fit *koine* Greek as well as they fit 20th-century English semantics.
[23] Ibid., 248 n. 1.

This is a very broad grouping of kinds of human experiences. When the domain is so broad, it is no wonder that subgroupings are necessary. Indeed, many of the NT Greek words and phrases treated in this lexicon do belong in several categories because they can evoke several separate domains. Domain 87 in this lexicon is *Status*; the subdomain to which ἀνάστασις is assigned is "High Status or Rank."[24] Domain 13 is *Be, Become, Exist, Happen*; Louw and Nida place ἀνάστασις in a subdomain they label "Change of State." But Louw and Nida have not gone on, or gone deeper, to analyze the physical experiential grounding of the notion of ἀνάστασις, nor do they indicate in this case the metaphorical quality of the word's usage in Domain 23-type usages, where reference to such an abstraction as the notion of resurrection from death only makes sense if one has in mind the physical, experiential concept of "going up" or "rising again."

These are the kinds of domain and subdomain categories that linguists have in mind when they refer to cross-domain mapping in metaphors. A more technical definition of metaphor, then, would refer to its 'cross-domain' features. Here, for example, is how Lakoff puts it:

> The word "metaphor" has come to be used differently in contemporary metaphor research. The word "metaphor" has come to mean "a cross-domain mapping in the conceptual system." The term "metaphorical expression" refers to a linguistic expression (a word, phrase, or sentence) that is the surface realization of such a cross-domain mapping (this is what the word "metaphor" referred to in the old theory).[25]

With these fundamental, theoretical category concepts in hand, the stage is set for an exploration of cognitivist understandings of the structure of metaphor and to an introduction of basic nomenclature and methods.

---

[24] The editors note that "In any analysis of *Status* a number of factors must be taken into account, for example, wealth, power, authority, fame, respect, occupation, and birth. [They omit gender!]. Furthermore, there are a number of semantic domains in which status is highly significant, though secondary to rank and role. For example, there are numerous ranks of priestly functionaries in religion, but these are treated under *Religious Activities* (Domain 53). The same is true of persons with various military ranks or statuses which are treated in *Military Activities* (Domain 55)." Ibid., 734 n. 1.

[25] Lakoff, "The Contemporary Theory of Metaphor," 203.

The Structure of Metaphor

Mapping

The method employed in this system for analyzing metaphor attempts to 'map' (in the mathematical sense) the ways in which one kind of thing—a 'Target Domain'—is being understood in terms of another kind of thing—a 'Source Domain.' These are mappings across conceptual domains. Typically, the 'Target Domain' is more abstract and the 'Source Domain' is more concrete.[26] The correspondences mapped are ontological correspondences, so that entities in the (typically more abstract) target domain correspond in a systematic fashion to entities in the (typically more concrete) source domain. Mapping metaphors is not merely a matter of noticing similarities. In fact, metaphors often create similarities where in actuality none exist.[27] To illustrate how this mapping method works, consider the following examples of statements that might make sense to members of the evangelical Christian subculture:

> The *Crusade* would not have been successful without the faithful work of our prayer *warriors*. Thanks to all the prayer *captains*. "Evangelism Explosion" is all about *winning* souls for Christ. We are called to *free the captives* from darkness and fear. He is a *Captain* in the Salvation *Army*. We need to *recruit* 10,000 missionaries for short- and long-term *volunteer service*. This soul-winning *campaign* is *targeting* young people.

Notice that in all these expressions, language about *war* or *the military* is used to describe Christian *evangelism*. A cognitive linguist would ask two basic kinds of questions about this set of linguistic expressions. First, the cognitive linguist asks if there is a general principle governing how these linguistic expressions about war are used to characterize evangelism. Second, the cognitive linguist asks if there is a general principle governing how patterns of inference about war are *used to reason* about evangelism in these expressions. An attempt would be made to answer these questions by doing a detailed mapping of the correspondences noticed.

---

[26] But such is not always the case. See the discussion of Joseph Grady's revision of the "concrete-to-abstract" rule of thumb in the section on Primary Metaphor, below.
[27] Regarding the roles and dynamics "similarities" play in conceptual metaphor, see Lakoff and Johnson, "The Creation of Similarity," in *Metaphors We Live By*, 147–155.

Notation and Naming Metaphors

It is important to remember that the 'name' of a metaphor is a sort of mnemonic device standing for the mapping itself, which is the set of correspondences, the conceptual pattern being noticed. I will be using three conventional forms for notation of conceptual metaphors, and intend to use them interchangeably throughout the study. The first form looks like this:

Target Is Source.

Bad Is Foul-Smelling, Evangelism Is War, and Knowing Is Seeing are examples. This form reads like an English sentence, but it is not technically a sentence; it is a name for a metaphorical mapping across conceptual domains. The second form of notation is a variation of the first. It puts the name of the conceptual metaphor in all caps:

EVANGELISM IS WAR.

I sometimes use this form for visual emphasis, to highlight the conceptual metaphors being discussed so that readers can locate them more easily.

The third notation form looks like this:

Source → Target

or

Target ← Source

I will use this form to indicate the direction of cross-domain mappings, and will often use this form to name *koine* Greek metaphors. It is important to notice the direction in which the arrow is pointing; it always points to the target domain. For example, κακός ← σκολιός would be read, "Κακός Is Σκολιός" and it would indicate that σκολιός represents the source domain, while κακός stands for the target domain. But the same metaphor could be named putting the source domain first, like this: σκολιός → κακός, and it would be read in the same way as the above example, "Κακός Is Σκολιός." An English translation would be something like, "Bad Is Crooked" or "Bad ← Crooked."

It is also acceptable to use a fourth form of metaphor notion, one that is similar to the first form, but uses quotation marks: "Evangelism is War" or "Bad is Foul-Smelling." Some of the material cited in this book uses this notation form, and there is no significant difference between the correspondences indicated in any of the four notation formats.

Directionality

"Evangelism is War," but it is not the case in the expressions before us that "War is Evangelism." Perhaps someone could devise an expression using such a metaphor, but it would seem a bit odd because it would violate the convention in place. In almost all cases, the movement in metaphors is from Source to Target, not the other way around. Nor does the relationship posed in a metaphor typically work in both directions. Linguists calls this feature of metaphor mapping 'directionality' and note that typically the mapping in metaphors is uni-directional.

While the Evangelism Is War metaphor does not show up in 1 Peter—and could not, since 'evangelism,' the particular target domain concept of that metaphor, is a modern (Euro-American?) one—Peter does employ language from a military domain to speak of non-military struggle. When Peter speaks of 'fleshly desires' that 'wage war against the soul' (2.11)[28] and counsels his readers to 'arm' themselves with the 'same intention' that Christ had (4.1),[29] he draws on conventional features of the domain of military struggle, in which antagonists with armaments vie, to speak of *moral* struggle. The metaphors in these two verses are not identical; they map differently. But they are related, because they both draw from the military source domain and evoke specific military scenarios. In each case, different features or properties of the source domain are picked out for mapping, and in each case they are mapped onto different targets.

Notice that the name of the metaphor is not simply 'war.' A traditional approach to metaphor study might have picked up the war language and said that there is a 'war metaphor' here. Cognitive metaphor analysis methods highlight the directionality and dual-domain nature of metaphor by including both the Source Domain, "War," or "Battle" and the Target Domain, "Moral Struggle" in the name devised to stand for the relationship being noticed. It also analyzes specific features or 'entailments' of the metaphorical comparison or transfer, 'mapping'. In the 2.11 example above, we could name the particular sub-metaphor in play, "Moral Struggle with Fleshly Desire is Struggle with a Mili-

---

[28] ἀπέχεσθαι τῶν σαρκικῶν ἐπιθυμιῶν αἵτινες στρατεύονται κατὰ τῆς ψυχῆς (2.11b). Woodenly translated: "hold off yourself from the fleshly desires that soldier against the soul." The NRSV has it: "abstain from the desires of the flesh that wage war against the soul."

[29] τὴν αὐτὴν ἔννοιαν ὁπλίσασθε (4.1b): "with the same insight arm yourself." NRSV: "arm yourselves also with the same intention …"

tary Antagonist" or, more concisely, "Fleshly Desire is an Antagonist."[30] Precise methods for executing such mappings and determining how to name the distinctive metaphors are demonstrated in Chapter 5.

Image Metaphors: Distinguishing Image from Conceptual Metaphor Mappings

There are two major kinds of metaphor mappings: conceptual mappings and image mappings. While conceptual metaphors like Evangelism Is War map one conceptual domain onto another, *image metaphors* work by mapping specific, more richly detailed image material. Image metaphors are more fleeting than conceptual metaphors; they are highly specific, 'one-shot' mappings of images.[31] They often map part-whole structure and relations (the head on a man; the spire on a church) or attribute structure and relations (e.g., color, shape) from one mental image to another. Lakoff and Turner give the following example of an image-mapping:

> My wife ... whose waist is an hourglass.[32]

Here the words evoke the mental image of an hourglass—its basic shape—and allow the reader to superimpose that shape, that image, on the wife's waist: "we map the middle of the hourglass onto the waist of the woman." Moreover, Lakoff and Johnson point out that "the words do not tell us which part of the hourglass to map onto the waist, or even that it is only part of the hourglass shape that corresponds to the waist. The words are prompts for us to perform mapping from one conventional image to another at the conceptual level."[33]

---

[30] Cognitive linguistic methods would, additionally, pick up a metonymic function here. In the injunction to "arm" oneself and the notion that desire "soldiers" against the soul, aspects of a scenario stand for, evoke, a huge conventional scenario—Moral Battle.

[31] George Lakoff and Mark Turner, *More than Cool Reason* (Chicago and London: University of Chicago Press, 1989), 90–91. Some traditional definitions of metaphor confine the denotation of the word to what cognitivists are calling "image metaphor." The distinction in definition is telling; cognitivists understand image metaphors to be related to conceptual metaphor—and Turner and Lakoff explain that image metaphors, too, actually work with conceptual material—but the term "metaphor is more properly attached to the more pervasive and deeper mental work performed via cognitive, conceptual metaphor."

[32] Lakoff and Johnson explain what they mean by "attribute structure" thusly: "such things as color, intensity of light, physical shape, curvature, and, for events, aspects of the overall shape, such as continuous versus discrete, open-ended versus completed, repetitive versus not repetitive, brief versus extended." Ibid., 90.

[33] Ibid.

Poets often employ such mappings, and biblical poetry uses them as well. The Song of Solomon, for example, uses image-mappings not unlike the hourglass waist one to describe another beloved:

> Your navel is a rounded bowl
>   that never lacks mixed wine.
> Your belly is a heap of wheat,
>   encircled with lilies. (7.2)

But there is a second kind of image metaphor, one that maps rich imagistic detail from a source domain onto a target domain that is less detailed and concrete, *creating* an image in the target domain. For example, in 1 Peter, the reader encounters this second sort of image metaphor in the poetic passage borrowed from the Septuagint (LXX) (Isaiah 40.6–8), at 1.24–25a:

> *All flesh is like grass*
>   *and all its glory like the flower of grass.*
> *The grass withers,*
>   *and the flower falls,*
> *but the word of the Lord endures forever.* (NRSV)

The Greek looks like this:

> πᾶσα σὰρξ ὡς χόρτος
>   all   flesh   like   grass
>
> καὶ πᾶσα δόξα αὐτῆς ὡς ἄνθος χόρτου
> and all splendor of it as flower of grass
>
> ἐξηράνθη ὁ χόρτος
> was dried out the grass
>
> καὶ τὸ ἄνθος ἐξέπεσεν
> and the flower fell out
>
> τὸ δὲ ῥῆμα κυρίου μένει εἰς τὸν αἰῶνα
> the but word of Master remains into the age-aeon

The words allow us to see a simple little picture of grass drying out, so that the flower 'fell out.' But the metaphorical dynamics here are anything but simple. The 'drying out' and falling of the grass flower is mapped onto the more abstract 'all flesh' *creating* an image in the target domain that allows the reader to 'see' πᾶσα σὰρξ ('all flesh') drying out like a tiny grass flower, falling. Then in v. 25, the image of the drying and falling grass flower is mapped onto a different target, the ῥῆμα κυρίου ("word of the Master"), which by contrast, μένει ('lasts,' 'remains'). There the visual image of the tiny grass flower drying and falling creates a contrasting image, impressing itself almost like a photographic negative onto the very abstract notion of 'word,' so that in the blend, the reader can get a picture of what the Master's word is *not* like.[34] This 'word' is *not* tiny and fragile and fleeting, but resilient and eternal.

The terms of the methodology can be confusing. When it is said that image metaphors work with images, in distinction from conceptual metaphors, this does not mean that an image metaphor is not also 'conceptual' in the sense of being a cognitive function or product. That is, the metaphorical dynamic is located not in the words themselves, but in the mental image evoked by the word.[35] But in image metaphors there is less inferential structure transfer than is the case with what are called 'conceptual' metaphors. Conceptual metaphors can carry fairly detailed or elaborate entailments from source to target—entailments grounded in the properties, relations, and specific kinds of knowledge that belong to that source concept. The ways properties and relations are structured in the source concept then inferentially lend structure in the target concept. Consider, for example, the conceptual metaphor, Life Is a Journey. The rich and interconnected properties of the source domain, "Journey" (a start, middle and end; obstacles encountered; topography; vehicles; solitary or in company, and so on) are available to structure entailments in the target domain, "Life" (which then has a beginning, middle, and end, and during which one may encounter obstacles, and so on). By contrast, image metaphors are not so loaded with specific potential inferential structure.

In image metaphors, words are "prompts" for us "to perform a conceptual mapping between conventional *images*"[36] or from a conventional image onto a more abstract target domain, creating an *image* in the target. Image metaphors are also related to more robust conceptual mappings in that they can "trigger and reinforce" conceptual metaphors.[37] In the example above, it is not that the details of the images—grass and

---

[34] See the discussion of counterfactual spaces and networks in Fauconnier and Turner, *The Way We Think*, 217–247.

[35] See Damasio, *Descartes' Error*, 105–108, regarding neural image mapping, thought processes, and words as prompts.

[36] Lakoff, "The Contemporary Theory," 230; emphasis mine. For more complete definitions and examples of image metaphor, image schema, image schema metaphor, and image metaphor mappings, see Ibid., 229–231, and Lakoff and Turner, *More than Cool Reason*, 89–100.

[37] Lakoff and Turner, *More than Cool Reason*, 92.

grass flowers—themselves conventionally stand for human beings. But People Are Plants is a conventional conceptual metaphor, as is Death Is Down; these conceptual metaphors are both evoked by the image metaphors in this poem.

Another term cognitive linguists use in metaphor analysis, *image schematic structure*, sounds like image metaphor and image-mapping, but describes a separate set of features.

Image Schema Mappings

In this metaphor-study system, it is important to distinguish image metaphors from image *schema* metaphors. While image metaphors map rich mental images onto other rich mental images, image schemas do not employ finely detailed images. Instead, they evoke more general structures like paths, containers and bounded regions. Lakoff and Johnson include a brief list of basic image schemas in their synopsis of current cognitive linguistic findings:

> [T]here is a relatively small collection of primitive image schemas that structure systems of spatial relations in the world's languages ... part-whole, center-periphery, link, cycles, iteration, contact, adjacency, forced motion (e.g., pushing, pulling, propelling), support, balance, straight-curved, and near-far. Orientations also used in the spatial-relations systems of the world's languages include vertical orientation, horizontal orientation, and front-back orientation.[38]

The information evoked by image schema mappings is more skeletal than that conveyed via rich image metaphors or robust conceptual metaphors, but that does not mean it is less important. 'Skeletal' is an apt description because the deep, basic structures image schemas evoke

---

[38] Lakoff and Johnson, *Philosophy in the Flesh*, 35. A more complete discussion of image schemas is found in Lakoff, *Women, Fire, and Dangerous Things*, 416–461. See also Johnson, *The Body in the Mind;* and L. Talmy, "How Language Structures Space," in H.L. Pick and L.P. Acredolo, eds., *Spatial Orientation: Theory, Research, and Application* (New York: Plenum Press, 1983). Regarding neuroscience modeling and research supporting this theory, see Lakoff and Johnson, *Philosophy in the Flesh*, 112–113; Srinivas Sankara Narayanan, "Embodiment in Language Understanding: Sensory-Motor Representations for Metaphoric Reasoning About Event Description," in KARMA: Knowledge-based active representations for metaphor and aspect (Ph.D. diss, Department of Computer Science, University of California, Berkeley, 1997), and Terry Regier, "A Model of the Human Capacity for Categorizing Spatial Relations," *Cognitive Linguistics* 6-1 (1995): 63–88.

are often not readily visible (unless one learns what to look for) in a text, yet they lend necessary support.

Image schemas often work in concert with more detailed image metaphors—as when, for example, in 1 Peter 2.21, the very basic image schema of a path is combined with a visual image metaphor to evoke a picture of footprints on that path:

> For to this you have been called, because Christ also suffered for you, leaving you an example, so that you should follow in his steps.

The 'footprints' or 'steps' part of the Greek looks like this:

> ἵνα ἐπακολουθήσητε τοῖς ἴχνεσιν αὐτοῦ
> so that you might follow *in the footprints* of him.

Notice that the dative τοῖς ('in the') evokes a space 'in' which one might follow, and that ἴχνεσιν ('footprints') allows the reader to imagine, to 'see' footprints on a path or road—even though there is no word 'path' here. The notion of following 'in' footprints is a mapping of image schematic structure. To actually follow someone's (or something's!) footprints is not metaphorical, but using words to evoke the image schema of a set of footprints one could follow is metaphoric.

Image schemas are often triggered by prepositions, and, conversely, cognitive linguists say that "the spatial senses of prepositions tend to be defined in terms of image schemas (e.g., *in, out, to, from, along*, and so on)."[39] This is as true in *koine* Greek as in English. But perhaps the most interesting features of the way image schemas function in the moral discourse of a NT letter like 1 Peter are the places where prepositions and moral behavior vocabulary combine to evoke very basic, gestalt structures 'in' which behavior is imagined to take place. Chapters 5–7 present a number of examples; here I point to just a few:

> ἐν ἁγιασμῷ πνεύματος
> in holiness of spirit (1.2 Dative)
>
> εἰς ὑπακοὴν
> into/for obedience (1.2 Accusative)[40]
>
> ἐκ τῆς ματαίας ὑμῶν ἀναστροφῆς
> from out of the futile your behavior (1.18 Genitive)[41]

---

[39] Lakoff. and Turner, *More than Cool Reason*, 99.
[40] NRSV: "sanctified by the Spirit to be obedient".
[41] NRSV: "[You know that you were ransomed] from the futile ways inherited from your ancestors."

In each case, the preposition evokes a rudimentary imaginary space, a zone or *schema*. It can be a zone in which holiness of spirit and obedience can take place or, conversely, out of which readers are prompted to move, leaving behind old ways of behaving.

Novel Metaphors, Alternative Mappings, and Interpretation

Traditional understandings of metaphor tend to confine the scope of 'metaphor' to expressions that seem new, as many image metaphors do, and to 'creative' figurative language. The cognitive approach makes room for novel expressions, but anchors them to the conceptual and primary metaphors with which they actually work. Cognitive linguists are finding that novel expressions are invariably extensions, novel instances, of conceptual and primary metaphors; they rely on conventional concepts even while they play with those conventions by extension or elaboration. In addition, often there is interplay in a text between novel extensions and traditional, conventional metaphorical expressions; they are found in conjunction with each other.[42]

Take, for example, one of the ways evil is portrayed at the end of 1 Peter, at 5.8:

ὡς λέων ὠρυόμενος
as lion   roaring

In Greek, ὡς ('as') can serve as a discourse marker signaling the presence of a metaphor, as it does here. Cognitive linguistic methodology identifies the 'roaring'—ὠρυόμενος—as a novel extension of a conventional conceptual metaphor, Evil Is a Wild Animal, specifically a *lion*. The elaboration 'roaring' is made up on the fly, tacked onto the stock metaphor.[43] 'Roaring' is a property of lions that usually is not mapped in the basic conceptual metaphor Evil is a Wild Animal / Lion. But because the stock metaphor exists, and "roaring" is a property belonging to lions, it is a potential source domain concept, and the reader

---

[42] See Ibid., 66–67, regarding novel metaphor. Lakoff and Johnson point out in this context that such metaphors require "a process of interpretation" even when they are readily understood.

[43] Ps. 21.14 LXX; Ps. 10, Ps. 17, Ps. 74; Daniel 6.23; Rev. 13.2. Notice the association of a prowling lion with concern for economic justice in Pss. 10, 17, and 74, and with moral accounting in Ps. 10. Mention in 1 Peter of a prowling lion could evoke such associations for readers familiar with these Psalms. Goppelt notes Qumran literature usage; Leonnard Goppelt, *A Commentary on 1 Peter*, ed. Ferdinand Hahn, tr. John E. Alsup (Grand Rapids, Mich.: Eerdmans, 1978, 1993), 360, n. 11.

has little or no trouble understanding what is being said here. The (aural+visual) image of a roaring lion creates, then, an image in the target domain of evil on the prowl, roaring and dangerous. 'Sleeping' is another property that can belong to lions, and that therefore could potentially be mapped onto a target domain. But, of course, a sleeping lion has very different entailments, carries different inferences, from those carried by a roaring lion. The point is that properties picked up in novel extensions of a metaphor bear interpretive weight (and require interpretation).

Notice also that 'lion' by itself is not a metaphor, nor does 'lion' always trigger a mapping onto the same target domain ("Evil"). The 'Lion of Judah' picks up some of the same qualities of this source domain—strength, cunning, ferocity—but also maps properties from the source domain that the Evil Is a Lion does not map: (projected) nobility, for example, and applies them to an entirely different target domain. No (sane) reader mistakes the Lion of Judah (Judah Is a Lion) for the lion that is evil (Evil Is a Lion), but if a writer were to say, "the Lion of Judah roared," a plausible meaning could be constructed. The novel extension works in either case.[44]

The Invariance Principle

Both conceptual mappings and image-mappings have been found to obey the Invariance Principle: "Metaphorical mappings preserve the cognitive topology (that is, the image schema structure) of the source domain, in a way consistent with the inherent structure of the target domain."[45] As it works out in practice, this principle means that there are constraints on correspondences. In a container schema, for example, source domain interiors correspond to target domain interiors; exteriors correspond to exteriors, and so on.

In the 1 Peter text, when the words ἐϰ τῆς ματαίας ὑμῶν ἀναστροφῆς ('out of the futile ways, behavior,' which the text says are 'inherited from your ancestors'; 1.18) evoke a container schema, the structure of the source domain matches structures in the target domain. If there is

---

[44] "As a roaring lion" is part of a complex metaphor, discussed in Chapter 7. Another way of analyzing these expressions is available in this methodology: they can be metonymies (Lion For Judah; Lion For Evil). See the discussion of religious symbolic metonymy in Lakoff and Johnson, *Metaphors We Live By*, 40.

[45] Lakoff, "The Contemporary Theory," 214.

an ἐκ ('out'), then there is an 'in.' The implication in this case is that one can move 'out of' or 'into' the container, the space constrained by 'futile ways' / 'worthless behavior.' The abstract domain, morality and ethics, is just that—quite abstract. It has some non-metaphorical, literal, structure of its own, but it is hard to pinpoint what that 'literal' structure is.[46] There are moral agents, but even 'agent' is metaphorical; morality is about behaviors and concepts, and some philosophers have theorized that there is a core, ideal or non-metaphorical notion, 'good.' But metaphor systems give us more structure, more ways to talk about morality and ethics.

Inference Structure

The whole range of linguistic expressions this methodology identifies—image metaphors and schemas, conceptual metaphors, and so on—contributes to the structure of any given linguistic communication. When we talk or write about morality and ethics, we talk about it in terms borrowed from other domains (health and physical strength, commerce and marketing, cleaning and washing). That much may be obvious, but what is perhaps not so obvious is that when we do that language borrowing, we also import *inferential* structure from those other conceptual domains. So the inferential structures of the physical health domain constrain and structure our talk and thinking about morality. We borrow the notion of physical strength-building training to talk about the process of becoming morally 'strong'; by implication, there is such a thing as moral 'weakness,' and also by implication,

---

[46] Lakoff and other cognitive linguists working on metaphor do use the term "literal" in distinguishing certain kinds of expressions from metaphorical ones, and in this study I will use the term, "literal," as well. But there are levels of "literalness." Lakoff says, "Although the old literal-metaphorical distinction was based on assumptions that have proved to be false, one can make a different sort of literal-metaphorical distinction: those concepts that are not comprehended via conceptual metaphor might be called 'literal.' Thus, while I will argue that a great many common concepts like causation and purpose are metaphorical, there is nonetheless an extensive range of nonmetaphorical concepts. Thus, as sentence like 'The balloon went up' is not metaphorical, nor is the old philosopher's favorite 'The cat is on the mat.' But as soon as one gets away from concrete physical experience and starts talking about abstractions or emotions, metaphorical understanding is the norm." (Lakoff, "The Contemporary Theory of Metaphor," 205). See also Lakoff and Johnson, *Metaphors We Live By*,13, 53; and Fauconnier and Turner, *The Way We Think*, 69.

such weakness might be due to lack of discipline, lack of effort, or bad 'coaching.'[47]

The strong claim here is that any human conceptual system contains thousands of these conventional mappings, and that metaphors form a highly structured subsystem of the conceptual system.[48] It is *not* being claimed that we perform these conceptual maneuvers consciously. In fact, as with the rest of speech and thought, the conventional conceptual metaphor system is used mostly unconsciously, and with no noticeable effort. Metaphor systems are central to our understanding of our experience, and to the ways in which we act on that understanding. Evidence amassed so far indicates that metaphorical mappings vary in universality.[49] Some seem to be quite widespread, occurring across languages and cultures, while others seem to be culture-specific. Linguist Kevin Moore summarizes the implications:

> Some metaphors are more or less directly motivated by experiences a person of any culture might have, while other motivations have to do with concepts that are culture-specific to varying degrees ... While there is a substantial amount of metaphor structure that is shared crosslinguistically, a full understanding of conceptual metaphor depends on properties of particular languages, communities of speakers, or individuals. Metaphor structure interacts with language use in important ways, and considerations of linguistic practice (Hanks 1990, 1996) have much to do with the nature of metaphorical language and plausibly with the structure of particular conceptual metaphors.[50]

Again, a key observation here is that people seem to *act* based on the ways in which we understand our experiences, and a key claim is that metaphor plays a significant role in the way we understand our experiences.[51] This potentially has far-reaching implications for morality and ethics. If it is true, then conceptual metaphor is likely to play a star-

---

[47] "Cross-domain mapping" is the term applied to the cognitive mechanism at work this kind of inference importing. Lakoff and Johnson differentiate between cognitive mechanisms and neural ones, and mention Narayanan's neural theory as one that is consistent with the cognitive linguistic findings. Lakoff and Johnson, *Philosophy in the Flesh*, 71.

[48] Ibid., 42.

[49] Linguist Kevin Moore's work on spatial metaphors for time indicates that ego-based time metaphors invariably have the future in front of ego; past in back of ego. Moore, "Spatial Experience and Temporal Metaphors in Wolof."

[50] Ibid., Abstract.

[51] Moore admits that linguistic responses vary even when the 'grounding' experiences seem similar: "To a very important extent, all people live within the same physical constraints involving things like human bodies and laws of motion. At the same time

ring role (or several starring roles) in our everyday perceptions of moral situations and our negotiations of options and actions available to us, as well as in our verbal expression and interaction around the moral aspects of our experience.

In addition to the kinds of metaphorical mappings presented thus far, for the purposes of biblical study it is helpful to have in hand a few additional tools from cognitive linguistic methodology and models: the notions of primary metaphors and scenes; the concept of metonymy, and the theory of conceptual and metaphorical blending.

Primary Metaphors

It should be clear by now that the term 'metaphor' is rich and multi-dimensional; by it I refer to much more than the word traditionally has denoted. Cognitive linguists and other scientists working on the various phenomena in the larger category I am calling 'metaphor' have noticed there are several levels of structure, correspondence patterning, and inferential mapping. While in their early work, George Lakoff and Mark Johnson theorized that metaphor was experientially based—grounded, they thought, in basic bodily experience—just how that happens, and how it could be true of the more abstract-level metaphors, is only now becoming clearer. In their more recent study, *Philosophy in the Flesh*, they provide a helpful overview of cognitive approaches to the issues of bodily experiential grounding and subjective experience inherent in metaphor; readers eager to learn more about this aspect of the study of metaphor should consult their chapter entitled, "Primary Metaphor and Subjective Experience."[52]

It will be useful for readers to have in hand a basic definition of Primary Metaphor:

> Primary metaphors are cross-domain mappings, from a *source domain* (the sensorimotor domain) to a *target domain* (the domain of subjective experience), preserving inference and sometimes preserving lexical representation.[53]

That is, a sensori-motor-level inference (e.g. what smells bad is rotten; what is dark is hard to see) is mapped onto a (non-sensori-motor) target.

---

there is extensive variation within those constraints." Ibid., 9.8. Basic physical human experiences constrain but do not determine conceptual metaphor.
[52] Lakoff and Johnson, *Philosophy in the Flesh*, 45–59.
[53] Ibid., 58.

Sometimes even the evocative word ("lexical expression") is kept in the process. For example, consider the expression, "That stinks!" By itself, this is not a metaphorical expression; it could be referring to some rotten meat. But uttered in the context of subjective evaluation of behavior—say, a boss firing someone unfairly—the expression is metaphorical. The theory is that primary experiences of being repelled by foul-smelling substances create or induce a correlation between subjective evaluative and olfactory experience. The metaphor could be named "Bad is Foul-Smelling."

What is important to notice at the primary level is the connection between sensori-motor experience and subjective experience.[54] There is research which suggests that some of the associations at this level are made so early and are so basic to human experience that they effectively comprise part of the human cognitive unconscious.[55] Responses to bad behavior ("That stinks!") can express an almost instinctual moral sensitivity. If one lacks moral sensitivity at this primary level, one lacks something basically human.[56]

Moreover, identification of primary metaphors and primary scenes that occur cross-linguistically (in a number of languages) may provide evidence of the kinds of conceptual metaphors that are 'universal.' Lakoff and Johnson provide a representative list of such metaphors in *Philosophy in the Flesh*. In addition to Bad Is Stinky, they list, for example, Help Is Support, Control Is Up, and Difficulties Are Burdens. Here is their entry for the latter primary metaphor:

---

[54] Joseph Grady theorizes that certain primary metaphors, based in sensori-motor experience, are at the core of most elaborate metaphors and blends. He pioneered methods for decomposing metaphorical complexes and devised a theory that each primary metaphor is associated with a *primary scene*—an iterated everyday experience. Grady, "Foundations of Meaning: Primary Metaphors and Primary Scenes." See n. 62, below, regarding blends.

[55] Lakoff and Johnson say that, "Primary metaphors are part of the cognitive unconscious. We acquire them automatically and unconsciously via the normal process of neural learning and may be unaware that we have them. We have no choice in this process. When the embodied experiences in the world are universal, then the corresponding primary metaphors are universally acquired. This explains the widespread occurrence around the world of a great many primary metaphors." Lakoff and Johnson, *Philosophy in the Flesh*, 56. See the bibliography in that volume for references to research data.

[56] Regarding research indicating possible neurobiological groundings of moral sensitivity, see Damasio, *Descartes' Error*, 124–126.

Difficulties Are Burdens
Subjective Judgment: Difficulty
Sensorimotor Domain: Muscular exertion
Example: "She's *weighed down by* responsibilities."
Primary Experience: The discomfort or disabling effect of lifting or carrying heavy objects.[57]

Could we list *koine* Greek examples that use this primary metaphor, as well? One only needs to look up 'burden' in the index to Louw and Nida's *Greek-English Lexicon* to find a number of clues that point to a positive answer. The listings under English 'burden' and 'burdensome' include Greek words that belong in both sensorimotor domains (86.1 weight) and domains dealing with subjective experience and judgment (25.239 anxiety; 22.4, 18, 26, 27, 30 hardship).[58] The fact that we share such primary metaphors helps explain how translation and cross-cultural, cross-linguistic understanding can happen at all.

The deeper theoretical implications here touch on the question of the nature and origin of 'universal' concepts, including moral or ethical universals. If "Bad is Foul-Smelling" is a concept acquired automatically and unconsciously, as part of the very early processes of neural association and learning, then it is no wonder that most of the time we are unaware that we operate with this conceptual metaphor. We take it for granted and we use it without having consciously chosen it. Cognitivists theorize that certain human bodily experiences are universal—the feeling of revulsion people have when we smell rotten meat, for example. If that kind of experience is universal, trans-cultural, then this helps explain how it could be the case that some corresponding primary metaphors are also universally acquired.

Accordingly, primary metaphor, and the embodied experience that grounds it, is a key to understanding the cognitive grounding of concepts that we may share with 1st-century readers (and the writer) of 1 Peter. While cultural and language differences are indeed significant, certain human experiences are so basic as to transcend (or subtend) culture. That is not to deny that 'universal' conceptual metaphors are indeed learned or historically transmitted; Lakoff and Johnson

---

[57] Lakoff and Johnson, *Philosophy in the Flesh*, 50, Table 4.1.
[58] Louw and Nida, *Greek-English Lexicon*, v. 2, 276. They note that βάρυς ("heavy, burdensome"), βάρος ("hardship, burden"), βαρέομαι ("to be burdened, to be troubled"), and ἐλαφρός ("light, not heavy") are sometimes used literally, as in Mt 23.4, while at other times they are used figuratively, as in Mt. 11.30 and 2 Cor 1.8. Ibid., v 2, 243–244, 733.

admit that they are not necessarily innate.[59] But cognitive linguists have located hundreds of linguistic universals (to which primary conceptual metaphors contribute), and the existence of these universals helps explain how understanding and translation can work across cultural differences and temporal distances as significant as the ones that loom between modern readers and the writers and first readers of the New Testament.

Complex Metaphors and Blends

When readers encounter a text like 1 Peter, the primary metaphors are most often cloaked. They are difficult to discern because they are combined with one another in the complex, composite metaphors in the figurative expressions that present themselves to us. Lakoff and Johnson liken the relationship between primary and complex metaphors to the atoms that combine to form molecules:

> A great many of these complex molecular metaphors are stable—conventionalized, entrenched, fixed for long periods of time. They form a huge part of our conceptual system and affect how we think and what we care about almost every waking moment.[60]

These kinds of metaphors are used every day, but linguists have observed that 'everyday' metaphors can be quite complex; the manner in which they are comprised of primary metaphors added to cultural models and beliefs is anything but simple. While their linguistic and conceptual complexity—and sometimes abstraction—sometimes makes it difficult to discern any direct experiential grounding for some expressions, most are nevertheless grounded in primary bodily or social experience.

Many of the metaphorical expressions encountered in NT texts—like 1 Peter—are complex in this sense, but there are other ways in which metaphors are composed and blended, too. When, for example, a reader encounters the expression ὡς λέων ὠρυόμενος ('as a roaring

---

[59] Lakoff and Johnson, *Philosophy in the Flesh*, 57. Regarding historical senses of words and the significance of etymology for current meanings, see Eve Sweetser, *From Etymology to Pragmatics: Metaphorical and Cultural Aspects of Semantic Structure* (Cambridge: Cambridge University Press, 1990). Joe Grady explains that "Historical senses of words are not necessarily relevant to the way those words are understood by contemporary speakers ... However, this information can sometimes shed light on the synchronic variety of the word's semantics." Grady, "Foundations of Meaning," 96.

[60] Lakoff and Johnson, *Philosophy in the Flesh*, 60.

lion') describing evil, it is not encountered in isolation. Its metaphorical dynamics cannot be completely understood without taking into account the other metaphors with which it is blended.[61] It is 'the opponent / plaintiff', [the] 'slanderer,' 'the devil' (ὁ ἀντίδικος ... διάβολος) who "prowls around like a roaring lion." This personification is a subcase of other sorts of personification; a slanderer is also a human being. So evil is portrayed here in overlapping (blended) metaphors from distinctive source domains:

> Interpersonal Conflict Domain:
> ἀντίδικος 'opponent, adversary'
>
> Legal Domain:
> ἀντίδικος 'accuser, plaintiff'
> διάβολος 'slanderer'
>
> Supernatural Beings and Powers Domain:
> διάβολος 'evil supernatural being'
>
> Animal Domain:
> λέων ὠρυόμενος 'roaring lion'

Notice that ἀντίδικος and διάβολος are listed under more than one domain. Words have the potential to trigger multiple domains, and therefore multiple mappings, at once. The reader or translator is faced with interpretive choices in these cases. One must pick up from contextual clues the subtleties of the potential mappings. A new kind of blended space is created as these source domains interact, such that there is an evil force and a legal edge to the accusatory, slanderous attack being described. Cognitive metaphor analysis methods allow us to notice how the blend itself exerts pressure, constraining and shaping how potential entailments in each target and source domain influence the picture that the composite metaphor presents. The whole is not a mere sum of the parts.

Fauconnier and Turner have devised a simple diagram to illustrate the basic dynamics of blending. In Blend Diagram 1, each circle represents a mental space—two *input* spaces, a *generic space* and a *blended space*:

---

[61] Fauconnier defines blending as "a cognitive operation ... that consists in integrating partial structures from two separate domains into a single structure with emergent properties within a third domain;" Gilles Fauconnier, *Mappings in Thought and Language*, 22; and see Ibid., 149–186. The conceptual blending concept was introduced in Gilles Fauconnier and Mark Turner, "Conceptual Projection and Middle Spaces," *UCSD Cognitive Science Technical Report* (1994).

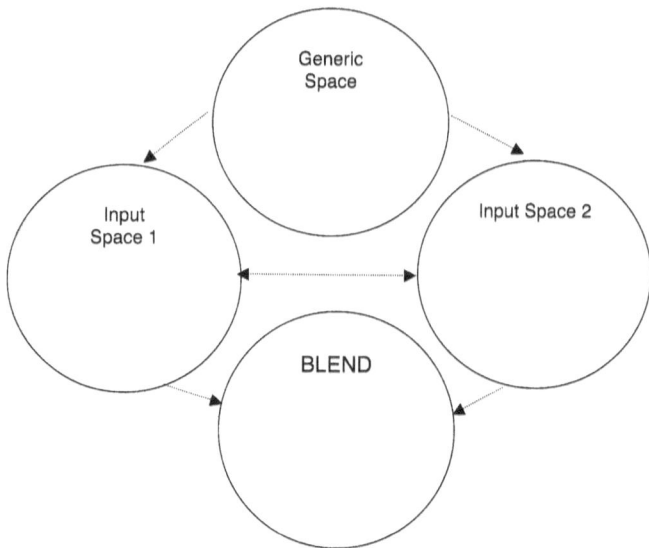

Blend diagram 1: Standard Blend

In the Roaring Lion Adversary example from 1 Peter, there are actually more than two input mental spaces, but for purposes of illustration, let us work with just two. Let Input Space 1 be the Lion Space. The words in the text evoke only a few of the many potential properties of lions available for mapping: wildness, roaring, prowling, seeking prey, intending to devour. Let Input Space 2 be the Legal Adversary Space. The Greek word ἀντίδικος can be simply 'an opponent,' but evokes here something like English 'slanderer' or 'legal opponent,' 'accuser.' There is a Generic Mental Space that maps onto each of these inputs and contains what the inputs have in common: an aggressive individual, potential danger, and an object of aggression. But this is *not* the 'blend.' Certain properties from each input space are projected into a fourth mental space, the Blended Space, so that now a composite picture emerges of a wildly aggressive force and a legal edge to the accusatory, slanderous attack. The blend could be diagrammed as described in Blend diagram 2.

Fauconnier and Turner note that a blend develops emergent structure that was not present in the separate inputs and that is much more elaborate than the common properties of the generic space. *This* legal adversary is on the prowl and intends to kill. *This* lion has the power to devour one's honorable standing in the community. In metaphorical blends like this one, each of the input spaces evokes a separate frame

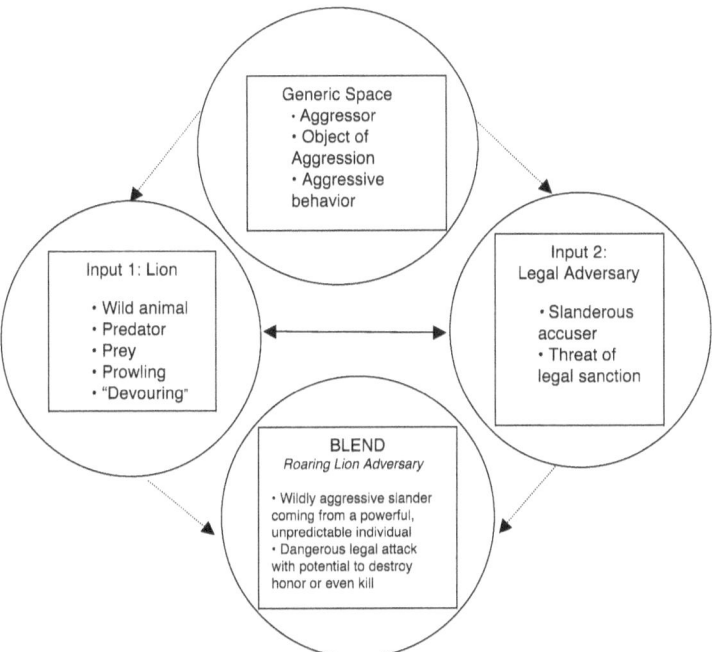

Blend diagram 2: Roaring Lion Adversary

(lion: wild animal frame; adversary: legal system). When we "run the blend," elaboration occurs, and a reader is prompted to imaginatively modify what was available in the inputs to produce a composite picture. Additionally, though, "The connections between the blend and the inputs never disappear. We work not just with the blend but with the entire integration network."[62] That is, the elements in each of the input spaces and in the generic space are not lost in the course of the blending operations.

We will encounter many such blends in the analysis of 1 Peter, and some of the nuances of mapping blends and discerning emergent structure will become clearer given those additional examples. What is most important to understand at this point is that metaphor and analogy are special kinds of conceptual blending and that while we perform these mental operations almost effortlessly much of the time, they are not magic, nor are they simple.

---

[62] Fauconnier and Turner, *The Way We Think*, 94.

Idiomatic Metaphors

Many idiomatic expressions contain figurative elements that can strike us as odd, random or arbitrary, especially when the origins of the idioms have been forgotten. Cognitive linguists argue that metaphorical idiomatic expressions are far from arbitrary; they work with conventional mental images and specific cultural knowledge evoked in connection with those conventions.[63] They also argue that such metaphors are far from 'dead'; they exert tremendous power to shape and constrain inferential patterns in discourse.[64]

For example, 1 Peter 2.12 uses an idiom for the Last Judgment:

ἐν ἡμέρᾳ ἐπισκοπῆς
"in the day of oversight (over-seeing)/ visitation"[65]

The idiom is a Greek (**LXX**: Septuagint) translation of a conventional Semitic expression. For readers familiar with this (Greek) expression, the words can evoke a conventional mental image—even an entire scenario—of a time and place in which God presides over the establishment of justice for the poor and oppressed; it can at the same time evoke a picture of the Final Judgment.[66] The idiom carries meanings that amount to much more than the sum of the parts 'in,' 'day,' and 'overseeing or visitation'—even though the parts are important aspects of the meaning of the idiom. Together they evoke specific Semitic, prophetic, and apocalyptic cultural knowledge. When these parts are combined in the idiomatic expression, a reader's associations are potentially much richer.

---

[63] Lakoff and Johnson, *Philosophy in the Flesh*, 67–69.

[64] Lakoff and Johnson note that "Examples like the *foot* of the mountain are idiosyncratic, unsystematic, and isolated. They do not interact with other metaphors, play no particularly interesting role in our conceptual system, and hence are not metaphors that we live by. The only signs of life they have is that they can be extended in subcultures and that their unused portions serve as the basis for (relatively uninteresting) novel metaphors. If any metaphorical expressions deserve to be called 'dead,' it is these, though they do have a bare spark of life, in that they are understood partly in terms of marginal metaphorical concepts like A MOUNTAIN IS A PERSON." Lakoff and Johnson, *Metaphors We Live By*, 55.

[65] The NRSV renders this sentence: "Conduct yourselves honorably among the Gentiles, so that, though they malign you as evildoers, they may see your honorable deeds and glorify God *when he comes to judge*."

[66] Eschatological meaning is carried by the phrase in Isa. 10.3; Jer. 6.15; Wis. 3.7–8; Lk. 1.68; 19.44. See Achtemeier, *1 Peter*, 178, n. 82. Idioms can become so entrenched that they function metonymically, and ἐν ἡμέρᾳ ἐπισκοπῆς may be a case in point. (Metonymy: "Day" For Eschatological Judgment).

Such metaphorical idioms are significant at a number of levels. They constitute clear evidence that metaphors and mental images are anchored in cultural and linguistic conventions; they are not random. People in the same linguistic community share stock metaphorical idioms, expressions that can convey pieces of a people's long-term cultural memory. In addition, Lakoff and Johnson note that such expressions "open the possibility that a significant part of the lexical differences across languages may have to do with differences in conventional imagery. The same metaphorical mappings applied to different images will give rise to different linguistic expressions of those mappings."[67] This has implications for lexical differences across the biblical languages and across modern English conventions in comparison with the biblical languages. While for English Bible readers familiar with biblical history, imagery, and expressions, the words 'Day of Judgment' may evoke images corresponding to those evoked in 1st-century readers of 1 Peter, such a correspondence is not guaranteed. Nor is there a lock-step, one-to-one correspondence certifying that all 1st-century readers would have understood the expression in one particular way. This metaphorical idiom is not merely a title or name for a single metaphorical mapping.

Moreover, some idiomatic metaphors are more local and may arise from novel extensions of conventional metaphors. The English idiom, 'to let the cat out of the bag,' for example, is a variation on a larger conventional conceptual metaphor, Knowing Is Seeing. To keep something secret, to make it inaccessible to others, is to contain it, to keep it out of the visual field, so Hidden Is Contained, and Secret Is Hidden from View, or Unknowable Is (Visually) Concealed. Another contemporary English idiom, 'to come out of the closet' is yet another extension of the same conceptual metaphors. If in *koine* Greek, to be seen is to be known, if judgment is to have one's deeds and true essence revealed, then perhaps in ἐπισκοπῆς ('Oversight') we have another instance of Knowing Is Seeing.

The images and knowledge about the images evoked by the expression 'in the Day of Oversight/Visitation' are contingent upon a reader's

---

[67] Lakoff and Johnson, *Philosophy in the Flesh*, 69. This cognitive understanding contradicts Ricoeur's construal of metaphor and linguistic community. He says, for example, "A metaphor is first and essentially an 'odd' predication that transgresses the semantic and cultural codes of a speaking community." Paul Ricoeur, *Figuring the Sacred: Religion, Narrative, and Imagination* (Minneapolis, Minn.: Fortress Press, 1995), 161.

stock of cultural knowledge and stock of conventional images; the metaphorical mappings will vary accordingly. In fact, the various translations of ἐπισκοπῆς—'Oversight,' 'Visitation,' or 'Judgment'—reflect alternative understandings of the contours of the source domain, and therefore, different mappings of this idiomatic metaphor. Such conventional idiomatic metaphors are not 'dead;' they contribute to the creation of meaning in the discourse. The associations they evoke spark readers' memories and anchor what is being said in this new setting to stories and mental images deeply embedded in the cultural memory.

The question arises, how conscious of such conventions and idioms does a reader need to be—or *can* a reader be? It is important to note that transparency and conventionality are not identical qualities. The Last Judgment is a conventional frame, but its conventionality may not be apparent; ironically, those for whom the convention is most powerful will likely be least conscious of it. It is, however, possible to educate readers to think about the differences between metaphorical expressions and broader conventions that might (or may not) be represented in a particular conventional linguistic phrase or expression.

Metonymy

Though the tag I am using for this general theoretical position is 'cognitive' or 'conceptual *metaphor* theory,' not every linguistic and conceptual relationship within the purview of this study is metaphoric, strictly speaking. Sometimes when one kind of thing is used to understand and experience—and talk about—another kind of thing, the 'things' compared or juxtaposed are *not* cross-domain entities. In some such cases, we are encountering *metonymy*, not metaphor. Metonymy uses one kind of thing to talk about an entity to which it is *related*. Traditional rhetoricians identified some of these mechanisms; *synecdoche*, for example, is the tag given to verbal expressions where a part stands for the whole. But cognitive linguistic research has uncovered aspects of metonymic processes that helpfully distinguish them from metaphoric processes and highlight their roles in our conceptual and linguistic toolkits. Lakoff and Johnson express the functional distinctions clearly:

> Metaphor and metonymy are different *kinds* of processes. Metaphor is principally a way of conceiving of one thing in terms of another, and its

primary function is understanding. Metonymy, on the other hand, has primarily a referential function, that is, it allows us to use one entity to *stand for* another.[68]

Metonymy is referential, but that is not the end of the matter. Metonymy is a pragmatic function mapping.[69] As with metaphor, metonymy also functions conceptually, is experientially grounded, is found to operate systematically and conventionally in languages—and both expresses and affects our thinking and our actions.[70]

Consider, for example, the functions in 1 Peter 5.9 of the word ἀδελφότητι (< ἀδελφότης < ἀδελφος 'brother' = 'brotherhood'). When one part of a category—the 'brotherhood' of the church—is selected to stand for the whole, that selected aspect or part evokes or draws the focus to itself. Metonymy is not inert or merely descriptive; it determines and is indicative of special focus in our understanding. What characteristics are highlighted, are mapped, when in 1 Peter 'brotherhood' stands for the church (male and female)? What is gained and what is lost if this is translated 'brotherhood,' 'brethren' (KJV), 'brothers' (NIV), 'your brothers and sisters' (NRSV), or 'Christian family' (New Century)? What shifts in a reader's understanding—and in potential actions prompted—when Peter chooses a different metonymy, a different part or aspect of the church, to stand for the whole—as he does when he names his readers ἀγαπητοί (< ἀγαπητός = 'beloved, loved ones') in 2.11 and φιλόξενοι (< φιλόξενος = 'stranger lovers') in 4.9? These are the kinds of questions cognitive linguistic methods prompt one to ask.

Metonymies, like metaphors, express and affect both our thought and our actions, including ethical thoughts and moral actions.[71] Accordingly, the investigation in Chapter 5 of the conceptual features of the moral discourse of 1 Peter will include coverage of several metonymies.

---

[68] Lakoff and Johnson, *Metaphors We Live By*, 36. See also Lakoff and Turner, *More than Cool Reason*, 100–105, for a discussion of the features of metonymy and ways of distinguishing it from metaphor.
[69] Gilles Fauconnier, *Mappings in Thought and Language*, 11.
[70] Lakoff and Johnson, *Metaphors We Live By*, 37, 39, 59.
[71] Ibid., 39. Lakoff and Johnson make the move from identifying metonymy as referential to revealing its significance and power as it informs and prompts action.

Cultural Models and Beliefs, Choices and Ethos

Cultural beliefs and models interact with metaphorical structures and functions. Even to introduce the concepts and methods of cognitive metaphor, it has been necessary to mention some of the cultural factors that inform source domain concepts, for example. But the matter is not simple; metaphors both absorb and display cultural models and beliefs. Cultural models constrain the kinds of metaphors that people in a culture use and understand, while the metaphors express the culture's expectations and beliefs. In the course of the 1 Peter study (Chapters 4–7), cultural beliefs will loom large as the metaphor system is exposed. Deep cultural convictions about honor and shame, gender roles, and social hierarchies shape the content and function of the metaphors in the text. But this study will focus on the implications of metaphorical dynamics at work in the formation and expression of cultural beliefs at more than one level or node.

First, at the level of reading and interpretation, it is possible to educate readers to notice the cultural models in play in a given text so that they become more aware of the features of their own native cultural models and assumptions. Readers can become aware of their own cultural 'father' models, for example, and notice the ways they map those properties and relations onto God. Moreover, given information about the 'father' models that might be in play in a NT text, readers can create different mappings and run alternative blends, perhaps those required for entry into the authorial audience.[72]

But the blending of cultural mental spaces in metaphors carries significance beyond its value in describing how reading and interpretive processes might work. These dynamics operate constantly in the interplay, the back-and-forth, between individual and society, as sociocultural ethos is shaped and transmitted, and as that ethos constrains and informs individuals' moral concepts. What Fauconnier and Turner say about the construction of meaning in general is true for moral and ethical models as well:

> The construction of meaning is like the evolution of species. It has coherent principles that operate all the time in an extremely rich mental and cultural world. Many, many, many new integrations are attempted and explored in an individual's backstage cognition, and in interchange by members of a culture, and most of them never go anywhere. But

---

[72] The notion of "authorial audience" is discussed in Chapter Four.

enough survive to provide all the languages, rituals, and innovations we see around us.[73]

It is the human ability to run blends that allows us to consider alternative scenarios—and imagine alternative consequences—sometimes in milliseconds. Moreover, we now have a history, or a set of cultural histories, of running such blends. Human cultural life is shaped by the conventional blends we have developed in our communities over time. Fauconnier and Turner put it this way:

> Conceiving complicated new scenarios in nearly any domain while making complicated new inferences and choices is now something that can be run as part of mental and cultural life. The cognitive capacities of modern human beings not only allow individuals a far greater power of concept and choice, they also allow cultures to transmit choices that have been made and tested by entire communities.[74]

1 Peter transmits some of the choices Christians have made; in our reading and response we both receive and test the inferences and choices displayed in this exemplar. Conceptual blending allows us to perform all of these tasks. But it is important to distinguish between the *function* of conceptual blending and the *cultural products* of that blending.[75] Cultural beliefs are both *products* of conceptual blending and powerful shaping *forces* in conceptual metaphor and other mental space blends. They affect reading and interpretation; they also operate when conceptual metaphor shapes an individual's moral conceptualizations and choices. Cultural models also constrain and compress conceptual metaphors at a communal level, at the level of the transmission of ethos. Reading 1 Peter with such beliefs in mind, checking for the ways

---

[73] Fauconnier and Turner, *The Way We Think*, 309.

[74] Ibid., 217. When they say "modern human beings" here, Fauconnier and Turner mean bio-evolutionarily modern, and therefore would include human beings in 1st-century Palestine and Asia Minor. People in the 1st century did not have Neanderthal brains. Regarding culture and collective memory, they say, "The bubble chamber of the brain runs constantly, making and unmaking integration networks. Cultures, too, running a bubble chamber over the collection of their members' brains, develop integration networks that can be disseminated because the members of the culture all have the capacity for double-scope integration. Very few of the networks tried out in these bubble chambers of brain and culture actually survive. A network that does survive takes its place in individual or collective memory and knowledge." Ibid., 396.

[75] Ibid., 215. Fauconnier and Turner say, "we need always to keep in mind the distinction between the *operation* of conceptual blending and the *cultural products* of conceptual blending."

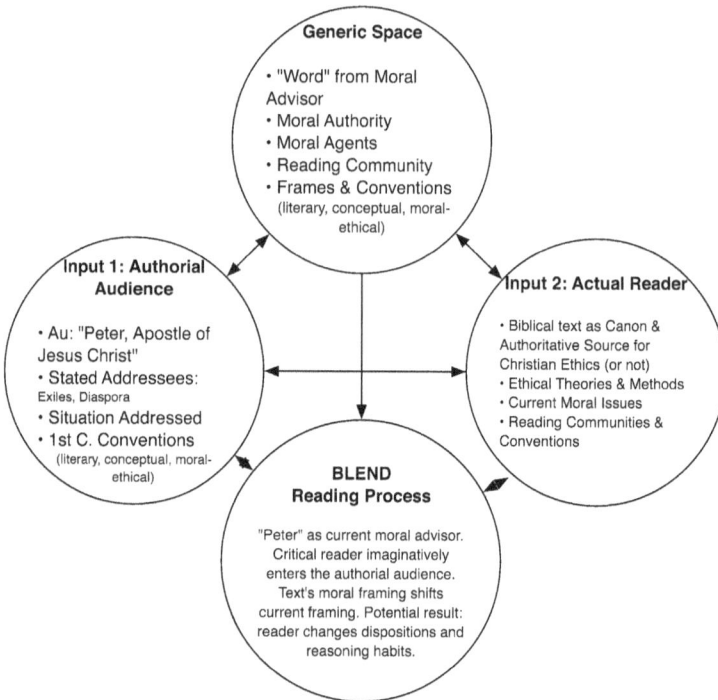

Blend diagram 3: Reading Moral Discourse as Blending

that cultural models inform metaphorical source domains, is a way to connect with and test culturally transmitted moral framings and choices.

Reading as Mental Space Blending

I have been using the terms of blended mental spaces and framing in reference to the reading and interpretive processes activated when modern readers encounter a text like 1 Peter. We could put some of the basic elements of that interactive process into a blend diagram.

When we run the blend, the reader's (or readers', plural, in a reading community) modern conceptions and conventions blend with input from the authorial audience space.[76] Features in each of the

---

[76] See Chapter 4, regarding 'authorial audience' and 'reading community.'

input spaces put pressure on the particular blend created. The degree to which modern readers are able to enter the authorial audience affects the outcome; some will hardly enter that audience at all. The blends such readers run will be barely affected by the conventions and concepts in the text. They might even attempt to project their own cultural (and literary, and moral) conventions onto the text, creating yet another input space, one that could not bear the label 'Authorial Audience.'

But when the blend is run well, when modern readers are able to enter the authorial audience even briefly, a conversation between the spaces can flow. Readers' conceptual structures and inference patterns can shift, and might be shaped or nuanced differently, as a result of the reading. Moral dispositions and conceptual structures that shape ethical inference patterns are potentially altered. This is the potential power of reading a text like 1 Peter.

Responses to Traditional Views

This contemporary theory of metaphor is in conflict with many basic tenets of the traditional views of metaphor surveyed in Chapter 1. In *More Than Cool Reason*, Lakoff and Turner outline six traditional positions regarding metaphor that they believe are mistaken:

1) the literal meaning theory
2) failure to seek general principles; focus on individual metaphorical expressions as though each were unique
3) the 'dead' metaphor concept: confusion between conventional metaphor and metaphors that no longer exist in a language
4) the claim that metaphors are "merely bidirectional linkages across domains"
5) the claim that the locus of metaphor is in words or linguistic expressions alone and not in conceptual structure
6) the claim that everything in language and thought is metaphorical.[77]

More needs to be said about each of these points and a few additional points of critique that have surfaced in more recent cognitive research.

---

[77] Lakoff and Turner, *More Than Cool Reason*, 110-111.

Literal Meaning Theory

'Literal meaning' is a *theory* inherited from our Enlightenment ancestors; it is the implicit working hypothesis underlying much traditional thinking about metaphor. Mark Johnson captures the core problem in this set of issues when he writes, summarizing his discussion of Ricoeur and of philosophical traditions with regard to the status and meaning of metaphor, "The underlying issue is whether 'reality' is objectively given, so that, as knowers, we can only stand apart and comment on it, or whether we have a 'world' only by virtue of having a language and system of value-laden concepts that make experience possible for us."[78] As he goes on to point out, these are questions about language, but they are not limited to the linguistic realm; they are fundamental epistemological and ontological questions. While philosophers have constructed highly complex and creative theories of language, many of their fundamental claims seem staked to beliefs and, to put it bluntly, fancy guesswork about how language arises and develops and works. But at least some of the core issues are not about what we wish were true or believe to be true about language (or truth). The question is how, empirically, do human beings create, acquire, and use language? Approaching these issues via study of metaphor and giving attention to the data gathered by cognitive scientists studying the way the brain works may help break up the philosophical logjam. At least some of the claims of the Literal Meaning Theory are empirically testable, and it is precisely a study of metaphorical phenomena that provides relevant data.

As Lakoff and Turner point out in *More than Cool Reason*, at least two of the implicit claims of the Literal Meaning Theory can be shown to be false. The first claim is that everyday language is conventional and referential (makes reference to ordinary reality) and semantically autonomous—and that ordinary language is not metaphoric. But this claim does not hold up against the overwhelming (and growing) evidence in the metaphor literature to the contrary. The data show that "conventional language and our conventional conceptual system are fundamentally and ineradicably metaphoric."[79] The data can account

---

[78] Mark Johnson, ed., *Philosophical Perspectives on Metaphor* (Minneapolis: University of Minnesota Press, 1981), 41.
[79] Lakoff and Turner, *More than Cool Reason*, 116.

for both conventional expressions—and the systematicity within and across domains—and poetic expressions; the Literal Meaning Theory cannot.

The second empirically testable claim of the Literal Meaning Theory is the Objectivist Claim:

> Conventional expressions in a language designate aspects of an objective, mind-free reality. Therefore, a statement must objectively be either true or false, depending on whether the objective world accords with the statement.[80]

But there is a wealth of evidence from the study of metaphor that this objectivist paradigm cannot explain:

The use of the same words across conceptual domains

How is it that we speak of someone 'making his way' in love, in business, and in sports? 'Objective' tests of truth or falsehood falter when it comes to evaluation of this kind of linguistic expression.

The use of the same inference patterns across conceptual domains

The Literal Meaning Theory cannot account for the inferential patterning and *function* of metaphor in language, not even in poetic language. These patterns rely on human cognitive processes and structures; they cannot be accounted for objectively.

The use of conceptual frameworks, many of which are metaphorical themselves

Lakoff and Turner (and the other researchers in the field) have shown that such frameworks do exist, and that in fact they are pervasive. Again, objective models fail to account adequately for such metaphorical frameworks.

In addition, they list some variations, or 'spinoffs' of the Literal Meaning Theory, and briefly outline their objections to these positions.

---

[80] Ibid., 117. In the same place, they observe that behind this claim is a "background assumption" that "'Objective reality' consists of states of affairs in the world independent of any human conceptualization or understanding ... [T]he world comes structured in a way that is objective—independent of any minds. The world as objectively structured includes objects, properties of those objects, relations holding among those objects, and categories of those objects, properties, and relations."

Because many of these spinoff positions underlie traditional and current critical practices in ethics and biblical scholarship, I list them in the Appendix, p. 357.

Methodology that Fails to Generalize Properly

Traditional approaches to metaphor have been methodologically flawed, usually in one of two ways. Some have used a case-by-case methodology, one that fails to recognize systematic principles by which metaphors are related to one another. Others have made what Lakoff and Turner call "the Source-domain-only Error," in which only the source domain is considered.[81] Many, perhaps most, biblical studies attempting to work with metaphor err in this way. They will say that the 'controlling' metaphor of 1 Peter, for example, is "Homelessness/Exile" or "Israel," or "Spiritual Household," naming a source domain without spelling out the various target domains onto which the notion of exile or homelessness is mapped in 1 Peter. Such a flawed method yields false or misleading generalizations but also prevents the elucidation of appropriate generalizations.

The Dead Metaphor Theory

The idea that metaphors that are conventional are 'dead'—that they are no longer metaphors—results in a failure to recognize metaphors active in ordinary, everyday language. Lakoff and Turner believe that "this mistake derives from a basic confusion: it assumes that those things in our cognition that are most alive and most active are those that are conscious. On the contrary, those that are most alive and most deeply entrenched, efficient, and powerful are those that are so automatic as to be unconscious and effortless."[82]

---

[81] Ibid., 128.
[82] Ibid., 129.

The Interaction Theory or Bi-Directionality Mistake

By this theory, if we say that "life is a journey," "we are merely comparing the two domains in both directions and picking out the similarities." But "if this were true, then our language should go both ways as well. We should speak of journeys conventionally in the language of life, perhaps calling embarkations 'births' and departures 'deaths.' ... The predictions made by the claim of bi-directionality are not borne out, since neither the logic nor the language of the target domain is mapped onto the source domain."[83]

The "Linguistics Expressions Only" Position

Behind the traditional distinction between metaphor and simile, lies an assumption that metaphor is a matter of linguistic expression, not of conceptual structure. But "the attempt to define metaphor in terms of syntactic form misses entirely what metaphor is about: the understanding of one concept in terms of another."[84]

The "It's All Metaphor" Position

This position comes in strong and weak forms. In the strong form, "Every aspect of every concept is completely understood via metaphor." Accordingly, all linguistic expressions are thought to be understood via metaphor. The weak form of the 'it's all metaphor' position is that all linguistic expressions involve a concept that is understood via metaphor, in some aspect. Lakoff and Turner say the weak position may be correct, but "it is the less interesting of the two," and that the strong position "seems false." It is agreed that metaphors allow us to understand one domain of experience in terms of another, but in order for metaphor to do this, there must be some "grounding."[85] That is, there must be some concepts to serve as source domains, concepts that are not completely understood via metaphor. Lakoff and Turner note that "there seems to be no shortage of such concepts" and they list,

---

[83] Ibid., 132–133.
[84] Ibid., 133.
[85] Regarding the "Grounding Hypothesis," see Ibid., 112–114.

for example, plants, departures, fire, sleep, locations, seeing.[86] Joseph Grady's work, discussed above, points to the fundamental significance of primary scenes and basic bodily and social experience underlying even our most primary metaphors.

In addition to the six positions outlined above, the contemporary theory clashes with a seventh position I will label the 'It's All Analogy' position.[87]

The 'It's All (or Mostly) Analogy' Position

Metaphor and analogy are related, and cognitive linguistic understandings of this relationship differ from traditional approaches. Does it matter how metaphor and analogy are defined in relationship to each other? This section summarizes some cognitive approaches to these issues, explaining why cognitivists argue that the traditional understanding of how analogy works in discourse is inadequate and inaccurate—and why this different understanding of analogy matters.[88]

Analogy and metaphor belong to overlapping conceptual spaces; they name related aspects of the way our minds work with networks of blended mental spaces that then are sometimes expressed in language.[89] But they are not identical. Analogy is the more general, over-arching term for comparison of (almost) any sort, while metaphor refers to a more specific set of ways category structures can be mapped onto each other. In this sense, it can be said that "analogy *includes* metaphor."[90] In *Reading Minds*, literary scholar Mark Turner explains that rather than being identical or competing terms describing exactly the same phenomena, analogy and metaphor are "like flip sides of a coin, interde-

---

[86] Ibid., 134–135.

[87] The designation of an "all-analogy" fallacy is my observation, not Lakoff and Turner's.

[88] David Tracy summarizes the differences between neo-Thomistic understandings of analogy and metaphor and his own process-oriented approach, underlining the metaphysical significance of these issues in *Blessed Rage for Order: the New Pluralism in Theology* (Chicago and London: University of Chicago Press, 1975, 1996), 160–162.

[89] "Varieties of meaning that on their faces seem unequal—such as categorizations, analogies, counterfactuals, metaphors, ritual, scientific notions, mathematical proofs, and grammatical constructions—turn out to be avatars of the spirit of blending." Fauconnier and Turner, *The Way We Think*, 106.

[90] Mark Turner, *Reading Minds: The Study of English in an Age of Cognitive Science* (Princeton, N.J.: Princeton University Press, 1991), 121; emphasis mine.

pendent upon each other."[91] What Turner says may not seem radical at first, but in making these claims he signals a decisive departure from the traditional understanding of analogy.

Aristotle is the father of the classical view, in which analogy works by locating dichotomies and indicating proportionate relationships or ratios. This classical understanding persists in modern philosophical definitions of analogy. For example, the language of mathematical proportion is used to define analogy in this 20th-century philosophical text:

> An analogy in its root meaning is a proportion, and primarily a mathematical ratio, e.g., 2:4::4:X. In such a ratio, given knowledge of three terms, and the nature of the proportionate relation, the value of the fourth term can be determined. Thus analogy is the repetition of the same fundamental pattern in two different contexts.[92]

Another 20th-century logician, I.M. Copi, represents the traditional approach when he defines analogy over against deductive reasoning, arguing that while analogy is ubiquitous in everyday inferences, and some analogy is argumentative, it nevertheless tends to be a 'looser' form of reasoning.[93] Classical understandings of logic and category structure persist when the logic of categorical syllogism is taken to be potentially (or inherently) more valid than the looser mode of argument by analogy. A dichotomy is thus set up between the supposedly tight (and reliable) logic of the categorical syllogism and the looser, vaguer mode of reasoning of analogical comparison or suggestion.

The problems with the classical, 'logically loose,' dichotomous definition of analogy are multiple. This one, over-arching dichotomy (categorical versus analogical) is often found in the company of—and even seems to endorse—a number of other questionable dichotomies: valid versus loosely inferential, literal versus figurative, real versus imaginary, true versus false, primary versus secondary.[94] Implicit is a notion that categorical syllogistic reasoning is more reliable than or somehow is

---

[91] Ibid., 122.

[92] Dorothy Emmet, *The Nature of Metaphysical Thinking* (New York: St. Martin's, 1945), 6.

[93] Irving M. Copi, *Introduction to Logic* (New York: Macmillan, 1968), 306–307. Copi follows classical (including Thomistic) categories, classing analogical conclusions as "probable inferences."

[94] M. Turner, *Reading Minds*, 121–122. Turner is speaking of analogical and *categorical* connections: "We tend to think of analogical connections as being opposed to categorical connections: for example, the analogical connections between electricity and water or between a journey and a life seem to us conjured or even whimsical, without legitimate claim on our category structures. I will argue that, on the contrary, categorical

to be preferred (because subject to validation?) over analogical reasoning. Again, because metaphor and simile are associated with analogical reasoning in this view, they fall into the category of the fanciful and the 'loose' and 'literary' over against hard, reliable, objective logic.[95]

Turner argues that the 'real' or 'true' versus 'false' dichotomy traditional views set up is itself untrue, because inaccurate. The similarities that analogies assert are not always logically false, nor are they sententially false.[96] In addition, the differences between metaphor and analogy consist not so much in *kind* (categorical versus analogical, read "loosely inferential") but in *degree*. Both analogy and metaphor work with cognitive category structures, but they differ in at least three ways: 1) degree of *entrenchment* of the category structures with which they work;[97] 2) degree and kind of *compression* they employ; and 3) relationship to organizing *frames*.

Let us take the third point first. Fauconnier and Turner observe that "the organizing frames in two [mental] spaces are analogous when there is a more abstract frame that applies to both of them. In that case, Analogy connects the organizing frames of the two mental spaces. For example, there is an Analogy mapping between the frame of a boxing match and the frame of a cockfight."[98] In highly conventional metaphors, by contrast, the two input spaces have *different* organizing frames, one of which gets projected into the blend.[99] The effect of this difference is that such metaphors can carry more detailed inputs, and the resulting inference patterns are more elaborated. Thus, Fauconnier and Turner note that metaphorical networks can go far beyond analogy.[100]

---

and analogical connections are not orthogonal to each other, but are more like flip sides of a coin, interdependent upon each other." Regarding the exclusion of figurative thought from "core meaning" in formal, analytic philosophy, see Fauconnier and Turner, *The Way We Think*, 14–15.

[95] Turner, *Reading Minds*, 139. Discussing the literal versus figurative dichotomy, Turner says it is "easily aligned with a range of other dichotomies: true versus false, real versus imaginary, conventional versus novel, dead versus live, stable versus unstable, categorical versus analogical, denotative versus connotative, fixed versus dynamic, primary versus secondary, and so on."

[96] Ibid.
[97] Ibid., 140.
[98] Fauconnier and Turner, *The Way We Think*, 106.
[99] Ibid., 126–127.
[100] Ibid., 128.

Secondly, Fauconnier and Turner theorize that analogy works with *compression*.[101] This kind of compression is operating when, for example, biblical scholars and Christian ethicists use the Two Worlds Metaphor. An enormous array of knowledge, properties, slots, and relations belonging to or displayed in the biblical texts are compressed into a singularity, The WORLD of the Text, or the World "behind" the text. A similar compression is performed on certain features—properties, knowledge, slots and relations—deemed significant in the modern context. These become The WORLD of the Readers, or the Modern World. Each World now seems unique, and its boundaries no longer look porous or penetrable.

In the analogy, the two compressed 'worlds' are provided a common, minimalist framing—a 'World' frame—so that the operations of analogical reasoning can be performed. The two Worlds are similar in some respects, but in many respects are disanalogous, and it is these disanalogous features that often have been of such interest to biblical scholars and ethicists.[102] The array of disanalogous factors is then compressed into a relationship of Identity with a quality of uniqueness that entails separation between the 'Worlds,' so that it makes sense to say (given this framing) that the modern or 21st-century World "split off" from or is "separated from" the ancient World. The 'Gap,' Lessing's Ditch, appears logically (by analogical reasoning) inherent.[103]

Moreover, Turner is interested in how people recognize analogy—in language in use. People do *not* generally recognize analogies by locating category "mistakes."[104] Instead, the dynamic he points to helps explain why analogies *seem* on the surface to be non-categorical or to disrupt conventional categories while actually relying on those conventions to work at all. Analogies often make *unconventional* connections between our mental models. "They exist," Turner says, "to make connections that are *not* already captured by our category structures."[105] But in order to do that, they work with our *conventional* mental mod-

---

[101] Ibid., 113–115; 314–317.
[102] Fauconnier and Turner's analysis terms Identity one of a set of Vital Relations. In the Two Worlds Analogy, identity is compressed into uniqueness to emphasize the radical distinction between the 'worlds.' Ibid., 314–315.
[103] Regarding Lessing's "Ditch," see Chapter 3, n. 43.
[104] "It is generally false that we recognize analogy by first recognizing categorization, then rejecting the categorization as false, and then doing secondary reconstructive work. On the contrary, under certain donations we prefer to recognize analogy first, as in 'A child is a mirror' or 'Language is a virus;'" (M. Turner, *Reading Minds*, 122).
[105] Ibid.

els, playing with them, suggesting alternative ways of looking at the conventional connections. Furthermore, just as not all analogies are argumentative, neither are all analogies playful. They themselves can become stock comparisons. When a physicist first suggested that light is a wave, the suggestion was disruptive of stock models and categories; now "light is a wave" is a stock analogy.[106] This is where the notion of degree of *entrenchment* comes into play. Standard analogies may be deeply entrenched in a community's conceptual structure; "new" analogies can feel less deeply entrenched, but they actually work with conventional frames and mappings.[107]

As Turner draws out the implications of his cognitive approach to analogy, he makes a number of significant claims that may prove useful for this study, both at the methodological and theoretical levels. Both analogy and metaphor work with cognitive category structures. Analogy does not operate, as the traditional view holds, outside or tangentially to, categories. In fact, analogies operate dynamically in language in use, influencing shifts in category structures and even sometimes generating new structures. The categories with which we think and with which languages work are not fixed, nor are they merely referential or reflective of 'real' categories in the world. In fact, "[C]ategory structures are dynamic and subject to transformation under the presence of analogy."[108] Analogies themselves provide evidence that our categories are products of human mental operations; they can inventively disrupt, influence, recast, or retune long-entrenched categories. But not all analogies are felicitous or novel; neither are they all emotionally charged or evocative of feeling. By the same token they are not all reducible in the sense in which mathematical ratios are; they are not all proportional comparisons.[109]

Analogies blend and make connections between categories, but not all cross-category or cross-domain connections are analogical. Many other kinds of blends work with multiple frames in the inputs, rather

---

[106] Ibid. Turner also points out that there are other, non-analogical, kinds of connections: mental space connections, identities asserting class containment, and equations contrasting mental models at the basic level.

[107] Fauconnier and Turner say, "Blends are often novel and generated on the fly ... but they recruit entrenched mappings and frames. Blends themselves can also become entrenched ... giving rise to conceptual and formal structures shared throughout the community;" *The Way We Think*, 49.

[108] M. Turner, *Reading Minds*, 125.

[109] Recall that even the classicists and their medieval adapters (notably, Aquinas) understood that people use a number of different kinds of analogical connections and

than with the single framing that analogy requires. The 'It's All- or Mostly- Analogy' position is untenable, then, at a number of levels and the cognitive linguistic critique of the traditional view of analogy is multifaceted. The conventional view is over-simplified and sets up (false) dichotomous categories. It therefore fails to account for the continuum and dynamic interdependence of analogous and metaphorical categories. To do that, it relies on an out-dated and failed theory of objective, immutable categorical truth. The literal / figurative dichotomy it sets up is at least questionable, if not *prima facie* false. It misunderstands how analogy is generated and fails to accurately describe or explain what happens when people make connections as they read (or listen or speak).

Perhaps the most significant aspect of this entire discussion is that if the cognitivists are correct, it is not just (or mainly) the surprising, shocking, novel connections or analogies that lend structure to moral discourse or are of interest when one wants to understand the roles 'analogical reasoning' plays in moral discourse. The deeper work and greater influence happens at another level, the more deeply entrenched level of cognitive metaphor. This level is "deep" because it is the level on the analogical thinking/mental space blend gradient where we often do not even notice cognitively constructed concepts as we use and encounter expressions. These are the cognitive categorical structures we take for granted. These are the very ones that wield most power in moral discourse. That is why it is important to know how metaphor and analogy work—respectively and interdependently. The terms 'analogy' and 'metaphor' are *not* interchangeable. This study, for the most part, attempts to look at the *metaphorical* level on the gradient, and not to stay at the more general level of analogy.

Finally, I prefer to use the term 'metaphor' or 'cognitive metaphor' instead of 'analogy' to signal the shift, the *paradigm* shift, from classical understandings—not just of these terms, but of how reasoning itself is understood. Using the term 'analogy' for all kinds of comparisons— and claiming that metaphor is essentially merely analogy—does not entail or signify that one understands or accepts that *cognitive* dynamics are at work. One can use 'analogy' for comparisons of many kinds and still buy into the traditional understanding of how metaphor and analogy operate. One might still suppose, then, that 'analogy' was an

---

comparisons. Recall also the reliance on the doctrine of essences in their explanation (and construction) of these different types of analogy. See Chapter 1.

argumentative maneuver or rhetorical device. Traditional 'analogy' can work with disembodied reason. That is what is unacceptable because it is inaccurate. It is inaccurate because, as Turner has said, "A statement is an analogy not with respect to the *world* but with respect to the *category structure* that is brought to bear upon it."[110]

The classical referential / objectivist view, in which analogies and metaphors are more or less (mostly lesser, looser) approximations, reflections or references to objective reality, relegates analogical 'poetic' reasoning to the para-rational realm and assumes that moral reasoning and the real work of ethics happens someplace else—in the sphere of reason or syllogistic logic. It is possible from that position to kindly tip one's hat to 'analogical imagination' or to admit that analogy and metaphor are rhetorically or motivationally useful adjuncts to logical ethical reasoning. But in that view, analogy and metaphor remain forever in an adjunct position.

Conclusion: Why Metaphor?

The survey in Chapter 1 revealed that Aristotle's view of metaphor has five major features: 1) transfer of names, 2) based on similarities, 3) involving deviance from ordinary usage, 4) in which "fittingness" or appropriateness it at issue. 5) All of this is a matter of intuition and perception. It was noted, in addition, that Aristotle posits (or assumes) a connection between metaphor and analogy. Conceptual metaphor theory clearly is at variance with the first four features in this list, calls into question traditional understandings of analogy,[111] and nuances the notion of perception in ways that contradict and demonstrate the inadequacy of traditional Greek faculty psychology.

The Augustinian strand of metaphor tradition does manage to see metaphor as a mechanism that transcends the words in which it is expressed, but it does that by valorizing metaphor as a mode of connection with a supernatural realm. The Thomistic strand tends to relegate metaphor or analogy to a para-rational function in ethical discourse. In

---

[110] Ibid., 148; emphasis mine.
[111] Ibid. See Lakoff, "The Contemporary Theory," 235–236. Turner suggests that the GENERIC IS SPECIFIC metaphor is the general mechanism at work in analogical reasoning, and that the Invariance Principle characterizes the class of possible analogies; Mark Turner, *Reading Minds*, 70–72, 161.

conceptual metaphor theory, metaphor is indeed connected with our capacity for imaginative thought, but it is grounded not in some supernatural realm, but in human, often bodily, experience.

This contemporary theory entails a different view of human reason from that with which Augustine and Aquinas were working. Thought is first of all *embodied*. That is, the core of our conceptual systems is directly grounded in perception, body movement, and physical and social experience.[112] Metaphors are ways people use their experience of one kind of thing to experience and understand another kind of thing. We use metaphors in systematic, conventionalized ways and the use of such conventions lends coherence and structure to our discourse, including our moral discourse. Metaphors are conceptual; before they are linguistic expressions, they are mental operations that blend and network mental spaces. The theory of metaphor articulated by Lakoff and colleagues represents a paradigm shift. Just what that might mean for ethics and biblical studies is the subject of the next chapter.

---

[112] Lakoff, *Women, Fire, and Dangerous Things*, xiv, xvi–xvii, 7–9, 31–32, 371–372.

CHAPTER THREE

TWO 'ANALOGICAL IMAGINATION'
APPROACHES TO METAPHOR AND NT ETHICS

the road to moral judgment is by way of the imagination
—A. Wilder[1]

In the fields of biblical hermeneutics and Christian ethics we often speak of a *problem*, the 'problem of Scripture and ethics.' The problem seems to have to do with the nature of Scripture, and the difficulties can be encapsulated in two words: *distance* and *diversity*. The historical-cultural distance between the biblical texts and the current modern context looms large. How can moral and ethical concepts and strictures arising from such culturally distant locations have bearing on modern moral issues? What help do these texts offer us as we face modern issues in bioethics or a global politics where weapons of mass destruction are brandished? Then there is the problem of *diversity*: Scripture speaks more than one language, both literally (Hebrew, Aramaic, Greek) and ethically (wisdom traditions, prophetic traditions, laws and maxims, narrative, and so on). The writings were composed and compiled over time, in various cultural and historical contexts. Their diversity seems to defy reification into a useful set of clear ethical or normative principles. These are the basic problems modern hermeneutics and Christian ethics grapple with in relation to Scripture.

But while our version of the 'problem' is new, since at least the time of Thomas Aquinas, Christian theologians have realized that difficult epistemological and hermeneutical issues surround the understanding and employment of the sacred texts in theological and ethical reasoning. Since at least Thomas's time, some theologians and biblical interpreters have thought that metaphor and analogy have important roles to play in these matters. In the current context, systematic theologians David Tracy and David Kelsey, historian Wayne Meeks, theological ethicists James Gustafson and Stanley Hauerwas, and biblical schol-

---

[1] Amos Wilder, *Early Christian Rhetoric: The Language of the Gospel*. Rev. ed. (Cambridge, Mass.: Harvard University Press, 1971), 60.

ars Dan Via and John Donahue are prominent and influential figures among the many who highlight the role of analogical and imaginative modes of reasoning in biblical hermeneutics, theology and theological ethics.

This chapter surveys the work of William Spohn and Richard Hays, two Christian scholars whose work belongs to this stream. In the course of this survey, an argument builds that while analogical imagination models are to be commended for giving attention to metaphor and analogy as well as for validating the usefulness of the imaginative in theological ethics and biblical hermeneutics, they remain in thrall to an objectivist historicism and fail to deliver sufficiently clear and workable analytical methods. Theoretical and methodological distinctions between cognitive linguistic approaches to metaphor and these analogical imagination models are highlighted, and it is argued that the cognitive model may have more to offer those working in the area of Scripture and ethics.

Scripture & the Analogical Imagination:
William Spohn's Go and Do Likewise

Roman Catholic moral theologian William Spohn was a kindred spirit with a passion for helping Christians come to a holistic understanding of Christian ethics and of the role of Scripture in moral formation and discernment, so that they can fully live the life offered in Christ. Though his books are accessible to non-specialists, they also represent important contributions Spohn made to the field of Christian ethics. Perhaps his core contribution lay in the way Spohn linked the ethics *of* Scripture to the role of Scripture *in* Christian ethics. To make those connections, he proposed revisions in the ways we describe the focus and scope of ethics and demonstrated a thoughtful way of reading the New Testament with issues of moral discernment and formation in view.[2] Declining to be confined by narrower definitions that implicitly discount the significance of moral formation, character, and community, Spohn widened the scope of ethics and explicated with real life

---

[2] Spohn's primary stated objective in *Go and Do Likewise* was to assist the faithful in making those connections, rather than laying out the methodological and theoretical fine points of this approach for professional ethicists. William C. Spohn, *Go and Do Likewise: Jesus and Ethics* (New York: Continuum, 1999).

examples what doing moral theology "in the light of Scripture" looks like in everyday life today.³

Spohn took his title from Jesus' comment at the close of his parable of the Good Samaritan: "Go and do likewise." *Likewise* becomes the key that opens the door to a way modern Christians can indeed faithfully follow Jesus today. To 'do likewise' is not to subscribe or submit to a code of rules, nor to attempt to copy exactly, but to accept an invitation to creative, dynamic, Spirit-inspired and enabled community. The Christian moral life, then, is life lived in the light of Jesus Christ, the 'concrete universal' whose life story is the master moral 'paradigm,' and is at the same time life empowered by the Spirit of Christ.⁴ This approach to Scripture and ethics was outlined in "Scripture as a Basis for Responding Love," a chapter in Spohn's earlier book, *What Are They Saying about Scripture and Ethics?*⁵ and developed more fully in *Go and Do Likewise*.

---

[3] The directive to do theology "in the light of Scripture" is a key Vatican II teaching. See the statement in *Dogmatic Constitution on Divine Revelation*, Vatican II, *Dei Verbum* (November 18, 1965), 24–25: Sacred theology rests on the written word of God, together with sacred tradition, as its primary and perpetual foundation. By scrutinizing in the light of faith all truth stored up in the mystery of Christ, theology is most powerfully strengthened and constantly rejuvenated by that word. For the Sacred Scriptures contain the word of God and since they are inspired really are the word of God; and so the study of the sacred page is, as it were, the soul of sacred theology. (3) By the same word of Scripture the ministry of the word also, that is, pastoral preaching, catechetics and all Christian instruction, in which the liturgical homily must hold the foremost place, is nourished in a healthy way and flourishes in a holy way. 25. Therefore, all the clergy must hold fast to the Sacred Scriptures through diligent sacred reading and careful study, especially the priests of Christ and others, such as deacons and catechists who are legitimately active in the ministry of the word. This is to be done so that none of them will become "an empty preacher of the word of God outwardly, who is not a listener to it inwardly" (4) since they must share the abundant wealth of the divine word with the faithful committed to them, especially in the sacred liturgy. The sacred synod also earnestly and especially urges all the Christian faithful, especially Religious, to learn by frequent reading of the divine Scriptures the "excellent knowledge of Jesus Christ" (Phil. 3:8). "For ignorance of the Scriptures is ignorance of Christ." (5) Therefore, they should gladly put themselves in touch with the sacred text itself, whether it be through the liturgy, rich in the divine word, or through devotional reading, or through instructions suitable for the purpose and other aids which, in our time, with approval and active support of the shepherds of the Church, are commendably spread everywhere. And let them remember that prayer should accompany the reading of Sacred Scripture, so that God and man may talk together; for "we speak to Him when we pray; we hear Him when we read the divine saying."

[4] Spohn, *Go and Do Likewise*, 2, 4.
[5] William C. Spohn, *What Are They Saying about Scripture and Ethics?* Revised and expanded ed. (Mahwah, N.J.: Paulist Press. 1995).

Spohn argued that Christian ethical "going and doing likewise" requires analogical imagination. While the spirit and basic orientation of our approaches is similar, I will argue that much of that which Spohn identified as analogical actually works via conceptual metaphor—and that both analogy and metaphor work by blending mental spaces. If one wishes to understand how analogical imagination works, then, the theory and methods of conceptual metaphor and blended space analysis will be indispensable. Our differences are not just terminological. Take the "test case" Spohn presents, the story of Jesus washing the disciples' feet (John 13). Spohn reads and applies this story analogically by providing a single frame (Rite, Worship) so that Rite in the text is analogically compared with Rite now. But how does a modern reader make sense of the text in the first place? Cognitive metaphor analysis would point to an array of conceptual metaphors at work and to the compression involved in the rituals.[6] Even the notion of 'going and doing' evokes several conventional metaphors for morality, a key one being Life Is a Journey. From a cognitive point of view, it is the modern reader's ability (or lack thereof) to pick up these conceptual metaphors that drives analogical imagination and allows the textual metaphors to shape moral disposition and inform choices.[7] So a central concern in this consideration of Spohn's work is his construal of how readers recognize and employ analogies and metaphors at all.

Spohn's Strengths

The virtues of *Go and Do Likewise* are many. First, I applaud as a necessary corrective to standard Euro-American Christian ethics in the liberal tradition Spohn's insistence on the need for a spirituality wedded to our ethic. He wisely and rightly counseled that before a propositional ethic could be articulated—whether that be a Kantian or utilitarian or some other style of ethic—came issues of moral character, disposition,

---

[6] Some of the conceptual metaphors are: Goodness Is Holiness; Goodness Is Purity; Water Is Cleanliness; Goodness Is Self-giving; Goodness Is Serving; Goodness Is Honor; Goodness Is Up (Status); Goodness Is Voluntarily Giving up Status—and the antitheses of these metaphors: Bad is Down; Bad is Dishonor; Bad Is Impure, and so on.

[7] Cognitivists recognize in ritual the action of blending and compression of mental spaces, especially of cause-and-effect compressions; see Gilles Fauconnier and Mark Turner, *The Way We Think: Conceptual Blending and the Mind's Hidden Complexities* (New York: Basic Books, 2002), 75–88.

and spiritual and moral formation. 'Ethics' properly is concerned with this whole gamut of issues.[8] He did this while insisting on the need for an ethic, for normative constraint, in Christian social ethical endeavors. That is, he located Christian ethics in Christian community as it is called together to embody the Gospel. "Communities are the primary locus of Christian moral discernment because the New Testament texts emerged from and were addressed to the communities of faith."[9] Christian ethicists and biblical scholars are first disciples of Christ, and 'Christian' ethics and questions of Christian morality properly belong not to the scholarly guilds but to this community first of all.[10]

Secondly, Spohn was one Christian ethicist who took with utmost seriousness the connection between Scripture and Christian ethics, and upheld Scripture as the church's book.[11] He did not discount the significance or weight of Scripture for constructive ethics and moral formation; he did not relegate Scripture to a fourth and last quadrant on a grid displaying sources of authority in Christian ethics. Nor did he isolate Scripture from other sources of authority; he took pains to demonstrate its connections and interplay with reason, experience, and tradition and how they work in concert over time to form Christian moral perception, dispositions, and identity.

Thirdly, Spohn was keen to counsel the reader who approaches the NT to be aware of the assumptions and expectations concerning the nature of the moral life and of ethics that are being brought to that reading. He was aware that readers bring much to the reading and interpretive process; there is no neutral or purely objective stance available from which to read these texts.[12] This is true in general, but it is also worth noting that the ethical frameworks and assumptions we bring to our readings of the NT shape our interpretations. Spohn asserted that they can distort our interpretations and appropriations, and counseled awareness, then, of our starting point.[13]

---

[8] Spohn, *Go and Do Likewise*, 13–14.
[9] Ibid., 22.
[10] Ibid., 14, 16, 22.
[11] Ibid., 10, 12–15.
[12] Ibid., 18.
[13] Spohn said, "The type of ethics assumed in the application frequently determines the selection." Ibid. This is in harmony with Thomas Ogletree's suggestion that recognizing one's point of view is a first step in the process of moral reflection on biblical texts. Thomas W. Ogletree, *The Use of the Bible in Christian Ethics: A Constructive Essay* (Philadelphia: Fortress Press, 1983), 3–4.

Spohn's Approach to the New Testament

In his reading of Scripture, Spohn began with the NT, and when he read the NT, he started with Jesus. While it is unfortunate that the OT got such short shrift in the process, I applaud the focus on the Gospels and the attempt to begin with Jesus. This starting point is a needed corrective to the ubiquitous use of Pauline theology or of an amalgamated anthology of "parenetic" passages as starting points for work on the ethics of the NT. Moreover, Spohn made a valiant effort to get past the composite Jesus that so many Christian ethicists tacitly address in their work or project onto the NT texts. Spohn tried to tease out the distinctive voices telling Jesus' story—Matthew, Mark, Luke, and John—and Paul. He looked at the whole story, the life story of Jesus, not merely at isolated incidents or sayings.

In addition, while Spohn's specialty was moral theology, he was well aware of certain developments in Jesus studies and of historical critical biblical methods. Spohn repeatedly reminded his readers that there are worlds of difference between our social and cultural *Sitzen im Leben* and Jesus of Nazareth's. On the other hand, Spohn from the outset made clear the limits of the historicity and objectivity upon which historical-critical method depended. "Historical method promised an objectivity it has been unable to deliver," he said.[14] Moreover, "the 'historical Jesus' constructed by scholarly research cannot function as the norm of Christian faith."[15] Having said this, though, Spohn affirmed a continued need for contextual approaches to Scripture-reading, and for historical and social-cultural information because it "provides a necessary background for normative debates of Christians today."[16] The worlds, then, were stuck held apart in Spohn's approach, for the purposes of determining ethical normativity.

In all of this, Spohn recognized that Scripture is not self-interpreting and he repeatedly invited Scripture-readers to be careful readers, paying attention to context (and genre?).[17] He was concerned to address the twin dangers of literalistic readings, on the one hand, and of unbridled, uncritical focus on the figurative, on the other. "Literal readings of biblical imagery can be unfaithful to their trajectory of meaning ...

---

[14] Spohn, *Go and Do Likewise*, 18.
[15] Ibid., 19.
[16] Ibid., 22.
[17] Ibid., 71.

[I]nvoking biblical images does not guarantee fidelity to the way of Christ."[18] Along the way, he modeled how faithful reading can be done, with a series of "show and tell" demonstrations of how he read certain passages with questions about the moral content and implications in mind.

Most germane to the *theoretical* issues taken on in this project is the central place Spohn carved out in Christian moral life and moral reasoning for narrative, for the imaginative, and for what Spohn called the 'analogical' mode of reason. His insistence that analogical reasoning is central, and that it is a form of reasoning, not just fanciful embellishment on an argument actually made more cogently and clearly elsewhere, is crucial.

> It seems that many of our assumptions that determined what is appropriate action are not based on articulated concepts or propositions. They are more likely contained in the analogies and metaphors that are operative in a culture rather than in explicitly formulated assumptions.[19]

It will be well to attend carefully to his construal of this analogical character of the task of reading and interpreting and applying Scripture in moral life, and to that I now turn.

Analogical and Moral Imagination

In *Go and Do Likewise*, Spohn explains how the 'moral imagination' moves analogically as it appropriates metaphorical frameworks from Scripture (and especially the story of Jesus' life) to apply to current contexts.[20] These Scriptural patterns—images and metaphors—are said to "correct our vision so we see others in a special way: as 'neighbor,' 'sister and brother,' and 'the one for whom Christ died.'"[21] "Analogical

---

[18] Ibid., 70. In this context, Spohn also offered an interpretive rubric: "Norms and paradigms that push the boundaries of cultural arrangements in their original biblical setting should not be used to canonize our present institutions."

[19] Ibid., 102.

[20] Ibid., 4. Spohn also said, "Christian moral reflection tries to imagine actions that will be appropriate to the problem at hand and faithful to the story of Jesus. The new actions will be analogical because they will be partly the same, partly different, but basically similar to the relevant portion of the story of Jesus." Ibid., 54. He acknowledged that this "formulation" had been articulated by David Tracy and cited his *Analogical Imagination: Christian Theology and the Culture of Pluralism* (New York: Crossroad, 1981), 88.

[21] Ibid.

imagination," then, guides the way we see our world and, through the "stories of Scripture," can even "shape our emotions to act in ways appropriate to the gospel."[22] He is not talking about sentiment or momentary, reflexive emotional reaction, but rather is interested in character formation, "steady qualities of character" that in the long run amount to identity.[23] His proposal is not simplistic, nor is the process he outlines easy. In fact, he counsels that living 'likewise' involves a sometimes-difficult journey, a progressive deepening, in both persons and communities.

The primary analogy Spohn was interested in was the one he believed needed to happen in the Scripture-reading and application process.[24] As modern Christians encounter Scripture and attempt to apply it to their moral lives today, they must make analogical connections or transfers between what they read in the text and what they experience in their own lives, and between the world of the text and their own worlds. Here is how Spohn schematized this analogical relationship:

NT text is to   ::   *Christian community is to*
its world   its world[25]

To explain how he saw this analogical process working, Spohn employed the traditional Thomistic vocabulary of 'proportional analogy' and of analogical over against 'univocal and equivocal' uses of language.[26] Spohn used this analogical formulation to drive home a key component of his analysis of the Scripture-and-ethics problem—and to point the way toward a solution to the problem. To see what Spohn was driving at, let us list the terms of the analogy and highlight his instructive commentary on the relationships pertaining between the terms:

(a) the biblical text in relation to
(b) its world and
(c) today's Christian community in relation to
(d) its world.

Spohn had this to say about the terms of this analogy:

---

[22] Ibid., 4.
[23] Ibid.
[24] Spohn called this "the basic analogy that guides Christian moral reflection on scripture." Ibid., 55.
[25] Ibid.
[26] Ibid. See Chapter 1 on Aquinas and analogy.

The classic analogical proportion involves four terms: not *a* to *a'* but *a* is to *b* as *c* is to *d*. The relations of the first two terms guides the pursuit for the fourth term, as in 2:4::8:X. Knowing *a*, *b*, and *c*, we try to figure out what *d* should be.[27]

That is, knowing what we know about the biblical text in relation to its world, and knowing what we do about our own Christian community, we try to figure out what *d* should be—what, in the light of the biblical text, we ought to do in our world. The interpretive movement Spohn advocated requires that readers not bypass considerations of the distinctions between two 'worlds'—the world of the biblical text, and the world of today's Christian community. His point was that to think we can move *directly* from the biblical text to drawing conclusions about moral and ethical matters in our world today is to dangerously oversimplify and distort the interpretive process. It would be to employ a false analogy, making an erroneous *a* to *a'* connection. This false equation, then, is behind modern readers' misreadings and misappropriations of Scripture.

Now, the relation holding between the biblical text and its world (*a* is to *b*) is the 'prime analogate' in this formula, and as such has *normative* status; it "sets the paradigm for the *analogue*" (*c* is to *d*).[28] Spohn explained this normative status and quality carefully; he worked very hard not to over-simplify complex interactions and relationships. Although he set out the major terms of the core analogical functions in this very clear, logical and mathematical model, Spohn insisted that he had in mind a kind of sensitive and artful listening for the "rhyme," rather than some strict and rigid formulaic read-and-apply program. Further, he counseled that "the moral implications are drawn less by strict logic than by a sense of what is appropriate and fitting."[29]

As I indicated earlier, Spohn used as a test case the story of Jesus washing the disciples' feet (John 13) to demonstrate the discernment process he had in mind. He compared and contrasted several specific modern "readings" in footwashing ritual designs, saying:

> The ritual is the analogue, and the scene in John 13 is the prime analogate. The tension between features in the analogue that are similar

---

[27] Spohn, *Go and Do Likewise*, 55.
[28] Spohn, *Go and Do Likewise*, 55.
[29] Ibid. But is, then, the analogical mode of reasoning being given a 'looser' and lesser status? See the section on analogy in Chapter 2.

to the prime analogate and those that are different sparks the graced imagination so see what should be done in response.[30]

The "graced imagination" is "sparked" by the analogical "tension;" a light dawns, and what "should be done" in response becomes clear. This now sounds like Augustinian language—the language of transcendent 'spark' providing enlightenment. But Spohn next turned to a consideration of how analogical imagination is grounded in the concrete. Relying on the expertise of David Tracy and literary critic William Lynch, he clarified the role of imagination as it moves between concrete and transcendent meaning. Spohn offered this Augustinian-sounding explanation from Lynch of how analogical imagination works with particular events, stories and objects:

> 'the plunge down *causally generates* the plunge up' into insight ... 'the mind that has descended into the real has shot up into insights that would have been inaccessible to pure concepts.'[31]

Spohn explained what this implies: "The stuff of ordinary life is not to be dismissed or transcended, but engaged. The Word is made flesh and cannot be found dissolved from flesh."[32] Engagement with life, connection with concrete reality, eschewing mystical transport to the transcendent—this is the way of analogical imagination in the key of Spohn:

> Since the pursuit of meaning and beauty passes through the narrow gate of particularity, we should not read the stories of Jesus as a code to transcendent meaning. We have to find ways of plunging into their particular characters, shape, and details so that the larger meaning is disclosed.[33]

It is precisely at this juncture that Spohn mentions cognitive metaphor and metaphor mapping.

---

[30] Ibid., 55.
[31] Ibid., 57. Spohn was quoting William F. Lynch, *Christ and Apollo: The Dimensions of the Literary Imagination* (New York: New Modern Library, 1963), 37–38. Spohn also quoted another Lynch statement in this context: "Our hope must be to discover such symbols as can make the imagination *rise* indeed, and yet keep all the tang and density of that actuality into which the imagination *descends.*" Ibid., 23.
[32] Spohn, *Go and Do Likewise*, 57.
[33] Ibid.

Metaphor in the Analogical Mix

Here is Spohn's most direct reference to cognitive metaphor:

> It takes a variety of analogies and metaphors to bring out the richness of experience. In the language of contemporary cognitive science, we need 'multiple metaphorical mappings' to grasp experiences.[34]

He is citing Mark Johnson's *Moral Imagination*. But in a footnote later in the chapter, Spohn reveals his evaluation of the cognitive approach:

> Like many others, Johnson uses 'metaphor' where it would be more accurate to use 'analogy.'[35]

This footnote belongs to a section entitled "The Kingdom of God: Metaphor and Analogy." There he explains that "God's reign is a metaphor that functions in two ways: it frames the disciples' view of the world, and it becomes a fruitful analogy in the parables of the kingdom."[36] Setting aside for a moment his problematical usages of the terms 'metaphor' and 'analogy' here, focus first on the way Spohn expresses a version of the 'it's all analogy' position.[37] While on the one hand, Spohn recognizes the need to get underneath sweeping generalities of the overarching analogies obtaining in Scriptural texts (and in the reading process?) to work with the richer level of detail provided in metaphorical mappings, on the other hand he seems to conclude that it is really analogy, not metaphor, that bears the cognitive load.[38]

But Spohn goes on to offer a (traditional) definition of metaphor and to assert that the "moral consequences" that follow analogical imagination-engaged readings of parables "flow integrally from the respective *metaphors* and the dispositions they engender." So the parables are both analogical and metaphorical.[39] The terms 'analogy' and

---

[34] Ibid., 57.
[35] Ibid., 201 n. 34.
[36] Ibid., 66.
[37] See Chapter 2 regarding the 'it's all analogy' position.
[38] Spohn recognized that certain metaphors were conventional and repeatedly used in Scriptural moral discourse. For example, he noted that 'walk' was a commonplace metaphor for living morally, journeying on the Way. Spohn, *Go and Do Likewise*, 25. What is missing here is an account of the role of such conventional, systematically used metaphors for morality in the analogical imagination. They seem merely to form a backdrop—he would sometimes say 'metaphorical frame,' or setting where the 'sparks' of imagination can fly.
[39] Ibid., 68, emphasis mine.

'metaphor' begin to collide, conflate, and morph. But before addressing the terminological issues, let us pick up the thread of Spohn's argument in his introduction to 'analogical imagination,' because it is important not to miss the strong claim here about the way encountering metaphors in the course of parable-reading might engender dispositions and have moral consequences.

Back to the Story, Forward to Appropriation

All of this discussion of the concrete and the transcendent and of specific, concrete metaphorical mapping fleshes out how Spohn's own discernment of the shape of a fitting and appropriate response to the John 13 story was enabled and constrained. Spohn described three performances that attempted to faithfully respond to that story. Each was a contemporary ritual enactment of foot washing. The first is set in St. Peter's Basilica in Rome, where the Pope washes the feet of twelve seminary students. The second occurs at Holy Spirit Parish in Berkeley, California, where the parish pastor washes the feet of a woman from the parish, and then the process is reversed. Next, these two wash the feet of a number of adults and children in the congregation, who then in turn wash other congregants' feet. In the third ritual, an Irish-American pastor in an inner city Baltimore church removes his chasuble and shines the shoes of twelve elderly African-American men.[40] Spohn then raised the question, "Which one of these rituals best conveys the example that Jesus gave in John 13?" Spohn explained how he discerned the rhyme in the rituals, saying that though each is an "exercise of analogical imagination," the third example would win the best-rhyme prize.[41] He concluded that the text itself engenders a question for Christians attempting to follow Jesus today: "If this is how Christians ought to love, what should we do about overcoming barriers of race and class, locating the Church in solidarity with the poor, and facing divisions within the parish itself?"[42] The level, then, of response and appropriation of Scripture that Spohn sought and taught, was far from simple or simplistic. Although his interpretation of the foot washing analogy began at the analogical level, using Rite as the overarching frame, he clearly understood that the

---

[40] Ibid., 52–54.
[41] Ibid., 54.
[42] Ibid., 55.

appropriation, the going and doing likewise, moved outside that analogical framing. But how? What inferential structure and interpretive process allows readers of the story to make those moves, to go from that story in John's Gospel, from a ritual framing to a broader one? Does the analogical imagination account suffice to explain these dynamics?

Conclusion: Cognitivist Responses and Questions

What does cognitive linguistic metaphor theory and method say to Spohn? Several observations and questions arise. Perhaps the first feature that stands out if one surveys Spohn's work from a cognitive metaphor stance is the metaphor-laden language Spohn employed (borrowed, really) to describe the current Scripture-and-ethics situation. He spoke of a 'problem' posed by the apparently inherent separation ('gap') between two 'worlds'—the 'world' of the scriptural text (then) and the 'world' of today's Christian community (now). These metaphors exert enormous power to frame the discussion and shape the proposed reading and interpretive methods Spohn offered. Now, to be fair, it has to be said that Spohn was simply using a set of metaphors that has become standard, stock metaphors in a certain linguistic community. In biblical hermeneutics circles as well as among Christian ethicists, this 'worlds' and 'gap' language evokes a certain image schema. Readers who belong to this linguistic community will likely be envisioning *the* 'chasm,' 'ditch,' or 'gap' that is (now, conventionally) assumed to exist between the 'worlds'—of the text and of the reader, of the historical and cultural milieu in which the NT texts were formed and the present.[43] I will return to a consideration of the power this set of metaphors wields in discussions of biblical

---

[43] In the 18th century, Gotthold Ephraim Lessing wrote, "That, then, is the ugly, broad ditch which I cannot get across, however often and however earnestly I have tried to make the leap. If anyone can help me over it, let him do it, I beg him, I adjure him. He will deserve a divine reward from me." Gotthold E. Lessing, "On the Proof of the Spirit and of Power," *Lessing's Theological Writings*, trans. & ed. Henry Chadwick (Stanford, California: Stanford University Press, 1967[1957]), 53–55. More recently, N.T. Wright has articulated the current challenge, however, which is to query "the existence of such a ditch in the first place." N.T. Wright, "The Letter to the Galatians: Exegesis and Theology" in *Between Two Horizons: Spanning New Testament Studies and Systematic Theology*, ed. Joel B. Green and Max Turner (Grand Rapids, Mich.: Eerdmans, 2000), 206. See my remarks concerning the Two Worlds Analogy in Chapter 2.

hermeneutical matters later in this chapter. Here I simply want to pose the questions Spohn's language raises for me: What understanding of the nature of sacred and ancient texts and of reading and interpretive processes is entailed in this language? Does the "gap between two worlds" metaphor fit the dynamic engagement Spohn in fact described and urged the Church to embody between Christian readers and performers of these texts?

A related set of questions concerns Spohn's language when it comes to talk referring to the Bible. When the talk is of Scripture as 'source,' and 'deposit,' this set of texts becomes an object and a container. The container holds resources. One wonders which properties of containers and their contents are indeed mapped when the Bible or Scripture is conceptualized this way. Does it confine the role of Scripture in Christian ethics to content-oriented, 'useful' and boundary making functions?[44] In this schema, who or what controls or decides what pieces of such "content" are in fact useful, relevant? More frequently, Spohn used the language of Scripture as story, narrative. Cognitivists would notice that these are not just genre labels, they are metaphors (Scripture Is a Story) with entailments.

Thirdly, some cognitivist observations concerning Spohn's analytical methods and working definitions could be offered. It must be said that the relationships between and distinctions among the terms *analogy* and *metaphor, frame, paradigm, image*, and so on, are difficult to understand and at points philosophically controversial. This reader finds that still to be the case after careful consideration of Spohn's construal. Where the proposed reading and interpretive method remains unwieldy and the working vocabulary of 'analogical imagination,' is muddled, one wonders whether it is not possible to devise more precise definitions and analyses of the functional properties of 'imagination.' In particular, reading Spohn spurs one to want to get at the particulars, the rich variety of concrete, enfleshed images and metaphors grounded in human

---

[44] Joel B. Green raises similar issues concerning view of Scripture and assumptions about its function in theology and ethics. Joel B. Green, "Scripture and Theology: Uniting the Two So Long Divided," *Between Two Horizons*, ed. Joel B. Green and Max Turner (Grand Rapids, Mich.: Eerdmans, 2000), 40. See also Joel B. Green, "Scripture and Theology: Failed Experiments, Fresh Perspectives," *Interpretation* 56, no.1 (January 2002): 5–20; and his essay on the authority of Scripture, "Scripture in the Church: Reconstructing the Authority of Scripture for Christian Formation and Mission," in *The Wesleyan Tradition: A Paradigm for Renewal*, ed. Paul W. Chilcote, (Nashville, Tenn.: Abingdon, 2002).

realities he suggests—following Lynch—make Scriptural texts sing with universal truth and beauty.[45] One longs for the workable methods for doing the detailed investigation of metaphor for which David Tracy, for one, has called.[46]

These queries about how 'imagination' works and how it might influence moral dispositions and ethical choices highlight a core issue. To put it plainly, is it the metaphors and images and analogies we are *conscious* of which hold ultimate sway over our moral imaginations and therefore wield the transformative power in moral dispositions? Spohn wanted to say—did say—that metaphorical frames "fund" our vision and shape our expectation. The "kingdom" frame, for example, "enriches and tutors our receptivity."[47] Here he quoted William James:

> *My experience is what I agree to attend to*. Only those items which I *notice* shape my mind—without selective interest, experience is an utter chaos.[48]

But this is precisely what the cognitivists deny, on empirical grounds. What if it is the largely *unconscious*, automatic, conventional metaphors and analogical frames we use effortlessly, constantly, that wield the deeper and more dynamic power—even to shape and define 'experience'? Cognitivists (Johnson, Lakoff) agree that, to the extent that we can become more aware of these dynamics, bring to conscious awareness this deep pool of expectations and presuppositions, we might be better able to selectively attend to certain inference patterns and then to change our minds. But they believe they can demonstrate the pervasive and fundamental force that conceptual metaphor and mental space blending wields at a mostly *un*conscious level.

Another set of questions concerns Spohn's use of 'proportional analogy.' Granted that proportional analogy is *one* way to look at the interactions, transactions, and imaginative and logical moves we make as we read and interpret and perform according to a text, two major questions nevertheless arise. 1) Does the particular proportional analogy Spohn proposed as the key analogy for solving the Scripture–and-ethics puzzle adequately reflect and fit the view of Scripture and the church to which he was committed? 2) Is the stated 'problem' (the 'gap') that

---

[45] Ibid., 57.
[46] David Tracy, *Blessed Rage for Order: The New Pluralism in Theology* (Chicago and London: University of Chicago Press, 1975, 1996), 77.
[47] Spohn, *Go and Do Likewise*, 88.
[48] Ibid., 88. Spohn was quoting William James, *The Principles of Psychology* (Cambridge, Mass.: Harvard University Press, 1983), 380–381. Emphasis mine.

this method hopes to address the actual (or main) issue facing contemporary readers and would-be performers of Scripture? That is, how is 'proportionate analogy' framing the issues and questions—and therefore constraining the answers proposed?

With regard to the first question, I think not. Spohn repeatedly insisted (urged) that contemporary Scripture readers can indeed take the "plunge" into the text, that the Bible is indeed Scripture, the Church's normative revelatory source. He was well aware that the Church has a rich and varied tradition, a history of interpretation and of attempts to perform according to what it reads in Scripture, to "go and do likewise." The Church has a rich memory and a history of having been read *by* Scripture, as well. So does not the 'gap' suggested by the divide, the blank space and the copula between "the text in its world" and the "world of the present Christian community" actually collapse? Is the text—and even some aspects of its "world"—not now indeed part of the 'world' of the present Christian community?

Moreover, one has to ask if the prime analogate he identified is actually available to modern readers of Scripture. That is, how can we actually know what the text meant or how it was received in that world? If we lack access to that knowledge, are the texts then unavailable to us—or are they only available to us to the extent that we accurately identify and honor the prime analogate? How might we better represent and investigate the cultural interplay that is entailed as modern readers encounter ancient texts? I query, then, the aptness of the proposed analogy, its fit, with the project and the proposals Spohn offered.

Concerning the relationship between analogy and metaphor, a few summary remarks can be made. Although in the places cited above, Spohn seemed to take the 'it's all analogy' position, he actually did more than mention metaphor and clearly had thought about the connections between analogy, paradigm, metaphor, and image, frames, and so on. From a cognitive linguistic perspective, while analogy does play an important role in moral discourse, analogy itself relies on cognitive metaphor. They are interdependent phenomena. Mark Johnson states a cognitivist understanding of the relationship between metaphor and analogy in relation to moral understanding:

> Metaphor ... constitutes a basis for analogizing and moving beyond the 'clear' or prototypical cases to new cases. It gives us constrained ways to pursue these metaphorical extensions. It thus allows us to learn from

experience in a way that is necessary if we are to grow in our moral understanding.[49]

Metaphor and analogy work in tandem, interdependently, to allow discourse to progress beyond conventional lines of moralizing so that revision and growth in moral understanding become possible. In the reading process, readers' category structures collide and meld with those of the text via cognitive metaphor and, sometimes, analogy.[50] Readers do express their perception, an intuitive "feel" that metaphor is more specific—and more 'figurative'—and that analogy is more general. Some expressions, especially those that cognitivists say are 'novel extensions,' simply "feel" more like metaphors. But is it the case, then, that we ought to follow Spohn's advice and effectively collapse the two terms?[51] The point is that this is not merely a terminological issue; theory of metaphor and meaning is at stake. Since I find Spohn himself making functional (but not always terminological) distinctions between general analogy and specific image metaphors, the need for more precise terminology *and* coherent theory is evident.

Since Spohn was aware—and concerned—that the ethical frameworks we bring to the text color our conclusions, what other kinds of frameworks might also be shaping our interpretations? Since he suggested that many of these pre-understandings were "customary" and "operating below conscious awareness," would it not be well to observe how cognitive scientists study these kinds of phenomena?[52] Cognitive linguists have amassed plentiful evidence detailing the patterns and functions of metaphors in language-in-use; it would be well to attend to this evidence. Cognitive theory leads us to expect that as we read 1 Peter, we will find that metaphor serves as a basis for analogizing, setting up constraints on analogies.

Finally, with regard to the language of (ethical) *norm* and *normativity*, cognitive linguistics might pose some interesting questions. Ethics bor-

---

[49] Mark Johnson, *Moral Imagination: Implications of Cognitive Science for Ethics* (Chicago and London: Chicago University Press, 1993), 10.
[50] See my discussion of the Two Worlds Analogy in Chapter 2.
[51] Spohn, *Go and Do Likewise*, 201 n 34. Regarding figurative 'feel,' when expressions "seem" fanciful, and its relationship to recognition of analogy and metaphor, see Mark Turner, *Reading Minds: The Study of English in the Age of Cognitive Science*, (Princeton, N.J.: Princeton University Press, 1991), 121–125. Also see Fauconnier and Turner, *The Way We Think*, 142.
[52] Spohn cites Ogletree on possible sub-conscious dynamics; *Go and Do Likewise*, 102.

rows the language of "norm" from the mathematical domain. What does this language make available to us, conceptually, as we consider how Scripture functions in ethics, moral formation and moral discernment? The field of ethics is understandably often concerned with "problems" and "problem-solving;" sometimes we use the language of "dilemma," but the focus is still on the "use" of Scripture as content or "source" for problem-solving. Spohn did well to lift up the narrative character of much of Scripture and to point to its fit in this regard with his own concern with moral formation and discernment. Scripture itself is not primarily problem-solving oriented. Does a focus on the great historical-cultural divide effectively and unnecessarily restrict the normative reach of Scripture?[53] I wonder about the fit of the notion of Jesus as "concrete universal" who functions in a "normative role" ("through faithful imagination his story becomes paradigmatic for moral perception, disposition, and identity") with the cultural-historical 'gap' schema.[54] Does this composite, constructed Jesus cohere with the biblical Jesus who speaks specific words and performs certain actions in given contexts—or does it, in effect, lift Jesus out of the text and out of context? While I doubt this was Spohn's intention, it may be one result of his proposed interpretation and application methods.

Spohn's language was of Jesus "setting the boundaries" and he said the life of Jesus "functions as [Christians'] 'norm' or standard, ... *paradigm* or exemplar that can be creatively applied in different circumstances." Can cognitive methods aid our understanding of how exemplars work or function "normatively"? That is, Spohn was concerned about the kinds of "false norms" that result when readers "[project] their own values and biases" onto the story of Jesus.[55] In this context, and throughout the book, he called for a "deeper reading of the Gospels" in order to "expose" such "counterfeits."[56] Again, I wonder what cognitive methods might offer us in that effort.

William Spohn's explication of the importance of analogical imagination for Christian ethics and for the function of Scripture in the moral formation and discernment of Christian communities is significant. Spohn made important contributions to the Christian com-

---

[53] On this, see Green, "Scripture and Theology," 40.
[54] Spohn, *Go and Do Likewise*, 2.
[55] Ibid., 70–71.
[56] Ibid., 11, 71, *passim*.

munity and to the field of Christian ethics as he reframed the role (function) of Scripture in constructive Christian ethics to focus on the life of Jesus as 'paradigm' and 'exemplar.' He offered a solution to both the distance and the diversity problems in Scripture and ethics work via analogical imagination. His work engenders further questions, and I want to take up his challenge, his suggestion, that it would be well for us to understand how the metaphors and analogies we encounter in Scripture might engender dispositions and have deep moral consequences. At this point in the study, it remains to be seen what actual contributions cognitive theory and methods might make to this project. I propose that Section 2 demonstrate the cognitive metaphor approach and that in the end we return to the questions about the relative merits of Spohn's approach and the one proposed here.

At several points in *Go and Do Likewise*, Spohn respectfully refers to NT scholar Richard Hays' work in *the Moral Vision of the New Testament*, and indicates affinity with certain of his methodological proposals.[57] In some respects, Spohn relies on Hays' notion of the 'paradigmatic' mode of discourse and its normative role in Christian ethics. I turn, then, to a review of Richard Hays' notion of Moral Vision.

Unified Moral Vision: Richard Hays' Approach to NT Ethics

New Testament scholar Richard Hays is concerned about some of the same problems that William Spohn addressed—merger and divorce. He is concerned about misreadings and misappropriations of Scripture that result from precritical or uncritical fusion, merger between the NT text and times and our own. But he is also concerned about Scripture's loss of status as normative and authoritative source in contemporary constructive ethics, a loss that seems to result from the radical divorce decreed by a historicism that insists on the unbridgeability of the 'gap.' Spohn and Hays deal with two gaps, really. There is the temporal gap between the text-times and our time, and there is the theological gap, the division of timeless, universal, theological truth from time-bound moral teaching and conventional wisdom. Like Spohn, Hays adopts

---

[57] In particular, Spohn relies on Hays' notion of 'paradigmatic' material and of the advisability of matching reading and interpretive strategies to the mode of discourse. Ibid., 23, 32, 190 n. 7.

a hermeneutics of appreciation, rather than one of suspicion.[58] Like Spohn, Hays leans heavily on the imaginative and metaphorical as he designs strategies for solving these inappropriate-fusion and radical-separation problems.

Section Overview

This treatment of Richard Hays' approach begins with an introduction to Hays' understanding of the problems he is addressing, followed by a synopsis of his working definitions of metaphor and a review of his proposed methods. Analysis of Hays' approach—and comparison and contrast with cognitive metaphor study methods—is integrated into each subsection, while the conclusion reviews these points.

The 'Problem(s)' and Hays' Goals

Hays says the primary goal of his work in *The Moral Vision of the New Testament* is "to engage the *theological problem of how the NT ought to shape the ethical norms and practices of the church in our time.*"[59] He sets his book up as an answer to a *problem*, a *theological* problem. He wants to think about *normative* hermeneutics, how the NT ought to shape the ethical norms and practices of the church today. Hay's title expresses the aim and scope of his project in this book: To outline the *moral* vision of the *NT*, but not to claim to have covered the entire canon or every aspect of its theology; to discern a *unified* vision ("*the* moral vision"); and to inquire after the *visionary* aspects of NT morality. When Hays writes of 'moral vision,' he has in mind first an investigation of the vision *of* the NT. He also considers ways in which that vision might function in (or for) the Christian community *normatively*—to shape, inform, and correct its moral vision:

> [C]areful exegesis heightens our awareness of the ideological diversity within Scripture and of our historical distance from the original communities (in ancient Israel and the earliest churches) to whom these texts were addressed. In other words, critical exegesis exacerbates the hermeneutical problem rather than solving it ... As Oliver O'Donovan once remarked, interpreters who think that they can determine the

---

[58] William Spohn coined the term "hermeneutics of appreciation." Spohn, *Go and Do Likewise*, 5, 17–18.

[59] Ibid., 9, emphasis his.

proper ethical application of the Bible solely through more sophisticated exegesis are like people who believe that they can fly if only they flap their arms hard enough.[60]

Hays wants the church to be able to fly, when it comes to proper ethical application of the Bible today, and not to be aimlessly expending futile energy in endless exegetical exercises. He warns readers ahead of time that the shortcomings of *sola Scriptura* cannot be remedied by what would amount to a *sola exegetica* approach.[61]

Definition(s) of Metaphor

Since attention to metaphor and imagery is so central to his task—and since metaphor study is the focus of this project—it will be well to attend to Hays' understanding of metaphor:

> Metaphors are *incongruous conjunctions* of *two images*—or two *semantic fields*—that turn out, upon reflection, to be *like one another* in ways not ordinarily recognized. They *shock us into thought* by positing unexpected *analogies—analogies that could not be discerned within conventional categories of knowledge.* Thus, *metaphors reshape our perception.*[62]

Similarity, incongruity, unconventionality, and "shock" value—these are components of traditional metaphor theories. But when Hays refers to conjunctions of images *or* of semantic fields, he may be moving beyond traditional views. Is he indicating agreement with a construal of metaphor that differentiates between image metaphors and conceptual metaphors? This is not clear. Perhaps he means that metaphors and images are identical, and that each image will be from a different semantic field. What is clear is that Hays is working with a mixed understanding of metaphor, combining features of traditional and contemporary views.

---

[60] Ibid., 3.
[61] Ibid. Hays has this to say in a later section on sources of authority in Christian ethics: "No matter how seriously the church may take the authority of the Bible, the slogan of *sola Scriptura* is both conceptually and practically untenable, because the interpretation of Scripture can never occur in a vacuum. The New Testament is always read by interpreters under the formative influence of some particular tradition, using the light of reason and experience and attempting to relate the Bible to a particular historical situation." Ibid., 209.
[62] Ibid., 300, emphasis mine. It is puzzling that Hays waits until the middle of his book to provide this definition of metaphor.

What difference does a 'mixed' understanding make? This will become clearer in the following sections, as we review the results of his study and certain features of the metaphors and images he finds become evident. At this point, let me simply raise some questions this working definition can engender. Are all metaphors alike in form and function? What is a 'semantic field,' and what would a semantic field have to do with a particular metaphor? Does Hays mean that every metaphor works with two entirely separate semantic fields? If so, then will he help readers understand how metaphors conjoin two semantic fields? Do metaphors always work with 'images'? Are 'metaphors' and 'images' identical? Does metaphor always "shock us into thought," or does it sometimes hardly ripple the surface of our conscious thought at all? That is, is metaphor always a phenomenon of which people are consciously aware? Are readers generally aware that they are encountering and interpreting images as they read? What is the function of metaphor in conventional categories of knowledge? Again, are metaphor and analogy identical, or is the relationship between the two complex? What is the function of 'perception' in metaphor?

From a cognitive point of view, Hays' definition is interesting but frustrating for several reasons. Hays knows that metaphors are somehow conceptual, not merely matters of linguistic expression. He also understands that they can cluster, and therefore that they can somehow be related to one another. The term 'mapping' is used at least once, but without explanation or demonstration of how cross-domain mapping works. One suspects that this is partly because Hays misses the unidirectionality of metaphorical mapping. But since he also almost always refers to an image or metaphor by its source domain only, one has to wonder if he does actually have the cross-domain, source-to-target mapping concept in mind. The assumption that metaphors work outside conventional categories will cause one to miss the systematic qualities of the ways metaphors do work with—and play with—conventions. If one expects images and metaphors to be shocking, and unusual, then the ubiquitous, characteristically *un*-shocking conventional conceptual metaphors will become invisible.

Hays on Analogy Versus Metaphor

Hays reveals his understanding of the relationship between metaphor and analogy in an endnote:

> The distinction between analogy and metaphor is often pressed much too strictly. In fact, both linguistic phenomena have to do with the mapping of one semantic field onto another. The major difference between them is that metaphor is usually held to entail a greater wrenching or distortion of conventional perception, resulting in a more radical restructuring of meaning. The difference, however, is one of degree, not of kind; both metaphor and analogy posit connections between disparate entities or fields. In the discussion that follows, I will not distinguish sharply between them. In general, however, I prefer to speak of the role of the NT in shaping Christian ethics as a process of metaphor-making, because the gospel proclaimed in the NT has an apocalyptic character: it shatters and defamiliarizes the business-as-usual world. Thus, linkages between the NT stories and our world will characteristically effect the radical re-orientation associated with metaphor.[63]

Two observations need to be made in response to this statement. First, one observes Hays' employment of some of the linguistic terminology ('mapping,' 'semantic fields,' 'conventional perception') as he constructs yet another mixed construal of metaphorical phenomena. In this construal, analogy and metaphor are really not very different, and this does help explain why in the course of his presentation, Hays does not distinguish between the two; he essentially treats analogy and metaphor as synonymous. Both work with "mapping of one semantic field onto another." What is clear is that by this definition, the wrenching- or distortion-factor is the major distinguishing feature between analogy and metaphor.[64] If, however, empirical evidence for metaphors that are *not* wrenching can be found, what becomes of the distinction between metaphor and analogy? While we can show that metaphor and analogy are related—and it may be true that the differences between them are matters of degree—this working definition conflates metaphor and analogy to an extent that is perhaps unhelpful.

The second observation concerns Hays' sweeping statement that the gospel "has an apocalyptic character" and his association of "metaphor-making" with that character. If analogy is the more prosaic, business-as-usual mechanism, over against the wrenching, world-changing dynamic of metaphor, then a stronger argument evidencing that

---

[63] Ibid., 311, n. 8.
[64] Hays seems to abide by the Interaction Theory and the notion of bidirectional linkages across domains. Hays cites several metaphor theorists and realizes that "the literature on metaphor is massive." The theorists listed: Wheelwright, Ricoeur, Johnson, McFague, Gerhart and Russell, Lash, Kittay, Soskice, Ollenburger, and Kraftchick. Ibid., 311, n. 8.

distinction ought to be made. These questions are not rhetorical; they can be answered with empirical evidence. One wonders if Hays' equivocation on the terms 'metaphor' and 'analogy' is confusing for readers who are unaware of the epistemological issues in play.

Hays' Analytical Model and Methods

To address the array of problems he has identified, Hays has designed a comprehensive, four-part process of textual investigation and reflection leading to moral action. He labels the four parts of the method "tasks," and names these *descriptive, synthetic, hermeneutical*, and *pragmatic*. Since the purpose of the present study is to consider the role of metaphor in the creation of meaning in moral discourse, my survey of Hays' voluminous work focuses on the roles Hays assigns to metaphor and imagination in each of these parts of his recommended process.

The Descriptive Task

Hays' first task in the process of discovering the unified moral vision of the NT is to attend to the distinctive features of each of the NT documents, rather than to elements they have in common. He fully intends to let this unified vision emerge from the texts, rather than to read his own vision into them.[65] Again, the purpose of undertaking this comprehensive survey is not primarily data collection. Hays seeks to discover in the NT a unified moral vision because he believes that Scripture's normative status and effective function depends on finding at least a core of agreed-upon values or approaches in this diverse collection of documents.[66]

---

[65] Ibid., 5, 194.

[66] How, he asks, can Scripture function normatively if it speaks not with one voice, but many? Contra Wayne Meeks, who sees in the NT an irreducible diversity of approaches and stands on moral issues, Hays argues that "the task of discerning some coherence in the canon is both necessary and possible." Ibid., 4. Meeks does, however, still find the NT to be a valuable and irreplaceable source of moral authority for the contemporary church community. He even asserts that "it was Paul, more clearly than any other who transformed this report [of Jesus' crucifixion and subsequent resurrection] into a metaphorical complex capable of shaping moral discourse." Wayne A. Meeks, *The Origins of Christian Morality: The First Two Centuries* (New Haven: Yale University Press, 1993), 86.

Hays specializes in the Pauline literature, and he begins his descriptive survey of the NT there. His rationale for beginning with Paul is that Paul predates the Gospels and articulates a more theologically cogent and systematic Christian ethics than the other writers do. Hays intends to cross-check his findings in Paul with the rest of the NT canon, beginning with the Gospels.[67]

The Daunting Ditch and Other Matters

Since Hays sets this project up as an attempt to investigate and solve a *theological* problem, his method for discovering Paul's moral vision is to look for "theological motifs" that "provide the framework for Paul's ethical teaching."[68] There is an attempt to incorporate metaphor analysis into this exegetical work, and Hays understands that metaphors might not only provide clues to Paul's theological commitments, but might also be part of a conceptual 'framework' of ethical teaching. But before Hays delves into the NT text itself, he finds it prudent to alert the reader to certain features of the theological and hermeneutical issues.

Having in his introductory pages alerted the reader to the general problematic of Scripture and ethics, Hays focuses in a slightly more detailed manner on the nature of this set of problems at the outset of his Descriptive Task section. His first 'description,' then, is of two major variations on the 'daunting ditch' argument that have had the persistent effect (at least in biblical scholarly and Christian ethics circles) of dismissing or discounting the value of the NT for contemporary constructive Christian ethics: Dibelius-type arguments and Houlden-style arguments. Dibelius thought he detected in the NT texts a split between the theologically significant material and what he called 'parenesis.'[69] The parenetic passages were judged to be conventional wis-

---

[67] Hays, *The Moral Vision of the New Testament*, 14. Hays says that in Paul, "the processes of moral logic are more on the surface … Beginning with the Gospels tends to create a perspectival distortion." But is Hays aware that the same could be said for the ramifications of beginning with Paul?

[68] Ibid., 14, 19.

[69] Ibid., 17. Regarding parenesis and a form-critical approach, see Martin Dibelius, *A Fresh Approach to the New Testament and Early Christian Literature*, The International Library of Christian Knowledge (London: Ivor Nicholson and Watson, 1936 [1926]), 143-144, 217-220. Hays mentions as an example of more recent NT scholarship in this stream Hans D. Betz's assessment of the ethic in Galatians: "Paul does not provide

dom gleaned from (Hellenistic) cultural stock. In this view, since there was nothing new in the ethics of the NT even *then*, when the texts were composed, there is certainly not much of value or of relevance for today in this material. Houlden, on the other hand, focused his attention on the eschatological and apocalyptic cast evident in many NT texts. The Houlden-style argument is that since the NT writers and original readers expected the imminent return of Jesus and were actively awaiting the end of the present αἰών or age, the ethic expressed in the NT is an *interim ethic*.[70] He finds Paul's moral judgments "inconsistent" and concludes that imminent eschatological expectation "deals a crippling blow to the ordinary processes of ethical argument."[71] In Houlden's estimation, then, apocalypticism begets moral quietism or zealous fanaticism—or both—neither of which renders Pauline ethical teaching rationally persuasive or apt.[72] That is, the behavioral expectations and the societal reforms envisioned (e.g., in Acts 2) are too radical to have been consistently practiced, or for anyone seriously to have expected them to be used as long-term ecclesial or social-political structural models.

Hays cuts through these arguments with relentless evidence to the contrary. Key to Hays' refutation of Dibelius- and Houlden-style positions is any evidence that the ethical teachings of Paul are indeed connected to his theology (imperative is tied to, not separate from, indicative) and that they go beyond—or are contrary to—cultural moral conventions. He is also, then, interested in any evidence for development within the canon, of elaboration or refinement (or divergence?) of moral stances and "moral teaching traditions" within the set of texts we call the NT.[73] All of this gives him reasons to investigate the texts with these issues in mind, and makes him keen to provide a 'thick descrip-

---

the Galatians with a specifically Christian ethic. The Christian is addressed as an educated and responsible person. He is expected to do no more than what would be expected of any other educated person in the Hellenistic culture of the time. In a rather conspicuous way Paul conforms to the ethical thought of his contemporaries." Hans Dieter Betz, *Galatians*, Hermeneia Commentary (Philadelphia: Fortress, 1979), 292.

[70] Hays, *The Moral Vision of the New Testament*, 21. The "interim ethic" thesis is developed in J.L. Houlden, *Ethics and the New Testament* (New York: Oxford University Press, 1973).

[71] Ibid., 28, 12.

[72] Dibelius- and Houlden-style approaches are often combined, as in the work of NT scholar Wolfgang Schrage, *The Ethics of the New Testament*, tr. David E. Green (Philadelphia: Fortress, 1988 [1982]).

[73] Hays, *The Moral Vision of the New Testament*, 3.

tion' of "the symbolic world of the communities that produces and received the NT writings."[74] At the same time, he rejects as "impossible" the Dibelius-type project of sorting "timeless" truth out from "culture-bound" advice.

Descriptive Evidence—Images and Metaphors

The writings themselves are his best evidence and source of data for the tasks entailed in discerning moral 'vision', thus the 'descriptive task' section of *The Moral Vision of the NT* is an attempt representatively to survey the NT. Hays does deal at least briefly with almost every book of the NT.[75] But since he begins with Paul and founds his hypothesis about the unified moral vision there, I will draw attention here to the particular metaphors and images, frames and symbols he identifies in the subsection on Paul's writings.[76] Here, then, is a list of the material identified as metaphorical (broadly conceived) in that section:

1) '*image* of new creation' (20)
2) '*thought-world* of Jewish apocalypticism' and apocalyptic '*motifs*' (20, 22); cosmic, apocalyptic "*frame*" (27);
3) battle *imagery* as characteristic of apocalyptic; Hope As Armor (23)
4) "Spirit as *arrabôn*, a kind of 'earnest money' or 'first installment'" (21)
5) cross as 'complex *symbol*' (27) and '*metaphor* for other actions (burden-bearing)' (28) with '*paradigmatic* role' (28)
6) 'Christ's self-giving' as a "*pattern ... projected ...* into an imperative for the community to serve" (28)
7) "The *koinonia* [fellowship, community] of his sufferings: that is Paul's *picture* of the life in X."
8) resurrection as *sign* of hope (28)
7) "the apostolically founded community *takes the place of* the Jerusalem *Temple* as the place where the glory of God resides." (34)
10) "*analogy* of the human body" as "*foundational metaphor* for the church's corporate life" ... 'the one body in Christ' *metaphor* ...

---

[74] Ibid., 4.
[75] Hays does not claim that this survey is comprehensive; he calls it "representative." Ibid., 13.
[76] Ibid., 16–59.

emphasizing the complementarity of different gifts for the common good (34, 36)
11) "The *metaphor* of 'living sacrifice' describes the vocation of the community" (36)
12) *'image* of corporate sacrifice' (36)
13) Paul "invokes the *metaphor* of himself as priest" (36)
14) 'sin *as* slavemaster' ... 'the slavery *metaphor*'(38)
15) [Jesus'] "death becomes *metaphorically paradigmatic* for the obedience of the community" (46)

Hays does not claim that this is a thorough survey of Paul's letters, and this metaphor and image list is hardly exhaustive. It is, however, representative both of some metaphors that a careful reader using the traditional approach to metaphor might notice in Paul's letters, and of the significance and merits of Hays' approach. There is not room here to comment on each item in this list, but a few explanatory comments are in order, especially regarding the metaphors that Hays will determine are 'focal' or 'key' metaphors in the entire NT canon.

Hays says 'new creation' (2 Cor 5:14B–18) is an *image* Paul uses repeatedly, and that "for Paul, *ktisis* ('creation') refers to the whole created order (cf. Romans 8:18–25)."[77] Hays argues that αἰών ('age') and κόσμος ("world") belong to an overarching category with 'new creation', and that the latter is the best candidate for the category title. Hays makes it clear that this 'new creation' is not about mere individual transformation. Its eschatological and apocalyptic 'framing' lifts the expression from individual, personal domain to the cosmic sphere. It remains unclear, however, how Hays knows that this is the framing, the domain, to which the expressions belong.

A cognitivist would ask what more could be said about the distinctive mappings of metaphorical expressions that use κτίσις αἰών, and κόσμος, respectively. Are these expressions actually always evoking identical source domains or schemas? Are they perhaps used to constitute clusters or blends of distinctive metaphors? What schemas or frames tend to be used in connection with these metaphors? Is 'new creation' an image? If it refers to or stands for the whole created order, is it functioning metonymically? In general, one is led to wonder what is gained—and what is lost—when a prototypical, central case image or metaphor is allowed to stand for an entire cluster of metaphors. Does,

---

[77] Ibid., 20.

then, reading every expression that uses the trigger words, κτίσις, αἰών or κόσμος through the single lens of "new" κτίσις focus or cloud the over-all picture? Hays' careful analysis has allowed him to distill from enormous volumes of material this one focal image. Having that distillate, identifying that core or overarching schematization, is indeed interesting and—to the extent that it can be empirically demonstrated to indeed hold true for the entire canon—significant. But the details of the entailments in the mappings of the variations on the theme are significant as well, and are lost in this focusing process. One wonders how—other than by sheer intuition—the decision is made that this is a *focal* image. Hays has presented some evidence indicating how he arrived at these conclusions, came up with this distillate. But in order to understand how such a process works, to replicate the process, analysis at another level would be necessary.

Hays has discerned patterns in the usages of language about the cross, as well. Again, cognitivists would applaud Hays' discernment of patterning, perhaps even of systematicity, in the uses of metaphors and images as well as his detection of the conceptual theological and ethical import of this patterned language use. Hays has discerned a conceptual metaphorical and metonymic pattern; he is not merely indexing (or confining his analysis to) uses of the words 'cross' and 'wood' (σταυρός, ξύλον) or to Paul's usage of related Greek verbal forms. But Hays' metaphor analysis terminology in this section of the discussion is somewhat confusing. He says, for example, that:

> Paul reads the cross as a *metaphor* for other actions (burden-bearing) that correspond *analogically* to the self-giving exemplified by Jesus' death. The *metaphorical interpretation* of the cross in Galatians 6.2 is exactly consonant with Paul's uses of the same *image* elsewhere.[78]

Granted that metaphor and analogy are interdependent, related phenomena. But what he is here calling a 'metaphor' actually sounds like a metonymy: The Cross For Burden-Bearing Actions. Is the cross an 'image'? Cognitive linguistic methods would draw a distinction between a one-time, one-shot image metaphor and this kind of ubiquitous metonymic use of a representative example—cross—for the entire category of behavior to which it may belong. But the most significant matter here is not about metaphor analysis terminology, but the way Paul uses the concept of Jesus' self-giving in the crucifixion to ground par-

---

[78] Ibid., 28; emphasis mine.

ticular points in his moral exhortation. Paul's analogical use, then, of the cross metonymy could serve current readers of these texts as an exemplar of how theological-ethical conclusions can follow from consideration of certain features of Jesus' life and death.

One detects the mixed understandings of metaphor with which Hays is working in another set of statements in this section on the cross:

> If we adopt a *more supple model of metaphorical correspondence*, the dissimilarities between Christ and his people are to be expected, because *metaphor always posits a startling likeness* between unlike entities. In Philippians, Paul offers a metaphorical reading of Christ's self-emptying and death; the power of the metaphor is precisely a function of its daring improbability.[79]

A "more supple model" sounds good. The cognitivist query here concerns the assumption that metaphorical correspondences *always* work with *daring, improbable* and *startling* likenesses. What if the power of the metaphor is also a function of its ordinariness and conventionality? One does not wish to discount Paul's daring or the remarkable qualities of this particular metaphorical (metonymic) correspondence. But if one confines one's metaphorical surveys and analyses to just those features that strike one as daring, improbable, and startling, one might miss other sorts of metaphors.

Cognitive metaphor analysis methodology is designed to pick out patterns beyond the designation of a 'ruling' metaphor, as well. Hays concludes, "the cross becomes the ruling metaphor for Christian obedience, while the resurrection stands as the sign of hope that those who now suffer will finally be vindicated by God."[80] The notion that there is a 'ruling' metaphor is, in fact, another metaphor, and one with very powerful entailments. Are metaphors related to one another hierarchically—in a linear fashion—or do they tend to cluster radially? The empirical evidence amassed to date supports the radial model, and suggests that prototypical metaphors at the center of such clusters exert some force on the structure of the category. But 'ruling' may not be an apt metaphor for the sort of influence of which we speak. These are some of the metaphor theory and terminological issues raised by Hays' statement.

But this 'ruling metaphor' statement raises another issue as well, one with more direct bearing on the ethical import of Hays' approach.

---

[79] Ibid., 30.
[80] Ibid., 31.

Granted that in Paul's discourse, Jesus' obedience in accepting the cross is a major motif. Is the cross then always (and mostly) about 'obedience'—in the entire NT canon? How would a reader-interpreter of these texts know that? Granted that by calling Jesus' willing, responsive action on behalf of others 'obedience,' obedience itself is redefined. It cannot be mere rule following or doing of duty. But are there not teleological and virtue-ethic casts to some of the entailments in the mappings of cross- related metaphors and metonymies in Paul and in the rest of the canon? It would be good to highlight these features of cruciform behavior as well. The holiness Jesus demonstrates in his suffering on the cross is not a holiness of duty.

Hays says the cross functions as a paradigm, complex symbol, and metaphor for other actions. While I agree with Hays that it is not merely the word—σταυρός ('cross')—that functions metaphorically and metonymically in Paul's writings, I am interested in thinking about how we decide what set of concepts and expressions belongs in an analysis of 'cross' language. Hays' analysis is thought-provoking, but he has not given us a clear set of methods for identification and analysis of various metaphorical, analogical, and metonymic functions. The terms—paradigm, metaphor, image, and complex symbol—begin to collapse into one another. In the confusion, details of the complexities of the transfers are lost. The social-cultural and theological-ethical symbolic power of Jesus' crucifixion transfers *what* into the moral discourse of Paul's letters? Confining that transfer mostly to the concepts 'obedience' and 'self-giving' seems inadequate.

Finally, I turn briefly to example #10, above, and Hays' treatment of the body as analogy and "*foundational metaphor* for the church's corporate life." Hays argues that it is the communal, corporate metaphor he dubs 'new community' that is the overarching one, The Church Community Is a Human Body being a subset in the cluster. Cognitive analysis would focus first on understanding in more detail how the source domains of Body and Household function separately and together as Paul expresses his vision of Christian community and its ethos.

Summary: Cognitive Perspectives on Hays' Descriptive Methods

Cognitivists would agree with Hays' intuition that metaphors, images, frames, and symbols are integral functional elements of the moral discourse—and the moral arguments—of Paul's letters. But from a cognitive linguistic perspective, Hays' mixture of terms—metaphor,

metaphor cluster, image, analogy, foundational metaphor, root metaphor, paradigmatic—is unwieldy and yields imprecise and incomplete data.

Hays' says he is aware of the cross-domain nature of metaphor, but he so often uses only the source domain half of an expression as a tag that it is hard to discern onto what precise target domain or concept he thinks each source image or concept is being mapped. Hays presumably has done his preliminary (or core) research with the Greek text, and sometimes points to features of the social-cultural domains within which the expressions arise. But could more be said about how modern readers can even read this material? Since he is clearly convinced of the truth of the Two Worlds hypothesis, and the radical cultural differences between the worlds of the texts and of modern readers, how might domain clash or mis-identification distort interpretations? Given this set of metaphors—the ones Hays identifies in his Paul section—has Hays actually explained how "the Word leaps the gap"? That is, if the particular source domains (slavery, crucifixion, Jewish Temple and sacrificial system; Greco-Roman communal structure; Jewish apocalyptic) from which these expressions arise are so completely foreign to 21st-century readers, how is it that the metaphors are even comprehensible?

The Synthetic Task

In the course of this descriptive representative survey of metaphorical material in the texts, Hays reveals his intuitive discovery of three 'focal images'—community, cross, new creation. Next, in his Synthetic Task section, he discusses in greater theoretical depth his discovery of these image (or metaphor) clusters in preparation for demonstrating, here and in the Hermeneutical Task section, their value as lenses through which to discern the unified moral vision of the NT canon. My present purpose is to review Hay's revelations about his theoretical approach to the role of image and metaphor in moral theology and hermeneutics in general and to reflect on possible coherences and differences in this approach from a cognitivist one.

Kelsey's 'Single Synoptic' Model

As methodologies for detecting the overarching theological themes of the NT go, Hays' approach is unorthodox. "Why," he asks, "look for *images* rather than concepts or doctrines, as a ground of coherence?"[81] First, Hays suggests this is a way to counteract certain adverse effects of form criticism. If certain images can be found in various forms and modes of discourse, then these images and metaphors are keys to recovering essential theological elements in materials that form critics have tended to separate in the process of identifying distinctive types or modes of discourse.[82] Hays suggests that the results of form criticism might be retained and respected, while he hopes that metaphor- and image-study will become a way to recover the core theological unity—and the linkage between the theological and the ethical, the indicative and the imperative—that has been lost or obscured in the critical shuffle. He hopes thereby to deliver a pragmatically useful framework for constructive ethics.[83]

But for Hays, the quest for the 'single synoptic' and the search for unified voice or vision is not (or not only) a matter of the nature of the canon or of texts. His methodology has been developed, at least in part, in response to David Kelsey's theory about the way images shape theological conclusions. Kelsey's claim, as Hays puts it, is that "every theological *reading* of Scripture depends upon 'a single synoptic imaginative judgment' in which the *interpreter* 'tries to catch up what Christianity is basically all about.'"[84] Hays proposes, then, to build

---

[81] Ibid., 194, emphasis mine.
[82] Ibid.
[83] Ibid., 5.
[84] Ibid., emphasis mine. Hays quotes Kelsey at length: "In short: at the root of a theological position there is an imaginative act in which a theologian tries to catch up in a single metaphorical judgment the full complexity of God's presence in, through, and over-against the activities comprising the church's common life and which, in turn, both provides the *discrimen* against which the theology criticizes the church's current forms of speech and life and determines the peculiar 'shape' of the position." David H. Kelsey, *The Uses of Scripture in Recent Theology* (Philadelphia: Fortress, 1975), 163. Hays admits that Kelsey uses different vocabulary ("ideational mode," "concrete actuality," and "ideal possibility"), vocabulary that may "suggest that he is thinking in terms of concepts (*Begriffe*) rather than images (*Vorstellungen*)." But does Hays understand the deep theoretical significance of this difference between his vocabulary choices and Kelsey's? Has he understood the conceptual claim here, and that Kelsey's focus is on the reader-interpreter's own presuppositions, the conceptual grid through which the texts are sifted? Ibid., 194.

on Kelsey's insight and develop a method for discovering images that "concretely represent [the] narrative coherence" of the NT within the texts themselves.[85] While he admits that this is indeed an imaginative exercise on his part, Hays seems to believe that what he is about is *discovering* (his word) images in or within the texts—not taking these images to his reading of the texts and trying them out as lenses through which to interpret, and certainly not imposing them on the texts.[86]

Hays expresses confidence in Kelsey's "single synoptic imaginative judgment" theory, and proceeds accordingly, full steam ahead. But can it be true that "*every* theological reading of Scripture 'depends upon a *single* synoptic imaginative judgment'"?[87] Such a claim would need to be backed up with empirical evidence. One must at least ask what kind of evidence, empirical evidence, would support this theory. If the moral theological discourse of the NT is indeed structured and constrained by certain key images—or even a 'single synoptic' one—this is important information to have.

Focal Images As Singular Synoptics

Setting aside for now certain problematical definitions of terms (are the three 'images' he picks out images?), let us focus on the matter of the nature and origin of these metaphor clusters or images. Here, again, are the three 'Focal Images':

- community—"the church is a countercultural community of discipleship."[88]
- cross—"Jesus' death on a cross is the paradigm for faithfulness to God in this world"[89]

---

[85] Ibid.
[86] Ibid., 193. 'Discovery' language also fits with other visually-based language Hays uses for this task: he "seeks" to find the images he is "looking for" and "discerning," believing that what he finds is "derived from the texts" while he, commendably, is zealous not to "artificially superimpose" images—or unity—on the texts (5, 194). This raises at least two questions: 1) Is it possible for a reader not to superimpose images on texts? 2) Has Hays in fact succeeded in avoiding doing this with his focal images?
[87] Ibid., emphasis mine. Hays states that Kelsey "has demonstrated" this theory, but does not offer a synopsis of the evidence or method of demonstration.
[88] Ibid., 196.
[89] Ibid., 197.

– new creation—"Paul's image of 'new creation' stands here as a shorthand signifier for the dialectical eschatology that runs throughout the NT"[90]

How does Hays select these particular focal images? In the course of his descriptive work, he notices that certain images appear repeatedly and begins to wonder what their function is in Paul's discourse.[91] He notices that even when expressions change in subtle ways—Paul does not, for example, always use exactly the same words each time he writes about the community of believers in Jesus—the underlying concepts are coherent. These are precisely the kinds of patterns that cognitive linguists might notice: repeated usages of certain images and metaphors, with variations in the actual words in the expressions. A review of the list of the metaphorical material Hays identified in his descriptive section on Paul, reveals how he is picking up metaphorical clustering:

Creation
1) "*image* of new creation" (20)
2) "thought-world of Jewish apocalypticism" and apocalyptic "motifs" (20, 22); cosmic, apocalyptic "frame" (27);
3) battle imagery as characteristic of apocalyptic; Hope As Armor (23)
4) "Spirit as *arrabōn*, a kind of 'earnest money' or 'first installment'" (21)
8) resurrection as sign of hope (28)

Cross / Community
5) cross as "complex *symbol*" (27) and "*metaphor* for other actions (burden-bearing)" (28) with "*paradigmatic* role" (28)
6) "Christ's self-giving" as a "*pattern ... projected ...* into an imperative for the community to serve" (28);
7) "The *koinonia* [fellowship, community] of his sufferings: that is Paul's *picture* of the life in X."

Community
7) "The *koinonia* [fellowship, community] of his sufferings: that is Paul's *picture* of the life in X."

---

[90] Ibid., 198.
[91] Ibid., 189.

9) "the apostolically founded community *takes the place of* the Jerusalem *Temple* as the place where the glory of God resides." (34)
10) "*analogy* of the human body" as "*foundational metaphor* for the church's corporate life;" ... 'the one body in Christ' *metaphor* ... emphasizing the complementarity of different gifts for the common good (34, 36)
11) "The *metaphor* of 'living sacrifice' describes the vocation of the community" (36)
12) "*image* of corporate sacrifice" (36)
13) Paul "invokes the *metaphor* of himself as priest" (36)
14) "sin *as* slavemaster" ... "the slavery *metaphor*"(38)
15) [Jesus'] "death becomes *metaphorically paradigmatic* for the obedience of the community" (46)

Notice that Hays groups cosmic, Jewish apocalyptic expressions and talk about 'ages' ('this present age,' the 'age to come'—αἰών) in the 'new creation' (κτίσις) image cluster. While in a close reading of Pauline material, the actual expression 'new creation' does not occur nearly so frequently (both in word count, and conceptually) as 'new *aeon*,' Hays argues that these images do indeed belong together and that to miss the apocalyptic framing of certain expressions would be to misread them.[92] Similarly, if centrality or overarching, 'focal' status of in an image cluster were to be determined by frequency of usage alone, 'new household' would trump 'new community.' Hays' argument for the adoption of 'community' as the overarching concept has some merit and actually relies on premises that agree with *conceptual* understandings of metaphor.[93]

Hays' discussion of how he has rejected certain images for 'focal' status is instructive, for in it he discloses the methodological processes by which he arrived at the focal image trinity. Each of these rejected images or metaphor clusters is significant, but is found to fit inside a yet larger category, and therefore not to deserve 'focal' status. More importantly, Hays indicates ways that mistaken, 'focal' use of these

---

[92] Ibid., 20. The specific argument is against individualistic readings of "If anyone is in Christ—new creation!" (2 Corinthians 5:17a). Hays discusses usages of κτίσις ("creation" or "creature") but does not choose to discuss metaphorical mappings of καινός ("fresh," "new").

[93] He admits that the word ἐκκλησία ("gathering") is used less frequently than the household and family vocabulary, but argues that the *concept* of new community is what Paul is driving at with the household talk.

lesser images distorts the picture, skewing one's construal of the NT's moral vision. So, for example, 'the orderly household' meets the criterion of frequency of use, but Hays discerns that it belongs inside the larger category of 'community,' and Hays cautions that focal use of this metaphor would cause distorted readings and appropriations, since "the church would be led to adopt hierarchical structures and practices that emphasize authority and stability."[94] By the same token, if one were to use as such a key image "freedom from Law and tradition," "the church would be led to reject authority structures and to adopt practices that emphasize Spirit-inspired spontaneity."[95] By a similar process, Hays rejects "love" and "liberation" as focal or key images. He asks if "love" is an image, and answers, "It is not really an image; rather, it is an interpretation of an image. What the New Testament means by 'love' is embodied concretely in the *cross.*"[96] So (to highlight the methodological move), is there a larger category to which "love" belongs? Yes. According to Hays, it belongs in the "cross" category.[97] Furthermore, in Hays' reading and evaluation, he has concluded that several NT writers fail ever to use any of the Greek words for "love," or even to mention the theme.[98] By a similar process, 'liberation' is found to belong to the 'new creation' category, and certain "dangers" of employing it as a focal image are posited.[99] Hays is seeing his focal image-lenses, then, as *corrective* lenses. But before taking a closer look at how he deploys these lenses when he turns to directly address hermeneutical issues, it will be well to consider Hays' terminology and the understanding of metaphor with which he tries to work. From a cognitive linguistic perspective, one notices that Hays most often uses the term 'image' in this section, rather than metaphor, and that he actually then often refers to a series of metonymies. Because he refers to images and metaphors by their source domains only, it is often unclear how he see the metaphors mapping.

---

[94] Ibid., 195.
[95] Ibid.
[96] Ibid., 202.
[97] This intuition is not, however, supported with semantic or linguistic evidence. This is not a linguistic argument but a theological one.
[98] Ibid., 200–201.
[99] Chief among these dangers is that if liberation is understood purely in political terms, the reader might lose "touch with the New Testament's emphasis on the power of God as the sole ground of hope and freedom … the delicate balance of the eschatological dialectic is lost." Ibid., 203.

Summary: Tri-focal Vision as Synthetic Model

While I marvel at Hays' perspicacity and intuitive sense of the importance of metaphor in the moral discourse of the NT, I wonder if a more detailed survey of the metaphorical and analogical features of these texts—the image-and conceptual metaphors, frames and schemas, the metonymies—would bear out his conclusions. Can it be demonstrated that these three features function tri-focally, as Hays suggests, in all the NT materials, across the canon? The empirical data Hays presents simply do not answer these questions. Instead, Hays has asserted his thesis, found some interesting but hardly thorough supporting evidence, and proceeded accordingly.

Further, I wonder how useful such overarching categories as these three focal images are for the hermeneutical and practical ethical work Hays has in mind. While understanding the general framing (or schematization) to which a particular image belongs will guard against certain kinds of mis-reading, this should augment or cap off, not bypass, investigation at a more detailed level. Metaphor functions in specific ways in the moral logic of each discourse, and a better understanding of those specifics will yield a deeper, and more deeply grounded, description of the general or overarching themes.

The Hermeneutical Task: Reading Other People's Mail

In the introduction to his book, Hays explains how he sees the hermeneutical problem the modern Christian faith community faces:

> These texts were not written in the first instance for residents of the United States at the end of the twentieth century. When we read Paul's letters to his churches, *we are reading the mail of people who have been dead for nineteen hundred years*; when we read the Gospels, we are reading stories told for the benefit of ancient communities whose customs and problems differed vastly from ours. Only historical ignorance or cultural chauvinism could lead us to suppose that no hermeneutical "translation" is necessary for us to understand these texts ... How can we *take our moral bearings* from a world so different from ours? If the New Testament's teachings are so integrally embedded in the social and symbolic world of first-century communities, can they *speak* at all to us or for us? Worse still, is the very effort to *derive guidance* from these texts doomed as an exercise in inauthenticity—either playacting or repressive heteronomy?[100]

---

[100] Ibid., 6, emphasis mine.

Here, again, we encounter the Two Worlds schema, and its looming, daunting historical abyss. Blended to this schema is an archeological discovery frame, in which some artifacts—ancient letters and other manuscripts in a foreign script, addressed to people in the Other World—have just been discovered. In order to read these documents, the archaeologists will have to decipher the language, and in order to translate them, they will have to try to understand as much as possible about the culture in which they were embedded. If that can be done, then modern people might be able to read these other peoples' mail.

Hay's picture is painted with the concepts of distance and of links, with language of 'daunting abyss,' 'chasm,' 'bridge.' But again the NT Is a Message that potentially 'speaks'—'into' the very separate sphere (container) that is our world, our time, our historical-cultural context. If (and only if) it can be translated so that it can speak our language, it can become a Source of Guidance for the Christian community's moral life (Life is a Journey; Moral Life Is A Journey). The NT Is Source Material for constructive Christian ethics. Ethics Is Problem-Solving, and hermeneutics is careful "conceptual *application*" of these source texts to current problems.[101]

Hays intuits that metaphor, the imagination, is an essential (necessary) linking force or device (another set of metaphors). In fact, hermeneutics itself is, essentially 'metaphor-making':

> The task of hermeneutical appropriation requires an *integrative act of the imagination*. This is always so, even for those who would like to deny it: with fear and trembling we must work out a life of faithfulness to God through responsive and creative reappropriation of the New Testament in a world far removed from the world of the original writers and readers. *Thus, whenever we appeal to the authority of the New Testament, we are necessarily engaged in metaphor-making, placing our community's life imaginatively within the world articulated by the texts.*[102]

I couldn't agree more. And less. I agree that metaphor is central to the imaginative process of engaging in moral discourse with the NT. But metaphors belong to the cultural and conceptual contexts in which they arise. If these contexts are far removed, then the metaphors from the one might not simply transfer to the other. How, then, *do* 21st-century readers ever make sense of 1st-century documents, let

---

[101] Hermeneutics as 'conceptual application' is mentioned, but the meaning of this term is not explained. Ibid., 6.
[102] Ibid., emphasis his.

alone "appropriate" them for constructive ethics in the new world? 'Metaphor' is not a magic word, and it is not necessarily, I'm afraid, a 'spark' that arcs the gap. At least, not quite so simply. But let us listen carefully as Richard Hays describes what he has in mind with regard to Scriptural metaphor's role in contemporary moral judgment.

'Using' the Texts; Moral Judgment as 'Metaphor-Making'

Hays extends his understanding of metaphor itself into a hermeneutical theory.

Consider the following:

> 'Metaphor is a mode of creating *dissonance* of *thought* in order *to restructure meaning relationships.*' That is what the New Testament, *read metaphorically* in conjunction with our experience of the world, does. The world we know—or thought we knew—is reconfigured when we 'read' it in counterpoint with the New Testament. The hermeneutical task is to relocate our contemporary experience on the map of the New Testament's story of Jesus. By telling us a story that *over-turns our conventional ways* of seeing the world, the New Testament provides the *images and categories* in light of which the life of our community (the metaphorical 'target domain') is reinterpreted. The temporal gap between the first-century Christians and Christians at the end of the twentieth century can be bridged only by a spark of imagination.[103]

Hays' statement here provokes many questions: Does metaphor work by creating 'dissonance' or by suggesting similarities—or both, or in some other way? What is 'dissonance of thought'? Is metaphor a linguistic phenomenon—a matter of word usage only—or is it a matter of thought, a mental or conceptual phenomenon? What are "meaning relationships" in a written text and in a reading process? What is a 'world'? How do the 'worlds' of readers interplay with text 'worlds' in the reading process? What would it mean to "relocate our contemporary experience on the map of the New Testament's story of Jesus"? Do metaphors and images work against or with conventional ways of seeing the world? How might metaphors and images that do work with conventional categories still manage to create 'dissonance of thought' and thereby effect re-structuring of the readers' categories and assumptions? Is the 'gap' between the 1st-century Christians and cur-

---

[103] Ibid., 302; emphasis mine.

rent Christians mostly temporal? If such a gap can be 'sparked' (arced?) by 'imagination,' what is 'imagination'?

Hay's theoretical (and theological) commitment is to the notion that there must be a coherent, canonical message. The temporal-historical-cultural gap interferes with the transmittal and appropriation of that message, especially on the moral plane. But since imagination and metaphor disrupt or transcend historical-cultural convention, they become the code-breaking keys to moral translatability. Hays relies on metaphor's *un*conventionality to transcend the conventions—the gap—and create cross-cultural coherence. The problems with this schema are manifold, but the clincher is that metaphors simply do not work in the way Hays suggests that they work.

Like Spohn, Hays seems to be trying to use the model of metaphor mapping itself as a metaphor—as a model for biblical hermeneutics. (Perhaps this is a metonymy: Metaphor Mapping For Biblical Hermeneutics). In this schema, the NT hermeneutical process is "reading metaphorically," and that means using "the images and categories" of the NT as one huge source domain and "the life of our community" as a similarly huge target domain. Hays' use of the terms of metaphor analysis is problematical at this point.[104] The trouble is that not *all* the images and categories of the NT can be mapped onto the life of our [Christian] community. That is, if—as he has said—metaphors work with cross-domain mappings, one needs to identify a target *domain*. "Our world today" or "the Christian community" or even "the Church in North America" is not a domain, in the semantic sense. A general analogical comparison can be suggested or posited, such that The Contemporary Church Is the NT Church. But this is so general an analogy that it does not get us very far. It is much more interesting to notice first how metaphors work within the text and then to attempt to analyze how readers make various mappings, how the metaphors get construed in the reading and interpretive process. A central methodological problem with Hays' proposal is that it seems to move to the macro—or meta- level without having done much spade-work, without noticing and analyzing how metaphorical mapping is happening *in the texts*.

To do that, one needs to have in hand the tools of metaphor analysis and to develop certain skills in the use of those tools. It is not enough

---

[104] Nowhere in the book does he explain for his readers what 'target domain' might mean, and he omits the term 'source domain' entirely. But these terms only make sense in tandem.

simply to state that metaphors work with cross-domain mappings and then to repeatedly identify and designate certain metaphors using one-word tags; both the target and source domains need to be indicated when a metaphor is named. (I would not argue with Hays on this point, except that he does use the terms 'target' and 'source'—although never in the same context, together—and he does talk about 'mapping' across semantic domains).

To the extent that the imagined or perceived 'gap' is real, then metaphor analysis will have to proceed very carefully, in several stages. One would need to attend to the cultural differences and to become familiar with the source cultures out of which the texts have arisen and in which the readers are embedded. Which metaphors could we have in common, given our shared humanity, our shared Greco-Roman cultural roots, our Judaic heritage, and so on? Which metaphors are foreign but understandable, translatable?

Modes of Appeal to Scripture: Rules, Principles, Paradigms, Symbolic World

Hays points to a variety of discourse types in which moral or ethical material is embedded in the NT, and he urges readers to match the 'mode' of their appeal to these texts or ethical appropriation of a text to the mode of discourse. It would be inappropriate, for example, to pull universal rules or principles out of parabolic material.[105]

There are several advantages to this approach over simplistic indicative-imperative dichotomies and the confinement of the ethical or moral to explicitly 'parenetic' passages. Hays recovers for ethics the entire array of discourse types. Each has something to offer; none is tangential or irrelevant. He does not dismiss as irrelevant the 'rule' category material, simply on the premise that ancient rules cannot be valid cross-culturally.[106]

Which mode does Hays sense is most 'metaphoric'? It seems that he is able to identify metaphors more easily in the paradigmatic and

---

[105] Ibid., 208. Hays' typology is a corrective adaptation of James Gustafson's model, which uses the terms *moral law*, *moral ideal*, and *moral analogy*. Gustafson proposed a dialectical method of "reflective discourse" using Scripture as "corresponding evidence" for ethical judgments made in the light of general theological and ethical principles. James M. Gustafson, "The Place of Scripture in Christian Ethics," *Interpretation* 24 (1970): 430–455.

[106] Contra Allen Verhey, *The Great Reversal: Ethics and the New Testament* (Grand Rapids, Michigan: Eerdmans, 1984), 176–177.

symbolic world modes, rather than the rule and principle modes. In his diagnostic checklist for evaluating theologians' use of Scripture in ethics, only under the 'Synthetic' category is there a question concerning metaphor.[107] Does he miss the conceptual metaphors employed in the expressions belonging even to the rule and principle modes? Does he understand that the names of each of these 'modes' is a metaphor?

Finally, use of the word 'mode' in the term Hays coined, "mode of moral discourse," is a bit problematical from the point of view of the ethics guild, since in its vocabulary, 'mode' refers to teleology versus deontology, and so on. Perhaps this terminological problem is indicative of a pervasive absence in Hays' work of attention to these particular distinctions. In general, Hays seems to assume that ethics is deontology. When it comes to the 'application' stages, then, of hermeneutics and his 'pragmatic' tasks, while he expresses concerns far beyond mere rule-following, his language is of 'ought' and 'obedience.' I grant that in Hays' usage and understanding, obedience is not lock-step, mindless doing of duty. In fact, he collapses into the term 'obedience' features of ethics of response, and these responses are often made in anticipation in view of a greater good to come. But the ethical language of teleology and consequence is missing in his analysis. Having perhaps failed to bring his own ethical point of view to critical consciousness, then, he has not been able to provide what Thomas Ogletree would say is a sufficiently "explicit account of salient preunderstandings of the moral life."[108]

Diagnostic Review of Five Approaches

In this hermeneutical chapter, Hays' proposes ten guidelines for NT ethics and uses them to structure his reviews of five contemporary scholars' use of the NT in ethical construction. (Reinhold Niebuhr, Barth, Yoder, Hauerwas, and Elizabeth Schüssler Fiorenza)[109] His analysis is keen when it comes to noticing each figure's selection and exege-

---

[107] Question II.D. reads, "What focal images are employed?" Hays, *The Moral Vision of the New Testament*, 213.
[108] Ogletree, *The Use of the Bible in Christian Ethics*, 4.
[109] For the list of guidelines, see Hays, *The Moral Vision of the New Testament*, 310–311. Metaphor and image are mentioned in items number four and nine.

sis of Scriptural texts. But his attention to the role of metaphor and imagination in each figure's work is confined mostly to attempts to discern each person's central, orienting metaphor—the 'single synoptic'. Does the focus on the *focal* image cause significant features of each thinker's approach to blur? One wonders what light might be shed on each one's characteristic mode of moral discourse by giving attention to a wider range of the metaphors they use before cutting to the 'single synoptic'. Perhaps Hays' conclusions about the core, orienting metaphors would be better supported with the kinds of evidence yielded by a more thorough survey of images and metaphors.

The Pragmatic Task

In his Pragmatic Task section, Hays demonstrates how he hopes the practical application and action component of his methodology will work. Here he addresses five contemporary ethical issues, admitting that only one of them—the renunciation of violence—is a central concern raised within the NT itself. Hays chooses his issues, he says, for purposes of methodological demonstration. But they are also issues that are especially inflammatory in the North American church context at the beginning of the 21st century. One wonders what might happen if a Christian community used Hays' methods to allow the NT to speak into their common life on the other three issues Hays says are in fact of central moral concern in the NT: "the sharing of possessions, the overcoming of ethnic divisions … and the unity of men and women in Christ."[110] That is, what would happen if rather than attempting to take to the texts issues from its own, 21st-century world and painstakingly extracting "answers," the reading-and-interpreting community allowed the texts themselves to raise ethical and moral issues? Hays is, of course, in favor of this latter move as well. But overall, Hays' approach in the Pragmatic Task section of his book perhaps inadvertently limits the normative reach of Scripture and fails to match up with some of the most powerful ways in which Scripture can (and does, sometimes) impact a reading community.[111]

---

[110] Ibid., 313.
[111] Joel Green suggests that when the focus is on Scripture's ability to solve current ethical problems, it often yields "an approach that severely curtails the normative

Conclusion: Hay's Moral Vision

Hays' read-and-apply method is careful, faithful, and elaborate. Some of his critics ask who (what local church community, what individual Christian, even what Christian biblical scholar or ethicist) would go to all the trouble of carrying out the 'tasks' as outlined, but that is a moot point. Perhaps a more apt diagnostic question would be to ask what would happen if we used Hays' version of the Kelsey 'single synoptic imaginative judgment' test in an analysis of Hays' own work. If one were to hone in on the one, single image or conceptual construct that controls Hays' work here, it would have to be the image of singularity, of unity itself. But I resist the requirement, the assumption, that one single image does in fact rule all. A single key might unlock the front door, but does not get us very far, if the goal is to discover what goes on in this house. Several other metaphors also wield enormous power in Hays' study of the NT's moral vision, and they turn out to be derived more from the auditory than from the visual domain.

In Hays' world, Scripture Is God's Spoken Word; Scripture Speaks. If Scripture Is a Message, it is no wonder that there is an assumption that there will be coherence in that message. The job of the reader-interpreter, and of the faithful, interpretive community, is to hear this word and, above all else, to obey.[112] Morality Is Obedience: this is the ethical filter through which Hays reads the NT and through which he characterizes the thematic unity of Christian morality and ethics. So while he is in fact able to point to deep, persistent teleologically-oriented expressions and themes (new creation, αἰών), they are muted and, I would venture to say, subsumed and distorted, by the clarion call of the obedient trumpets. It is a metaphor, a set of auditory metaphors, that constrains the 'vision' Hays "discerns"—that limits what he is able to see and the 'rhyme' he hears in the texts.

Looked at through the Morality Is Obedience and Scripture Is a Message filters, certain aspects of the texts stand out while others fade to the background or disappear. If Morality is Obedience, then

---

role of Scripture in the theological enterprise and that runs against the grain of how Scripture actually communicates." Green, "Scripture and Theology," 40.

[112] It is no coincidence that hearing and obeying occur in tandem. See the discussion of English and Indo-European sense-perception verbs in Eve Sweetser, *From Etymology to Pragmatics: Metaphorical and Cultural Aspects of Semantic Structure* (Cambridge: Cambridge University Press, 1990), 32–35.

154   CHAPTER THREE

no wonder one needs to find a unified voice, and no wonder one fears that normative status is lost for Scripture absent that unified voice.

But there are other powerful metaphors at work here, are there not? One of them is the metaphor that Scripture Is A Source for Christian ethics. These metaphors have the effect of limiting the function of Scripture in ethics to that which is practically applicable. While there is talk in Hays' work about shaping the imagination of the faithful community, of entering the symbolic world of the texts or of their generating cultures, his core metaphors for morality and ethics effectively steer us toward the applicable and the pragmatic.

That is why it might be well to attend to the details again, to go back to the descriptive process. It is also why it would be well to attend more carefully to what Kelsey was highlighting when he drew attention to the role of the reader-interpreter-theologian in such a "discovery" process. What, in fact, are the relationships between concepts (*Begriffe*) and images (*Vorstellungen*), and between images and metaphors, between metaphors and analogies and paradigms and frames? Underneath the terminological muddle in Hays' attempt to deploy metaphor study methods, is perhaps a more serious muddle. Has Hays understood that Kelsey's focus is on the reader-interpreter's own presuppositions, the conceptual grid through which the texts are sifted?[113] Had he applied to his own work that kind of analysis, one wonders if this bias toward singularity and deontology might have been discovered and corrected.

Cognitive theory makes better, more complete sense of the patterns Hays is noticing in the data and provides more workable terminological distinctions as well as delivering a methodology that allows one to attend to the level of detail in the data that will allow better evaluation of one's hypotheses concerning the structure—the metaphorical structure—and systematic uses of images and metaphors in the moral discourse.

Hays' commitments control his method. He is committed to the notion that there is a theological unity to the NT and to the necessity of a core univocal ethics of the NT that founds its normativity—"*The Moral Vision of the New Testament*"—and he sets about finding support for those commitments.[114] The Two-Worlds Paradigm, in which

---

[113] Ibid., 194.
[114] Hays says that if he had discovered significant divergence from the unified vision

the temporal and cultural gap is assumed to be prohibitively daunting, defines the nature of the 'problem' of NT ethics. It keeps Scripture always at arm's length, separating the tasks of critical historical investigation ("exegesis") from the 'application' of these findings and construal of its "significance for today."

Hays' introduction of the notion of symbolic worlds of the notion of social construction of reality is admirable, but incomplete. The question remains, is anything *transcultural*? Do our symbolic worlds share any features or qualities—and how do any such shared features contribute to our understanding and appropriation of the texts? While he has attempted representatively to survey the NT canon, Hays' results leave unanswered many questions about the role of metaphor and analogy within the texts themselves.

I agree with Hays that reading first-century texts takes imagination, but I see a different role for metaphor study in NT interpretation. A first-level metaphor-conscious process is to notice how metaphorical mapping happens in the text but also in the reading process. Where things get interesting is in the determination of what does and does not 'map,' in noticing the systematic ways in which metaphors are related, and in noticing the inference patterns. Hays quotes Amos Wilder, to the effect that "the road to moral judgment is by way of the imagination" but he seems content to leave mostly to the imagination how that might work.[115] Neither is his zeal to ground the normative functionality of Scripture necessarily arising from a negative, niggling drive to legitimate certain conservative moral positions or to license moral policing. The impetus behind this work is a desire to aid the contemporary church's perception of the moral vision of the NT so as to enable the church to be guided by that vision as it acts creatively in appropriating it now. Hays is to commended for his tremendous effort in assisting the faith community in becoming doers of the Word, and not just hearers only.

---

in the general epistles and Hebrews, he would have given them more complete treatment. Ibid., 13.

[115] Ibid., 73.

Questions and Issues Raised by 'AI' Approaches

Both William Spohn and Richard Hays employ the concept of analogical imagination to make thoughtful, sustained efforts to solve the Scripture and ethics problems set up by the Two Worlds Gap schema. The intuitive understanding guiding both proposals is that in the reading and interpretive process, the metaphorical—an analogical imaginative force—enables the Word to 'leap the gap.' Both outline for us particular processes, programs of text reading-observation, interpretation, and application incorporating the imaginative and relying on the analogical to close the gaps. Each is motivated by a concern to recover and revitalize the normative status and function of Scripture for constructive Christian ethics in communities of Christian faith.

At the end of the day, however, many unanswered—or incompletely answered—questions remain. How well does the read-and-observe, interpret, and apply method fit what can be empirically demonstrated about how reading processes work? That is, does it fit how texts actually communicate? If all reading is 'reading in,' when does interpretation take on the kind of quantum leap character that Hays claims 'leaps the gap'? When does it become what Spohn calls 'graced imagination' that simultaneously takes the 'plunge' up into insight and down into the 'real'? How, in these construals, does one identify misinterpretation, misreading? Can more be said about how 'analogical imagination' functions, about how metaphors, images, paradigms, frames, and analogies work and are related to each other? We need a more precise metaphor-study terminology and methodology than those Spohn and Hays have provided. We need a more coherent account of how the "miracle" of understanding ever happens, because the mystery and miracle of reading and interpreting ancient texts like the NT is that we ever "get it" at all. The shortcomings of AI approaches are not simply semantic, not rectifiable by the provision of a better glossary (though that would help). The problem is theoretical, paradigmatic. We in the Scripture and ethics field need a deeper, more coherent theoretical understanding of metaphor, one that is empirically grounded.

The major problem with these analogical imagination approaches may be with the primary analogy that is allowed to define the situation, The Problem. I refer to the Gap, to the Two Worlds Schema, and to the way it constrains the construal of the Scripture and ethics situation, in the first place. I refer to the historicism driving the schema, but also to the attempt to understand biblical hermeneutics as one huge, overarching metaphor or analogical frame. The primary analogy with which both Hays and Spohn work assumes the Gap. Each then calls on metaphor, and analogy itself, to be a catalyst (if not The catalyst) that allows the Worlds to creatively commingle or to be the spark that arcs the gap. But given the working definitions of metaphor with which each works, it remains unclear how metaphor is supposed to be able to perform this function, to provide this force. If the metaphors are in the texts, they belong to that Other World, the old world, the world of the text and its original readers. How, then, does noticing these metaphors or even noticing patterns in their usage solve the Gap problem? Scripture, in this schema, is an artifact from the Old World. It is an object that is—the recovery movement insists—still usable as a 'source' in contemporary ethics. But such read-interpret-apply methods may inherently limit the normativity of Scripture even while they so valiantly attempt to recover and assert its current applicability. It is the pragmatic expectation of 'applicability' of what is still basically viewed as "other peoples' mail" that remains problematic. While both Spohn and Hays beg off the (impossible) task of sorting out the culture-and-time-bound from the timeless, each actually relies on a core analogy that asserts, assumes, a time- and culture-boundedness of the entire canon. Often the 'normative', then, is reduced to general boundary-setting functions, to vague indications of general principle. Its well-intentioned proponents do sincerely have in mind recovering current applicability of Scripture for Christian ethics today. But does not the Two Worlds Gap, wedded to this set of analogical procedures, leave open an option of reduction of normativity to what seems inoffensive to us now? Entailed is a sifting process of careful (or not so careful) sorting—into 'relevant' and 'irrelevant', 'applicable' and not, 'useful' and 'timeless' or 'culturally-bound' and 'no longer binding.' Richard Hays has put his finger on one of the core problems with this approach: Culture is ubiquitous. The task of sorting 'timeless' from 'culture-bound' is impossible; everything human is culture-bound.

With analogical imagination, we are back to the indicative / imperative split that is the inevitable outcome of the separation of meaning *then* from significance for today. With these approaches Scripture is still problematized; the *diversity* problem is not solved via Hays' unified vision or Spohn's composite Jesus, and the *distance* problem persists in the Separate Worlds paradigm.

I suggest that we need to take Spohn's tip and move beyond querying to defying the hegemony of a historicism that has distorted our understanding of the actual Scripture and ethics situation. With N.T. Wright (and many others, now), let us unmask the Two Worlds Schema for what it is—a metaphorical schema that both speaks and hides truth. Surely there are significant differences between 1st-century Greco-Roman Palestinian (and Asia Minor) cultural-historical settings and those in which any 21st-century readers live. There is no use denying the differences. But is nothing cross- or transculturally human? If not, how has it ever been possible to translate and understand these texts at all? Perhaps a too-rigid, overstated social constructivism (wedded to radical historicism) has been allowed to obscure and deny what actually can and does happen in moral discourse when modern, even 21st-century, readers interact with the NT texts as Scripture.

Concluding Question: Interdisciplinarity?

The Spohn and Hays models leave a second set of unresolved issues, ones surrounding the inherent interdisciplinarity of any approach to Scripture and ethics. The Hays and Spohn methodologies are complicated but—each would admit—still incomplete. Spohn makes a valiant attempt to push (or at least invite) the ethics guild to admit that virtue ethics and moral formation do indeed belong to its purview. He has informed himself about many current issues in biblical studies, so that he begins to critique the hegemony of radical historicism, and to point to its effects upon Christian ethicists' attitudes and approaches to Scripture. But his Scripture-study methods remain at an elemental borrowing level. Hays, the NT scholar, has borrowed from ethics the language of norm, normativity, and warrant. While he is zealous to deliver to that guild a normative source of authority, his model accepts the disciplinary divide and status quo for the most part. Can a less awkward interdisciplinary model for work in Scripture and ethics be found?

Alternative Model of Interdisciplinarity for Biblical Ethics: Scripture as Exemplar

The most prominent model or approach—the one that is often taken for granted—assumes that certain 'gaps' exist, the most glaring (gaping) being two: 1) the gap between the 'original' meaning of the biblical text and its 'significance' today; 2) the gap between 'facts' and 'values.' These assumed gaps shape the questions and methods of

Scripture and ethics work. In extreme (but very real) cases, a Christian ethicist can say (and mean) that Scripture is of no use in constructive ethics today. On the other hand, other Christian ethicists will say that 'the original' ('historical') meaning 'controls' the meaning now. But that 'original' meaning was *never* univocal and is beyond our reach. The problem does not lie solely with the ethicists; biblical scholarship "has tended to reduce the meaning of those texts to their historical referents and/or to their historical witness, without remainder."[116]

I propose that cognitive linguistic theory offers an attractive alternative to the analogical imagination / hermeneutics of analogy model. In particular, cognitive theory fits certain developments in biblical studies and in theology and ethics. In biblical studies, it effectively addresses the following issues:

- The collapse of the House of Objectivity and the modernist "dream"
- The erasure of the distinction between exegesis and interpretation
- The focus on the role of the reader (in history and today)[117]

Cognitive linguistic theory and methods also answer David Tracy's call for attention to the need in hermeneutics for metaphor study methods:

> If the historian can reconstruct the texts in question, then the next problem becomes the need to discover what discipline will allow one to determine the meanings of those metaphors, symbols, and "images" used in the New Testament texts to express the religious significance of the proclamation that Jesus of Nazareth is the Christ.[118]

Tracy goes on, however, to express a traditional understanding that splits the metaphorical off from the conceptual. But what if metaphor and concept are *not* separate? What if metaphor itself is, at base, *conceptual*? What if language is language, and even religious language is still susceptible to investigation via linguistic methods?

I propose, then, in Section B, to demonstrate how a cognitive linguistic approach to metaphor might work for investigators of biblical ethics.

---

[116] Max Turner and Joel B. Green, "New Testament Commentary and Systematic Theology: Strangers or Friends?" in *Between Two Horizons: Spanning New Testament Studies and Systematic Theology* (Grand Rapids, Mich.: Eerdmans, 2000), 13.

[117] Turner and Green list these issues in their introduction to *Between Two Horizons*, 8–9.

[118] "Much of the language of the New Testament is metaphorical, symbolic, and parabolic as distinct from conceptual." D. Tracy, *Blessed Rage for Order*, 50.

I offer this methodological demonstration on one level as just that, a proposed methodology. But inherent in this proposal is a paradigm shift as well, a theoretical sea change. Biblical scholars do not need yet another method to come to its rescue in those stormy seas between the Gap. What if we admit that the Gap has been overstated—that though there are significant cultural and linguistic differences to contend with, these are yet all human cultures? The gap is a little "g" gap, if it is a gap at all. If language—including metaphor and analogy—works *conceptually*, if human concepts are rooted in human experience, how do we need to approach Scripture? I propose that we go to the texts with greater awareness of our own core metaphors for morality, looking for *trans*cultural conceptual stock, noticing interesting *cross*-cultural variations on themes common to identifiable domains of human experience-grounded concepts.

All of this leads me to suggest the following thought experiment: Erase the Gap. Draw a new picture; adopt a different paradigm. Accordingly, I propose, as well, that we experiment with the notion that the NT text we call "1 Peter" is not merely a 'source' for Christian ethics; it is itself an exemplar of the Christian ethical task. If 1 Peter "model[s] the instantiation of the good news in [a] particular locale and with respect to historical particularities," then how do current readers' tasks and questions change?[119] I suggest that Joel Green is on the right track when he suggests how reading changes when we go beyond the Two Worlds model:

> [O]ur task is not simply (and sometimes not at all) to read the content of the message of (say) 1 Peter into our world, as though we were merely to adopt its attitudes toward the state or its counsel regarding relations among husbands and wives. We are interested rather (and sometimes only) in inquiring into how 1 Peter itself engages in the task of theology and ethics. These texts, 1 Peter included, have as their objective the formation of communities that discern, embrace, serve, and propagate the character and purpose of Yahweh.[120]

This new model changes the questions. Instead of presenting modern problems to the Scripture and judging it deficient if it cannot resolve them to our satisfaction, we could investigate how the NT texts themselves define moral issues and problems. What kinds of experiences are construed as moral conflicts and challenges in their lives? To honor

---

[119] Green, "Scripture and Theology," 41.
[120] Ibid.

the texts as exemplars does not entail a denial of our differences, but rather seeks to uncover the cultural and conceptual clashes and blends, the congruencies and divergences in the interest of discerning what the Spirit might be saying to the churches today. We turn, then, to the methodological demonstration section with these questions and goals in mind.

PART B

CONCEPTUAL METAPHOR IN 1 PETER: METHODOLOGICAL DEMONSTRATION

INTRODUCTION

Although cognitive linguists work primarily with current language in use, a number of them (Sweetser, Turner) have applied cognitive theory and methodology to the special tasks of reading and understanding older texts. Before reading 1 Peter as moral discourse, then, it will be enlightening to consider how cognitive linguists understand reading and writing in general, and the reading of older texts in particular. I will first consider the significance for NT scholarship and ethics of certain cognitive linguists' views (Sweeter, Turner, Lakoff): that reading and writing are acts of the human mind; that social, linguistic, and literary conventions and communities are connected; that belief matters; that reading is political; and that moral discourse is about much more than ethical persuasion or moral advice. I will also borrow language and understandings about the roles of readers and authors, and the nature of the reading and interpretive process from literary scholars James Phelan and Peter Rabinowitz, scholars who are not cognitivists but whose work is compatible with cognitive approaches. All of these issues and questions form my pretext for reading 1 Peter as moral discourse.

Turning to the tasks of reading 1 Peter, I propose to examine the text, seeking what cognitive metaphor theory and methodology reveals and listening for the questions this methodology raises. Of particular interest are what conceptual metaphor study can tell us about how the moral argument is framed and constrained, the ways in which the moral discourse is grounded in basic bodily and primary social experience, and the connections between the cosmology and the politics of 1 Peter. Throughout, I explore some of the mechanisms by which 21st century readers can understand and misunderstand, misread, 1 Peter.

In a final section, after reading 1 Peter, I will reflect on what the methodology has revealed about the differences between translating and understanding, about the framing of moral discourse, about moral imagination, and about moral politics. I will argue that lively moral discourse can happen when 21st-century readers interact with 1 Peter and interact with one another using 1 Peter as an exemplar. The moral value, the ethical weight, of 1 Peter as moral discourse is not restricted to a set of opinions, instructions or bits of advice that can be accepted or rejected. It is in examining the *how* of moral discourse—both within the text and in the interaction entailed in reading, interpreting, and discussing the text—that the fundamental value of cognitive linguistic metaphor theory and methodology lies. That is why it would not be enough merely to use this methodology to enhance our understanding of *what* 1 Peter says about morality or Christian social ethics. It would not suffice simply to catalog and connect the metaphors the author employs in 1 Peter, to do 'descriptive' work, though the powers of this method in that regard are considerable. It is not even enough to supplement such descriptive results with insights about our respective perspectives, worldviews, and symbolic worlds in order to suggest how we can and cannot 'apply' 1 Peter's moral advice today. Cognitive metaphor theory and method draws our attention to metaethical and hermeneutical issues at a deeper, more constitutive level.

CHAPTER FOUR

BEFORE READING 1 PETER

> *When we see words on a page, do those words stand directly for external realities?*
> *No ... words and the patterns into which words fit are triggers to the imagination.*[1]

> To learn a belief without belief is to sing a song without the tune. *A yielding, an obedience, a willingness to accept these notes as the right notes, this pattern as the right pattern, is the essential gesture of performance, translation, and understanding. The gesture need not be permanent, a lasting posture of the mind or heart; yet it is not false. It is more than the suspension of disbelief needed to watch a play, yet less than a conversion. It is a position, a posture in the dance.*[2]

The major task of Part B is to deploy cognitive metaphor methods in order to discover what they reveal about 1 Peter as moral discourse. But before that study can be undertaken—before reading 1 Peter as exemplar of moral discourse—it is necessary to set out some basic understandings about the nature of moral discourse and the reading process. The moral discourse of 1 Peter is not merely an entity contained in the text of 1 Peter, not an inert object that awaits discovery as though readers and interpreters were miners or archaeologists beginning to dig for gold or artifacts. Discourse is dynamic; it is an event or an activity more than it is an entity or an object. One of the central questions this study addresses is whether moral discourse can indeed *happen* as 21st-century readers encounter 1 Peter. Given the apparent gaps—cultural and temporal, linguistic and philosophical—can modern readers engage in lively discourse as they read 1 Peter?

---

[1] Gilles Fauconnier and Mark Turner, *The Way We Think: Conceptual Blending and the Mind's Hidden Complexities* (New York: Basic Books, 2002), 146; emphasis mine.
[2] Ursula K. LeGuin, *The Telling* (New York: Harcourt, 2000), 97–98; emphasis original.

Excursus on Discourse

The terms 'discourse' and 'discourse analysis' have been used in so many ways that a working definition is needed to specify their meaning in this context. I will use 'discourse' to refer to naturally occurring connected speech and written texts, and 'discourse analysis' to refer mainly to linguistic analysis of speech and written texts. This study focuses on a written text, 1 Peter, and on twenty-first-century readers' interaction with that text.

In the 1980s, linguist Michael Stubbs surveyed the landscape of usages of the term discourse analysis, and located three main streams of definition:

(1) study of the use of language in units larger than the single sentence or utterance,
(2) study focused on interrelationships between language and society, and
(3) study of interactive or dialogic properties of everyday communication.[3] These three streams persist in the scholarly guilds, and one reason discourse analysis defies simple definition is that scholars in a number of disciplines (mostly humanities and social sciences) have used the term improvisationally, so that hybrids have developed.

My use of the term is colored by the disciplines from which I borrow, linguistic pragmatics and cognitive linguistics. Pragmatics, as a sub-discipline of linguistics, is concerned with the relationships between language use and the language user in a situational context.[4] Discourse analysts are interested in how language is used in social contexts, particularly in interaction between speakers. More recently, one key area that pragmatics has been concerned with is the study of presuppositions.

> The pragmatic interest in the implicit meaning dimensions of language use has been extended to include meanings which are logically entailed

---

[3] Michael Stubbs, *Discourse Analysis: The Sociolinguistic Analysis of Natural Language* (Oxford: Basil Blackwell, 1983), 1.

[4] "Pragmatic" refers to the social actor's capacity to adjust to situational circumstances. Stef Stembrouck surveys the history of the development of pragmatics, summarizing: "Initially, pragmatics was mainly bracketed by analytical philosophy, as the first themes it developed were indeed speech act theory and the study of principles of information exchange." Stef Stembrouck, "What Is Meant by Discourse Analysis?" available from http://bank.rug.ac.be/da/da.htm; Internet; accessed April 2001.

on the language user by the use of a particular structure ... The study of presuppositions therefore often concentrates on meaning dimensions which are 'taken for granted' in an utterance or a text, and hence this area of pragmatic research offers an instrument which is well-suited for examining the links between language and ideology.[5]

Cognitive metaphor study is one tool that pragmatics has developed for doing research on presuppositions.

I will use the term *moral discourse* to mean naturally occurring connected speech and written discourse that contains material pertaining to how people in various social contexts conceptualize and explain how they should live.[6] Analysis of 1 Peter as moral discourse is also metaethical inquiry, since it entails research into the presuppositions within a text whose aim, theme, and content is human morals. Moreover, since cognitive metaphor analysis can aid a scholar in locating within a text evidence of systematic use of conventional metaphors for morality, such analysis can ground determinations of the extent to which a given text's content or focus is moral and ethical.

My specific interest here is in the use of language in particular social contexts, (1) *within* the epistle of 1 Peter itself and in the social interaction between the writer(s) and intended recipients of the letter, so far as these can be discerned; (2) *between* the text and twenty-first-century readers in the US, especially the interactive and dialogic qualities thereof. Conceptual metaphor study is one set of tools discourse analysts can use to reveal and explain what a text evokes and how readers respond to the text.

Reading and Writing as Acts of the Human Mind

Conceptual metaphor study is predicated on cognitive scientific evidence that language and literature are acts of the human mind.[7] Language requires human cognition, and literature displays how people

---

[5] Ibid.

[6] This statement adapts for ethical and moral discourse a similar but more general definition articulated by Stembrouck, Ibid.

[7] Mark Turner, *Reading Minds: The Study of English in the Age of Cognitive Science* (Princeton, N.J.: Princeton University Press, 1991), 6. Regarding the cognitive processing involved in reading, see Fauconnier and Turner, *The Way We Think*, 146, 166–167, 210–211. Words, Fauconnier and Turner say, "are prompts we use to try to get one another to call up some of what we know and to work on it creatively to arrive at a meaning

think.⁸ This being the case, students and scholars of biblical literature and ethics would do well to study biblical language and literature as human cognitive and linguistic acts, expressions of the human conceptual apparatus.

Cognitive linguists approach what happens when people engage a written text—reading—as fundamentally an encounter between minds.⁹ The dynamic encounter of discourse displays how both writer and readers are thinking, and cognitively-oriented scholars are interested in understanding that *how* and that *thinking* as best we can. But three cautions are in order.

First, care must be taken when using the word 'mind.' A cognitive approach to the notion of 'the human mind' differs from the New Critical understanding. New Critical working definitions of 'mind' and 'human' tended to ignore or obscure grounding in physical experience and social, historical, and political factors, whereas cognitive linguistic (and cognitive scientific) data and analysis constitutes direct refutation of the adequacy of those New Critical understandings. Mind and reason are embodied, not disembodied—so much so that, to put it in the words of Lakoff and Johnson, "the very structure of reason itself comes from the details of our embodiment."¹⁰ Mind, human reason,

---

... Words by themselves give very little information about the meaning they prompt us to construct." Ibid., 146.

⁸ Antonio Damasio, a neurobiologist, writes: "Both words and arbitrary symbols are based on topographically organized representations and can become images. Most of the words we use in our inner speech, before speaking or writing a sentence, exist as auditory or visual images in our consciousness. If they did not become images, however fleetingly, they would not be anything we could know." Antonio R. Damasio, *Descartes' Error: Emotion, Reason, and the Human Brain* (New York: Penguin Putnam, 1994; HarperCollins, 2000). This book includes a good beginning bibliography on philosophy of mind and cognitive neuroscience.

⁹ *Reading Minds* is the title of English literature scholar Mark Turner's introduction to a cognitive linguistic approach to literary study, op. cit. "Minds" in a cognitivist understanding are embodied. Antonio Damasio says: "The body, as represented in the brain, may constitute the indispensable frame of reference for the neural processes that we experience as the mind ... The mind exists in and for an integrated organism; our minds would not be the way they are if it were not for the interplay of body and brain during evolution, during individual development, and at the current moment. The mind had to be first about the body, or it could not have been. On the basis of the ground reference that the body continuously provides, the mind can then be about many other things, real and imaginary." Damasio, *Descartes' Error*, xvi.

¹⁰ George Lakoff and Mark Johnson, *Philosophy in the Flesh: The Embodied Mind and Its Challenge to Western Thought* (New York: Basic Books, 1999), 4. See Damasio, *Descartes' Error*, 223–234.

is emotionally engaged, evolving, mostly unconscious, and inextricably linked to and interactive with our everyday lives as social beings.[11] When cognitive linguists and scientists speak of the human mind, then, they are not referring to some detached, intrapsychic, 'universal' Mind. But neither does a simplistic, absolutist version of the social construction of reality cohere with cognitive scientific findings. Linguist Eve Sweetser, for example, finds in her research on blended spaces and performativity that there are degrees of social constructedness and admits that cognitive linguists and others struggle to understand what is and is not socially constructed.[12]

The second caution concerns the Intentional Fallacy. Though perhaps a majority of scholars of biblical literature no longer officially or rigidly subscribe to New Critical doctrines of the autonomy of texts, at least one New Critical tenet persists in some circles: the notion that authorial intention is irrelevant to valid and sound interpretation. Traces—and bolder streams—of this erroneous notion still are to be found in current literary and biblical scholarship wherever textual autonomy is uncritically assumed. Moreover, if attempting to identify the meaning of a text by discovering an author's intention is fallacious, why would biblical scholars want to use a cognitive linguistic theory and methodology which admits that its primary interest is in understanding what an author or speaker is saying and how he or she is thinking? The answer has to do with how 'thinking' is defined and what qualities of the human mind and intentions are being studied. When cognitive linguists say they are studying language as an act of the human mind, they do not imply that they are attempting to uncover an author's internal, psychological intentions, nor are they assuming that the meaning of an utterance or text could be located in that manner. That was what the New Critics rightly warned against. A cognitive linguistic approach is, however, compatible with the project Peter Rabinowitz (in this respect agreeing with Roland Barthes) observes is what most *actual readers* attempt: trying to understand what the author is saying.[13] This study will demonstrate some of the ways cognitive linguistic

---

[11] Similar points are made by Damasio, *Descartes' Error*, xvi, and Lakoff and Johnson, *Philosophy in the Flesh*, 16–44.

[12] Eve Sweetser, "Blended Spaces and Performativity," in *Cognitive Linguistics* 11–3/4, (Special issue on blended spaces, ed. Seana Coulson and Todd Oakley, 2000), 305–333.
Regarding cognitivist understandings of social factors in meaning construction, see also Fauconnier and Turner, *The Way We Think*, 189–190, 309–310.

[13] Peter J. Rabinowitz, *Before Reading: Narrative Conventions and the Politics of Interpretation*

metaphor theory and methodology can help us understand what an author is saying and how communication between author and reader happens.

A third cautionary note concerns the interaction of this cognitive approach with another aspect of New Critical dogma, namely the New Critical suppression and mistrust of readers' responses to a text. Descent into what was termed the 'Affective Fallacy'—so the theory went—rendered unsound any interpretation that relied on observations about reader response. By and by, other literary critics (Fish) asserted, alternatively, that meaning could not be created or communicated *without* readers. A cognitive approach departs from both New Critical dogma and strong versions of 'reader response' theory.[14] Nor does it line up with Holland's psychoanalytic approach, which guesses that reading activates readers' fantasies.[15] The activation of mental spaces and conceptual blends is part and parcel of the way people think all the time, not just when they fantasize. Reading does, however, require activation of the kind of imagination Fauconnier and Turner investigate and schematize in *The Way We Think;* accordingly, this study will make use of some aspects their methodology.

To summarize, cognitive linguistic theory and methodology is not suited to any project that attempts to understand what authors are saying in texts as if texts were autonomous objects divorced from the people who constructed them, or as if readers' or hearers' responses were irrelevant. In fact, cognitive linguistic metaphor study demonstrates that neither the New Critical doctrine of the autonomy of the text nor a strong version of reader response theory squares with empirical evidence about how language and communicative processes like reading work. If the New Critical orthodoxy "ruled readers' responses

---

(Columbus, OH: Ohio State University Press, 1987), 25, 33. Philosopher Francis-Noel Thomas points out that we only bother to read a text on the assumption that someone, a writer, intended it to mean something. Reading as an intentional activity depends on taking writing as an intentional and purposeful activity: *The Writer, Writing* (Princeton: Princeton University Press, 1992).

[14] E.D. Hirsch, *Validity in Interpretation* (New Haven: Yale University Press, 1967); "Three Dimensions of Hermeneutics," *New Literary History* 3 (1972): 245–261; "Current Issues in Theory of Interpretation," *Journal of Religion* 55 (1975): 298–312; Stanley Fish, *Is There a Text in This Class? The Authority of Interpretive Communities* (Cambridge, Mass.: Harvard University Press, 1980).

[15] Norman Holland, "Literary Interpretation and Three Phases of Psychoanalysis," *Critical Inquiry* 3 (1976): 221–233; *5 Readers Reading* (New Haven: Yale University Press, 1975).

irrelevant to sound interpretation," cognitive empirical evidence will rule that doctrine inadequate.[16]

What, then, are the positive features of a cognitive approach to texts, to reading, and to interpretation? First, writing, reading and interpretation are acts of the human mind. They arise out of experiences of human beings who live (or have lived) in human bodies and in human social environments. Embodiment and the rootedness of all language in primary human bodily and social experience are starting points for cognitive approaches to language and literature.[17] Every feature of the process of written communication is anchored in everyday linguistic and conceptual frameworks. Communication requires conceptual framing and processing all along the way—in the writer's mind before she even begins to write, through the writing and revisions and editing, to the receptive processes of reading and interpretation.

Who is Reading? Conventions and Communities: Conceptual, Linguistic, Literary

Actual readers try to understand what an author is saying, but it also matters who the readers are, what kind of understanding is being sought, and how readers go about their tasks. Sometimes readers, upon encountering an ancient text like 1 Peter, acutely feel its strangeness and their cultural outsider status. There is a strong sense that this is 'other,' foreign, that its language is, even given careful translation, odd. On the other hand, sometimes 21st-century readers can readily join the authorial audience of such a text as 1 Peter, by entering the "dance" that LeGuin describes, and Phelan and Rabinowitz outline. This happens when readers adopt the beliefs that allow authentic performance—of understanding, of translating, of allowing the text's conceptual structures to move them, to shift their thinking at a deep, plate-tectonic level.[18] Still, modern readers must learn this dance, and

---

[16] James Phelan, foreword to Rabinowitz, *Before Reading*, xiii. Unlike Hirsch, Phelan and Rabinowitz are concerned with reading conventions and implicit rules—with what readers know and do before they read.

[17] Mark Turner says, "The human mind is linguistic and literary; language and literature are products of the everyday human mind." Turner, *Reading Minds*, vii.

[18] I refer to the LeGuin quote at the start of this chapter, which begins, *"To learn a belief without belief is to sing a song without the tune,"* and ends, "It is a position, a posture in the dance." Le Guin, *The Telling*, 97–98. Emphasis original.

they can also step aside from the text in ways that the first recipients of the letter could not. There are perhaps elements of 'performance' required of current readers that were not required of the earliest readers of the letter.

To understand the issues involved, it will be helpful to borrow some language and concepts from literary critics and linguists. First, consider the distinction drawn by literary scholar Mark Turner, a cognitivist, between *special* understanding and *common* understanding. Members of natural linguistic communities (for example, native Basque speakers or literate, upper-class Elizabethan English speakers) share specific linguistic skills and conceptual resources that enable understanding to flow relatively easily, seemingly naturally, when the text they are reading or the speech they are auditing comes from that same linguistic base. Most of the time our use of language and even our reading takes places at this level. But there are other, more specialized language communities. These communities share certain conceptual structures and linguistic skills, and they often seek—and perhaps sometimes find—what Turner calls 'special understanding.' This is the kind of understanding enjoyed within special language communities of novelists, dramatists, poets, and their most sophisticated readers. There are even subsets within larger specialized communities. For example, within the set of modern fiction readers, there are writers and readers of detective novels.

The point is that biblical scholars and Christian ethicists comprise (alas, mostly separate) language communities that often seek and sometimes enjoy special understanding. These are not the only language and reading communities that are interested in 1 Peter, nor are they mutually exclusive, as though a reader had to choose one reading community, one reading posture. That is only half of the point, however. What Turner and other cognitively oriented literary scholars want us to realize is that—linguistically—special understanding is dependent on ("an exploitation of" says Turner) common understanding, and can be analyzed and evaluated accordingly.

A particular twist on this notion of linguistic community for biblical scholars is that though scholars belong within their own linguistic community—the set of those who use and understand the vocabulary and concepts and conventions of professional biblical study—they cannot claim to belong to the linguistic communities of the biblical texts, not in a natural and straightforward manner, anyway. Scholars cannot avoid bringing to the texts, even as specialized readers, the conceptual and linguistic frameworks and conventions of our own native linguistic communities. One basic task for biblical scholars, then, is to investigate what is and is not shared in language and thought with the biblical writers and their natural linguistic communities. Another important set of tasks cognitive linguistic discoveries and methods entail for biblical scholars is to develop analytic instruments for investigating the resources of the ordinary language and conventional thought of the Bible. Conceptual metaphor theory and method offers a subset, perhaps a start-up kit, of those tools.

Literary scholar Peter Rabinowitz explains that in order to read with understanding, readers have to enter what he calls the *authorial audience*—to attempt to approximate the beliefs and conceptual framework of the audience the author had in mind. To do this readers must share (or learn) the conventions—linguistic and literary—with which the author was working and thinking. Sometimes that sharing of conventions happens seemingly naturally, as the communication can flow when author and reader belong to the same linguistic community. But often the task of entering the authorial audience is harder, as it moves by fits and starts when our linguistic communities overlap to varying degrees with that of the author. James Phelan, in his Forward to Rabinowitz's *Before Reading*, suggests that an understanding of the literary conventions the author is using is necessary for the quality of understanding enjoyed by the authorial audience.[19] I will turn momentarily to a consideration of how some aspects of *epistolary* conventions affect reading. But the focus at this point is on what metaphor theory has to do with reading theory. Cognitively oriented linguists and literary scholars like Turner say that literary conventions are anchored in everyday linguistic and conceptual (metaphorical) frameworks. The word 'biblical' could be inserted in front of 'language' in what Turner says about tools readers need for understanding:

> Given a bit of language, a discourse, or a text, how does a reader understand it? Given alternative readings, what were the different processes that led to those alternative understandings? The most amazing phenomenon our profession confronts, and the one for which we have the least explanation, is that a reader can make sense of a text, and that

---

[19] "Reading in the authorial audience ... involves an effort to determine which conventions the writer is working with or against." James Phelan, "Forward" in Rabinowitz, *Before Reading*, xiv.

there are certain regularities across the individual senses made of a given text. How do readers do that?[20]

Cognitive metaphor study attempts to give some answers to those questions. What cognitivists find interesting is that despite divergent interpretation, there is massive convergence in readers' understandings of texts written by members of their own linguistic community. The question, the challenge, is how to explain the seemingly effortless, automatic understanding that so often does take place. Even with texts of more distant provenance (in culture, temporal origin), the scholarly arguments are circumscribed. Although Scripture scholars might disagree about the significance of what is said to have happened on the Damascus road or what walking on water is about, we do *not* fight over whether Jesus taught in Galilee or about what it (literally) means to walk down a road—or whether Paul was converted to Christianity. Our discussions of authorial intent and nuances of meaning proceed from a bedrock of shared understandings even from a distance of two thousand years.

Is Nothing Sacred? The Role of Belief in Reading 1 Peter

If entering the authorial audience requires one to adopt certain beliefs, more needs to be said about what kinds of beliefs we are talking about. When the 'belief' strand is pulled out, one discovers that it is no monofilament, and it is woven through the fabric of meaning construction in multiple ways.

Beliefs about the general structure of reality shape the way readers respond to a text. There may be some aspects of 1st-century Greco-Roman cosmological beliefs, for example, about which 21st-century English-speaking readers would need to have information, were they to understand what Peter is saying in his letter. If that is so, then in a sense, 21st-century readers have to drop some beliefs and adopt others in order to enter the authorial audience of a text like 1 Peter. Readers might have to un-learn, or suspend, their customary 21st-century versions of the Great Chain of Being, for example, in order to try on the tighter microcosm / macrocosm interactions that shape the moral implications of the Great Chain in the 1st-century version. A

---

[20] M. Turner, *Reading Minds*, 19.

reader might need to imaginatively adopt certain beliefs (an apocalyptic view of history, perhaps) in order to enter the audience that the writer addresses.[21] Perhaps we could adapt a suggestion offered by Rabinowitz to fiction readers who want to figure out what the *narrative audience* of a particular work is. He invites them to ask, "What sort of reader would I have to pretend to be—what would I have to know and believe—if I wanted to take this work of fiction as real?" In the present case, perhaps the question could be, "What sort of reader would I have to imagine myself being—what would I have to know and believe—if I wanted to take this letter as real, as addressed to me?" Even further, "What sort of reader shall I become, as I accept this letter as addressed to me?"[22] If we cannot imagine ourselves as part of the authorial audience, or—to quote Rabinowitz again—"if we misapprehend the beliefs of that audience, we are apt to make invalid, even perverse, interpretations."[23]

Belief operates in the special reading community of biblical scholars, as well. Belief in the tenets of a certain theoretical perspective and set of methods has so shaped biblical studies that it has become the *sine qua non* of the profession. How heretical any challenge to the validity of the historical critical paradigm sounds. Adherence to a scholarly guild's assumptions about its canon, methodology, tasks, and epistemology—subscription to the beliefs of this scholarly community—constrains interpretation.[24]

Belief shapes the expectations of readers and interpreters of the Bible in the professional Christian ethical guild. In particular, beliefs about the status and function of scripture as a source of authority in ethical argument influence approaches and responses to this letter. If one believes that the Bible is Scripture, and that as such, it functions as one source of authority in constructive Christian ethics, these beliefs entail

---

[21] Rabinowitz, *Before Reading*, 33.

[22] Joel Green suggests that for readers within the Christian faith community, the kind of "pretending" posture Rabinowitz describes is not strong enough to describe the stance taken by readers for whom this texts is Scripture. He quotes Ursula K. LeGuin, "To learn a belief without belief is to sing a song without the tune." Joel B. Green, "Scripture and Theology: Failed Experiments, Fresh Perspectives," *Interpretation* (January 2002): 9.

[23] Rabinowitz, *Before Reading*, 96.

[24] The situation in biblical studies is not unlike that in which literature professor Mark Turner sees in his guild: "Belief, with its power to admit the believer to our elite Disney World for literary critics, substitutes for touching home base." Turner, *Reading Minds*, 15.

expectations that shape interpretation and response in the reading.[25] If one, in addition, is a member of the reading community which recognizes the continuity of its own life with the lives that gave rise to 1 Peter, if it is read as one continuous story, then the linkages are indeed potentially profound. If one believes that valid sources of authority for ethics ought to conform to a certain (modern) discursive style (or logical form) in order to be useful, then those beliefs will constrain one's response to 1 Peter.

All of these kinds of beliefs constrain and engender expectations. Philosophical and theological assumptions, especially unexamined ones, color interpretations, and this observation has become almost a commonplace. But the point here is that many kinds of expectations are necessarily in play when we read. What cognitive metaphor study offers is one way (or a set of ways) to examine, and analyze what R.N. Ross called 'structures of expectations.'[26] Linguist Deborah Tannen explains: "on the basis of one's experience of the world in a given culture (or combination of cultures), one organizes knowledge about the world and uses this knowledge to predict interpretations and relationships regarding new information, events, and experiences."[27] Metaphor study helps us locate those structures, to understand that which is cross-cultural, and to locate what is potentially transcultural.

Reading 1 Peter As a Letter

Πέτρος ἀπόστολος Ἰησοῦ Χριστοῦ ἐκλεκτοῖς παρεπιδήμοις διασπορᾶς
Peter   apostle of Jesus Christ to select   transients   of dispersion

The opening words of 1 Peter could be translated as follows:

From: Peter, apostle of Jesus Christ
To: The elect Diaspora, resident aliens

---

[25] The approach taken here is congruent with the hermeneutical "key" that James McClendon offers, when he refers to "the Bible's own linking device, the Bible's tropic way of holding its great story together." James McClendon, *Doctrine: Systematic Theology, Volume 2* (Nashville: Abingdon, 1994), 45. Some of what McClendon attributes to the "mystical" I suspect happens via mental space evocation and conceptual blending in its many manifestations.

[26] Robert N. Ross, "Ellipsis and the Structure of Expectation," *San Jose State Occasional Papers in Linguistics* 1 (1975).

[27] Deborah Tannen, ed. *Framing in Discourse* (Oxford: Oxford University Press, 1993), 16.

One prerequisite for entering the authorial audience of 1 Peter is to read it *as* a letter. It should be read as a letter because that is what it is—just as a mystery novel should be read as a mystery and not as a criminological report. The author writes this piece of prose in a certain form—epistle—to a certain audience. It would appear to be a category mistake to read this piece of writing as anything but a letter from a certain person (the apostle Peter) to the stated recipients. In that sense, 21st-century readers looking over this document would be at best reading someone else's mail, reading over the intended readers' shoulders.[28] But the matter is a bit more complex than that.

Linguistic Community and Convention

Consider the matter of the particular letter-genre conventions to which this document conforms.[29] By 1st-century Greco-Roman convention, the stated author (Πέτρος ἀπόστολος Ἰησοῦ Χριστοῦ—"Peter, apostle of Jesus Christ") of this epistle may be a fiction, of sorts.[30] The first recipients of this letter may quite naturally (seemingly naturally, that is, because they knew the convention) have understood right away that they were to read this letter *as if* it were from the apostle Peter, the former Galilean fisherman. No matter how one calculates the probability that this might be the real Peter writing, the authorial

---

[28] See Richard Hays, *The Moral Vision of the New Testament* (San Francisco: HarperSanFrancisco, 1996), 6, and my discussion of Hays' approach in Chapter 3, above. See also M. Eugene Boring, "Interpreting 1 Peter as a Letter [not] Written to Us," *Quarterly Review* 13 (Spring 1993): 89–111. Boring says, "Our name does not appear in the address of 1 Peter. Not only was this letter not written to us; nothing in the New Testament was written to us. The first principle of biblical interpretation, a hermeneutical principle that corresponds to the scandalous particularity of the incarnation, is simply this: Nothing in the Bible was written to us ... when the people of Cappadocia received it, they did not say, 'What is this strange document? Maybe we should form a study group.' It spoke directly to them. And this is the key difference between them and us when we read this letter." (Ibid., 93–94). He goes on, however, to discuss the significance of the letter's canonicity and the senses in which 1 Peter is for us. See also Gary A. Phillips and Danna Nolan Fewell, "Ethics, Bible, Reading As If," *Semeia* 77 (1997): 1–22.

[29] See Rabinowitz, *Before Reading*, concerning levels of pretense or imagination required of readers.

[30] But by 1st-century standards, it wouldn't *feel* fictional, even if the letter is pseudonymous. For a summaries of authorship issues, see Paul J. Achtemeier, Hermeneia, *1 Peter: A Commentary on First Peter* (Minneapolis, Minn.: Augsburg Fortress, 1996), 1; and see David G. Horrell, "The Product of a Petrine Circle? A Reassessment of the Origin and Character of 1 Peter" in *Journal for the Study of the New Testament* 86 (2002): 29–60.

audience is cued that it is expected to imagine (or accept) that the document is from Peter. It appears likely that Peter enlisted the help of Silvanus (1 Peter 1.1, 5.12), someone schooled in Greek and aware of the Greek version of the Old Testament. It is quite possible that Peter did substantially author the letter, but that Sylvanus wrote it down, using his literary skills. But what that sort of pseudonymous strategy signified then (legitimate tie-in to recognized authority) is not what it might signify now, in our culture (fraud, deception?). Likewise, the addressees. What an odd beginning. When we read 1 Peter from our own contexts, are we reading someone else's mail, trying to look over (1st century) shoulders? Yes and No. Everything depends on who is reading and why, to what end.

Yes, as Eugene Boring says, 1 Peter, on one level is a letter *not* written to *us*. Its language and culture is foreign to us; it was sent to someone else, and its original recipients must have understood it in ways we cannot.[31] But no. This letter is now part of our culture, as well. Even those outside the faith community which holds this book as canonical Scripture, understand that it has sacred status for some. As Joel Green affirms:

> Even though we recognize that each book of the Bible was written to people and in places far removed from us in time and culture, when we approach the Bible as Scripture we take seriously the faith statement that this book is our Book, these scriptures are our Scripture. We are not reading someone else's mail—as though reading the Bible had to do foremost with recovering an ancient meaning intended for someone else and then translating its principles for use in our own lives. When we recall that *we* are the people of God to whom the Bible is addressed as Scripture, we realize that the fundamental transformation that must take place is not the transformation of an ancient message into a contemporary meaning but rather the transformation of our lives by means of God's Word.[32]

That is, if the readers (Green's "we") are the church, they constitute a linguistic community that reads 1 Peter *as* a letter written both *then*—to *them*, the 1st-century recipients—and heard again afresh *now* in such a way that it feels as if it were indeed written to *"us."* Given this

---

[31] Boring, "Interpreting 1 Peter as a Letter [not] Written to Us."

[32] Joel B. Green, "Scripture in the Church: Reconstructing the Authority of Scripture for Christian Formation and Mission," in *The Wesleyan Tradition: A Paradigm for Renewal*, ed. Paul Wesley Chilcote (Nashville: Abingdon, 2002). This perspective is consistent with James McClendon's *"this is that"* hermeneutic. James McClendon, *Ethics: Systematic Theology, Volume 1* (Nashville: Abingdon, 1986), 33.

reading community, the letter is still current. This linguistic community would not be reading the letter as *voyeurs*. Even so, to read with understanding we must imaginatively put ourselves in the place of the original readership—and put the original author(s) in the place of Peter—not as a game but for the purpose of reading the text, for the purpose, that is, of entering the authorial audience.

Other reading communities—professional Christian ethicists, biblical scholars, historians—might read the letter *as* moral discourse or ethical treatise, *as* an artifact, or *as* primary source material. The wise reader becomes aware of reading *as*, and the critical reader will want to think about how the meaning construed is thus affected.

Blended Spaces, Multiple Reading Communities

Readers have several options in this regard, since they might belong to several reading communities. Each way of *reading as* opens up a particular kind of blended space.[33] Some disagreements about how 1 Peter ought to be read—and even about its status as source of authority for contemporary ethics—are disagreements about (or uncertainty about) the status of these blends. Underneath these disagreements are varying beliefs about the social authority that gives shaping authority to a writer or speaker ("Peter, apostle of Jesus Christ") or to a text (is it Scripture or Bible or 1st-century artifact?).

When 1 Peter is read as a letter and as Scripture (and as an artifact from another culture) we combine conventional knowledge and inference patterns from more than one domain to yield a new category, to create a new space. This is a matter of linguistic community. When church parishioners are taught to read 1 Peter 'as if' it were a letter to them (and if they believe it is Scripture for them), they may no longer feel the 'as if.' The text gains enormous power in such a community, since performativity is dependent on the status of the speaker (or text).

Clearly, there are a number of ways of reading a document like 1 Peter; there are optional blended spaces for readers to inhabit. But there are constraints on the blends, not an infinite number of legitimate

---

[33] For an introduction to blended spaces, see Eve Sweetser and Gilles Fauconnier, "Cognitive Links and Domains: Basic Aspects of Mental Space Theory," in *Spaces, Worlds, and Grammar*, ed. Gilles Fauconnier and Eve Sweetser (Chicago and London: University of Chicago Press, 1996), 1–28.

options. If readers gather information about the source domains operating in this text, they will become aware of what 1 Peter is *not* (and therefore how *not* to read 1 Peter). 1 Peter is not: a Greek philosophical dialog, though it has some affinities with that form; it is certainly not a 21st-century letter or memo written directly from the apostle Peter to modern Christians. But it *is* a letter that belongs to the church's Scriptural canon.

So What? Moral Politics and Why Reading 1 Peter Matters

1 Peter—this little letter (ὀλίγων ἔγραψα—'brief writing') that Peter writes to "the exiles of the Dispersion in Pontus, Galatia, Cappadocia, Asia and Bithynia"—is very much about politics and morality. The politics Peter deals with are multiple; he addresses social relationships at every level, from husband and wife to parent and child, church leader to member, minority group to larger culture and government. His writing brings to awareness questions raised by the presence of Christ in the believers' lives and minds, questions about systems of power relations and the ethics of social structures. Peter writes about the decisions people can make and dispositions people can take on in the face of exile and enslavement, gender hierarchy, and church hierarchy. As Peter Rabinowitz reminds us, these kinds of social systems "may be in part formalized (for instance, through law)" but they "are always in part invisible." One of the functions of written discourse can be to legitimate invisible power relationships simply by 'naturalizing' them.[34] It is at least partly via conceptual metaphor that the letter communicates and displays these social and political values.

George Lakoff states a core warrant for the use of cognitive linguistic methods to investigate moral discourse:

> The most fundamental values in a culture will be coherent with the metaphorical structure of the most fundamental concepts in the culture ... our values are not independent but must form a coherent system with the metaphorical concepts we live by.[35]

If Lakoff is right, cognitive metaphor analysis should contribute data that will help answer a question the NT scholarly reading community

---

[34] Rabinowitz, *Before Reading*, 5.
[35] George Lakoff and Mark Johnson, *Metaphors We Live By* (Chicago: University of Chicago Press, 1980), 22.

has been batting around for decades: Does 1 Peter uncritically employ conventional Greco-Roman moral thinking and assumptions or does the author alter and subvert those conventions? Certain members of the NT scholarly community have read in 1 Peter an attempt to Hellenize, to acculturate Christianity to Greco-Roman values.[36] From this perspective, the moral message of 1 Peter is repressive and backtracks significantly from the household values of Christianity's Jewish origins.[37] But other readers in this community argue that the letter does *not* counsel accommodation to Greco-Roman culture or espousal of its ethical ideals.[38] Some of these arguments have been based on what scholars have noticed about the shaping power of certain metaphors in the letter. Yet another reading sees the language of 'strangers,' 'exiles' whose home is heaven and hears a message counseling quietism.[39] These perspectives cannot all be correct. One aim of this study is to use conceptual metaphor analysis to clarify the social-ethical message of the letter and, secondarily, to locate with more precision the role metaphor plays in communicating that message.

---

[36] Thus in a mid-'80s piece, David Balch says: "1 Peter ... stresses 'doing good' as praised by Roman governors and living harmoniously in Greco-Roman households ... Petrine Christianity accepted Hellenistic social values in tension with important values in Jewish tradition (in the Torah) and even in tension with the early Jesus movement, changes that raise questions about continuity and identity in early Christianity." David L. Balch, "Hellenization / Acculturation in 1 Peter," in *Perspectives on 1 Peter*, ed. Charles H. Talbert (NABPR Special Series 9; Macon, Georgia: Mercer University Press, 1986), 81.

[37] Balch concludes that 1 Peter's household code "reflects the cultural change from the Mosaic story of salvation to Greek politics ... The household values in Israelite society were radically different from the structure of the Greco-Roman house, and the Jewish author of 1 Peter is acculturating." David L. Balch, "Early Christian Criticism of Patriarchal Authority: 1 Peter 2:11–3:12," *Union Seminary Quarterly Review* 39 (1984): 97.

[38] Thus Achtemeier concludes that the "controlling metaphor" is "the Christian community as the new people of God constituted by the Christ who suffered and rose." Paul J. Achtemeier, "New-born Babes and Living Stones: Literal and Figurative in 1 Peter," in M.P. Horgan and P.J. Kobelski, eds., *To Touch the Text: Biblical and Related Studies in Honor of Joseph H. Fitzmyer* (New York: Crossroad/Continuum, 1988), 224. Achtemeier is also arguing with John H. Elliott, who says that the *oikos* (house, household) terminology "coordinates" the traditional metaphors 1 Peter employs; *A Home for the Homeless: A Sociological Exegesis of 1 Peter, its Situation and Strategy* (Philadelphia: Fortress, 1981), 228. Achtemeier's suggested "controlling metaphor" is a complex blend.

[39] Victor Paul Furnish, "Elect Sojourners in Christ: An Approach to the Theology of 1 Peter," *Perkins School of Theology Journal* 28 (1975): 1–11. Elliott judges Furnish's "pilgrim motif" reading to have spiritualized away the Christian's actual social-political estrangement and thereby erased Peter's call to social engagement. Elliott, *A Home for the Homeless*, 128–129.

Conclusion: Disposition Before Reading Matters

Reading 1 Peter is a sometimes complex dance. Readers belonging to multiple reading communities will read it in more than one way. Some will read the letter as if it were not written to them. Then they will notice its 'otherness,' its foreign qualities, and perhaps step back or to the side, looking at it critically. Perhaps sometimes the reading experience might resemble the visual and perceptive shifts one undergoes upon viewing a figure-ground picture or a three-dimensional graphic that gives the viewer a sensation of actually entering the space of the picture. The frame fades, the flat dimensionality of the object collapses or telescopes, and perceptual fusion is felt.

One of the greatest gifts 21st-century readers can bring to this text is our outsider-ness. We are in a position—as cultural outsiders always are—to notice what might have been invisible, what was conventionalized, naturalized, in the moral logic and the politics of Peter's day. This study will use conceptual metaphor methods to locate and analyze such conventions. But by the same token—or the flip side of the same coin—one of the greatest gifts 1 Peter brings to us is its strangeness. If we let it touch us, our own conventions and moral logic may be called into question. Is it possible to hold all of these factors together, the strangeness and the immediacy, the sacred authority and our questions and objections? That is the challenge of the dance that is exemplary reading.

CHAPTER FIVE

METAMORAL METAPHORS: MORAL
ACCOUNTING AND AUTHORITY

> *our impartiality is kept for abstract merit and demerit, which none of us ever saw.*[1]

About Metaphors for Morality

The language 1 Peter uses to talk about morality and immorality is odd and confusing at many points. At the same time, for some readers its language—at least in English translation—is familiar. The sense of strangeness or of familiarity in readers' responses is significant; it can indicate the degree of cross- or transcultural conceptual clash readers encounter. To illustrate what is potentially strange and hard to understand, here are some examples, translated from the Greek:

> To the *exiles of the Dispersion ... sanctified* by the Spirit *to be obedient to* Jesus Christ and to be *sprinkled with his blood.* (1.2)
>
> For this reason the gospel was proclaimed even to the dead, so that, though they had been *judged* in the *flesh* as everyone is *judged*, they might live in the spirit as God does. (4.6)
>
> If you endure [pain] for doing wrong, what *credit* is that? (2.20)[2]

Although the biblically literate may assume they understand these expressions well enough, for the general reader—or even a 21st-century, university-educated North American—certain elements could raise questions. What is the meaning of 'in the flesh' and 'sanctified,' and what do they have to do with sprinkled blood? Why does the author switch from this language of blood and flesh to that of credit? How can one be 'obedient' to someone who has already died? For many readers, this will be strange language indeed. But for other readers, familiarity with the language—not its strangeness—may mask the actual foreign-

---

[1] George Eliot, *Middlemarch* (London: Penguin Classics, 1994 [1871–1872]), 408.
[2] Except where otherwise indicated, I will use the New Revised Standard Version.

ness of the concepts in play. Many modern Christians will bring to the reading extensive understanding of what modern Church communities think 'obedience to God' or 'Christ's blood' may mean, as those concepts have evolved over centuries. These readers may assume they know what is meant here; the questions raised above will not occur to them.

In either case, these expressions from 1 Peter carry with them and evoke certain patterns of thought, certain entailments about the nature of human moral life and its consequences. Linguist George Lakoff would say these expressions contain *conceptual metaphors*, and some of them are metaphors for morality that "come with built in *inference patterns*."[3]

Cognitive linguists have become interested in investigating the systematic features of such metaphorical language and inference patterns.[4] They are looking for patterns within and across languages in the ways people talk and write when they try to express ideas about good and evil, moral and immoral conduct. They find that in many languages immoral behavior is spoken of as if it were a *disease* that can *spread* and *infect* society, for example, and that in some of the same languages people talk as though they think when someone offends them they are *owed* an apology or when someone helps them, they ought to *pay back* the kindness.[5] Cognitive linguists want to understand how these linguistic expressions and inference patterns are related. I am interested in inquiry at this linguistic level, but I am more interested in using this linguistic methodology to understand the inference patterns built into

---

[3] George Lakoff discusses moral implications of built in inference patterns: "The Metaphor System for Morality" in *Conceptual Structure, Discourse, and Language*, ed. Adele E. Goldberg (Stanford, Cal.: CSLI Publications, 1996), 249. Emphasis mine. I am indebted to Prof. Lakoff's work in the cited article for providing a method of presenting data and analysis.

[4] George Lakoff is at the forefront of the research on metaphors for morality, but he has collaborated with philosopher Mark Johnson and literary scholar Mark Turner, as well as certain of his graduate students, notably Sarah Taub and Chris Klingebiel. In addition to the chapter in Goldberg, cited above (n. 2), cognitive linguistic research on Moral Accounting is reported in the following: Sarah Taub, "Moral Accounting" (UC Berkeley, unpublished ms., 1990); Chris Klingebiel, "Moral Arithmetic" (UC Berkeley, unpublished ms., 1990); Mark Johnson, *Moral Imagination: Implications of Cognitive Science for Ethics* (Chicago: University of Chicago Press, 1993); George Lakoff, *Moral Politics: What Conservatives Know that Liberals Don't* (Chicago: University of Chicago Press, 1996); and George Lakoff and Mark Johnson, *Philosophy in the Flesh* (New York: Basic Books, 1999).

[5] These are examples Lakoff has used widely. See "The Metaphor System," 249.

the moral discourse of the New Testament (NT).⁶ It is a way of getting at how the writers of the NT were thinking as they worked out ethical issues and taught people about moral behavior. It can also give us clues about what happens when modern readers encounter these texts.

With this chapter, I begin to demonstrate how certain linguistic methods for locating and understanding conceptual metaphors can be used to enhance our understanding of the moral discourse of 1 Peter. It focuses on the logic and language of one major set of moral schemes in 1 Peter, Moral Accounting, and addresses certain questions: What evidence is there that a general Moral Accounting metaphor is used in 1 Peter? Does 1 Peter simply add to the data confirming the mappings linguistic analysts have devised, or does it entail alterations, refinements or variations on those mappings? I argue that Moral Accounting figures into the discourse of 1 Peter in a number of ways, and that social-cultural variations in experiences modify the ways accounting and finance source concepts bind with various target concepts to create metaphors for morality in this text. Noticing these features also reveals points of potential misreading and skewed interpretation. Readers' depth of awareness of their own cultural constructs (the source domain construals they tend to superimpose on the text) are bound to affect interpretations. But by the same token, readers' degrees of familiarity with certain 1st-century social structures and practices—among them the slavery system, patron-client relationships, a justice model whose concern is restoration of honor and social balance, and remedies for debt centered on 'release' and 'deliverance'—influence the extent to which they are able to enter the authorial audience. To situate this analysis of 1 Peter within the larger discussion of metaphors for morality,

---

⁶ See the Excursus on Discourse in Chapter 2, above. I use a cognitive linguistics understanding of *discourse*, which attempts to correct the distortions created by the tendency in linguistics and philosophy to study features of thought and language by separating them into components (e.g., syntactic, semantic, pragmatic). Linguist Gilles Fauconnier has pointed out that these component-based approaches trap one into attempting to study the grammatical or meaning structure of expressions independently of their function in building up discourse, and independently of their use in reasoning and communication. I agree with Fauconnier when he says, "In fact, discourse configurations are highly organized and complex within wider social and cultural contexts, and the *raison d'etre* of grammatical constructions and words within them is to provide us with (imperfect) clues as to what discourse configurations to set up." Gilles Fauconnier, *Mappings in Thought and Language* (Cambridge: Cambridge University Press, 1997), 6.

I turn first to a presentation of some basic cognitivist understandings—groundedness in human bodily and primary social experience, and inferential systematicity.

The Experiential Basis of Metaphors in Moral Discourse

Systematic linguistic research into the ways people talk and think about morality is just beginning, but some results are already in. The data amassed to date leads Lakoff to theorize that metaphors for morality have their basis in certain ways people experience material or physical well-being. As he is using the term, 'well-being' is defined and constrained as follows:

> Other things being equal, you are better off if you are
> *healthy* rather than sick,
> *rich* rather than poor,
> *strong* rather than weak,
> *safe* rather than in danger,
> *cared for* rather than uncared for,
> *cared about* rather than ignored,
> *happy* rather than sad, disgusted, or in pain,
> *whole* rather than lacking,
> *beautiful* rather than ugly,
> if you are experiencing *beauty* rather than ugliness,
> if you are functioning in the *light* rather than the dark, and
> if you can stand *upright* so that you don't fall down.[7]

These are some of the everyday human experiences of well-being that get used in most if not all languages to talk about moral goodness. One will immediately have recognized that the flip side of this well-being list would be a list of ways we experience the opposite of well-being, harm in its various manifestations. It is evidence of the systematicity of metaphors for morality, Lakoff theorizes, that immoral behavior is thought about and talked about in terms of physical harm: sickness, poverty, weakness, danger, and so on.

At this point we are looking at a very basic level. At some point complicated moral norms need to be considered, and the qualification at the top of Lakoff's list—"other things being equal"—is important. For each of the items in the list, one could also locate special cases, circumstances in which these general statements would not be true, and

---

[7] Lakoff, "The Metaphor System," 250.

Lakoff is well aware of this.[8] Still, people seem to use these basic human experiences of well-being to talk about and think about moral well-being, goodness. We will want to ask whether or not this set of aspects of well-being fits the 1st-century Greek document studied here.

Linguists have also noticed that moral language goes beyond this physically or materially grounded level to a more abstract one. There are words and concepts like *virtue, justice* and *fairness* for which it is difficult to locate a simple experiential or physical basis or grounding.[9] Still, cognitive linguists notice that if they look closely they can find ways in which such abstract words and concepts are physically and experientially grounded.[10]

Moral Language and Moral Logic

Lakoff theorizes that "[metaphorical] moral schemes provide the rational skeletons for moral reasoning."[11] This means that metaphors do much more than merely illustrate or embellish rational, propositional statements that could somehow stand on their own. Metaphors, says Lakoff, "define moral ground rules" and "give structure to abstract moral thought."[12] The kinds of moral schemes Lakoff is talking about are distinct sets of concepts and expressions, grounded in certain semantic domains, each scheme carrying a logic of its own.

> There is a logic of moral strength and uprightness, of moral fiber and standing up to evil and keeping oneself from falling. There is a different logic of moral debts, moral credit, and moral bankruptcy. And a still different logic of moral purity and filth and disease. The logics

---

[8] Ibid.

[9] Joseph E. Grady points to the inadequacy of the term 'abstract.' He demonstrates that experiential bases can be located for certain "abstract" words and concepts like *happiness* and *difficulty* (which he calls *primary target concepts*) but that finding such grounding is far more difficult for words like *justice*. It is not the case that, as Lakoff had earlier theorized, conceptual metaphors always use experience or understanding from a "concrete" domain to understand and experience an "abstract" one. Joseph E. Grady, "Foundations of Meaning: Primary Metaphors and Primary Scenes" (Ph.D. diss., University of California at Berkeley, 1997).

[10] Lakoff says, "Every form of metaphorical morality has its source in experiential morality. Consequently we shall speak of abstract morality as being 'grounded' in experiential morality, that is, in the promotion of experiential well-being." Lakoff, "The Metaphor System," 251.

[11] Ibid.

[12] Ibid.

come from 'source domains'—from what we know about strength and uprightness, about debits and credits, about filth and disease.[13]

The language of moral discourse varies according to which moral scheme is being used. Expressions like "You're going to *get what's coming to you!*" and "Get your mind out of the *gutter!*" are linguistic reflections of two different metaphorical modes of thought—a financial accounting one and a purity-based mode. The same two modes of thought are expressed in the lyrics of a hymn: "Jesus *paid* it all/ all to him I *owe*./ Sin had left a *crimson stain*;/ he *washed it white as snow*."[14] Good Is Pure and Bad Is Impure. Here, these basic metaphors for morality are extended in novel fashion, so that the impurity is a 'crimson stain.' Particular properties of the source domain concepts—the way a bright red stain shows up, how hard it is to remove such stains—are mapped onto the target domain of goodness and morality. In this way, the language evokes particular understandings and ways to frame the experience of obvious and lasting moral consequences and the need for rehabilitation, for 'cleansing.' In some uses of the moral purity scheme, individuals or groups who have not undergone moral rehabilitation are therefore still impure, and potentially contaminating (though this is not *prima facie* implied in these lyrics). In the song, the Morality As Purity set of concepts is juxtaposed to, or blended with, the notion of moral debt. The implications of that scheme are distinct from the purity ones. A person who is morally 'debt-free' might then be free to 'forgive the debts' of her own moral debtors, for example. These individual transactions could have far-reaching social consequences. The assessment of the moral problem, and the solution to that problem, differs with each framing.

Cognitive linguists think metaphorical structure is operant in abstract moral discourse both at the level of language and at the level of logic, and that the two are inseparable.[15] They also find metaphorical structure at work in ordinary, everyday discourse. In fact, abstract,

---

[13] Ibid. Mark Johnson presents a somewhat different way of mapping this metaphor system in *Moral Imagination*, 44–50. He does locate a commodity transaction/legal connection within the Moral Accounting metaphor when he maps "Fair exchange/payment" onto "Justice." Ibid., 45.

[14] The lyrics continue to use these financial and purity frames: "For nothing good *have* I/Whereby Thy grace *to claim*,/ I'll *wash* my garments *white*/In the *blood* of Calv'ry's Lamb ... And now complete in Him/ My robe His *righteousness*,/ Close sheltered 'neath His side,/ I am divinely blest."

[15] Lakoff, "The Metaphor System."

technical moral discourse uses the same metaphorical structures that are found in ordinary discourse.

First Peter contains an amazing array of metaphors and the moral logic of the letter is complex and multi-layered. My goal in the rest of this chapter is to begin to characterize the systematic use of two moral schemes in 1 Peter, Moral Accounting and the Great Chain of Being. I will use cognitive metaphor methods to see what they reveal about how the logic and language of Moral Accounting and the Great Chain contributes to the moral discourse of 1 Peter.

Moral Accounting: The General Metaphor

Cognitive linguists researching language for morality in a number of languages are finding that virtually all languages conceptualize morality as well-being and that *wealth* is one way well-being is conceptualized. We could begin to diagram the metaphorical interactions this way:

Source	Target	Grounding
WEALTH →	WELL-BEING	{Experiences in which access to food, shelter, clothing, etc., correlate with financial status or property holdings.}[16]

Figure 1: Conceptual Metaphor
(WELL-BEING IS WEALTH)

Notice that wealth is the 'source domain.' What is known about concrete, actual wealth is used as a source to help people understand and talk about the more abstract concept, well-being (the 'target domain'). Cognitive linguists looking at expressions like "He has a *rich* life" and "an inheritance that is imperishable" (1 Peter 1.4) see the metaphor Well-Being Is Wealth at work.[17]

---

[16] I am indebted to Joseph E. Grady for this type of notation, which he calls a *binding table*. It is designed to show some of the ways primary metaphors can be combined and elaborated to yield the kinds of specific imagery we have seen in the examples above. Grady, "Foundations of Meaning," 67–68.

[17] See Ch 2, 81, for a definition of primary metaphor. Some of the primary metaphors that ground the more elaborate metaphors for judging and moral accounting are: Considering Is Weighing, Analyzing Is Cutting, Reasoning Is Adding and Subtracting, Knowing Is Seeing, Being In Control Is Being Above, Social Status Is Vertical Elevation, Viability Is Erectness, and Assistance Is (Physical) Support.

I have said that conceptual metaphor researchers say wealth and well-being are linked metaphorically, but I still have not explained how *morality* is connected with well-being. Cognitive linguists have found that another very general metaphor blends with the wealth and abundance metaphors to create a complex metaphor. This catalyst-metaphor has to do with how causal action and interaction are conceptualized. A set of causes or a causative agent is thought of as *giving* an effect to an affected party, as in "That chili *gave* me heartburn." Or a preschool teacher complains that his students 'gave' him a cold, as though this were a transfer of objects. For those of us interested in how moral discourse works, a fascinating aspect of this complex metaphor system begins to emerge when we notice that expressions used to talk and think about how people interact morally often include words from the monetary or marketing domains. The expression, "She *owed* me an apology and she finally *gave* it to me," implies that I have *gained* some kind of moral and social capital in the interaction.[18] This is how moral action and causality is often conceptualized, in terms of financial transaction or commodity exchange. We could diagram it in the following manner:

Source	*Target*	*Grounding*
FINANCIAL TRANSACTION	→ MORAL INTERACTION	{Experiences of gain and loss in actual monetary or marketing transactions correlate with experiences of gain and loss of moral "capital."}

Figure 2. Moral Transaction Metaphor
(MORAL INTERACTION IS FINANCIAL TRANSACTION)

The next step is where *accounting* comes in. Just as financial transactions and their consequences (*the bottom line*) can be recorded in a ledger, so people have had a set of understandings about the incremental and lasting consequences of moral interactions. In a number of languages

---

[18] 'Capital,' is a modern term, evoking modern concepts of wealth and monetary exchange. I use it here as shorthand for 'accumulated wealth' and because it is part of the vocabulary of cognitive linguistic treatments of Moral Accounting. 'Estate' may be a more apt English translation of the Greek concept here, since it carries status connotations. Other appropriate Greek vocabulary is considered below.

and cultures people use the language and inference patterns of financial accounting when they talk about moral obligations and consequences. The basic metaphor works like this:

Financial Source Domain: →   *Moral Target Domain*
FINANCIAL ACCOUNTING   MORAL ACCOUNTING

Figure 3. General Moral Accounting Metaphor
(MORAL ACCOUNTING IS FINANCIAL ACCOUNTING)

One can hear this metaphor at work in English expressions like "The President ought to be *held accountable* for the way his personal conduct has side-tracked the nation" or "Sure Sally made a mistake, but *take into account* all the good things she has done lately. Don't judge her so harshly." This very general metaphor is instantiated in a plethora of ways and can be combined with still other metaphors so that it becomes a very handy conceptual resource. Both the general metaphor and many of its spin-offs have become part of our stock of conventional conceptual metaphors, concepts that we use every day in both ordinary and formal discourse.

These kinds of metaphors for morality do not necessarily directly indicate what actions are good or bad. Instead, their influence in moral discourse is over-arching or pervasive, often in a behind-the-scenes fashion. George Lakoff calls them *metamoral* metaphors, and notes that "when combined with other metaphors, they generate moral conclusions about various kinds of behavior."[19] The question is, do the *metamoral* metaphors in 1 Peter mesh with our own, or not? Where they differ, can we yet understand the 1st-century concepts well enough to respond to them? To answer those questions will not be easy, but some answers can be found, given certain kinds of empirical evidence. The following sections of this chapter begin to consider that evidence.

Linguistic Evidence: The General Moral Accounting Metaphor in 1 Peter

Turning again to 1 Peter, consider the following expressions as evidence of the general Moral Accounting metaphor at work in this discourse. The NRSV translation is in bold print as are the Greek words potentially evoking accounting metaphors:

---

[19] George Lakoff, *Moral Politics*, 44.

(1) ὁ κατὰ τὸ πολὺ αὐτοῦ ἔλεος   ἀναγεννήσας   ἡμᾶς εἰς
He by the much of him mercy having given birth again us into

ἐλπίδα ζῶσαν
hope living

By his great *mercy* he has given us a new birth into a living hope ... (1.36).

(2)   εἰδότες   ὅτι οὐ   φθαρτοῖς   ἀργυρίῳ ἢ χρυσίῳ
Having known that not incorruptible silver or gold

     ἐλυτρώθητε   ἐκ τῆς ματαίας ὑμῶν ἀναστροφῆς
you were redeemed from the futile of you behavior

πατροπαραδότου
given over by fathers

You know that you were *ransomed* from the futile ways *inherited* from your ancestors, not with perishable things like silver or gold, (1.18).

(3) Ὑποτάγητε πάσῃ ἀνθρωπίνῃ   κτίσει   διὰ τὸν κύριον,
Be subject to all humanlike creation for the sake of the Master,

εἴτε   βασιλεῖ ὡς ὑπερέχοντι, εἴτε ἡγεμόσιν ὡς   δι'   αὐτοῦ
whether to king as excelling or to leaders as through him

πεμπομένοις εἰς   ἐκδίκησιν   κακοποιῶν ἔπαινον δὲ ἀγαθοποιῶν.
 being sent for bring out right of bad doers praise but doing good

For the *Lord's* sake accept the authority of every human institution, whether of the emperor as supreme, or of governors, as sent by him to *punish* those who do wrong and to praise those who do right (2.13–14).

(4) τοῦτο γὰρ χάρις εἰ   διὰ   συνείδησιν θεοῦ ὑποφέρει
    this for favor if through conscience of God endures

     τις   λύπας πάσχων ἀδίκως.
someone griefs suffering unjustly

[F]or it is *a credit to* you if, being aware of God, you endure pain while suffering unjustly (2.19).

(5) μὴ ἀποδιδόντες κακὸν   ἀντὶ   κακοῦ ἢ λοιδορίαν
    not giving back bad in place of bad or abuse

      ἀντὶ   λοιδορίας τοὐναντίον δὲ εὐλογοῦντες
in place of abuse   on the contrary but speaking well

Do not *repay* evil for evil or abuse for abuse; but, on the contrary, *repay* with a blessing (3.9).

(6) Καὶ εἰ πατέρα ἐπικαλεῖσθε τὸν ἀπροσωπολήμπτως
    And if father you call on the not receiving face

κρίνοντα   κατὰ   τὸ ἑκάστου ἔργον, ἐν φόβῳ τὸν τῆς
one judging according to the of each work in fear the of the

παροικίας ὑμῶν χρόνον ἀναστράφητε
exile   of you   time   behave

If you invoke as Father the one who *judges* all people impartially *according to* their deeds, live in reverent fear during the time of your exile (1.17).

(7) οἳ ἀποδώσουσιν   λόγον   τῷ ἑτοίμως ἔχοντι κρῖναι
    who will give back accounting to the ready one having to judge

ζῶντας καὶ νεκρούς
living and dead

But they will have to *give an accounting* to him who stands ready *to judge* the living and the dead (4.5).

These examples highlight some of the difficulties as well as the promise of this kind of study. First, there are differences between the Greek text and the English translations. While #2 contains vocabulary that relatively clearly belongs to the financial domain, the rest are not so transparently about commodities or exchange. In #4, the English (NRSV) uses 'credit' for χάρις. But does the Greek expression belong to the financial domain? Cases would have to be made that each example does belong to Moral Accounting.[20] Moreover, one intuits that there are both commonalities and differences between these expressions. The language of *ransom* from *inherited* and futile ways of living (1.18) is not the same as that of *judging* (1.17; 4.5), but are they entirely unrelated when they occur together like this? Is the 'accounting' in #7 about financial accounting or story-telling? Beyond (or underneath) the language, some readers detect logical contradictions between the basic ideas expressed. How can the same God both *ransom* and *judge* evildoers? How is it that God sends some people to *punish* wrongdoers (2.13–14) and that the same God exhorts other people (through the apostle, Peter) *not to repay* evil when it is done to them (3.9)?

With only a cursory look at examples from 1 Peter, already so many questions have arisen. To understand how these expressions fit in the general Moral Accounting system at work in 1 Peter, I propose to employ some methods linguists are developing to analyze the dif-

---

[20] The primary text is the Greek text (with its variants) of 1 Peter and the metaphor system of the Greek text is the first object of study. But Christian ethicists and educators and NT scholars also have to work with the metaphor systems of the English texts that inform the Christian community of moral discourse.

ferences and connections or coordination between metaphors. One set of methods highlights variations in expressions that indicate how semantic framing and schematization operates in a piece of discourse. These methods help analysts locate sub-categories of the general Moral Accounting metaphor. Lakoff calls the sub-categories 'moral schemes' and uses them to parse varieties of moral logic.[21] These parsing methods, though, need to be supplemented with another set of methods that will help explain the blending and networking that lend coherence when these disparate parts come together in the discourse. I turn first to some methods for detecting distinctive facets of Moral Accounting, then to the blending and networking methods.

Sub-Categories: Moral Accounting Schemes in 1 Peter

Researchers working on Moral Accounting metaphors in a number of languages have found the following sub-sets of interacting metaphors, or schemes:

- Reciprocation
- Retribution
- Restitution
- Altruism
- Bookkeeping

This is not an exhaustive list, but it is a start. The next few sections survey 1 Peter for expressions that evoke each of these schemes and analyze some of the inference patterns transferred to the moral domain from the monetary one.[22]

---

[21] Lakoff's method is a top-down flow chart, working from the general metaphor, Moral Accounting, to the more specific sub-categories. Actual analysis of written discourse, however, usually works from sub-categories to larger ones. That is, one notices specific expressions and metaphors and then the connections between them.

"Scheme," "schema" and "frame" are often used interchangeably in the linguistic literature. Lakoff and Turner define "schema" as "knowledge structured in ... a skeletal form" and point to the conventionalized, automatic, and even unconscious use of such schemas as *journey*; George Lakoff and Mark Turner, *More than Cool Reason: A Field Guide to Poetic Metaphor* (Chicago: University of Chicago Press, 1989), 61–62. See also Gilles Fauconnier and Eve Sweetser, *Spaces, Worlds, and Grammar* (Chicago: University of Chicago Press, 1996), 5–6, where "frames" are defined as "structured understandings of the way aspects of the world functions." See also Chapter 2, above.

[22] Among the moral schemes Lakoff and Johnson list in *Philosophy in the Flesh* are: reciprocation, retribution, revenge, restitution, altruism, karma, 'turning the other

Reciprocation and Retribution

"One good turn *deserves* another."[23] That idea of *deserving* something is the basic concept operant in one Moral Accounting scheme. Lakoff offers examples from everyday speech in English: "If you do something good for me, then I 'owe' you something; I am 'in your debt.' When I do something equally good for you, we are even, and the moral books are balanced."[24] When people use these kinds of expressions, moral interaction is being conceptualized as though it were about *giving* something of positive value. By the same token, in this moral scheme immoral action towards another is either *taking away* someone else's moral capital or is *giving* something of negative value. Moral reciprocation is conceptualized using monetary or property-related concepts.

But beyond the borrowing of language, what is more interesting is that a whole set of inferences can be borrowed from the structure of the financial domain and applied to the moral domain.[25] This scheme carries several such entailments. Just as financial debts have to be paid, so in the moral domain one is required to pay one's moral debts. This imperative can have the positive effect of generating responsible behavior in a social system. But the social down-side of the logic of this scheme is that the sense of indebtedness can accrue in a negative sense as well: one *bad* turn *deserves* another. Cycles of revenge and retribution rely on the legitimating power of this logic. Notice, then, how Peter uses this particular moral scheme as he exhorts his readers:

> Do not *repay* (ἀποδιδόντες) *evil for evil* or *abuse for abuse*; but, on the contrary, *repay with a blessing. It is for this that you were called—that you might inherit a blessing* (εὐλογίαν κληρονομήσητε). (3.9)

---

cheek,' justice as 'fairness', and rights as moral I.O.U.'s. In *Moral Politics*, Lakoff calls "reward and punishment" another 'basic moral schema.'

[23] Mark Johnson sees this English expression as an instantiation of a related metaphor, Moral Balance Is Balance of Transactions. *Moral Imagination*, 46.

[24] Lakoff, "The Metaphor System," 253. See also the analysis of "turn the other cheek" in Taub, "Moral Accounting."

[25] Accounting practices in the 1st century were not, of course, identical to those used today, and the details of mappings will potentially vary accordingly. But at the generic level—where most metaphorical work happens—the basic features are not that different; even in computerized spreadsheet software, records are kept (now more meticulously than ever), debits and credits are recorded, and someone audits the "books."

Peter is asking his readers to notice the way they have been thinking—in terms of wrongs done to one *deserving payback*—and to choose to change the way they think. He is exhorting them to eschew their rights as holders of moral capital, especially with regard to the down-side: One bad turn may deserve another, and if one person has wronged another, the wrongdoer may be in moral debt to the person he has wronged. But the injured party does not have to cash in that claim. One can choose a different logic, a logic that has the effect of undermining the revenge-cycle. It is a logic grounded in one's trust that in the higher, nobler economy of God's household, those who belong to the Father are assured of the inheritance and blessing coming to them, and can therefore afford to absorb the temporary, surface-level setbacks of petty insult. Even more, they can afford to display their honor by responding to insult with blessing, rather than in kind.[26]

The language of material reciprocation is still used in moral discourse to talk about moral obligation.[27] But in 1st-century Palestine and Asia Minor, the notions of reciprocation and retribution were powerful and complicated social constructs. The moral arithmetic at work in retributive action had the force of moral duty and principle behind it: To let someone 'get away with' harming another (dishonoring) would be to renege on one's responsibility to maintain the proper balance, the moral and social balance, of the group. There was a sense of social obligation to maintain a carefully delineated balance of honor and deserts, rooted in an assumed social hierarchy. It is important not to over-simplify a social system that was complex, and metaphor study cannot explain all the details involved, but it can help us locate the use of the social and moral logic of retribution and revenge in moral discourse and parse it.

---

[26] Regarding honor-shame social structures, see: J.G. Peristiany, ed., *Honour and Shame: The Values of Mediterranean Society*, The Nature of Human Society Series (Chicago: University of Chicago Press, 1966; London: Weidenfeld and Nicolson, Midway Reprint, 1974); and David D. Gilmore, ed., *Honor and Shame and the Unity of the Mediterranean*, A Special Publication of the American Anthropological Association, 22 (Washington: American Anthropological Association, 1987).

[27] See Mark Johnson, *Moral Imagination*, 47, for examples.

Restitution

What a wrong-doer *owes* can be made up for in very specific ways. A thief can literally pay back what he took by returning the stolen items or by working off his debts. The notion of compensating for what has been taken away in *moral* capital operates in the logic and in the expressions of moral discourse around other kinds of wrongdoing as well.[28] One can see it operating in Peter's moral exhortation:

(a) Love cancels (καλύπτει: *covers*) a multitude of wrongs. (4.8)
(b) But let none of you *suffer* (πάσχω) as a murderer, a thief, a criminal, or even as a mischief maker (ἀλλοτριεπίσκοπος). (4.15)

Peter's advice with regard to this part of the Moral Accounting system seems to be both positive and preventative. In (a), the positive, debt-canceling value of good actions is evoked. 'Love' here takes the form of certain kinds of good action and honorable behavior: "Be hospitable to one another without complaint ... serve one another ... speak as one speaking the very words of God" (4.9–10). These kinds of actions, moral goods, will 'cover' or cancel moral debts, sins. In (b) it is as if Peter were saying, Do not even get in the position of needing to make restitution for these kinds of moral offenses. Notice, too, that the scheme can operate without the presence of obvious financial or marketing language. In 1 Peter, a major variation within this scheme is the notion that *payment* (source domain concept) is sometimes related to *suffering* (target domain concept) for wrongdoing (see 2.21–24); when that is the case, Suffering Is Payment. While it is beyond the scope of this study to cover all that is being said about the connections between suffering and morality in the letter, any further research on the question would do well to attend to the metaphorical mappings and entailments involved.

Altruism

By the rules of basic moral arithmetic, one good turn deserves another, but beneficence adds another factor to the equation. If someone has done something good for me, he has given me something of positive value and I am in his debt. The altruistic moment comes when I choose

---

[28] The term 'literal' here means concrete, experiential, rather than metaphorical, but does *not* imply the old 'literal-figurative' split. Regarding cognitive linguistic understandings of 'literal' as opposed to 'metaphorical,' see Chapter 2.

to cancel the debt. If I have given freely, I do not expect the favor to be returned. There is, however, a twist or a positive spin for the benefactor, because this transaction allows the beneficent one to accrue *moral* credit.

The NT abounds with examples of the use of the altruism scheme. Recall one negative moral stereotype from the Gospel of Matthew—the kind of benefactor who toots his own horn, the 'hypocrite' who likes everyone to notice his generosity (Matt 6.2–4). Jesus exposes the selfish motives underneath false altruism, saying, "they have *received* their *reward in full.*" The result of self-serving, hypocritical giving is that instead of building up moral credit, one acquires serious moral debt. In the Matthew example, it is the lack of earthly reward which builds up credit in heaven.

In 1 Peter, it is God who is the ultimate altruist; he is the one who cancels moral debts and rewards altruistic actions. The gift of ransom (release from patterns of immoral behavior 'futile ways') by God the Father through Jesus' suffering, death (Suffering Is Payment), and resurrection amounts to *mercy* (ἔλεος) that is not repayable and for which Christians owe a (metaphorical) debt of gratitude. Then as now, ransom involved an exchange of goods, as the English expression, 'ransom payment,' suggests.

The Petrine language that evokes the altruism metaphor scheme—and aids in the recognition of a commodity transaction / financial source domain factor—is the language of *mercy* (ἔλεος 1.3; ἐλεέω 2.10) and of the Father who is 'the God of all *grace*' (πάσης χάριτος < χάρις, '[material] gift') who 'will himself restore, support, strengthen, and establish' the believers (5.10).[29] All of this he gives, not expecting payment in kind.

When Peter speaks of mercy that forms a people into God's own people (2.10), he may evoke for some readers the traditional Jewish notion of God's *hesed*, his steadfast love, sometimes translated ἔλεος in the Septuagint (LXX), and translated 'steadfast love' (RSV), 'loyalty' (NEB), 'mercy' (KJV) in English. *Hesed* is rooted in deep, abiding

---

[29] Regarding financial or commodity associations in usages of ἐλεέω see Walter Bauer, *A Greek-English Lexicon of the New Testament and other Early Christian Literature*, 2d ed., tr. and ed. by William F. Arndt, F. Wilbur Gingrich, and Frederick W. Danker (Chicago: Chicago University Press, 1979), 249. Also see "ἐλεέω," in *A Greek-English Lexicon*, compiled by H.G. Liddell and Robert Scott, Rev. ed. (Oxford: Clarendon Press; New York: Oxford University Press, 1996), 531.

relationship, and is not directly concerned with financial transaction or status, but concrete actions that display *hesed* include intervention for debtors.[30]

Matters become even more complicated when we realize that in the 1st-century, altruism is wrapped up in social practices of patron—client relationships, where reciprocity and balance were of utmost importance. But in 1 Peter, God does not expect payment in kind.[31] God does not expect to be repaid, because this is impossible. An important set of reciprocal actions are appropriate responses, however, in the form of honor and service (1 Peter 2.9–12).

Related 1st-century Schemes: Debt Slavery and Ransom

Lakoff and Johnson (and Taub and Klingebiel) were working with modern languages and cultures when they compiled their lists of variations on the general Moral Accounting metaphor. Since in 1 Peter we are looking at a 1st-century *koine* Greek document, it is perhaps not surprising that the 20th/21st-century moral scheme list needs to be modified in the light of older data. In fact, it should be more surprising that there is such relatively easy understanding across these languages and cultures (ours and the 1st-century Palestinian, Greco-Roman) with regard to Moral Accounting. The variations are grounded in different basic social experiences, everyday experiences of wealth and poverty or indebtedness.

Debt Slavery Frame

In Greco-Roman culture, as in most modern ones, it would be assumed that, other things being equal, it is better to be *free* rather than en-

---

[30] In the subsection on *hesed* in her article on "Love (OT)," Katharine D. Sakenfeld surveys the range of OT usages and identifies central case components: "critical situational need, unique opportunity to assist, and freedom of decision" [on the part of the giver]. She also notes the tight connection of many usages of *hesed* with issues of communal justice and judgment. *Anchor Bible Dictionary*, 4 ed. David Noel Freedman, et al. (New York: Doubleday, 1992): 377–380.

[31] On patron-client social dynamics, see Richard P. Saller, *Personal Patronage Under the Early Empire* (Cambridge; New York: Cambridge University Press, 2002), and Andrew Wallace-Hadrill, ed., *Patronage in Ancient Society* (London; New York: Routledge, 1989).

slaved.[32] This, then, should be added to the list of aspects of well-being: Well-being Is Freedom. A lot of metaphors for morality in the NT—and 1 Peter is no exception—are grounded in the common experiences of slavery at that time. Slavery was common; perhaps fully twenty percent of the population of republican Rome, for example, was enslaved.[33] While it beyond the scope of this study even to survey the slavery systems operating in 1st-century Palestine and the larger context of the Roman Empire, it will be well to recall the kinds of circumstances that resulted in enslavement. Some were simply born into slavery; their mothers were slaves. Others were enslaved in the wake of war; they were part of what the victors "won." At least some slaves had been exposed (abandoned), as infants or young children, or were sold by their parents to pay off debts. Still others became slaves as a result of judicial action; they were sentenced to slavery. But many were 'debt slaves,' who in order to pay off their own debts, agreed to a period of servitude. Temporary enslavement to one's creditor for the purpose of working off one's debt was a legitimate and even honorable aspect of the social system.[34] I will argue that this latter category of slave provides significant source domain material for the Moral Accounting system in 1 Peter. The debt slavery system was as much a given in the 1st-century Greco-Roman context as our system of buying on credit with little plastic cards is for us. As such, it provided a set of conventional social roles and relations—a stock frame—from which people drew as they thought about and talked about moral behavior and its consequences.

In 1 Peter, these widespread cultural experiences around slavery of various sorts operate at both the literal level—in the everyday experi-

---

[32] The qualification "other things being equal" is important here. Some slaves enjoyed higher status and general well-being than some "free" people.

[33] Everett Ferguson, *Backgrounds of Early Christianity*, 2d ed. (Grand Rapids: Eerdmans, 1993), 56.

[34] Regarding the complexities and ambiguities of slavery in Greco-Roman society: Scott S. Bartchy, "Slave, Slavery," *Dictionary of the Later New Testament and Its Developments*, ed. Ralph P. Martin and Peter H. Davids (Downer's Grove, Ill.: InterVarsity, 1997): 1098–102; M.A. Dandamayev, "Slavery (Ancient Near East) (Old Testament)," *Anchor Bible Dictionary* 6:58–65; Moses I. Finley, *Ancient Slavery and Modern Ideology* (New York: Viking, 1980); Keith Hopkins, *Conquerors and Slaves* (New York: Cambridge University Press, 1978). For evidence of education among slaves in the Greco-Roman period see Suetonius *Vit.* 6.2.3., and Pliny, *Letters and Panegyricus*. 2 vols, The Loeb Classical Library (Cambridge Mass: Harvard University Press, 1969): 8.1. and Plutarch, *Plutarch's Lives*, tr. Bernadotte Perrin, The Loeb Classical Library (Cambridge, Mass.: Harvard University Press, 1914–1926): 17.3. See also William V. Harris, *Ancient Literacy* (Cambridge, Mass.: Harvard University Press, 1989), 255–259.

ence of the people Peter is addressing—and metaphorically. Peter writes to literal slaves (οἰκέται) and actual slave-holders, masters (δεσπόταις). (2.18–25) But metaphorical usage is evident when Peter enjoins his readers to think of themselves *as* 'servants,' or more accurately, 'slaves' of God (ὡς θεοῦ δοῦλοι):

> As *servants* of God, live as *free people*, yet do not use your *freedom* as a pretext for evil. (2.16)

These slaves are not necessarily 'debt slaves.' But notice that even when Peter addresses literal slaves, advising them to endure harsh treatment, he moves into metaphorical territory when he uses a Moral Accounting metaphor:

> For it is a *credit* (γὰρ χάρις) to you if, being aware of God, you endure pain while suffering unjustly. If you endure when you are beaten for doing wrong, what *credit* (γάρ κλέος) is that? (2.19–20a)

Here certain words are potential triggers for the financial domain, and therefore perhaps evoke *debt* slavery. That is, literal slaves who had no hope of paying off their debt and gaining release might not be concerned with accruing 'credit' with their masters. Moreover, to what kind of account is this unjust suffering and endurance being credited? Actual debt-slaves do not accrue actual credit on their accounts with their creditors for enduring harsh treatment.[35] That is, their enslaved state itself does pay a literal debt, but a beating will not lessen their literal owners' degree of ownership. Suffering literal pain does not accrue literal credit leading to actual freedom from servitude. Instead, Peter is offering actual slaves an alternative way of thinking about the moral significance of their plight. He asks them to consider someone besides their literal masters to be their (metaphorical) real Master, and to live accordingly.[36] If they are *slaves* of God (2.16), if God fills the *master* role in the slavery frame, or if Jesus is Lord (κύριος, 'Master'), then their everyday lives as literal slaves can be recast.[37]

---

[35] It is the use of certain vocabulary (χάρις) as well as the repeated reference in the letter to ransom or deliverance (λύτρωσις), that leads me to frame the slavery here as debt-slavery.

[36] See the other metaphorical uses of slave in 1 Peter 4.10–11; 5.6.

[37] Variations on the slavery scheme are superimposed upon each other or blended in 1 Peter. In 1 Peter 2.21–24, the *suffering* slot is filled by Jesus. It is preeminently as a suffering one, serving God above all others, that Jesus becomes the model, the *typos*, that Christian servants are encouraged to follow. They are invited to imagine putting themselves in the suffering servant slot, and thinking about their plight accordingly. But

The metaphor breaks down when it is run to its logical conclusion; Peter is *not* advising his readers to endure unjust treatment in order to accrue so much credit on their divine accounts that they *earn* their freedom from God or from Jesus. That scenario would be contrary to the deeper logic of the grand narrative to which this discourse continually refers, and we will have more to say about this as the analysis proceeds.

A lot is going on in this example, but the most important point here is that in 1 Peter even Christians who are not actually slaves are invited to think of themselves *as* slaves, and to conceptualize whatever suffering they are undergoing in that light. A literal debt-slave's suffering takes on a different value in the present as it is reframed in view of Jesus' suffering, resurrection, and future glory. But so does the suffering of people who are not literal slaves, but are now thinking of themselves *as* 'servants,' *slaves of God*. The metaphor can be named:

Christians Are Slaves of God

Χριστιανός ← Θεοῦ δοῦλοι
"Christians"   of God slaves

(4.16)   (2.16)

As the standard slavery frame is altered, the logic, the inferential structure, of the source domain is also transferred to the target domain, the domain of morals and moral accountability. The next section considers some of the ways that inferential structure is altered.

Variation on the Scheme of Debt Slavery: Ransom or Deliverance

Once readers become aware that sometimes in 1 Peter 'slave' can be metaphorical, they may infer a certain moral accounting logic. Readers familiar with versions of the concept of ransom from slavery to sin that are clearly operant in the Gospels (e.g., John 8) and in Paul's writings are apt to use that knowledge as source input and assume they know what Peter means. Here is my sketch of one potential scenario readers might blend with 1 Peter as they read:

---

filling the *slave* slot with *the individual Christian believer* alters the frame so that the *master* is God or Jesus.

The moral debt each individual has accrued (actual "sin" incurs metaphorical, not literal "debt") is so great that it would be impossible to work off, even by an especially long period of debt-slavery. Jesus intervenes; he is the redeemer who *ransoms* (λυτρόωμαι 1.18) the sin-debt slaves. Ransom is effected when Jesus *pays* sinners' *moral debts* by suffering on the cross (1.19; 3.18), freeing evildoers from the old master, Evil. Christians are therefore indebted to Jesus and bound to him as their new master. Slavery under this new master/lord is "freedom": freedom from enslavement to sin ("the futile ways inherited from your ancestors" 1.17) freedom from the overwhelming burden of debt too deep to pay, freedom for service to others in the name of the new master.

This scenario fits well with the basic Moral Accounting metaphor system whose contours linguists have sketched according to their analyses of modern moral discourse. Its focus is the moral status of individual moral agents, and it offers what is, at least on the surface, a plausible account of how moral debt might be dealt with—via 'payment.' Even so, it is different from the modern account in some important ways. Its unique 1st-century flavor is detected in the introjection of the notions of slavery and ransom; the individual debtor is rescued from the seemingly inevitable and interminable consequences of moral debt when someone else 'pays' for his release.

But while this construal of the moral accounting logic can make sense of some features of this discourse, it fails in significant ways to fit the contours of the 1st-century source domains in play in this Greek text. Instead, it conflates modern cultural notions with 1st-century ones, producing a confusing and ultimately incoherent collage. Modern readers' experience of individual guilt and blame-based justice systems, perhaps combined with their association of 'slavery' with American chattel slavery, and even of ransom payments in hostage situations, can be commingled with the modern doctrines of atonement to yield a picture that makes modern sense but misses much in 1 Peter. To enter the authorial audience deeply enough to pick up the nuances of the Moral Accounting system, some modern baggage needs to be shelved, at least temporarily. The trick is to become aware of the competing (modern) metaphor schemas and framings that we bring to the reading. If we are to enter the authorial audience, we must try on the 1st-century versions, let them come to the foreground.

While certain sets of modern assumptions need to be bracketed, acquisition of certain sets of 1st-century source domain knowledge can aid deeper entry into the authorial audience. The range of concepts and inferences that λυτρόωμαι—'deliverance/ ransom' might evoke must be considered. Looking at those issues will highlight the need to consider further how contextualized concepts of justice and household intersect and interact with financial accounting, with debt slavery as a nexus of this interaction. My aim in what follows is twofold: 1) to highlight the cognitive linguistic methodological tools that might yield corrective construals of the penal substitution-style scenario sketched above, and 2) to see what light cognitive methods can shed on how such misreading happens, in the first place.

λυτρόωμαι—*Ransom Reconsidered*

The 'ransom' word occurs in 1.18–19:

    εἰδότες   ὅτι οὐ   φθαρτοῖς ἀργυρίῳ ἢ χρυσίῳ
    Having known that not in corruptible silver or gold

    ἐλυτρώθητε   ἐκ τῆς ματαίας ὑμῶν ἀναστροφῆς
    you were redeemed from the futile of you behavior

    πατροπαραδότου ἀλλὰ τιμίῳ αἵματι ὡς ἀμνοῦ ἀμώμου καὶ
    given over by fathers but in valuable blood as of lamb blameless and

    ἀσπίλου Χριστοῦ
    without stain Christ

You know that you were *ransomed* from the futile ways inherited from your ancestors ... (1.18).

In addition to the language that may evoke the wealth and finance domain ('silver' and 'gold,' and 'precious'), the co-text contains another potential financial or accounting domain trigger: δι' ὑμᾶς 'on your account,' or 'for your sake' (1.20). Overlaid with these finance/wealth domain triggers are words evoking a separate domain, that of sacrificial rite or worship:

    τιμίῳ ἅματι < τίμιος + αἷμα 'precious blood' 1.19
    ἀμνοῦ < ἀμνός '(sacrificial) lamb' 1.19
    ἀμώμου < ἄμωμος 'without blemish' 1.19
    ἀσπίλου < ἄσπιλος 'without spot' 1.19

Readers understandably construe this, then, as a *payment* (in blood) for individual sinners' moral debts.[38]

---

[38] The precise meaning in 1.18 of ἐλυτρώθητε—and in particular of its relation to the sacrificial language has been a matter of debate among NT scholars. When van Unnik, for example, proposes that the Jewish proselyte ceremony is the key to correct interpretation, he is proposing that framing and running a blend that he believes

But λυτρόομαι has the potential to evoke a wider range of source concepts. Louw and Nida considered the contexts of the word's usage in the NT and assigned it to the subdomain, "Release, Set Free," in a domain they labeled, "Control, Rule."[39] Λυτρόομαι is related to λύω—'to release from control, to set free.' The other vocabulary in this subdomain includes the following words:

> λυτρωτής 'deliverer, liberator, redeemer'
> λύτρον, αςντίλυτρον 'means of release, ransom'
> ἀγοράζω, ἐξαγοράζω 'to buy; to redeem, to set free'
> ἄφεσις 'release, liberty'
> ἐλευθερία 'to be free, freedom'
> ἐλεύθερος 'free, to be free'
> ἐλευθερόω 'to set free, to release'
> καταργέομαι 'to be freed, to be released'
> ἄνεσις 'some freedom, some liberty'
> δικαιόω 'to release, to set free' especially from *moral* state or consequences

While some of the sense of this expression in 1.18–19 may be about release from 'debt'—the financial domain—the expression is embedded in a text replete with allusions to the salvation history of Israel and to the story of Jesus' life. Potentially, 'deliverance' is associated with God's liberation of his people from Egyptian bondage—the Exodus— and to Moses as *typos*, as prototypical Deliverer. It is in the light of Moses' actions on behalf of his people that Jesus' actions for the new people of God are to be interpreted. If that mental space is evoked here, the reference to 'blood,' recalls the Passover, and lamb's blood as sign of deliverance from slavery and from death itself. There is an unmistakable socio-political edge to this deliverance.[40]

Moreover, Hellenized Judaic and Greco-Roman cultural models of divine sacrifice offer readers yet more source concepts potentially feeding into the complex blends in play. But if all of this sacrificial and accounting vocabulary is being filtered through modern (19th and 20th-

---

lends coherence. But that proposal is not the only way of constructing meaning here. W.C. van Unnik, *Sparsa Collecta: The Collected Essays of W.C. van Unnik*, 2, Supplement to *Novum Testamentum* 29 (Leiden: E.J. Brill, 1980), 3–82.

[39] Johannes P. Louw and Eugene A. Nida, eds., *Greek-English Lexicon of the New Testament Based on Semantic Domains*, 2d ed. (New York: United Bible Societies, 1988, 1989) 487–489, §37.127–139.

[40] Here I agree with the argument put forward and the conclusions drawn by Mark Baker and Joel Green in *Recovering the Scandal of the Cross: Atonement in New Testament and Contemporary Contexts* (Downers Grove, Ill.: InterVarsity Press, 2000), 99–106.

century) doctrines of individual substitutionary atonement, readers will miss the unique flavor of the Petrine version of λύτρωσις 'ransom' or 'deliverance' of a *people*, and might make false inferences. Why does this matter? The danger in substitution of an individualistic, pietistic frame (or imposition of this kind of filter) is loss of the social-political ethical dimension of Peter's message. That mode of reading fails to connect Peter's discourse with the larger story it is rooted in, the story Scripture tells throughout the canon of a God who does *hesed*, shows mercy, and enacts deliverance from slavery at all levels—literal and metaphorical.

To understand some key components of how slavery blends with Moral Accounting in 1 Peter, though, input from at least two more domains needs to be considered. I turn now to an exploration of Moral Accounting connections with legal justice and the cultural model of the household.

Judgment and Moral Bookkeeping

All of these moral schemes—reciprocation, retribution, restitution, altruism, ransom/deliverance—refer to or overlap with an over-arching scheme, that of moral bookkeeping. But, as is perhaps already apparent, 'bookkeeping' and 'accounting' are misleading tags to put on all of the assessing and evaluating that seems to be going on around accounting for behavior in 1 Peter. That is at least partly because the evaluation strand is no monofilament; it draws on more than just the financial-accounting domain for its source concepts. Since other aspects of the cultural model are in play, the connections and interactions between the schemes are complex and are therefore difficult to map. In addition to input from the financial-accounting domain, evaluation and assessment source concepts are coming from at least two other domains—from 'judging' in the legal domain, and from the kind of oversight and care a father exercises over those in his household. To illustrate, consider how these conceptual metaphorical dynamics function in one of the expressions from 1 Peter: "If you invoke as *Father* the one who *judges* all people impartially *according to* their deeds, live in reverent fear during the time of your exile." (1.17; #6 above).

Καὶ εἰ πατέρα ἐπικαλεῖσθε τὸν ἀπροσωπολήμπτως
And if father you call on the not receiving face

κρίνοντα κατὰ τὸ ἑκάστου ἔργον, ἐν φόβῳ τὸν τῆς παροικίας
one judging according to the of each work in fear the of the exile

ὑμῶν χρόνον ἀναστράφητε
of you time   behave

It may be helpful to look at potential triggers in 1 Peter for the financial, legal and household domains in connection with morality, then to think about how modern readers can run the blends in 1.17. First, there is input from the financial-accounting domain. As previous Moral Accounting research leads us to expect, some of the properties and roles pertaining to financial record-keeping are indeed borrowed for the moral domain, and this can be discerned from some of the specific Greek vocabulary Peter uses, vocabulary that potentially triggers these source concepts:

Input Space 1: Finance	Greek Triggers in 1 Peter
Account ledger	λόγος, λόγον, ἀπολογία 3.15
Debt	ἁμαρτάνοντες 2.20; [ὀφειλή]
Credit	κλέος 2.20; χάρις 2.19, 20
Debtor	[χρεοφειλέτης—Luke]
Creditor	[δανιστής, τραπεζίτης]
Cancel a debt	[χαρίζομαι, ἀφίημι]
Account Reviewer	ἔχοντι κρῖναι 4.5 οἰκονόμος 4.10, 17
Accounting Event: Auditing	κρίνοντα κατὰ τὸ ἑκάστου ἔργον 1.17 ἀποδοκιμάζω 2.4; ἐποπτεύω 2.12, 3.2; ἐπίσκοπος 2.25 ἐδίκησιν κακοποιῶν ἔπαινον δὲ ἀγαθοποιῶν 2.14

In 1.17, the notion that the judge will 'evaluate according to each deed' or 'each one's deeds' evokes the kind of incremental accounting that financial bookkeeping entails. But specific parts of the same expressions can evoke legal domain concepts:

Input Space 2: Law, Justice	Greek Triggers in 1 Peter
Evidence, account	λόγος, λόγον, ἀπολογία 3.15
Legal Offense /charge	ἁμαρτία: ἁμαρτάνοντες 2.20 ἐκζτέω 1.10; ἀνομία, ἄθεσμος
Legal Offender—Defendant	κακοποιός 2.12; ἁμαρτωλός 4.18
Legal Troublemaker	ἀλλοτριεπίσκοπος 4.18 φονεύς, κλέπτης, κακοποιός 4.15
Legal Defense—evidence; claim one's legal right	ἐπικαλοῦμαι 1.17; καλῶν ἔργων 2.12
Accusing, asking for proof	αἰτέω 3.15; ἐπερώτημα 3.21
Accuser—Plaintiff?	καταλαλοῦσιν ὑμῶν ὡς κακοποιῶν 2.12 ἀλλοτριεπίσκοπος 4.15

210   CHAPTER FIVE

Accuser—Attorney?   ἀντίδικος 5.8
Judge   κρίνοντα 1.17 ἐποπτεύω 2.12, 3.2
Judgment / verdict   κρίμα 4.17
Accounting Event: Judging   κρίνω: κρίνοντα κατὰ τὸ ἑκάστου ἔργον 1.17
                            ἐποπτεύω 2.12, 3.2 ἐδίκησιν κακοποιῶν ἔπαινον
                            δὲ ἀγαθοποιῶν 2.14

Some of the vocabulary in 1.17 that evoked financial domain concepts can also evoke the legal framework, with its entailments. Note the question marks after 'plaintiff' and 'attorney,' in the chart, however. The specific cultural version of legal 'judging' in 1 Peter needs to be noticed and displayed in the mappings. Are not terms such as 'attorney,' 'plaintiff,' and 'defendant,' being imported from modern cultural experiences of legal processes in this proposed mapping chart? Some revisions are in order, but what features of 1st-century justice structures in 1 Peter need to be expressed in the charting? To answer that question, it will be best to look first at a third source domain impacting this 1st-century version of Moral Accounting, the household domain—and in particular, the roles of the household manager and the *paterfamilias*:

Input Space 3: Household   Greek Triggers
Shame   αἰσχύνομαι 4.16; δόξα 1.7, 11, 21, 24, 4.11,
                                   13, 14, 5.1, 4, 10; δοξάζω 1.8, 2.12, 4.11,
                                   16; δόκιμος; δοκιμάζω 1.7; καλός 2.12,
                                   4.10; καταλαλιά 2.1, 12; 3.16;
Honor   τιμή 1.7, 2.7, 3.7; τίμιος 1.19; τιμάω 2.17;
                                   ὑποτάσσω 2.13, 18, 3.1, 5, 22, 5.5;
                                   φοβέομαι 2.17, 3.6, 14; φόβος 1.17, 2.18,
                                   3.2, 14, 16
Family: extended household   γενεά; γένος 2.9; οἰκιακός; οἶκος 2.5, 4.17;
                                   πατρῷος; ῥίζα; σάρξ 1.24; σπέρμα;
                                   συνοικέω 3.7
Family members   ἀδελφός 5.12; ἀδελφότης 2.17, 5.9;
                                   ἄνδρος 3.7; ἀνήρ 3.1, 5, 7; αἰκός;
                                   ἀρτιγέννητος 2.2, βρέφος 2.2; γυνή 3.1, 5;
                                   7; θυγάτηρ; μάμμη; μήτηρ; σκεῦος 3.7;
                                   συγγενής; τέκνον 1.14, 3.6; υἱός 5.13;
Inherited family 'ways'   πατροπαράδοτος 1.18
Offended outsider
Outsider who offends, slanders   καταλαλέω 2.12, 3.16; κατάλαλος
Household owner, master   οἰκοδεσπότης
Household builder   οἰκοδομέω 2.5, 7

Father	πατέρα 1.17; πατήρ 1.2, 3, 17; [προπάτωρ]
Household manager/ accountant	κύριος 1.3, 25, 2.3, 13, 3.6, 12, 15; οἰκονόμος 4.10
Accounting Event: Fatherly Action to Restore Honor	κρίνοντα κατὰ τὸ ἑκάστου ἔργον 1.17 ἐποπτεύω 2.12, 3.2

If one just one slot is pulled out—οἰκονόμος, the accountant/manager in the Household frame—and mapped onto the moral domain, what are the entailments?

Source Domain: Household   Target Domain: Morality

Slot: Household manager   →   Moral Authority / Evaluator

When the accounting and management functions of the household manager are emphasized, a 'bottom line'-style Moral Accounting scenario emerges. The οἰκονόμος manages the household books and oversees the workers' accounts. He is aware of the details, the actual debits and credits accruing on each line, in each category. He must balance the books; he must guard the honor of the household.

Indeed, if one were to consider further how honor-shame cultural models might be expressed in the discourse, a different version of accounting-judging emerges. In the 1st-century household, the father's honor must be maintained, and the οἰκονόμος, the manager-accountant, is himself a servant of this *paterfamilias*. Moreover, if in an honor-shame-based culture, a judge's role is also to restore communal relational balance—honor—the inference patterns potentially differ from those in the finance domain mapping in isolation. That is, the goal of the evaluation is less likely to be assignation of guilt, focusing blame on an individual, isolated offender, and meting out punishment— features of our own cultural justice model. Instead, the just judge takes the wide view, and designs consequences for dishonorable behavior accordingly—ones that will restore harmony and balance to the group, consequences that have the potential of restoring offenders' status in the family. One can hear these honor-shame chords resonating in such Petrine expressions as:

> For the *eyes of the Lord are on* the righteous, and his *ears are open* to their prayer. But the *face of the Lord is against* those who do evil … Keep your *conscience clear*, so that, when you are maligned, those who abuse you for your good conduct in Christ may be *put to shame*. (3.12, 16b)

Could it be that in the 1st-century context, where the judge role entails assessing and presiding over maintenance of communal honor, of 'right'

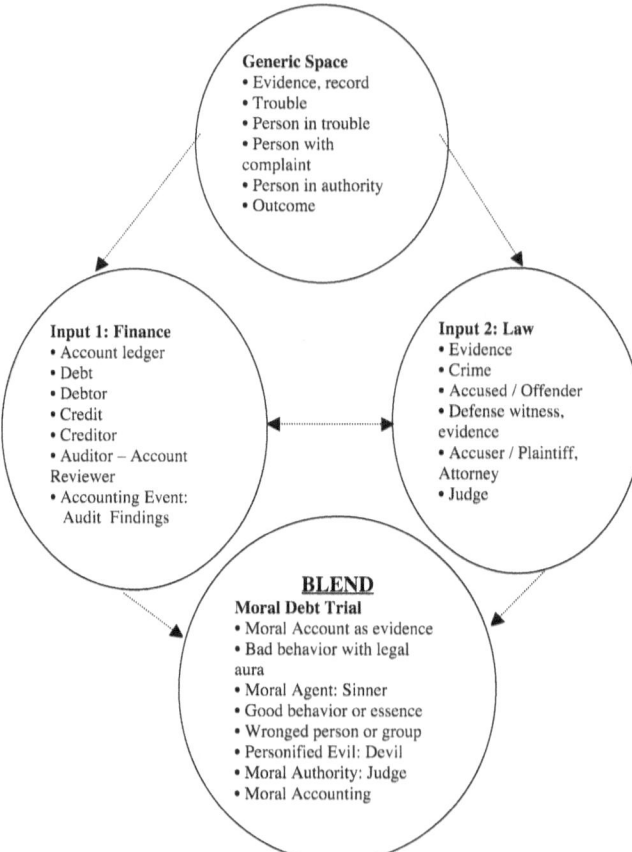

Moral debt trial blend.

Running the Blend: Bad moral behavior and character of a moral agent (individual or group) has lasting effects and liabilities. Moral debt is recorded and audited; eventually a debtor must be made to account for it. The assessment is like a financial audit with legal penalties. An evil, accusing– even slanderous– force brings charges before the ultimate moral, Authority, The Judge who reviews the Books. In 1 Peter, the final Judge and Auditor. (Overseer) is God

relations and 'balance,' the prototypical overseer/moral authority was the *paterfamilias*? In the text, the discourse repeatedly shifts from legal framing (judge) to household framing (father), creating a blended space in which these respective roles and relations are combined. These shifts and blends are especially prominent in the first two chapters of the letter, but they persist through to the end—and lend coherence, thereby, to the discourse as a whole. The resultant complex blend could be diagrammed in a number of ways; here are two Fauconnier-Turner style blend diagrams of the interactions.[41] The first shows the interactions when the legal and financial domain concepts blend in the moral domain.

Notice that there are two 'input spaces'—the financial accounting source domain material, on the one hand, and the legal account-judgment domain, on the other. Not everything that pertains to financial accounting would map onto the legal domain; in this diagram only some of the features that have potential to blend are listed. Notice, too, that there is a 'generic space,' where more generalized, abstract notions common to both input spaces are listed. The spaces hold these qualities in common, but this is not the 'blend.' The blended space is where the more interesting action happens. The blend borrows specific features from each of the input spaces and combines them in such a way that the whole is more than a sum of its parts. That is, when the blend is 'run,' novel inferences and interesting spins on the (relatively bland) input space material can pop up.

In 1 Peter, the devil is a slanderer, an accuser (from the legal domain). In fact, this blend is further elaborated by this factor. Bad behavior (and perhaps bad character) is a *caused* effect, and in this discourse, conceptual metaphors suggest at one point that a personified evil force is such a causative agent.

Next, consider what happens when certain properties, roles, relations, and knowledge from the Household domain blend with these legal and financial domain inputs. The Megablend diagram is one way to display some of the links and blends.

Now when we run the blend, the honor of the Household is at stake, and the *paterfamilias* blends with the account-overseer and the judge to produce a Moral Debt Trial blend with a distinctively 1st-century flavor.

Slots and Relations: Alternate Method

Blend diagrams display very general kinds of connections between mental spaces that are potentially opened up as one reads a text like 1 Peter. But they do not allow for detailed explication of how source

---

[41] Gilles Fauconnier and Mark Turner, *The Way We Think: Conceptual Blending and the Mind's Hidden Complexities* (New York: Basic Books, 2002).

214 CHAPTER FIVE

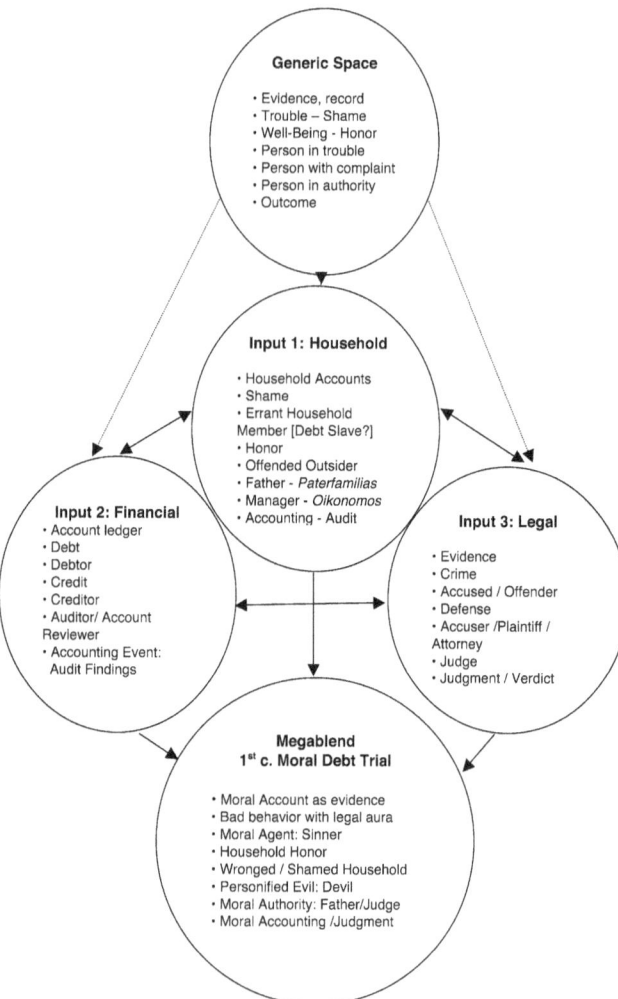

Megablend diagram: 1st Century Moral Debt Trial

domain factors influence target concepts in the moral domain. I offer the mappings in the Appendix as another way to chart out the Moral and Financial relationships discussed above. It is an adaptation of a method devised by Turner and Lakoff[42] to display the structures of schemes and to indicate the way metaphorical systems work. Four

---

[42] Lakoff and Turner, *More than Cool Reason*, 63–65.

facets of each scheme are charted: 1) slots—basic elements of a scheme that are to be filled in; 2) relations, (3) properties and (4) knowledge—in the source domain that get mapped onto relations, properties, and knowledge in the target domain. Notice in the Moral Bookkeeping Schema Charts (Appendix to Chapter Five) that the items in the slots column on the far left all have to do with bookkeeping. They are basic objects, roles, or actions involved in financial accounting, and they have nothing directly to do with ethics or morality per se. In fact, they are sometimes used in the NT without directly referring to or having bearing on any moral issue or argument. But in the metaphors that use bookkeeping to talk and think about morality, various aspects of the bookkeeping domain are mapped onto moral factors, agents, and actions (the middle column). In the right-hand column are listed examples from 1 Peter, with a few additional examples from other NT books. These are included to indicate what Greek vocabulary tends to evoke the scheme as well as to indicate the contextual adaptability of these conventions. Not every slot in the source /slot column is instantiated in 1 Peter; cognitive linguists would say these slots are "not filled." Some slots, however, are filled in more than one way. This is where the mappings get complicated and interesting. The 'Accountant' slot is a case in point. It matters very much who is doing the final auditing of the moral books—a Father God who is nurturing and merciful, or a by-the-book accountant god whose idea of how to rectify the books is punitive *quid pro quo*. It matters, additionally, that human rulers are delegated by God to keep the moral books in society, in the present—and that they in turn are ultimately accountable to God (2.14).

Charts 2 and 3 detail the way relations and properties in the source schema are mapped onto relations and properties in the target domain. Notice that when the logic of relations between debtors and their debts is mapped into the moral domain, particular ways of talking and thinking about responsibility and agency emerge. Notice, too, that the relations are keyed to culturally embedded experience. The way debtors and creditors related in the 1st-century Greco-Roman context informs and constrains the mapping here. Obviously, the more we can find out about how those relations worked—between clients and patrons, for example—the better we will understand the conceptual metaphors that use those relations as source concepts in 1st-century texts. Items listed in the properties chart (#3) work in the same way. Just as debits and credits in an actual ledger accrue incrementally, so individual deeds might be thought of as contributing to one's character or moral standing in incremental fashion. Just as a debtor must answer to the creditor and, if the debt is not paid, eventually to a judge, so those who do evil must answer to legitimate moral authorities.

In Chart 4, certain kinds of source domain knowledge maps onto the target domain so as to create conventional ways of talking and thinking about moral knowledge. Some features of the source domain concepts in this category are relatively general kinds of knowledge, and pertain in both the 1st-century cultural model and in ours. Indebtedness can be temporary now, as it could then. But again we are attempting to work with 'knowledge' of the way financial accounting actually worked in the 1st-century. Features of everyday experience and knowledge of the ways things worked in their context—like debt slavery—quite directly figure into and constrained the ways that knowledge can be used to talk about and think about moral accountability and indebtedness.

Variations on the Themes of Moral Accounting

This analysis keeps running into variations on various slots and relations and so on. Cognitive linguists would not be surprised that this is so, nor that the metaphors blend and collide in innumerable ways. But they could help us notice what some of the major options and tendencies are.

The Books and the Account Holders

There are at least two versions of the moral books. In the first version, each person has a ledger, an account book. Good and bad deeds are recorded as they happen, and in some variations this recording is constantly being done by a heavenly over-seer (3.12?). In a second version of the Moral Accounting books, there are two comprehensive books—one containing the names of the good people, and the other listing those who are evil. In 1 Peter, we may have yet another variation in play—one where the accountable subject is a group (a household, a nation, a People, or a church; 4.17).

But a basic metaphor is at work in both the individual and collective versions: *Legal* Records Are Financial Ledgers/Account Books. There is no direct, logically necessary connection between one's legal status and one's financial standing—and between those kinds of 'books' and moral standing, the moral books. Unless, of course, a person has committed financial fraud or gotten into such deep debt that—in our culture—he lands in bankruptcy court or—in the 1st century, he winds up a debt slave. Such a scenario is, then, one way financial and legal records can blend in literal, and then in metaphorical ways.

Source domain data skews mappings of the Account Holder slot, as well. If people in 1st-century Palestine and Asia Minor tended to conceptualize and experience identity in terms of group belonging rather than holding the autonomous, individuated self that is our ideal, then the preferred mappings will differ.

The Day or Time of Judgment

This variable was alluded to above, when it was noted that the account can be a running account, monitored constantly or on a regular basis, of an individual or a collective subject. In 1 Peter, regular accounting seems to be delegated to earthly authorities—governors in the social realm and elders in the church household. But Peter also uses language that evokes an apocalyptic convention of final judgment or Day of Reckoning that involves 'nations' or people groups. Is this blended with individual judgment after death?

Peter seems to hold all of these pictures—interim judgment in the present, plus ultimate judgment after death or at in an end-of-history Day, so that moral behavior has both incremental and cumulative consequences. His exhortation, moreover, is directed both to individuals and to groups of people. The judgment will begin (is beginning!) with the household of God—and the rest of the people are next! Individuals and churches ought to assess their behavior and change what needs changing. Peter's teaching is compatible with Jesus' when he taught that both individuals and nations would be judged at the end of time (Luke 13:1–5, Matt 19:28). This formative Christian teaching is in keeping, too, with Peter's (and Jesus') Jewish heritage.[43]

---

[43] See J. Gwyn Griffiths, *The Divine Verdict: A Study of Divine Judgement in the Ancient Religions* (Leiden and New York: E.J. Brill, 1991), 351.

The Offenses: Shame versus Guilt

There is more than one kind of human experience of social and legal offense, and since specific source domain properties map onto any target domain usage, it is important to pay attention to source domain variations. Perhaps the most powerful variation on the legal offense moral offense/sin mapping is the set of issues around Honor/Shame versus Guilt/Blame. The prototypical legal case in modern Western legal systems is about righting a wrong done to an individual. Cases are brought against individuals, built on evidence centered on specific harmful acts. Assignment of blame and successful prosecution of the offender leads to punitive judgment. 'Justice' is done when this blame-assignment and punishment process renders a clear verdict and the offender 'pays' the 'debt' he 'owes' to the offended individual and to society. But 1 Peter comes to us from a culture in which judgment and offenses were experienced differently. In an honor-shame based system, prototypical offenses concern disharmonious behaviors within or between people groups. Instead of being focused on specific acts, the sense of offense is more often tied to revelation of anomaly or impurity. An individual who acts contrary to group values and standards, who disrupts the status system or fails to comply with reciprocity expectations, brings shame upon himself and dishonor on the group. Appropriate sanctions in these societies tend to center on ostracism or ridicule, with the juridical process exerting pressure on offenders to conform and demonstrate their worthiness and readiness to rejoin the group. In extreme cases, only exile will remedy the situation, restore group honor. But an arbiter's goal would have been to find a way to restore honor and harmony in the social, relational system.

Words from the legal domain ('judge,' 'judgment,') are potential prompts for Western 21st-century readers of 1 Peter to map their own social-cultural experience of law and punishment onto this 1st-century text. If readers fail to notice cues that the authorial audience views judgment differently, interpretive mistakes—and, in particular, mistaken mappings of Moral Accounting metaphors—will result. In this regard, cognitive linguistic analyses and mappings of Moral Accounting based on modern, Western guilt/blame source domain experience, do not fit 1 Peter.

The Account Judges

In 1 Peter the ultimate judge of moral status and determiner of consequences is God. He is the final judge of the accounts and the account holders. But what kind of judge is God? Remember that a judge's goal, in an honor-shame scenario, is to restore harmony and honor where shame has disrupted it; to restore relational equilibrium. A good judge attends to the relational dynamics of the group or groups. In 1 Peter, it is God's all-seeing, all-knowing eye (3.12) that potentially evokes this kind of caring and very powerful judge.

It matters very much to the moral logic of this discourse which kind of judge and what kind of father properties in the Source Domain blend to create Peter's active source concept. Some evaluative, judging activity is delegated to human leaders—governors, managers, and leaders in the church—so that the 'judge' slot is actually filled in a number of ways in 1 Peter. God is the End-of-time Judge, but interim judging is also carried out by 'Gentiles' or 'nations,' masters, household managers, husbands, and the readers of the letter. The *implied* judges are readers who will take Peter's points about the significance of their actions, assess their own moral accounts, and change their behavior accordingly.

The purposes of all this moral accounting, of judgment, and even of negative consequences for bad behavior, are many. Certainly punishment is in the picture (2.14), but The Judge in 1 Peter, God the Father, "cares for you," and "will himself restore, support, strengthen, and establish" anxious Christians (5.7, 10). The overall goal of the interim judgments and punishments and of warnings about final accountability seems to be corrective nurturing towards authentic goodness, wholeness of character, in both individuals and groups, in churches, households and larger people groups (ἔθνος 'nation').

Significance of Accounting and Judgment

Deeds may be counted and assessed according to 1 Peter, but this does not necessarily imply a simple *quid pro quo* (punishment meted out for individual infractions; rewards given for each good deed). If that were the case, humanity would be caught in an endless cycle of punishment and occasional reward, inducing despair and anxiety. Instead, in 1 Peter deeds reveal the true character and moral status of the people and of their Lord (2.9). Provision is made for restoration of honor—for individuals and for people groups—under the watchful eye of the Father God whose judgment is trustworthy and fair.

Human behavior *counts;* it matters what people do to and for one another. It counts in the present. Personal well-being and societal cohesion and safety, the common good, are at stake. In 1 Peter, human behavior counts ultimately, in the future, even the future after death. People have moral obligations as individuals and as churches and as nations, and there are consequences for failure to meet those obligations.

Summary: Moral Accounting Schemes and 1 Peter

In the beginning, the following questions were raised: What evidence is there that Moral Accounting is used in 1 Peter? and Are there variations or special ways in which financial or marketing or accounting concepts and language are used in this epistle—usages that would surprise the linguists—or does 1 Peter simply add to the data supporting the working theory? In a number of ways, Moral Accounting figures into the discourse of 1 Peter, but social-cultural variations in experiences significantly modify the way accounting and finance source concepts bind with target concepts to create metaphors for morality. At least two features need to be added to the list of well-being markers: *free* rather than enslaved, and *honored* rather than dishonored. In order to understand the way Moral Accounting works in 1 Peter, it is necessary to take into account the culturally specific manner in which altruism and reciprocity are shaped by such social structures as client-patron relationships and the debt slavery system.

Moreover, while it is clearly the case that in 1 Peter it is better to be debt-free than to be indebted, and better to be free or to be a master rather than enslaved, is Wellbeing Wealth? In the senses just mentioned, at least, one could say yes. To receive a vast, 'undefiled' *inheritance* is surely to enter into well-being in 1 Peter (1.4). But caution is advisable in such cross-cultural research. If one were to attempt to name the Wellbeing Is Wealth metaphor using Greek vocabulary that most closely parallels English vocabulary, it might be something like

εὐδαιμονία ← πλούσιος
Well-being Is Wealth

But this specific vocabulary is absent from 1 Peter. That does not mean a concept like Well-being Is Wealth is missing; we have shown that a version of it is operating in the discourse.[44] Moreover, well-being is not always wealth, even in English. What words in 1 Peter evoke the notion, the *target concept* most like the one we name in English 'well-being,' and in conjunction with what *source concepts* is it found? This is a question that will be kept in mind as this study proceeds, in Chapter 6, to investigate an array of metaphors for morality in 1 Peter.

Cognitive linguists would not find it surprising that cultural variations in experience—specific features of the source domains—modify the metaphors, nor does this data undermine the basic theory of cognitive metaphor. The data does, however, call into question some of the generalizations that have been made about the inference patterns and implications of Moral Accounting metaphors. Several conventional signs of well-being are turned upside-down or are played with in 1 Peter. Researchers who are used to finding expressions that employ the 'rich, rather than poor' convention might be surprised at the alternative ways financial or material well-being figures in the moral discourse of 1 Peter. They might also be surprised at the way suffering figures into the account. Sometimes it serves as payment for evil deeds, but in other passages this is precisely not the case. Suffering is not valorized or valued intrinsically in 1 Peter, but when it is done 'in Christ' it becomes a sign of solidarity with Christ and a path to glory.

In Peter's version of the Moral Accounting scheme, suffering is not necessarily a 'payment,' a sign or consequence of bad behavior or being cursed. In this way, conventional wisdom is over-ruled. For Peter, suffering in the course of doing good can be a mark of belonging to and living in Christ, and that becomes the ultimate sign of well-being. Suffering on another's behalf can be *effective*, but it is not a *quid pro quo* payment. Peter uses the language and logic of Moral Accounting to make moral sense of the suffering of Christ and of the righteous who will follow him. He thus seeks to induct his readers into his own discourse community. Induction into that community will have specific behavioral consequences grounded in altered understandings of Moral Accounting. These understandings are framed and expressed in the metaphors Peter offers in place of then-current conventions.

---

[44] Further research on Well-being Is Wealth in the NT is called for; a range of words and phrases that may evoke the concept should be considered. In addition to εὐδαιμονία, candidates for core 'well-being' vocabulary include: εὐάρεστος, μακαρισμός,

Two additional features of Peter's spin on Moral Accounting stand out. Blending features of a nurturing father with the judge who oversees accounts and renders final verdicts yields a composite picture of judgment which carries distinctive tones of grace and merciful care. There is also a role, a slot, which is *not* part of the conventional Moral Accounting scheme in our culture: the redeemer, who ransoms. This additional slot's presence in Peter's discourse is the key to the apparent paradox of the God who both judges according to deeds and saves, forgives.

The systematic use of Moral Accounting metaphors lends coherence to the moral discourse of 1 Peter. The way Peter weaves what people know about debt and accounts and credit into what he is trying to say about morality is so tight that the elements are inseparable. That is, these conceptual metaphors are part and parcel of the moral argument, not mere embellishment and elaboration. This moral argument cannot take place without these conceptual metaphors. Noticing the details of the interplay between financial and moral concepts helps us pay attention to the socio-cultural grounding of the moral discourse. Noticing the intricacies also highlights what is odd to us: the assumptions that Peter seems to make about the legitimacy of certain social structures and practices, among them the debt slavery system, patron-client relationships, and household hierarchy. Oddities notwithstanding, however, this twenty-one-century-old document is remarkably readable and understandable. Conceptual metaphor theory says that is because we share with the writer and first readers basic human experiences of credit and debt, of ledgers and days of reckoning and because given information about the culturally specific particulars of their experiences in that domain, we can understand the connections they were making with moral concepts.

Moral Authority and the Great Chain of Being

The Moral Accounting Schema implies that there is a structure of legitimate moral authority. If there is accounting for moral action and

---

εὐφροσύνη, χαρά, καιρός, εἰρήνη, τιμή. "Wealth" vocabulary includes: γάζα, εὐπορέομαι, εὐπορία, τιμότης, οἰκία, οὐσία, πλούσιος, τὰ ἀγαθά, χρῆμα and βίος; βιοω 4.2; βίωσις. But the investigation will need to include a range of phrases and narrative descriptions, not merely these potential trigger words.

METAMORAL METAPHORS: MORAL ACCOUNTING AND AUTHORITY 223

inaction, who has the right—and the power—to do that accounting? This section considers the role of conceptual metaphor in the moral authority structure with which 1 Peter works.

Literal Authority

Sometimes the moral discourse of 1 Peter refers to actual authority figures. Various hierarchical structures of the 1st-century Roman Empire are in evidence—actual hierarchy both at the level of imperial government as it impacts the everyday lives of people in outlying provinces of Asia Minor and at the level of the ordinary household. Here are four examples.

1) Emperor βασιλεύς (2.13) and

2) Governors ἡγεμόνος—*hegemonos* (2.14):

Ὑποτάγητε πάσῃ ἀνθρωπίνῃ κτίσει διὰ τὸν κύριον, εἴτε
Be subject to all human-like creatures through the master, whether

βασιλεῖ ὡς ὑπερέχοντι, εἴτε ἡγεμόσιν ...
to king as excelling or to governors/ leaders ...

NRSV: For the Lord's sake accept the authority of every human institution, whether of the emperor as supreme, or of governors ...

3) Husbands ἄνδρες (3.7):

Οἱ ἄνδρες ὁμοίως, συνοικοῦντες κατὰ γνῶσιν ὡς ἀσθενεστέρῳ
The men likewise, dwelling together by knowledge as to weaker

σκεύει τῷ γυναικείῳ, ἀπονέμοντες τιμὴν ὡς καὶ συγκληρονόμοις χάριτος
pot the woman assigning value as also co-inheritors of favor

ζωῆς ...
of life

NRSV: Husbands, show consideration for your wives in your life together, paying honor to the woman as the weaker sex, since they too are also heirs of the gracious gift of life ...

4) Masters, slave owners δεσπότης (2.18):

Οἱ οἰκέται ὑποτασσόμενοι ἐν παντὶ φόβῳ τοῖς δεσπόταις,
The household servants being subject in all fear to the masters

οὐ μόνον τοῖς ἀγαθοῖς καὶ ἐπιεικέσιν ἀλλὰ καὶ τοῖς σκολιοῖς.
not only to the good and gentle but also to the crooked

NRSV: Slaves, accept the authority of your masters with all deference, not only those who are kind and gentle but also those who are harsh.

The statuses named in these examples are actual, not metaphorical, societal roles—cultural behavioral conventions. But people use conceptual metaphor to experience and understand even actual, literal social hierarchy. The governmental and household hierarchies only work if they make sense for people, and one way that seems to happen is via the primary metaphors BEING IN CONTROL IS BEING ABOVE, and SOCIAL STATUS IS VERTICAL ELEVATION (or, in shortened form, Status Is Up). That is, people use their experience of the relative physical power advantage of being above others or bigger than others to understand and legitimate social hierarchies.

Also notice that this conventional hierarchy, though it is assumed, is altered or amended in each case in 1 Peter. With respect to the governmental stratum, even the Roman emperor's authority is qualified. Ordinary Roman citizens (readers who have already been asked to imagine they are exiles or resident aliens rather than Roman citizens, 1.2) are addressed as though they had the power to accept or reject the emperor's authority! In Peter's construal of the Great Chain, Governors Are Agents of God. The Chain extends upwards, into the cosmic realm, so that even the highest human authority is beneath divine authority. Peter advises Christians in Asia Minor—in the outlying Roman provinces there—to live by certain metaphors: to consider governmental authorities as *agents* of God, sent to *punish* bad behavior and *reward* good behavior. They are advised to act, first of all, "for the sake of the Lord, Jesus."

Husbands are addressed, but only briefly in comparison to the amount of ink spent on wives, and when they are addressed they are enjoined to *pay honor* to their wives and show consideration for them, regarding them *as heirs* (!). The cultural conventions maintain sway—it is assumed that it is in the nature of women to be weaker, "the weaker sex" and that honor is one of the highest values. But the conventions are amended when wives are honored as heirs and when masters are not even addressed directly. Only by reading what is said about Jesus as Master and what is said to slaves can we, by implication, work out what role slave-holders and household masters have in Peter's authority structure.

Moral Authority

Now the analysis touches on what is the more interesting dynamic here—that 1 Peter makes metaphorical use of *social* authority structures to understand and discuss *moral* authority and responsibility. One level of metaphorical dynamic is in evidence when Peter discusses the moral authority of the emperor and of local governors. Their authority is now to be "*accepted* … for the *Lord's sake*," and they are to be thought of "*as* sent by him [the Lord] to punish those who do wrong and to praise those who do right" (2.13, 14). Reward and punishment for good and evil behavior comes sometimes in the form of governmental sanction, but in this discourse that governmental sanction has carries even higher authority—the divine. But the logic also entails that the 'lord' who 'sends' governmental agents is above even the Roman emperor. Over-arching moral authority is thus vested in Jesus the Κύριος, who delegates it to Roman governmental authorities. A complex set of blended metaphors is at work here, but the effect of this complex conceptual blending is to quickly produce a simple, clear picture of the way in which the coming (and dying and rising) of the man Jesus is thought to have radically altered the conventional Chain of Being.[45]

Κύριος *and Authority in Households*

Peter also adapts conventional cultural models of the household to frame (metaphorically) the believers' relationships to one another. Their leaders he calls 'elders,' while the rank-and-file are 'younger brothers' (5.5, 9). These expressions evoke a simple family frame—a set of understandings based on everyday experiences of family in this specific sociocultural location—so that the authority structures belonging to actual families can be used to understand and experience authority structures in the church, among the Christians as (metaphorical) brotherhood or family. [Christians Are Brothers in a Family] If Jesus is Κύριος of this household, then the very idea of 'master' is recast, is it not? While Peter is quite aware that some masters are 'crooked,' (σκολιός) in character, and that some of the readers may be suffering in such actual house-

---

[45] There is a vast literature on κύριος in the NT. Regarding its use in 1 Peter and to its Christological significance, see Paul J. Achtemeier, *1 Peter: A Commentary on First Peter*, Hermeneia (Minneapolis: Fortress Press, 1996), 141–142, 147, 227.

holds, that crooked kind of mastering is in no way condoned; instead, Jesus becomes the Master master. It is his way of bearing authority, of caring for his household, that is offered as the model for all other leading. That is, in conceptual metaphor terms, Peter proclaims Jesus the prototype of the radial category, 'Masters.' He is the central case, the 'pattern' (ὑπογραμμός 2.21). For hearers and readers of these words, there are some implications. If the prototype Master suffers and dies on behalf of those in his care in order to free them, then what ought other, lowlier (or less central) masters do? There is no directive, no overt declaration initiating a social reform program here, but the ethical implications of these conceptual metaphors are powerful, and potentially transformative.

Peter draws the family frame wide, as one would expect in the Roman context. Moreover, οἶκος—'house' (actual structure) stands for the family, the relational network (House For Family; Οἶκος For Συγγένεια). As the Household frame is employed in Peter, many, but not all, of the slots are filled. Some of the slots that play significant roles in the moral argument are given more complete treatment in Chapter 8; here I highlight the impact of household framing on the moral authority structure of the church. Here is the basic metaphor:

> Χριστιανός ← Οἶκος
> Christians   Are   a Household

In the Household cluster belong a number of additional conceptual metaphors, including the following:

> God Is a Father
> Jesus Is Master (Κύριος) of a Household
>   (Metonymy: Role For Actor)
> Church Leaders Are Overseers of Household Slaves
>   (Metonymy: Central Activity For Job)
> Christians Are Household Slaves
> Christian Are Freemen

Authority is culturally vested in the father, the *paterfamilias*, and in household managers or overseers.[46] These actual authority structures are transferred—via metaphor—first to God, and then to the church

---

[46] 'Father' evokes socio-cultural models and readers' own understanding and experience of fathers. Modern readers easily blend their own 'father' concepts into the text, but competent readers who enter the authorial audience will take their cues from Peter, whose father concepts are rooted in traditional Israelite experience, in the scriptures of these people, and in his own Hellenized Judaic contextual experience.

'elders' (who may or may not actually be older in years or higher in actual, everyday status in actual day-to-day work roles). Consider also one major extension or elaboration Peter uses: Church Leaders Are Shepherds of the flock (The Church Is a Flock of Sheep); by extension, Jesus is the Chief Shepherd.[47] OT allusions abound—to God as shepherd of the Flock Israel.[48] Peter thus schools any readers who might be Gentile converts in traditional Israelite scriptural metaphors for God.[49] How do we know this is a metaphor? There is no intrinsic relationship between shepherds or shepherding and moral authority among human beings. A few properties of shepherds—that they take care, that they lead, that they feed and protect, and that they are held responsible by the owner of the sheep, the master of the household, for what happens to the sheep—are borrowed from the sheep-herding domain and mapped onto the church domain.

The Great Chain of Being

In order to understand this moral authority structure, a reader needs to have a certain cultural model in mind—a basic, classic Western form of the Great Chain of Being. A reader could have this model "in mind" either unconsciously, as would be the case if one belonged to 1st-century Greco-Roman culture, or deliberately, as would be the case if a 21st-century, First World reader acquired the requisite knowledge about that 1st-century model in order to enter the authorial audience. This is not to deny that the Great Chain persists even in the 21st-century; in fact the model's persistence opens up one wide avenue of

---

[47] The metaphor may be (The Christian) Household Is a Flock, where Οἶκος ← Ποίμνιον.

[48] Gen. 49.24, Ps. 23; 77.20; 78.52; 79.13; 80.1; 95.7; 100.3; Ezek. 34.22; Isa. 40.11; Jer. 23.4; 31.10; 50.19; Mic. 2.12–13; Zech. 10.3.

[49] I will use the phrase 'traditional Israelite scripture' to denote the writings and tradition from which Peter Finding adequate terminology to indicate Peter's native tradition is not easy. He quotes from and alludes to passages from the Septuagint (LXX; Greek translation of certain Hebrew texts). But 'Hebrew' is a linguistic term, not a cultural one, and Peter does more than quote or allude to texts; he relies on the grand narrative, the story line, of his people. 'Judaism' has not developed in his time, nor have the writings yet been compiled into a canon. 'Old Testament' is also inappropriate, since it is a term that implies relationship to a 'new' testament that had yet to be compiled (and, in some cases, authored) by his time. draws. ∎
word?

understanding when current readers encounter 1st-century texts.⁵⁰ But current readers tend not to be aware that their cognitive modeling repertoire even includes the Great Chain (myth: we have evolved beyond it)—or to deny its power. It would be interesting to think about how differences in Great Chain models might affect the social and political, and ethical conclusions readers reach. For now, let it be said that current elaborations on the Great Chain carry crucial differences from 1st-century versions, differences this study will highlight. Since The Great Chain cultural model is a complex metaphorical set of frames (or schemas), and is the over-arching conceptual construct at work in the moral authority structure of this discourse, the next section offers a brief tour of the 1st-century Greco-Roman version.

The Basic Great Chain

In the Great Chain cultural model, everything in the cosmos has an assigned place in a hierarchy of beings. At the top of the classic Greco-Roman hierarchy are beings and forces with cosmic power—e.g., the Fates. Just below them is Zeus, the father of the gods, and the Olympic Pantheon, then semi-divine beings, human beings, animals, plants, inanimate objects.⁵¹ The hellenized monotheisms—Judaism, Christianity—adapt this model, and in early Christian thinking God is Father—θεός, 'God' and πατήρ, 'father'—albeit without a Jovian-style cohort and sans certain character qualities Zeus displays. The Judeo-Christian God is holy, not sexually profligate; the Christian version of Father God is often tender, nurturing, acting always for the well-being of humanity. God is above the angels and above human beings because his character, his most salient properties of being, are superior, higher. At each level on the (vertical) scale, a being's best, strongest (metaphorical) attributes—its *essence*—assigns its place in relation to other beings.⁵² The kinds of properties by which placement is awarded are considered 'higher' properties—ability to reason, aesthetic sensibility, and moral tenor. God is on the top by virtue of the ultimate holiness of his

---

⁵⁰ Regarding the persistence of the Great Chain in Western culture, see Lakoff and Turner, *More than Cool Reason*, 208.

⁵¹ See Lakoff and Turner, *More than Cool Reason*, 166–181 regarding basic and elaborated Great Chain models.

⁵² Regarding 'essence,' see Lakoff and Turner, Ibid., 168–169. For discussions of the connections between theories of essence in philosophical ethics and practical morality, see Lakoff and Johnson, *Philosophy in the Flesh*, 368–371, 430–432, 544.

character, his wisdom and awesome cognitive ability, as well as his power to affect the beings below him.

In practice—for example, in a discourse like 1 Peter—the notion of essences is elaborated into an informal working theory of causation. There is a set of assumptions at work, assumptions about the nature of things.[53] Lakoff and Turner use the word 'ensemble' to characterize the way The Great Chain Metaphor combines with this notion of essences or the nature of things.[54]

What is significant for this study is that an elaborated version of this basic cultural model underlies or over-arches—pervades—this moral discourse in such a systematic, conventionalized manner that, minus the Great Chain, it would be impossible to understand how metaphors for morality are at work here. As the model is elaborated, social relationships are defined, and human status constrained, via the structures of a scalar scenario. Again, the claim is not that the author consciously crafted his discourse with a Great Chain chart in hand. The shaping force of such a cultural model is so strong precisely because it is largely taken for granted; it is mostly an unconscious set of associations and relationships, part of the cultural presupposition pool. Moral Accounting and Great Chain metaphors do not so much tell people what to do as set the moral stage; they are *metamoral* metaphors. Deep ethical concepts like justice, fairness, and the notion of the fitting rely on these kinds of metaphors.[55]

It will be necessary to become aware of the way these and other *metamoral* metaphorical models shape the moral discourse of 1 Peter; accordingly, this study points to evidence of the Moral Accounting and of the Great Chain's sway—and of breaks with the conventions—in each of the 'living spaces' outlined in Chapters 6 through 8.

---

[53] Lakoff and Turner, *More than Cool Reason*, 173.
[54] Other members of the ensemble are The Maxim of Quantity (a Gricean communicative principle which says, Be only as informative as necessary) and the Generic is Specific Metaphor; see Ibid., 162, 171–180.
[55] As I mentioned near the outset, in *Moral Politics*, George Lakoff notes that "When combined with other metaphors, [metamoral metaphors] generate moral conclusions about various kinds of behavior." *Moral Politics*, 44.

Moral Implications: Macrocosm and Microcosm

Before turning to that survey, we need to consider the notion of Macrocosm and Microcosm and its role in yet another cultural model at work in 1 Peter, Honor and Shame.[56] The basic Great Chain Model describes a macrocosmic hierarchical scale. But as the model is extended, sub-hierarchies are elaborated at each level of being, so that the microcosm mirrors macrocosmic order. Animals are above plants, true enough. But among animals, the lion is king while mice are lowly; perhaps cockroaches and lice are the untouchables. The elaborated social hierarchies on the human plane mirror the order above and below.

The Macrocosm and Microcosm aspect of the model also implies that compliance with authority in a lower sphere is referenced to maintenance of correct order above. In addition, exercise of appropriate authority over those below maintains balance, right relationship, harmony. That kind of harmony is spelled 'honor' in this cultural system. In this way, certain cultural conventions about what seems to be the 'natural' order of things—what *is*– control assumptions about what *ought* to be, how beings at each level ought to behave to maintain the integrity and harmony of the system. If the shape of the good is scalar and if maintaining that shape is harmony, then well-being will result only when lower beings submit to higher ones. That is why in this sub-system a key metaphor for morality (perhaps *the* key metaphor) is Morality Is Submission or Obedience

TD: Morals		SD: Great Chain
Καλόν ἀναστροφή	←	Ὑποτάσσω
Good behavior	Is	"To Be Under," Submission[57]

If obedience in the microcosm mirrors and expresses right relationship (righteousness) to the beings above, disobedience signals gross disorder and rocks the system off-balance. Dominance and submission patterns are assumed to be part of the essential nature of the cosmos, so that to subvert the hierarchy at any level—even at the microcosmic level of one's own household—is to challenge the correctness of the macrocosmic, the cosmic order.[58] Knowing one's place and behaving

---

[56] On macrocosm and microcosm, see Ibid., 209.
[57] The metaphor is a counterfactual composite that relies on primary metaphors: STATUS IS UP; CONTROL IS UP. Also in play in this text is the notion that goodness is holiness, ἁγιασμός; see 1.15.
[58] Ibid., 210.

accordingly is the basic conventional moral program, and it is no wonder, then, that this conventional 'order' finds its primary focus in the οἶκος, the household.

Caution: beware importing inappropriate models—or missing the way the basic patterns of the models are instantiated in this particular text. I name these cultural models here and sketch their profiles so that readers are prompted to detect their traces. But it will be important to notice Peter's riffs—so that when Peter gives his advice to slaves and masters, wives and husbands, he is signaling affinity with the models but may also be offering alterations of any of these cultural templates. In this discourse the prototypical Master is Jesus and the central case Account-Judge is the Father God who watches over his household with loving concern, and the cultural models shift dramatically in the process. The ethical implications of these conceptual metaphors are powerful, and potentially transformative.

Peter's Point

By now it is apparent that Peter is answering a tacit question about the place of Jesus in this Chain of Being and by implication in the Moral Accounting and authority structures that accompany the Great Chain. If Jesus is 'Christ' and if he is 'Lord,' where does he fit in the hierarchy—and what does that imply for the status of beings below him? How does one make sense of a Christ or a Lord whose Father is God himself, but who suffered an ignominious death? How is honor to now be understood? In 1 Peter, honor and shame are being redefined, re-referenced, in light of Jesus Christ.

Summary

The moral authority structure with which 1 Peter works is framed in conceptual metaphors before it is instantiated verbally in certain image schemas and metonymies.

Certain properties of literal accountants and creditors, governors and slave masters, are transferred to the moral domain, where they are used to reason about moral authority and the nature of moral accountability. The properties and knowledge employed in the conceptual metaphors are culturally and socio-politically grounded. 1st-century experience of the connections between financial/marketing transactions and legal standing, and well as culturally specific knowledge of hierarchies in various spheres (government, household) constrain the mappings. It would be impossible to understand the moral discourse of 1 Peter without taking into account (!) the clusters of conceptual metaphors that express and constrain the way moral authority is being understood. They constitute (or reflect) conventional assumptions—the presupposition pool—of the discourse.

In Moral Accounting and the moral authority structure to which is it keyed, we now have in view some major features of the moral landscape of 1 Peter. But what are the specific behaviors and moral character traits by which all of this accounting is undertaken in 1 Peter? Chapter 6 addresses this question by displaying an array of conceptual metaphor networks that frame and focus Peter's moral teaching on the character of Jesus Christ.

CHAPTER SIX

LIVING IN CHRIST

τὴν ἀγαθὴν ἐν Χριστῷ ἀναστροφήν
your good behavior in Christ

The moral behavior that Peter declares will be accounted for and judged does not happen in a vacuum or in abstraction. In his discourse, certain living spaces open up via conceptual metaphors that elaborate, blend, and network to create a comprehensive picture. The composite picture is of a place where goodness is possible, where would-be followers of Jesus the Christ can indeed go and do as he taught and did. The moral-ethical implications of Peter's teachings in this epistle are contested and debated in biblical scholarly circles and among some Christian ethicists, and many of the debates are essentially about the status of metaphors, mappings, and blends, and the implications of the inferences each scenario evokes. From a cognitivist point of view, the metaphors display the ethos of the culture, and the moral discourse of the text is coherent to the extent that the metaphors are coherent. That is, since "the most fundamental values in a culture will be coherent with the metaphorical structure of the most fundamental concepts in the culture," paying attention to the specific metaphors by which Peter urges his readers to live should allow us to clarify the values with which he works.[1]

This chapter surveys one major metaphor system in 1 Peter, behavior 'in Christ.' This metaphor cluster constitutes a certain kind of 'living space' wherein moral (or immoral) behavior is displayed and constrained. The aim here is to show some of the ways conceptual metaphor and other mental space-blending functions shape the moral discourse of this epistle. Chapters 7 and 8 will survey four additional 'living spaces': in time; in/among the peoples, in the household, and in the body. The hope is that looking at these living-space metaphors will generate nuanced answers to two questions: How are moral issues

---

[1] George Lakoff and Mark Johnson, *Metaphors We Live By* (Chicago: Chicago University Press, 1980), 22.

defined and addressed in this letter? How can modern, 21st-century Christians engage this early exemplar of Christian moral discourse? In pursuit of answers to those questions, I turn first to Peter's fundamental framing of 'good behavior in Christ.'

Good Behavior 'in Christ'

The moral conceptual content of the discourse comes into focus at 3.16. Here Peter, still speaking of the evidence upon which interim and ultimate moral accounting and judgment takes place, uses the phrase, τὴν ἀγαθὴν ἐν Χριστῷ ἀναστροφήν—'[your] good behavior in Christ'.[2] That is, even though now the Christians are being slandered, ultimately those who are accusing them will be 'ashamed of their slander' because the truth that is being enacted in the Christians' 'good behavior in Christ' will be revealed. Interim moral accounting and judgment is being rendered, but by people who lack legitimate moral authority. But when the ultimate accounting takes place, these would-be moral authorities will be exposed as slanderers. The truth enacted in the Christian's behavior will exonerate them.

But what does 'good behavior in Christ' mean, exactly? Is the notion unique to 3.16? The phrase activates a cognitive linguist's metaphor detection radar because it makes no literal sense. Even at the time this letter was written, Jesus of Nazareth was already dead; Peter's first readers could not have literally lived *with* Jesus. Moreover, the preposition here is not μετά ('according to', or 'with') or σύν ('with'), or κατά ('according to') but ἐν ('in'). How does one person—or a group—live 'in' another person? Commentators have puzzled over the phrase for centuries, deeming it ambiguous. Funk said it "defies definite interpretation."[3] Attempts have been made to compare and

---

[2] Given the honor-shame cultural model with which the discourse works, 'moral, honorable way of life' or 'honorable behavior' may be a better translation of τὴν ἀγαθὴν ... ἀναστροφήν than 'good behavior.' Peter uses classical, stock Greek moral vocabulary for 'good': ἀγαθός.

[3] F. Blass and A. Debrunner, *A Greek Grammar of the New Testament and Other Early Christian Literature*, tr. and rev. by Robert W. Funk (Chicago and London: University of Chicago Press, 1961): 118. Paul Achtemeier correctly intuits that this is dative of sphere and concludes that "the phrase is probably best understood as signifying what the adjective 'Christian' does in English: to think and act within the sphere of the influence of Christ." Paul J. Achtemeier, *I Peter: A Commentary on First Peter*, Hermeneia (Minneapolis, Minn.: Augsburg Fortress, 1996), 236–237. Elliott rehearses

contrast Peter's usage and meanings with Paul's usage of 'in Christ' and of 'Christ in you.' More recently, William Barcley reviewed the scholarly treatment of Paul's usage of 'in Christ' and of 'Christ in you' and concluded that the majority of scholars have erroneously collapsed the terms and treated them as functionally and even conceptually equivalent.[4] Cognitive metaphor analysis will not clear up all of the ambiguities; rather, it helps explain the nature of the ambiguity and situates certain earlier analyses on firmer ground.

Various NT Uses of ἐν

First, consider the preposition ἐν. Cognitive linguistic analysis of prepositions reveals that words like English 'in' and 'with,' 'on' and 'over'— and Greek ἐν, μετά, ἐπί, ὑπέρ—are used to express schematic spatial relations.[5] Moreover, they are often used *metaphorically* to allow abstract concepts to be understood in terms of physical objects and spatial relations. For example, politicians and their parties can be 'out' of power; bell-bottoms were 'in' style, then 'out' of style (now they are back 'in' in some regions); and people fall 'in' and 'out' of love.[6]

Similarly, Greek prepositions express schematic spatial relations, and a single word like ἐν can evoke multiple image schemas. Consider the following uses of ἐν:

---

the theory of Pauline coinage of the term and asserts that "the Petrine author ... employs it as a stock phrase" that is the Christians' "self-designation," in distinction from "Christian", which was a label given them by outsiders. John H. Elliott, *1 Peter: A New Translation with Introduction and Commentary*, Anchor Bible 37B (New York: Doubleday, 2000), 632. Norbert Brox anchors an argument for Pauline influence on 1 Peter in usage of ἐν Χριστῷ: "zeigt aber ein weiteres mal das paulinische Kolarit des 1 Peter," N. Brox, *Der erste Petrus brief*, Evangelish-Katholischer Kommentar zum Neuen Testament, 21 (Zurich: Benziger Verlag; Neukirchen-Vluyn: Neukirchener Verlag, 1979), 16. Goppelt sees thematic connections in the three usages of 'in Christ' in 1 Peter, saying they "describe modally the shaping fellowship with Christ that is a central theological tenet of the letter." Leonhard Gopppelt, *A Commentary on 1 Peter*, ed. Ferdinand Hahn, tr. John E. Alsup (Grand Rapids, Mich.: Eerdmans, 1993), 245–246.

[4] William B. Barcley, *Christ in You: A Study in Paul's Theology and Ethics* (Lanham, N.Y.: Oxford University Press of America, 1999).

[5] Image schemas evoke general mental space structures like paths, containers and bounded regions. See Chapter 2.

[6] On English 'in,' see G. Lakoff and M. Johnson, *Philosophy in the Flesh: The Embodied Mind and its Challenge to Western Thought* (New York: Basic Books, 1999), 31–32.

1) κηρύσσων ἐν τῇ ἐρήμῳ τῆς Ἰουδαίας
   preaching in the desert the Judean

   in the wilderness of Judea proclaiming (Matt 3.1b)

Here ἐν refers to an actual spatial location, working with the domain of direct human experience of location in a place, a given terrain. This use of ἐν is *not* metaphorical.

2) ὑπάρχων   ἐν βασάνοις
   being, belonging in torment

   In Hades, where he was being tormented (Luke 16.23a)

Now ἐν refers to a physical and emotional state or condition, to the domains of both physical and emotional experience.

3) σπείρεται   ἐν φθορᾷ   ἐγείρεται ἐν   ἀφθαρσίᾳ
   it is sown in a state of being mortal,   it rises in a state of being immortal

   What is sown is perishable, what is raised is imperishable (1 Cor 15.42)

In this case, we have moved to an even more abstract realm of reference, to a theoretical state or condition.

4) ὅτι ἐν ἐμοὶ ὁ πατὴρ κἀγὼ ἐν τῷ πατρί
   that in me the father and I am in the father

   that the Father is in me and I am in the Father (John 10.38b)

'Ἐν here seems to be used in reference to a (theoretical) social association, or even a theological distinction. But note again that it is not clear exactly how in this case one person can be 'in' another.

5) ἔφυγεν   δὲ   Μωϋσῆς ἐν τῷ   λόγῳ   τούτῳ
   escaped, fled but Moses because of word-account this

   because of this report, Moses fled (Acts 7.29)

In this case, ἐν refers to an instrumental cause or reason—*because of* the account or report, Moses fled.[7] Similarly, in 4.16 ἐν τῷ evokes a cause or reason: '*because of* this name' you will suffer.

What do cognitive linguists make of the multiple usages of the word (grapheme) 'in' or ἐν? The word is the same in each case, but the conceptual structuring is different. In #1, the concept of ἐν simply and directly emerges from the physical experience of being in

---

[7] Zerwick translates this ἐν 'at,' saying it refers to "both occasion and cause." Max Zerwick, S.J., *A Grammatical Analysis of the Greek New Testament*, 4th ed. (Rome: Editrice Pontificio Instituto Biblio, 1993), 372.

a location, in a given terrain—from spatial experience. This is not a metaphorical concept and the usage of ἐν here is not metaphorical. Rather, it is just this sort of ordinary experience of being in a particular place that grounds other, metaphorical, usages of ἐν. Examples # 2, 3, and 4, above, are instances of the metaphorical, conceptual use of ἐν.[8] The actual physical experience of being spatially located helps us conceptualize what it is like to have a certain emotional experience, the experience of being tormented (#2), to describe the differences between being alive and being dead (#3), to think of one being's relationship to another (#4), or to express what we are intuiting about cause and effect (#5). Cognitive linguists say that we do not have five (or more) different, homophonous words, ἐν. Instead, we have one *emergent concept* 'EN, one word for that emergent concept, and multiple metaphorical concepts in which 'EN serves to partially define emotional states, theological relationships between beings, the nature of instrumentality, and so on.[9]

Ἐν in 1 Peter

To return to 1 Peter, in 3.16, ἐν is used in a way that looks most like the usage in #4, above. One way cognitive metaphor analysis explains what is happening here is to point out that ἐν Χριστῷ ('in Christ') evokes a particular kind of *image schema*, a *container schema*. The words ἐν Χριστῷ evoke this container schema (a bounded region in space), and along with it an elementary structure: there is a boundary, an inside and an outside. This basic structure is a gestalt structure; the parts make no sense without the whole.[10]

Container Schematic Logic
– If there is an 'in', then there is also an 'out' or 'outside.'
– The experience of containment typically involves protection from, or resistance to, external forces.

---

[8] Examples # 2, 3, and 4 also employ the conceptual metaphor States Are Locations.
[9] Regarding emergent metaphors and emergent concepts, see Lakoff and Johnson, *Metaphors We Live By*, 59–60.
[10] Regarding Gestalt perception and structure see Lakoff and Johnson, *Philosophy in the Flesh*, 27–28, 37, 77, 90–91, 116. Regarding container schematics and logic, see Mark Johnson, *The Body in the Mind: The Bodily Basis of Meaning, Imagination, and Reason* (Chicago: Chicago University Press, 1987), 22.

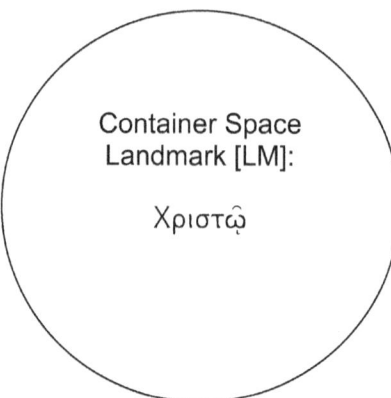

The 'in Christ' Container

- Containment limits and restricts forces within the container.
- This restraint of forces gives the contained object a relative fixity of location.
- Relative fixing of location within the container means that the contained object becomes either accessible or inaccessible to the view of some observer.
- We experience transitivity of containment: If B is in A, then whatever is in B is also in A.

Such spatial relations carry built-in rudimentary (but crucial) logic. If there is an 'in', then there is also an 'out' or 'outside.' Just as physical objects may or may not be placed in—or fit into—containers, so metaphorical objects may or may not fit 'in' the metaphorical container. Behavior may or may *not* be 'in' Christ. This container schema is conceptual; the logic of the schema is evoked from the image, and one does not have to stop (reading) and perform symbolic logical operations in order to elicit the logical entailments. As one reads the text, this conceptual schematic logic appears self-evident.

This schema carries with it several built-in constraints. Actual, physical containers have certain properties, and these may or may not be used in any given metaphorical or conceptual container schema. Consider the properties of containers such as cartons, rooms or bowls. A container can hold objects in a way that confines or protects. It can restrict motion or provide a safe space, and it might do both at once. The sides or lid of a box can hide objects—block visual perception.

Characters as Conceptual Landmarks

Fauconnier and Turner observe that narrative characters and historical figures become basic cognitive cultural instruments. A specific character from the cultural stock can be projected—moral essence intact— into a conceptual space where it serves as a 'landmark' reference, potential cognitive shorthand for particular moral qualities. In this case, the character 'Christ' is projected into the space eon opens up. When the graphemes ἐν Χριστῷ prompt for these conceptual operations, everything the reader associates with Χριστός—stories of his life, his sayings, his character, even his manner of death—is potentially put into a conceptual container.[11] The *moral* character the reader associates with Χριστός becomes a landmark that aids (or prompts for) recognition of Χριστός-like behavior on the readers' own part.

Metonymy 'in Christ'

'Christ' may metonymically stand for the Church (Christ For Church), as well. In that case, the social group, the church, is a container, conceptualized as a bounded spatial region (The Church Is a Container/Bounded Space). This is the way in which Peter uses 'in Christ' as he closes the letter:

εἰρήνη ὑμῖν πᾶσιν τοῖς ἐν Χριστῷ
Peace to you all the ones in Christ.

"Peace to all of you, those in Christ." (5.14b)

Here the collective, all those who now believe and live in reference to Christ, are grouped all together, 'in' Christ. The Greek *word* we often translate 'church,' ἐκκλησία, does not appear in 1 Peter, but the *concept* that the individuals who name the name of Christ constitute a social group, and that this group can be thought of as a kind of container, a space for living within certain boundaries, is operating throughout the letter. A stock conceptual metaphor is at work: Social Groups Are Containers. Recall that the letter began by naming the readers 'strangers' of the 'Diaspora' in a specific politico-geographical territory—Pontus, Galatia, etc. But recall, also, that the first and last

---

[11] Gilles Fauconnier and Mark Turner, *The Way We Think: Conceptual Blending and the Mind's Hidden Complexities* (New York: Basic Books, 2002), 250.

regions listed (Pontus and Bithynia) were no longer separate regions by the time this letter was composed. This address, then, implicitly calls into question the status of the authorial audience's belonging and the nature of their true identity. 1 Peter ends with a concise and dramatic declaration of the letter's core claim: the re-named, re-framed identity of the believers 'in Christ': εἰρήνη ὑμῖν πᾶσιν τοῖς ἐν Χριστῷ (5.14).

Usage of ἐν in Reference to Conduct or Behavior

In order to understand *how* ἐν Χριστῷ is working as a container schema in the letter, we have to refer to co-textual clues, particularly to other uses of ἐν with reference to a realm or sphere of conduct. From the outset—that is, beginning with the salutation—Peter declares that in the physical region and societal reality of Pontus, Galatia, Cappadocia, Asia and Bithynia, Peter's readers are 'elected transients' or 'resident aliens' ἐκλεκτοῖς παρεπιδήμοις διασπορᾶς—'to select transients of dispersion' (1.1). But even geographical terms that look literal may not be; by the time this letter was written, Pontus and Bithynia had merged. The author may be deliberately using a out-dated designation to raise readers' awareness that the provenance of the letter is unusual, potentially prompting readers to realize they must imagine, in effect, metaphorical addressees living in metaphorical space.[12]

---

[12] About the issues of provenance, Joel B. Green says, "Peter deploys a range of images to characterize his audience, to map their identity ... Among these, the one we might be tempted to read in the most literal fashion is the list of geographical locations enumerated in 1:1: 'Pontus, Galatia, Cappadocia, Asia, and Bithynia.' A straightforward reading is not without its problems, however, since ... Pontus and Bithynia had by the time of 1 Peter long been a single province, having been combined under Pompey in 63 BCE. The whole area to which Peter refers would have marked out the northern half of Asia Minor, but there is little suggestion in historical reminiscence, and even less within the letter itself, regarding the significance of this particular collocation of regions. The diversity otherwise characteristic of this part of the Empire—degree of Hellenization, latitude in natural and economic resources, and the extent of Roman administrative and military presence, for example—was well on display in these environs. Given that geography is socially defined space, it is important to push further, though, to inquire into the role of this locale (these locales) within Peter's rhetoric." Joel B. Green, "Faithful Witness in the Diaspora: The Holy Spirit and the Exiled People of God according to 1 Peter," in *The Holy Spirit and Christian Origins*, edited by Graham Stanton, Stephen Barton, and Bruce Longenecker (Grand Rapids, Mich.: Wm. B. Eerdmans; Edinburgh: T. & T. Clark), forthcoming.

The letter's odd opening sets up a question: If the addressees do not belong there, if they are 'diaspora sojourners' and 'exiles' in Asia Minor, where *do* they belong?[13] Peter essentially answers that question: ἐν Χριστῷ—'in Christ.' But that clear label or demarcation does not come until 3.16. Long before the reader reaches that point, Peter has used ἐν many times to assist in setting out image schemas for spheres or arenas of behavior. Right away, in 1.2, we see this happening:

1) ἐν ἁγιασμῷ πνεύματος εἰς ὑπακοὴν καὶ ῥαντισμὸν
in holiness of spirit for obedience and sprinkling

αἵματος Ἰησοῦ Χριστοῦ
of blood of Jesus Christ

NRSV: sanctified by the Spirit to be obedient to Jesus Christ and to be sprinkled with his blood.

Many translators render this ἐν as 'instrumental dative'—that is, they read ἐν as evoking a cause-and-effect framing—and therefore translate it with English 'by'—as in the NRSV '*by* the Holy Spirit'. But another reading is possible. Ἐν ἁγιασμῷ πνεύματος might evoke a (metaphorical, not actual) spatial sphere. When that is the image schema evoked, then the meaning is different: 'inside the container/ sphere/ realm' of (the) Holy Spirit, believers are enabled to be obedient to Jesus Christ and to be sprinkled by his blood. One way of understanding what is at stake in translation issues is just this—recognizing that words can evoke multiple framings. What we do when we translate, then, is report what the words evoke for us—and report the multiple framings evoked, when that happens.

2) λυπηθέντες ἐν ποικίλοις πειρασμοῖς
having been grieved in various pressures/suffering

NRSV: "even if now for a little while you have had to suffer various trials" (1.6)

The NRSV translation slides over or combines framings, erasing the Greek ἐν. What does ἐν evoke? Is it closer to English 'by' or 'in'? Is the picture that the various pressures and sufferings *caused* the grief or that the grief was due to having lived *in the sphere of* various pressures or suffering? In 1 Peter, one can still be 'in Christ' and be 'in suffering'—

---

[13] The NIV translation, 'strangers in the world,' introduces a framing not strictly supported by the Greek in this verse.

suffering is not a sign of moral failure or of judgment; rather it can be a sign of belonging 'in Christ.'

3) ἅγιοι ἐν πάσῃ ἀναστροφῇ γενήθητε
holy ones in all of behavior/conduct become

"become holy people in all your behavior" (1.15b)

Here is another use of ἐν with ἀναστροφῇ ('behavior', 'way of life', or 'conduct'), lending credence to the notion that with ἐν there is sometimes an evocation of a conceptual sphere or container or region in which behavior can take place.[14] The essential quality, the moral character, with which the Behavior Sphere is to be filled is holiness, Godly holiness. The behavior sphere is to be so fully of holy essence that the Christians can be called, that they become ἅγιοι, 'holy ones.'[15] As Achtemeier has observed, "'Holiness' is therefore not something one can 'achieve' by moral effort; rather it is a separation from former culture for God that entails certain behavior appropriate for this situation. Thus the command 'become holy' (ἅγιοι ... γενήθητε) means to live a life worthy of God."[16]

Peter's admonitions (3.2) to Christian wives with non-believing husbands uses similar (or identical) framing. He says that even if some of these men 'disobey the word,' they might be won over ('gained') with words—when they have noticed their wives' conduct. This conduct, or behavior, is done 'in holy/pure fear/awe'—not abject fear of their husbands, but in the awe appropriate to living in the presence of, in light of, God's presence.

---

[14] This fits with the image schema that ἀναστροπή can evoke: Behavior Is Moving Back and Forth.

[15] See Achtemeier's discussions of the 'holy' vocabulary in 1 Peter; *1 Peter*, 120–121, 135. While he is correct to cite Beare (Francis W. Beare, *The First Epistle of Peter: The Greek Text with Introduction and Notes* [3d ed.; Oxford: Blackwell, 1970] 98; cf. 168) that the word ἁγιασμός "does not necessarily contain etymologically any necessary connotation of morality," Achtemeier is also correct to point out that "the moral content [container metaphor!] is ... to be derived from the nature (κατά) of the God who has called and separated them from their former culture." Ibid., 121. Compare this insight with Mark Johnson's observation that "via metaphorical projection, social or interpersonal agreements, contracts, and obligations are treated as bounded entities" Johnson, *The Body in the Mind*, 35.

[16] Again, see Fauconnier and Turner's work on social-cultural and literary characters as basic cognitive cultural instruments that can serve as 'landmarks,' filling conceptual spaces: Gilles Fauconnier and Mark Turner, *The Way We Think*, 250. And see Chapter 8, below.

Achtemeier, *1 Peter*, 121.

4) ἐποπτεύσαντες τὴν ἐν φόβῳ ἁγνὴν ἀναστροφὴν ὑμῶν
   having observed the in fear/awe pure behavior your

   NRSV: when they see the purity and reverence of your lives (3.2)

So in 3.2 it is behavior in reverent purity that is desirable; the image schema evoked uses a complex blend—a spatial schema characterized by φόβῳ (reverent fear) and ἁγνὴν (purity) creates a conceptual space in which ἀναστροφή (behavior), can take place. Again, ἐν is the marker, a signal, for evocation of a conceptual spatial sphere. Again, a word evoking the notion of moral conduct, ἀναστροφή, is superimposed on or blended into that spatial sphere—so that a complex image schema emerges. With this example, Peter also signals that the kind of cultural separation he has in mind does not necessarily entail disengagement from non-Christian society, especially not from one's own family (husband!). Holiness modeled after the God who is present and engaged in human life—preeminently in Jesus—is a holiness that enters into life among the suffering and lowly, and is expressed in action to effect their liberation. This will become more apparent as this analysis proceeds.

In 4.19, a very different Greek word evoking the notion of moral conduct, ἀγαποποιέω—'doing/making good'—is used with ἐν:

5) ὥστε καὶ οἱ πάσχοντες κατὰ τὸ θέλημα τοῦ θεοῦ πιστῷ
   So that also those suffering by the will of God faithful

   κτίστῃ παρατιθέσθωσαν τὰς ψυχὰς αὐτῶν ἐν ἀγαθοποιΐᾳ
   creator let set along the (souls) of them in good-doing

   NRSV: Therefore, let those suffering in accordance with God's will entrust themselves to a faithful Creator, while continuing to do good. (4.19)

Here again Peter employs classic Greek moral vocabulary—ἀγαθός. But notice also that again the preposition is ἐν. What is the framing here, causation and instrumentality or spatial sphere? If Peter had wanted to indicate causation—the notion that *by* doing good the believers could secure connection to the faithful Creator—he could have used κατά. But here he uses ἐν, evoking a different meaning. Having already entrusted themselves—τὰς ψυχὰς αὐτῶν—to the will of a faithful Creator, sufferers should continue to live out their lives *in the sphere of* good-doing.

6) ἐν τῇ ἀγνοίᾳ ὑμῶν ἐπιθυμίαις
   in the not-knowing your desires

   "in your ignorant desires" (1.14b)

The emotional and physical state of being that is ἐπιθυμία—'desire' (here, 'desires,' plural) is blended with the concept of ἄγνοια ('not knowing', 'ignorance'). The blend qualifies or characterizes a conceptual, metaphorical space, ἐν—a space in which, Peter reflects, the Christians no longer live. Coherent with this picture is what he says a little further on, at 1.17–18:

> Καὶ εἰ πατέρα ἐπικαλεῖσθε τὸν ἀπροσωπολήμπτως κρίνοντα κατὰ τὸ
> And if father you call on the not receiving face one judging by the
>
> ἑκάστου ἔργον, ἐν φόβῳ τὸν τῆς παροικίας ὑμῶν χρόνον
> of each deed/work in fear/awe the of the transiency of you time
>
> ἀναστράφητε, εἰδότες ὅτι ... ἐλυτρώθητε ἐκ τῆς
> behave/conduct having known that you were redeemed from the
>
> ματαίας ὑμῶν ἀναστροφῆς πατροπαραδότου
> futile your behavior/conduct given over by fathers

> NRSV: If you invoke as Father the one who judges all people impartially according to their deeds, live in reverent fear during the time of your exile. You know that you were ransomed from the futile ways inherited from your ancestors ...

'Fear' of God, behavior 'during the time of' their sojourn (cf. 'behavior in Christ') is contrasted with the 'futile ways' of their former lives and of their ancestors, which they are 'being redeemed out of'—ἐλυτρώθητε ἐκ.

Consider, further, the much more concrete way in which Peter expresses what he means by living 'in Christ' at 2.21:

> 7) εἰς τοῦτο γὰρ ἐκλήθητε, ὅτι καὶ Χριστὸς ἔπαθεν ὑπὲρ
> into this for you were called, that also Christ suffered on behalf
>
> ὑμῶν ὑμῖν ὑπολιμπάνων ὑπογραμμόν ἵνα ἐπακολουθήσητε
> of you to you leaving behind pattern that you might follow on
>
> τοῖς ἴχνεσιν αὐτοῦ
> in the footprints of him

> NRSV: For to this you have been called, because Christ also suffered for you, leaving you an example, so that you should follow in his steps.

The preposition εἰς evokes a bounded space *into* which the reader is invited, even *called* to move, a zone whose content is χάρις ('grace, favor') from God connected with (but not strictly caused by) doing good and enduring suffering (ἀγαθοποιοῦντες καὶ πάσχοντες ὑπομενεῖτε, v. 20). Then Peter gives us the notion of Christ as a pattern to follow, and the picture of actually walking, following, in the footsteps of Christ.

To unpack the ensemble of conceptual metaphors at work in this seemingly simple sentence is a complicated task. To focus here on the aspects which evoke spatial, container schemas, and connect them with moral conduct, we note simply that in the metaphorical *expression* 'follow in his footprints' several *conceptual* metaphors are at work. If one can follow 'in' (dative: τοῖς) someone's footsteps, then A Footprint Is a Container, or, at the more primary conceptual level, A Path Is a Bounded Space. A reader needs to have the conventional conceptual metaphor Life Is a Journey in hand so that the more specific The Life of Christ Is a Journey and The Life Journey (Path) of Christ Is a Moral Pattern blends can work.

By way of contrast, consider a place where Peter makes use of the concept of a spatial sphere and a path, again connected with morally significant behavior, but where the moral content is negative, and the target domain is more abstract.

> πεπορευμένους ἐν ἀσελγείαις, ἐπιθυμίαις, οἰνοφλυγίαις, κώμοις,
> having traveled in debaucheries, in desires, drunkennesses, carousings,
>
> πότοις καὶ ἀθεμίτοις εἰδωλολατρίαις
> drinking and unlawful idol services
>
> NRSV: (You have already spent enough time in doing what the Gentiles like to do), *living in* licentiousness, passions, drunkenness, revels, carousing, and lawless idolatry. (4.3b)

Not all bounded spaces in 1 Peter are associated with the good; not all paths or journeys are good. In fact, the reader is tacitly exhorted to choose between paths, to choose to leave one for another—or at least to remember having been on that other (bad) road. The NRSV has translated πεπορευμένους, 'living in.' A rendering retaining the conceptual metaphor would be a more periphrastic one, to be sure, but I prefer to risk wordiness and put it, 'traveling down the path of.' In fact, the notion of movement along a path persists in the next sentence, where Peter uses an expression that plays with it a little:

> ἐν ᾧ ξενίζονται μὴ συντρεχόντων ὑμῶν εἰς τὴν αὐτὴν
> in which they think strange not running with you into the same
>
> τῆς ἀσωτίας ἀνάχυσιν βλασφημοῦντες
> of the dissipation pouring out insulting
>
> BH: They think it is strange that you are not running along the same paths with them any more, in that way of life that is characterized by drunkenness and being out of control—so they insult you, and in so doing, blaspheme. (4.4)

The NRSV translates this, "They are surprised that you no longer join them in the same excesses of dissipation, and so they blaspheme." But this translation obscures the conceptual metaphors at work. In the Greek, the conceptual metaphors A Path Is a Bounded Space and Life Is a Journey are blended with moral content, so that the space is filled, in this case, with Immorality Is Impurity, Lawlessness, and so on. Thus, the qualities of being 'in' and 'out' of the 'in Christ' container are given broad definition.

Coordinated Spatial Metaphors: In and Out, Into and Out of

The domains Peter urges his readers to live 'in' are coordinated, and contribute to the coherence of the large picture of Christian moral life he paints.[17] The positive zones ("live here, this way") are more clearly seen and understood in contrast to the negative zones or containers—'in the futile ways'—in which Peter urges his readers not to live. In fact, he declares them ransomed, brought *out of*, that other space.

Perhaps the clearest example, and a summary one, of this coordination of spatial metaphors where moral content is concerned is found at 2.9b:

ὅπως τὰς ἀρετὰς   ἐξαγγείλητε   τοῦ ἐκ σκότους ὑμᾶς
so that the virtues you might announce the from   dark   you

καλέσαντος εἰς τὸ θαυμαστὸν αὐτοῦ φῶς
having called into the   marvelous   of him light

NRSV: in order that you may proclaim the mighty acts of him who called you out of darkness into his marvelous light. (2.9b)

BH: [all the preceding titles, identity tags, are being transferred to you] so that you might proclaim the virtues of him who called you out of darkness into his marvelous light.

---

[17] I am indebted to Eve Sweetser for the notion of co-orientation of metaphorical mappings, and for the suggestion that Morality Is Up and In. See Eve Sweetser, "'The suburbs of your good pleasure': Cognition, culture and the bases of metaphoric structure" in G. Bradshaw, T. Bishop and M. Turner (eds.), *The Shakespearean International Yearbook, vol. 4: Shakespeare Studies Today* (Aldershot, England: Ashgate Publishing, 2004), 24–55.

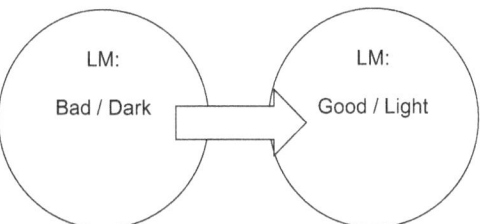

Concept: Move *out of* one space *into* another.

Where the NRSV has 'mighty acts,' the Greek is ἀρετάς (< ἀρετή), a word evoking rich classical Greek ethical associations.[18] To name some of the conceptual metaphors at work here, let us begin with ἀρετή—Morality Is (Physical) Strength. But the word also carries the more visually rooted sense of Glory or Wonder.[19] Perhaps more to the point—regarding container schemas, and the coordination of the spatial metaphors that evoke container schemas—we have here side by side an 'in' or 'into' and an 'out of'—εἰς and an ἐκ. Members of the authorial audience will know, by convention, that Good Is Bright/Good Is Light and Bad Is Dark. So even if the moral vocabulary word, ἀρετή, had not already evoked a moral flavor—but especially since it has—the light and dark vocabulary would clue us in about how to fill in the container. It tells us what the conceptual content of the container is. For that reason, one might be justified in identifying the target domain as at least having a moral component. We might name the metaphor "Taking on Christian Identity Is Moving from One Container/Bounded Space into Another," where the containers are labeled "Bad Is Dark" and "Good Is Light". So the complex blend is "Taking on Christian Identity Is Going from Dark into Light".

Particular features of 'in' and 'out,' good/in the light versus bad/in the dark behavior are specified in the rest of the discourse.[20]

---

[18] Regarding the significance of ἀρετή and ἀγαθός see Alasdair MacIntyre, *A Short History of Ethics* (New York: Collier Macmillan, 1966), 5–12, 14. 18.

[19] Bauer notes that the LXX sometimes uses ἀρετή to translate Hebrew 'glory' and 'praise;' Walter Bauer, *A Greek-English Lexicon of the New Testament and other Early Christian Literature*, 2d ed. Translated and edited by William F. Arndt, F. Wilbur Gingrich, and Frederick W. Danker. (Chicago: Chicago University Press, 1979).

[20] It is not that a negative quality is always associated with ἐκ ('out of' or 'from'). Readers are enjoined to 'love one another from/out of clean hearts' (1.22) and character is judged ἐκ τῶν καλῶν ἔργον ('from/ on good works'; 2.12). See also uses of ἐκ in

Via this re-framing, these offers of alternative schematics, Peter calls for re-thinking of the overarching framing of readers' ethical life and moral obligations. Coordinated, overlapping conceptual spatial metaphors, schemas, lend coherence to the discourse at the same time that they allow for complex nuancing. The claim here is not that there is big one container (e.g., Good Zone) evoked by each of these words but that the containers evoked are congruent or complement each other, thereby enhancing overall narrative coherence.

Summary: 'in Christ' Demonstrated; Four Coordinated Domains

To summarize: By itself, the phrase 'in Christ' is quite abstract, but by the time he uses the phrase to close the letter, Peter has described in specific detail what behavior and peace 'in Christ' looks like in the concrete. He has outlined how he thinks readers could live 'in Christ' as ordinary citizens (and non-citizens) vis-à-vis non-Christian society. With the simple phrase 'in Christ' Peter evokes the shape of the pattern connecting various pieces of moral advice and gives the pieces a depth of field they would otherwise lack. In the process, he is urging them to take on particular moral stances in their families, their church, and in their society. But these are stances that find their coherence insofar as they cohere with the character of Christ—with the life, the suffering, the death, and the resurrection of Jesus Christ.

Peter does all of this by evoking four additional overlapping conceptual spaces in which his readers live, employing four major clusters of source domain material: 1) time and events, 2) a nation or people group, 3) households, and 4) the human body. To understand how conceptual metaphors operate to create meaning in this moral discourse, attention must be paid to the ways Peter associates moral behavior and its consequences with each of these four domains. Each domain becomes, in effect, a *living space*—an arena in which one lives 'in Christ.' Accordingly, we turn next to conceptual metaphors employing the domains of time and events.

4.11, 1.3, and 1.21. Peter also uses εἰς—'into' to evoke container schemas (1.3 into 'living hope'; 1.4 into inheritance incorruptible and undefiled and unfading, kept in [ἐν] the heavens; into 'salvation' σωτηρίαν 1.5).

CHAPTER SEVEN

TIME AND EVENTS: STRUCTURED SPACE FOR MORAL LIVING

> ἐκ τῶν καλῶν ἔργων ἐποπτεύοντες δοξάσωσιν τὸν θεὸν ἐν ἡμέρᾳ ἐπισκοπῆς
>
> *so they may see your honorable deeds and glorify God when he comes to judge (2.12c)*

Behavior 'in Christ' happens in time. Subsequent sections of this chapter elucidate how Peter structures his exhortation around behavior in the *nation*, in the *household*, and in the *body*. But the placement of those pieces in the larger picture will make more sense if attention is first paid to an over-arching domain, one that permeates the rest. That domain is *time;* Peter roots Christian morality *in* time. It is on the basis of behavior *in the present time* that the *future* judgment will be made. Moreover, Peter urges his readers to change their behavior, to eschew certain behaviors patterns of the *past*, all of this in view of certain *events* he argues ought to motivate them to make these changes. That much may be obvious to observant readers even without conceptual metaphor study.

But underneath the obvious time structure of the letter lies an inferential structure, and this is much more interesting than the plain facts of verb tense changes. Peter uses concepts of time and space and motion to structure and communicate his moral exhortation. This section considers some of the complexities of the time metaphors Peter uses, focusing on what they contribute to his moral discourse. Though the time metaphor structure is complex, it is coherent. Its coherent cognitive metaphorical structure lends structure to the discourse as a whole and, in particular, to the moral exhortation of 1 Peter. I will argue that, because Peter repeatedly connects time and events with moral action and its consequences, time constitutes a morally significant *living space* that is qualified in specific ways.

Events and Time: About the Domains

I just made reference to 'the' domain of time, but we ought to be aware that 1 Peter arises from a specific language community—and this should alert us to the possibility that Peter's time concepts might not be identical with their own 21st-century, 1st-World concepts.[1] Throughout this section, then, attention will be paid to distinctive features of the time concepts employed in this 1st-century document. But I will argue that, via conceptual metaphor, 21st-century readers are able to understand what Peter is saying, even with regard to such a fundamental concept as time.

Method: How to Read for Time Concepts

What does time have to do with morality? Curiosity is aroused when the (cognitive metaphor-aware) reader notices places in the text where talk about moral accounting and judgment for good and bad behavior is found in conjunction with explicit *time* vocabulary—words like χρόνος, ἡμέρα, καιρός, αἰών. A set of questions forms: Is there some pattern here? Are time and moral accounting and behavioral exhortation connected in some coherent manner in this discourse?

In order to answer those larger questions, cognitive linguistic methodology prompts queries about patterns in the ways prepositions, adverbs, and verb tenses and moods operate in the discourse to evoke ways of thinking about time. The patterns cognitive linguists have noticed in time expressions indicate that people tend to use both metonymy and cognitive metaphor to schematize time and that these dynamics can be discerned by paying attention to certain linguistic features. The next sections outline basic features of their findings about time metonymies and metaphors before moving on to asking whether and how these properties are in play in 1 Peter.

---

[1] On variations in language communities' time concepts and mappings, see Joseph E. Grady, "Foundations of Meaning: Primary Metaphors and Primary Scenes," (Ph.D. diss., University of California, 1997), 119; and Lakoff and Johnson, *Philosophy in the Flesh*, 141, 150.

Metonymy and Definitions of Time

'Time' is such a basic set of concepts that it is difficult to define and impossible to isolate and observe experimentally in and of itself. In *Philosophy in the Flesh*, Lakoff and Johnson assert that "we define time by metonymy."[2]

> We cannot observe time itself—if time even exists as a thing-in-itself. We can only observe events and compare them. In the world, there are iterative events against which other events are compared. We define time by metonymy: successive iterations of a type of event stand for intervals of 'time.' Consequently, the basic literal properties of our concept of time are consequences of properties of events:
>
> > Time is directional and irreversible because events are directional and irreversible; events cannot 'unhappen.'
> > Time is continuous because we experience events as continuous.
> > Time is segmentable because periodic events have beginnings and ends.
> > Time can be measured because iterations of events can be counted.
>
> What we call the domain of time appears to be a conceptual domain that we use for asking certain questions about events through their comparison to other events: where they are 'located' relative to other events, how they can be measured relative to other events, and so on. What is literal and inherent about the conceptual domain of time is that it is characterized by the comparison of events ... our real experience of time is always relative to our real experience of events ... our experience of time is dependent on our embodied conceptualization of time in terms of events.[3]

The question is, how much of this is true of time concepts in the 1st-century Greco-Roman context—and how might this be detected in the 1st-century document on which this study focuses? A major task will be to discern how these metonymic features are or are not in evidence in 1 Peter.

The Metaphorization of Time

Linguists have found that, in addition to the metonymic features just mentioned, certain conceptual metaphors are frequently used for time and can be detected in their linguistic expressions. People seldom talk

---

[2] Lakoff and Johnson, *Philosophy in the Flesh*, 138.
[3] Ibid.

about time in purely temporal terms. Instead, across language groups, people use experiences of motion through space to ground thinking and facilitate talking about time. The key source domains for time metaphors, then, are the domains of motion (especially of objects in motion) and space (including spatial orientation). The following sections survey the moral discourse of 1 Peter for expressions evoking Spatial Time, Time Is Motion, and Time Is a Substance.[4]

Spatial Time

Consider how time talk is connected with notions of location or spatial sphere. In *koine* Greek as in English, one central concept is that time is something people can be *in*. In both language communities, people talk as though time is a (physical) place or region or location—a space. Take, for example, how Peter writes about the time when ultimate moral accounting will take place:

ἐκ   τῶν καλῶν ἔργων ἐποπτεύοντες   δοξάσωσιν   τὸν θεὸν ἐν
from the   good   works   observing   they might give glory the of God in

ἡμέρᾳ   ἐπισκοπῆς
day   of oversight (2.12c)

NRSV: they may see your honorable deeds and glorify God when he comes to judge.

BH paraphrase: so that by observing your good deeds they will give glory to God in the Day of Oversight (Final Judgment or Reckoning).

Just as with the 'in Christ' examples of the preceding section, the Greek preposition ἐν ('in') evokes a bounded space. But here the space is a 'day' (ἡμέρᾳ) in which the final Accounting will take place. In that day of 'oversight' (ἐπισκοπῆς, meaning 'reckoning,' not 'over-looking') the ultimate moral consequences of all the peoples' present good works will come to light. The connection with moral behavior (τῶν καλῶν ἔργων, 'good deeds') is unmistakable. The major point here is that a specific period or unit of time, a day, is used to evoke the conceptual notion of a bounded space *in* which moral consequences are ultimately rendered.

---

[4] See the analysis of time metaphors in Lakoff and Johnson, *Philosophy in the Flesh*, 137–169.

Readers alert to these kinds of patterns will notice that Peter uses several stock time nouns with the dative ἐν. For example, he can use ἐν with χρόνος:

εἰς τὸ   μηκέτι   ἀνθρώπων ἐπιθυμίαις ἀλλὰ   θελήματι   θεοῦ τὸν
for the no longer of humans   desires   but   want /will of God the

ἐπίλοιπον ἐν σαρκὶ βιῶσαι χρόνον.
remaining in flesh to live time (4.2)

NRSV: so as to *live for the rest of your earthly life* no longer by human desires but by the will of God. (4.2)

In this case, time is again clearly linked with issues around how one ought to live (no longer out of human desires but by the will of God). This blend of σαρκός ('bodily, fleshy') with βίος ('biological life') and χρόνος ('clock-time') yields a limited sphere or space in time:

βιῶσαι χρόνον < βιόω 'live' (aorist infinite) βιῶσαι
+
χρονος 'time' (accusative of extent) χρόνον

= 'time to live'

The inferential structure of the blend yields a rich conceptual picture: the span of one's biological lifetime is limited, but it is where one lives and moves and has one's physical being. This spatial, biological lifetime, then, is a living space in which one's moral character develops and is displayed.[5]

Past Time as Place: Behavior then

Peter is also capable of arguing that choices made and attitudes taken toward one's physical deportment in the present can take their bearings from choices others have made in the past. Consider the way time figures into his suggestions for women's behavior towards their husbands.

οὕτως γάρ ποτε καὶ αἱ ἅγιαι γυναῖκες αἱ ἐλπίζουσαι εἰς θεὸν
thusly for then also the holy women the ones hoping in God

ἐκόσμουν   ἑαυτὰς   ὑποτασσόμεναι τοῖς ἰδίοις ἀνδράσιν
were adorning themselves being subjected to the own men (3.5)

NRSV: It was in this way long ago that the holy women who hoped

---

[5] Other time words in this sentence evoke Time Is a Substance and the notion of limited duration: 'no longer' μηκέτι; 'remaining' ἐπίλοιπον.

in God used to adorn themselves by accepting the authority of their husbands.

In this case, the Greek time word is an adverb, ποτέ ('when; then; once upon a time').[6] If this enclitic particle evokes the notion *then*, it also connotes the spatial concept *there*.

Peter's language suggests that behavior of women in the past—albeit exemplary ones—sets a moral precedent for behavior in the reader's present. The force of this dynamic is not merely argumentative. Invoking the past in this manner contributes to a quality of this moral discourse that is akin to *narrative* flow. Peter invites the reader to place herself in a certain story line, to view her own choices within that version of the past, allowing the behavior of those particular women then and there to inform her own behavior here and now.[7]

Beyond the Present Here and Now: Life in Eternal Spatial Time

Moreover, a people's behavior in the present has lasting significance because it is actually lived in a larger time frame, a container that subsumes or surpasses the present 'age.' Consider how Peter writes with larger time frames in mind.

Ὁ   δὲ θεὸς πάσης χάριτος ὁ   καλέσας   ὑμᾶς εἰς τὴν αἰώνιον
the but God of all   favor the one having called you into the eternal

---

[6] The NRSV translation '*long ago*' introduces a separate conceptual metaphor—Time Is a Path. This shift of metaphors is perhaps innocuous, but it is a shift. See Johannes Louw and Eugene Nida, *Greek-English Lexicon of the New Testament Based on Semantic Domains*, 2d ed. (New York and London: United Bible Societies, 1988, 1989) §67.9, 67.30, 67.40.

[7] William Spohn makes the connection between time and narrative: "[A] narrative *locates people in space and time*, often to an *ultimate framework*. Myths define origin and destiny so that the members of the group can understand where they came from and where they are going. They grasp their personal story within the framework of the larger narrative. When cultures change and diversify, however, no single narrative gets passed down. Individuals have to choose which narrative makes sense, or they may pick and choose among them. The result is often a kaleidoscopic, shifting identity or a self without clear boundaries or bearings.

Narrative theologians and literary critics have shown that story is the appropriate vehicle for human experience because both *unfold over time* and through choice and suffering. *Human identity seems to require a temporal framework.* A blueprint or program will not do; we need some structure with selves at the center who progress through a beginning, middle and end. In other words, we need a story." William Spohn, *Go and Do Likewise: Jesus and Ethics* (New York: Continuum, 1999), 173–174, emphases mine.

αὐτοῦ δόξαν ἐν Χριστῷ ὀλίγον παθόντας αὐτὸς καταρτίσει,
of himsplendor in Christ, few having suffered himself will put in order,

στηρίξει, σθενώσει, θεμελιώσει.
will strengthen, will invigorate, will found. (5.10)

NRSV: And after you have suffered for a little while, the God of all grace, who has called you to his eternal glory in Christ, will himself restore, support, strengthen, and establish you.

In this example, the temporal space is evoked not by 'in' (ἐν) but by another preposition, 'into' (εἰς), telling readers they are called '*into* his eternal … glory *in* Christ.'

The sentence creates a complex blend whose main elements are tagged with the words

εἰς αἰώνιον, δόξαν, ἐν Χριστῷ
into + eternal + glory + in Christ

One way to understand how this blend works is to notice that first a spatial time container is opened up, which then is nested into another container:

1) Spatial Preposition + (time Adj. + Noun) → Spatial Time Container

εἰς   αἰώνιον δόξαν
into   eternal glory

2) Spatial Preposition + Noun (proper name) → 'in Christ' Container

ἐν   Χριστῷ
in   Christ

Each of these containers opens up a large living space that (entailed in the properties of αἰών) inherently elevates to ultimate significance human behavior lived out in that space. In fact, the writer next promises that God himself will actively assist those who live in this blended space.

Καιρός: Blending Divine and Human Time

Consider yet another way in which this discourse has the divine and the everyday human intersect and interact in time.

εἰς κληρονομίαν ἄφθαρτον καὶ ἀμίαντον καὶ ἀμάραντον,
into inheritance incorruptible and undefiled and unfading,

τετηρημένην ἐν οὐρανοῖς εἰς ὑμᾶς τοὺς ἐν δυνάμει θεοῦ
having been kept in the heavens for you the ones in power of God

φρουρουμένους διὰ πίστεως εἰς σωτηρίαν ἑτοίμην ἀποκαλυφθῆναι ἐν
being guarded by trust into deliverance prepared to be uncovered in

καιρῷ ἐσχάτῳ
season last

> NRSV: And into an inheritance that is imperishable, undefiled, and unfading, kept in heaven for you, who are being protected by the power of God through faith for a salvation ready to be revealed in the last time. (1.4–5)

In 1.4–5, Peter's language links the notion of a heavenly place or realm existing in a divine spatial time zone (ἐν οὐρανοῖς) with the notion of the believers' having received 'in due time / the right season' (ἐν καιρῷ) an 'incorruptible, undefiled' inheritance. This rich blend of specially qualified spatial times entails that heavenly moral purity is a defining characteristic of the identity and way of life that accompanies their earthly deliverance 'into salvation' (εἰς σωτηρίαν).[8]

Καιρός evokes a spatial time zone, the specific qualities of which can be modified in a given co-text. In 4.17, for example, καιρός is the 'season' for judgment to begin, and it is coterminous with the 'end' (τέλος) for those who disobey. But in 5.6, καιρός is the 'due time' or 'right season' for the faithful ones who are humbled now to be 'elevated; lifted up.' This immediate co-text includes an invitation to readers—to cast all their anxieties on the one who cares for them, along with a moral exhortation to stay 'balanced, sober, awake, alert' to the devil's sneaky, predatory ways. Καιρός, then, is spatial time, due time, for living out the good, for moral behavior.

Spatial Time: Summary

The notion that Time Is a Space is *conceptual* and this concept can be evoked by a variety of linguistic expressions. In *koine* Greek, certain prepositions (ἐν and εἰς) can evoke such spatial times when they are found in conjunction with words from the time domain—αἰών ('age' or 'era'); βίος ('living'); χρόνος ('time'); ἡμέρα ('day'). At several points in 1 Peter such spatial time is evoked in connection with moral exhorta-

---

[8] In 1.10–11, Peter again announces the arrival of the 'season' (καιρὸν) for 'deliverance' (σωτηρίον) the prophets had spoken of, a season—spatial time—which becomes the arena in which they are to consider themselves to be living and making moral choices (1.13).

tion, so that time is conceived as a space in which behavior takes place or, alternatively, where the consequences of previous behavior are ultimately brought to bear. These spatial times contribute to the narrative feel or framework of the letter.

The Moving Time Metaphor

A second major set of conceptual metaphors for time combines the concept of spatial time with the notion of movement, creating a stock schema. In this schema, a stationary observer faces in one direction in a given bounded space. Time is conceptualized as an object (or set of objects) that is coming toward and then moving past the observer.[9]

Consider, then, how Peter uses the concept of Moving Time as he urges his readers toward moral reform:

Πάντων δὲ τὸ   τέλος   ἤγγικεν, σωφρονήσατε οὖν καὶ
Of all but the completion has neared think soberly then and

νήψατε   εἰς προσευχάς (4.7)
well-balanced in   prayers

NRSV: The end of all things is near; therefore be serious and discipline yourselves for the sake of your prayers.

In 4.7, the time domain vocabulary is τὸ τέλος ("the end"). The "end" in view is clearly The End, and it is *coming toward* the observer.[10] While another time-and-motion metaphor has an observer moving toward a stationary point in time, here it appears that τὸ τέλος, not the observer, is moving.[11] The End has not yet arrived, but its motion towards the observer is steady and inevitable. There is a vast literature discussing various denotations and connotations of τέλος, and it is beyond the scope of this study to adjudicate amongst them. Suffice it to say that in this example, τέλος may signify the final moment or a last period of time.[12]

---

[9] Lakoff and Johnson, *Philosophy in the Flesh*, 140–142. Their explanation uses a separate Time Orientation metaphor which they think is combined with the Moving Time metaphor.

[10] ἤγγικεν pf < ἐγγίζω (< ἐγγύς 'near'—'approach,' 'be at hand').

[11] Regarding the Moving Time versus Moving Observer metaphors, see Lakoff and Johnson, *Philosophy in the Flesh*, 145–148.

[12] Τέλος encompasses the notion of the completion of human history at the *end* of human history (or of a given period of human history). It does not connote the end of space-time as it is constructed and conceptualized in the 21st-century West.

The general Moving Time metaphor can be broken down into constituent parts, such that the salient feature in this example can be named Moments In Time Are Objects in Motion, or to be even more specific, The End /Time of Completion (τὸ τέλος) Is an Object in Motion. The conceptual metaphorical work accomplished with these expressions is deep. What is known from the source domain (motion) about the motion of objects coming towards and nearing an observer is mapped onto the inference structure of the target domain (the passage of time). In English, as in some Greek expressions, the present moment is *here* and *now*. Such a concept of time in motion implies change, the possibility of development, and carries a note of urgency into the moral exhortation that follows: "Be serious! Discipline yourselves ..." In 1 Peter, time is not simply a static or inert space, it can be dynamic, moving. But the End has not yet arrived, so there is still time for those whose identities are grounded in Jesus to change their ways to fit the pattern of his ways.

The Time-Substance Variation

Sometimes a Moving Time mapping picks up certain features of the notion that time is an object, treating *time as a substance* that can be measured. When that concept is at work, we speak of, for example, haing a given "amount" of time in which to do something.[13] This conceptual metaphor is at work in 5.10:

Ὁ δὲ θεὸς πάσης χάριτος, ὁ   καλέσας   ὑμᾶς εἰς τὴν αἰώνιον
the but God of all   favor   the one having called   you   into the eternal

αὐτοῦ δόξαν ἐν Χριστῷ, ὀλίγον   παθόντας   αὐτὸς   καταρτίσει,
of him glory in Christ,   few   having suffered himself will put in order,

στηρίξει,   σθενώσει,   θεμελιώσει.
will strengthen, will invigorate will found. (5.10)

NRSV: And after you have suffered for a little while, the God of all grace, who has called you to his eternal glory in Christ, will himself restore, support, strengthen, and establish you.

With ὀλίγον ('a little [while]'), the *duration* of their suffering is characterized as being 'few, short in time,' in comparison with the notion

---

[13] See the way Lakoff and Johnson chart the mapping; *Philosophy in the Flesh*, 145.

of eternality, expressed by 'into eternal' glory.[14] So, Time Is a Substance whose total amount is limited; Duration Is Amount. Again, behavior in this brief period of suffering is happening *in* the present time. Peter promises that God will act on their behalf *in* the future, personally providing restoration, support, strength, and a firm foundation.

Timely Metonymies

Time metaphors are often found working in concert with metonymies, and this happens at some important junctures in 1 Peter. Notice how in 2.12c, the conventional term ἡμέρα ἐπισκοπῆς ('day of oversight/reckoning') functions metonymically. The conventional *name* given for an event ('The Day of Oversight / Reckoning') *stands for* the *event* or process (moral accounting). This metonymic action could be tagged, 'The Day' *For* Process of Rendering Ultimate Moral Consequences.[15,16]

Days for Era or Lifespan: Metonymic Definitions of Time

Something *conventional* and *conceptual* is going on in the use of 'day' and 'days' in this discourse, something that has to do with the ways morality is connected with time as space or container. Notice how these conceptual conventions work in another sentence using ἡμέρα.

ἐκήρυξεν   ἀπειθήσασίν   ποτε ὅτε ἀπεξεδέχετο ἡ τοῦ
he announced to ones having disobeyed then when   awaited   the of

---

[14] εἰς τὴν αἰώνιον (< αἰών 'age').

[15] Here the underlying conceptual metonymies are Name of Day For Event, Event For Process and Event For Time. Regarding the Event For Time metonymy, see Lakoff and Johnson, *Philosophy in the Flesh*, 155–156.

[16] "We define time by metonymy: successive iterations of a type of event stand for intervals of 'time.'" Lakoff & Johnson, *Philosophy in the Flesh*, 138. There is nothing inherent in the word ἡμέρα ('day') that dictates it must stand for the entire process of final moral accounting; rather, the metonymy "Day For Final Accounting" works by cultural and linguistic convention. In traditional Israelite culture, there was concept that in the 1st-century was still developing, a tradition about 'The Day' of judgment and of vindication. This tradition did not develop in a conceptual vacuum. There are qualities, properties, of the inferential structure of a 'day' that makes it an apt candidate for supplying (or evoking) inferential structure in another kind of time period or space (metaphor). When the 'day' stands for that other spatial time, it is functioning metonymically.

θεοῦ μακροθυμία ἐν ἡμέραις   Νῶε
God long temper in   days   of Noah (3.19b–3.20a)

NRSV: (v. 19) he made a proclamation [to the spirits in prison] … (v. 20) who in former times did not obey, when God waited patiently in the days of Noah.

A timespan is a space in which people live—*in* the days of Noah—and the writer characterizes the shape of their living with moral evaluative terms: ἀπειθήσασίν (< ἀ—πειθέω), 'dis-obey.' But *days* also stand (metonymically) for *lifespan* or era (Days For Era), and An Era Is a (Living) Space/ Container in which people display behavior—in this case, very bad behavior. One can see this same metonymy at work in 3.10:

ὁ   γὰρ   θέλων   ζωὴν   ἀγαπᾶν
The one for wanting   life   to love

καὶ ἰδεῖν ἡμέρας ἀγαθὰς
and to see days good

παυσάτω τὴν γλῶσσαν ἀπὸ κακοῦ
let stop the   tongue from   bad

καὶ χείλη τοῦ μὴ λαλῆσαι   δόλον
and lips the not to speak dishonesty

NRSV:

Those who desire life
and desire to see good days,
let them keep their tongues from evil
and their lips from speaking deceit.

Whereas in the previous example, the 'days' in question were decidedly evil, here 'days' stand for the remainder of a lifetime ('days' parallel 'life') the moral character of which is still malleable. These 'days' are yet to be seen (by the Moving Time Metaphor, they are in motion, coming toward the observer, but are not yet in visual range), still in the future.[17] Since this is the case, this conventional moral exhortation implies that there is *still time* to affect the outcome, to qualify the moral living space 'days' stand for.

---

[17] Another key metaphor at work here: Knowing Is Seeing.

Blended Metaphors and Metonymies

Peter's discourse employs all of these timely metaphors and metonymies in concert. To understand the conceptual metaphorical and metonymical structure of the discourse, it has been necessary to locate and separate the distinct elements or voices in that concert. But in order to grasp their inferential heft, it is also important to see how time metaphors and metonymies are blended and juxtaposed in the discourse. Notice, then, how Peter blends time concepts to create space for moral living and judgment—moral consequences—in 1.17.

Καὶ εἰ πατέρα ἐπικαλεῖσθε τὸν ἀπροσωπολήμπτως κρίνοντα
And if father you call on the not receiving face one judging

κατὰ τὸ ἑκάστου ἔργον, ἐν φόβῳ τὸν τῆς παροικίας ὑμῶν
by the of each work in fear the of the transiency of you

χρόνον ἀναστράφητε (1.17)
time behave

NRSV: If you invoke as Father the one who judges all people impartially according to their deeds, live in reverent fear *during the time* of your *exile*.

Here Peter exhorts his readers to be aware of the time in which they live and to behave (ἀναστράφητε) accordingly. To understand how the blend works it must be broken into its components and then re-assembled. Here are some of the keys.

Strictly speaking, the ἐν here is ἐν φόβῳ ('in fear' or 'in reverent awe').[18] But that fear or awe is qualified, described as that kind of awe appropriate to the *time* (χρόνος), the chronological duration, of their 'transiency' or 'exile' (παροικίας).[19] Thus the chronological time,[20] the present in which they live, is blended with the notion that they are in exile. If Time Periods Are Containers / Bounded Spaces, then this time period—of exile as a *time to stay* in a foreign country—is an arena in which behavior is acted out. That arena for behavior has specific

---

[18] ἐν evokes a bounded space *containing* the state or emotion φόβος: Awe Is a Container < Emotional States Are Containers.

[19] The Greek word NRSV translates into English 'exile' (παροικίας—'transiency or exile' < παρ + οἰκία—a *stay* in a foreign country) evokes notions both of limited duration and bounded space or specific location. That is, the word evoking a State (παροικίας) also stands for the Time, the *duration* of time in which they remain in this status (Amount of Substance Is Duration Of Time; States Are Locations).

[20] Χρόνον < χρονος 'time' *Chronos*-type time evokes measurable time. The conceptual mechanism is Time Is a Substance; blended with παροικίας, 'exile' or 'sojourn,' the notion of limited, finite duration emerges.

features, the limitations, entailments evoked by παροικία or exile. In the resultant idealized, cognitive blended space their moral behavior is constrained and qualified, given specific meaning.

For readers aware of the larger, canonical Scriptural narrative, this language may well evoke images of Israel in Exile, and contribute to the coherent 'narrative quality' of the epistle. It is with the pervasive blending of 'stranger'—'exile' language with declarations of special Peoplehood status with State As Location metaphors that Peter locates his readers within the Israel-in-Exile narrative; this study will attend to further features of this blending dynamic as it proceeds.

Moreover, Peter exhorts readers to consider human behavior now as being in view of the πατέρα ('father'), God who judges (κρίνοντα) all—in the present tense—according to their deeds (κατὰ τὸ ἑκάστου ἔργον). Later in the letter, Peter will also bring into play the *final* judgment—and it may be that even here he means his readers to have that final judgment in mind. But in 1.17, his point is that *in the present* the 'father-judge' is actively evaluating human behavior.

Summary: Time and Morality in 1 Peter

Some important claims were set out in the opening of this Events and Time section, claims which now have been examined and supported with discursive evidence:

- Underneath the obvious time structure of the letter lies an inferential structure.
- Peter uses concepts of time and space and motion to structure and communicate his moral exhortation.
- The time metaphor structure is complex, but it is coherent. This coherent cognitive metaphorical structure lends structure to the discourse as a whole and, in particular, to the moral exhortation of 1 Peter.
- Because Peter repeatedly connects time and events with moral action and its consequences, time constitutes a morally significant *living space* that it is qualified in specific ways.
- Via conceptual metaphor 21st-century readers are able to understand well enough what Peter is saying—even with regard to such a fundamental concept as time.
- Metonymic features are used in time language in 1 Peter.

Above all, in 1 Peter there is room, there is time, for good living in this world. That time-space for living is both adequate and limited. Human beings have choices to make about how they will mark their time, how their time will be marked. A person's own limited Lifespan Is a Space in which good is worked or evil done. This is also true of a People's lifespan together; they can work together for good or evil. In time, a People confronts evil, endures suffering, and creates a communal character. They become known by their behavior over time, in the long run. Behavior in time past matters. Patterns are developed; a people develop a moral character by which they are known and whose consequences affect their descendents.

Heavenly time-space is the ground and the border of biological lifetimes in 1 Peter. Καιρός evokes the permeation of heavenly, godly time into ordinary time in such a way that the godly time-space is interwoven with χρόνος, so that there is no purely secular time.

There will come a Day, a day for ultimate Moral Accounting. The inevitability of that specific future's coming is communicated via conceptual metaphor. In this case, the inferential structure of a time domain concept makes it possible for author and reader to share or notice certain notions of the features of ethical consequences.

Each of these time and event conceptual threads is significant in its own right, worth noting and considering. But perhaps most significant is the way they are interwoven, creating major features of the texture of the letter. Peter weaves a thick and ornate time tapestry. In this tapestry, coordinated and contrasting time concepts display some of the foundational notions of his moral universe. When one steps back after examining the work at the detailed level, the effect is stunning. The overall effect of these accumulated, blending, clashing time framings and concepts is that the discourse offers a (conceptual) Story line. Peter invites the reader (3.1–6) to place herself in a certain story line, to view her own choices within that version of the past, allowing the behavior of those particular women then and there to inform her own behavior here and now.

1 Peter is an epistle, not a story. But with all of his time talk, Peter creates a coherent conceptual structure with *narrative* qualities, one that invites readers to own a shared history and to locate themselves amongst a new People of God, called together in this time and place.[21]

---

[21] "[A] narrative locates people in space and time." Spohn, *Go and Do Likewise*, 174.

He writes with a particular version of spatial time and in view of a particular framing of—story about—this people's past, present, and future. As he offers (urges) his readers to reform their moral lives, he presents a grand narrative set in a cosmic, ultimate framework that lends dignity and purpose to everyday behavioral choices and to their suffering 'in Christ' and in time. At the outset of this section, it was remarked that Peter urges his readers to change their behavior, to eschew certain behaviors patterns of the *past*, all of this in view of certain *events*. Those touchstone events stand out when the discourse is read with an eye for the conceptual structure around time. The life—especially the suffering unto death—and the resurrection of Jesus the Christ happen(ed) in earthly χρόνος. But in 1 Peter, χρόνος and καιρός intersect and when they do, events and present-tense behaviors are given larger, cosmic-time framing. While Peter argues that these events ought to motivate his readers to make specific behavioral changes, the thrust, the dynamic force, of this conceptual framing goes much deeper than what is usually denoted by the term 'motivation' in professional ethical discourse today. Peter invites readers to take on a new identity, to be formed into a People of God whose time has come and is coming.

The next chapter focuses on how conceptual metaphor structures what Peter says about moral behavior in three basic arenas—in nations or people groups, in households, and in the body. Each of these arenas is qualified by Peter's vision of living—his metamoral metaphors—of doing good in the present time, in the καιρός moment that has dawned 'in Christ.'

CHAPTER EIGHT

LIVING IN THE NATION, IN THE
HOUSEHOLD, AND IN THE BODY

> τὴν ἀναστροφὴν ὑμῶν ἐν τοῖς ἔθνεσιν ἔχοντες καλήν
> *Conduct yourselves honorably among the Gentiles (2.12a)*

Ἐν τοῖς ἔθνεσιν: *Christian Morality In Social-Political Reality*

Peter begins his letter with words that open up a large landscape—literally, virtually all of Asia Minor; figuratively, the whole socio-political world; theologically, a cosmos that stretches into heavenly space and moves outside ordinary time. The intended range of recipients of this letter is wide; neither is the scope of its moral discourse small:

> To the exiles of the Dispersion in Pontus, Galatia, Cappadocia, Asia, and Bithynia, who have been chosen and destined by God the Father and sanctified by the Spirit to be obedient to Jesus Christ and to be sprinkled with his blood: May grace and peace be yours in abundance (1.1–2).

This salutation evokes a question Peter will answer in his letter: Who are the 'exiles of the dispersion,' and to whom and *where* do they belong? This section of the study focuses on the way Peter uses certain experiences and understandings from the socio-political domain to shape his moral discourse. Foregrounded here are the primary social understandings that arise from people's experience of peoplehood itself—of belonging to a nation or ethnic group. The way such experiences constrain identity and behavior is a central component of Peter's message.

I will argue that Peter essentially answers the where-do-believers-belong question: you belong 'in Christ' (ἐν Χριστῷ). As followers of Jesus, they now belong, above all other allegiances and identity markers, ἐν Χριστῷ. But that belonging, that identity, is also expressed in the language of national and ethnic identity; the 'Christians,' Χριστιανός (4.16), are also the 'People of God,' λαὸς θεοῦ (2.10). If 'in Christ' answers the 'where' question, 'the People of God' answers a to-*whom*-

do-they-belong question. Moreover, those questions and answers cannot be rightly heard without considering the nuanced social-cultural framing Peter proposes when he invites readers to 'live in reverent fear/awe during the time of your *exile*.'[1]

Attention is turned in this section, then, to the conceptual metaphorical dynamics of this belonging at the level of peoplehood. The aim is to find out what conceptual metaphor analysis reveals about the ways in which Peter's moral discourse relies on a reframing of group identity and to consider some potential inferences this reframing or schematization might evoke for readers of the letter.

People Who Belong As A People

Peter directly addresses the tacit identity question raised by the salutation in the portion of the letter that immediately precedes his plunge into specific ethical advice.

> Ὑμεῖς δὲ γένος ἐκλεκτόν, βασίλειον ἱεράτευμα, ἔθνος ἅγιον, λαὸς εἰς
> You but *kind   select*,   kingly   priesthood, *nation holy*, *people for*
>
> περιποίησιν, ὅπως τὰς ἀρετὰς   ἐξαγγείλητε   τοῦ ἐκ
> *possession* so that the virtues you might announce out the from
>
> σκότους ὑμᾶς καλέσαντος εἰς τὸ θαυμαστὸν αὐτοῦ φῶς. οἵ ποτε
> dark   you having called into the marvelous of him light. who then
>
> οὐ λαὸς νῦν δὲ λαὸς θεοῦ, οἱ οὐκ   ἠλεημένοι   νῦν δὲ
> *not people* now but *people of God*, who not have mercy shown now but
>
> ἐλεηθέντες.
> having received mercy.
>
> NRSV: But you are a *chosen race*, a royal priesthood, a *holy nation*, God's *own people*, in order that you may proclaim the might acts of him who called you out of darkness into his marvelous light. Once you were *not a people*, but now you are *God's people*; once you had not received mercy, but now you have received mercy (2.9–10).

Into this short section Peter packs a number of powerful metaphors that map geo-political and ethnic religious source concepts onto a target domain he names only 'you.' But clearly, 'you' stands for the Christians as a group, the collectivity that later would be named the church and that in this epistle is named 'Christian' (Χριστιανός, 4.16).

---

[1] ἐν φόβῳ τὸν τῆς παροικίας ὑμῶν χρόνον ἀναστράφητε (1.17b).

Some conceptual metaphors, metonymies, and blends relying on social group source domain concepts can already be identified:

> Christians Are a Nation / Christians Are a People Group
> The Church Is a Chosen Nation/ Chosen People
> Christians Are a Royal (or Temple) Priesthood
> 'Priest' For the Essence of a People
> Christians Are a Holy Nation
> (The Chosen) People Are Possessions of God
> (God Is a Person)

Peter speaks of the collectivity, the believers, as a group, implying that they have the status and belonging, the communal identity entailed in peoplehood or nationhood. Notice that the vocabulary translated into English 'people' or 'nation' shifts slightly—

> γένος ἐκλεκτόν—'elect/chosen people/nation'
> ἔθνος ἅγιον—'holy people / holy nation'
> λαὸς εἰς περιποίησιν—'a people for possession/belonging'
> λαὸς θεοῦ—'people of God'

NT scholars (Elliott, Achtemeier, Michaels, et al.) have carried on a lively discussion about the significance of these various collective titles. A cognitive linguist listening in would observe that the discussion is about how to identify and map the distinctive metaphors, and how to run the complex blends that emerge. Distinctions between γένος, ἔθνος and λαός are grounded in the properties of the schemas they evoke. What persists, no matter the Greek 'people' word used, is the notion that the Christians' new set of relationships with one another and with God—their group identity—is like that of a distinctive people group.[2] Though they are spread throughout the Roman provinces of Asia Minor, perhaps in small cell groups meeting here and there, they are encouraged to think of themselves *as* a distinctive People, a legitimate Nation, even a nation located in an imaginary geo-political region.

---

[2] Contra Elliott, who says "the believers are not said to constitute a 'new people' but, rather, are declared the eschatological realization of Israel as God's elect and holy people." John H. Elliott, *1 Peter: A New Translation with Introduction and Commentary*, Anchor Bible 37B (New York: Doubleday, 2000), 447. And see his discussion of the collective titles in John H. Elliott, *A Home for the Homeless: A Sociological Exegesis of 1 Peter, Its Situation and Strategy* (Philadelphia: Fortress, 1981), 227. My reading agrees with Paul J. Achtemeier, "Newborn Babes and Living Stones: Literal and Figurative in 1 Peter," in *To Touch the Text: Biblical and Related Studies in Honor of Joseph H. Fitzmyer, S.J.*, ed. M.P. Horgan and P.J. Kobelski (New York: Crossroad/ Continuum, 1988), 224–231.

When Peter attributes peoplehood to his readers (the plural 'you' to whom he writes), it is not just any people group Peter has in mind, but *the* nation, the people of Israel.³ In Peter's cultural context, that particular 'Chosen' people or holy nation is the prototypical nation, the central case. Here Peter, himself a Jew, transfers certain attributes and responsibilities of the people of Israel to the collectivity that he is now addressing, the church in Asia Minor. So, in effect, The Church Is Israel or The Church Is the New Israel.⁴ Moreover, notice how Peter asserts that his readers (who likely are mostly Gentile Christian converts) once 'were *no people*'—a very Jewish perspective on Gentiles. He defines 'people' status both positively and negatively, using a counterfactual that opens up and demarks negative space.⁵ To do that, Peter alludes to a saying of the prophet Hosea. Hosea 2:23 reads:

> And I will have pity on *Lo-ruhamah (Not pitied)*,
> and I will say to *Lo-ammi (Not my people)*, 'You are my people';
> and he shall say, 'You are my God.'"⁶

The basic sensibility is a pervasive one in human cultures.⁷ We insiders are the People; outsiders are 'no people.' The ethnic boundary drawn entails a container concept; there is a metaphorical bounded space within which the People dwell.

---

³ Regarding the meaning and significance of ἔθνος see Achtemeier, *1 Peter*, 70, 164, 281; and Elliott, *Home for the Homeless*, 98, 119–127, 133, 153–155, 227–229, 284.

⁴ Achtemeier concludes that this is the 'root' metaphor of 1 Peter, contra Elliott, who thinks church as οἶκος is the controlling metaphor. Discussion of the pitfalls of 'root' and 'controlling' metaphor terminology are discussed below. See Achtemeier, "Newborn Babes and Living Stones," 213, 224–229. See also Achtemeier, *1 Peter*, 69–71.

⁵ On definition via counterfactuals, and counterfactuals' use of negative space blends, see Gilles Fauconnier and Mark Turner, *The Way We Think: Conceptual Blending and the Mind's Hidden Complexities* (New York: Basic Books, 2002), 240–241.

⁶ Greek ἔθνος seems to be the word of choice when the task is translating Hebrew (LXX) *goyim* and *'ammin*, but λαός can also be chosen. Walter Bauer, *A Greek-English Lexicon of the New Testament and other Early Christian Literature*, 2d ed. Translated and edited by William F. Arndt, F. Wilbur Gingrich, and Frederick W. Danker. (Chicago: Chicago University Press, 1979), 217. Compare Peter's scenario with Ephesians 2:11–21, where Paul articulates an early Christian perspective on Gentiles. It reads, in part: "Remember that you were at that time without Christ, being aliens from the commonwealth of Israel, and strangers to the covenants of promise, having no hope and without God in the world. But now in Christ Jesus you who once were far off have been brought near by the blood of Christ" (2.12–13). In Romans 3.29, he asserts that God is God even of the Gentiles. In 9:24–25, Paul quotes the Hosea passage to which Peter also alludes. Paul renders Hosea, in part: Καλέσω τὸν οὐ λαόν μου λαόν μου—"I will call those who were not my people, 'my people.'"

⁷ Peoples' names for themselves as a collectivity often translate into English 'the

But now the Christians (Χριστιανός, 4.16) are not only a people, they are a *holy* people, and a people *belonging to* God. The purpose, the responsibility entailed in that identity is 'to declare (by their just and righteous ways together) the virtues of God, who called them out of darkness into the light.' This People, then, has both its identity and its destiny framed in moral terms, in holiness and manifesting the 'virtues' (ἀρετή), the mighty and good acts, of its God.[8] They are to think of themselves as a possession of God (λαὸς εἰς περιποίησιν; λαὸς θεοῦ). These expressions work via conceptual metaphor: The Church Is an Object; The Church Is a Possession of God (where God Is a Person). The moral advice Peter is about to give makes sense only in light of this re-framed identity. 'As Christians' (ὡς Χριστιανός), they can expect to suffer, but they must not bring dishonor upon the national household (A Nation Is a Household): 'let none of you suffer as a murderer, a thief, a criminal, or even as a mischief maker.' (4.15) Their honor consists in 'bearing this [family] name' (ἐν τῷ ὀνόματι τούτῳ, 4.16), and behaving accordingly.

People who are Exiles

Christians (ὑμεῖς 'you,' pl.—2.9) Are The People, The Holy Nation, God's Chosen, God's Possession. But how does that cluster of metaphors square with the language of 'strangers,' 'resident aliens,' 'exiles,' 'sojourners,' 'diaspora' (παροίκους- 2.11; παρεπιδήμοις διασπορᾶς—1.1)? 'Diaspora' is an important clue. In the light of the schematic metaphor, The Church Is the New Israel, Peter's salutation makes a certain kind of sense. When he writes to 'exiles of the dispersion' he is not writing to literal diaspora Jews. No, he writes to Christian converts who are (mostly) non-Jews, people who until they joined the 'Christian' way belonged in the ordinary sense—whether or not they each had Roman citizenship—in their native land. But now that they belong to a new 'Nation,' they have become 'exiles' in their own country. It is as though they had become 'resident aliens' without having actually moved.

---

people' (e.g., Navajo *di'nay).* Terms for outsiders, foreigners can be blunt, as in this text 'no people' (cf. Japanese *gai jin).* Thus Elliott: "For ideological purposes all inimical outsiders were reduced to one common social ('Gentile,' 2:12; 4:3) and demonic (5:8–9) denominator." *Home for the Homeless,* 81. But 'ideology' is anachronistic.

[8] See also the discussion of the meaning of 'holiness,' Chapter 6, above.

But there is also a twist, a variation on that schematic theme, a twist that has been a point of scholarly contention. The argument has to do with how the metaphors are mapped. If the frame is Exile, then how is the 'home country' slot filled? How does the filling of that slot affect the logic, the moral logic, of the schematic? First consider the shape of the basic source frame, Exile:

Exile: SD

SLOTS
displaced person or group
home country
sending-out or banishing force, usually a ruler
reason for banishment (offense; condition)
host country
boundaries
journey
length of stay in host country

RELATIONS
exiles are caused by a ruling force to leave their homes
exiles are or are not welcomed by hosts
exiles do not belong in the host or foreign land
exiles do or do not assimilate
exiles belong with each other (within their own group)
rulers have power over exiles
in a host country, exiles are not full citizens
exiles usually have lower status than full citizens

PROPERTIES
exiles have a variety of resources that affect the way they deal with their situation:
a group of exiles has more power and resources than an individual exile
exiles have a kind of independence that native citizens cannot—an odd kind of freedom

KNOWLEDGE
exile is the opposite of being at home, belonging
exile is more than just being away from home, it is banishment
exiles are unwanted in the home country
exiles might not be wanted in the host country
there is an assumption that one would want to return home
exile is an 'unnatural' state
issues of low status surround exile
    questionable identity
    questionable worth
    questionable honor

exile is a temporary condition
a JOURNEY is entailed, usually across BOUNDARIES / GEOPOLITICS

Exile Source Domain Frame

The second slot is a 'native' or 'home' country. Many readers have noticed that sometimes Peter seems to fill that slot with ἐν οὐρανοῖς 'in the heavens.'[9]

If Peter always filled the 'home' slot with 'heaven,' what would that do to the logic of the discourse? If home is heaven, one does not truly belong here on planet Earth. One ought to behave as though one belonged to God—be holy—but perhaps one might be impatient with earthly difficulties, including moral difficulties—moral 'impurities.' The holiness envisioned might be an angelic, other-worldly holiness. If one's true home is in heaven, one might also be impatient with the long process and struggle involved in reform of unjust social structures. One might split one's identity off from the here and now, and become (in modern terms) a 'pie in the sky' believer. That is the fear John Elliott expresses in *A Home for the Homeless*, when he calls into question the way some people seem to be reading 1 Peter.[10] That is why Elliott insisted

---

[9] Potential 'heaven as home' triggers (some working via negative space, counterfactual blends) in 1 Peter include: 'into an inheritance that is imperishable ... kept in heaven for you' εἰς κληρονομίαν ἄφθαρτον ... τετηρημένην ἐν οὐρανοῖς εἰς ὑμᾶς (1.4); 'the time of your exile' τῆς παροικίας ὑμῶν χρόνον (1.17b); 'you have been born anew, not of perishable but of imperishable seed' ἀναγεγεννημένοι οὐκ ἐκ σπορᾶς φθαρτῆς ἀλλὰ ἀφθάρτου (1.23); 'to live for the rest of your earthly life' τὸν ἐπίλοιπον ἐν σαρκὶ βιῶσαι χρόνον (4.2b); 'you will win the crown of glory that never fades away' κομεῖσθε τὸν ἀμαράντινον τῆς δόξης στέφανον (5.4b); 'so that he may exalt you in due time' ἵνα ὑμᾶς ὑψώσῃ ἐν καιρῷ (5.6b).

[10] Elliott was responding to Victor Paul Furnish's 'pilgrim motif' reading, which concluded that "Christians are the elect of God and thus only temporarily residents in this present world." Victor P. Furnish, "Elect Sojourners in Christ: An Approach to the Theology of 1 Peter," *Perkins Journal* 28 (1975): 3. See Elliott, *A Home for the Homeless*, 129. Elliott insists that "1 Peter is not offering its readers a theological recipe for escaping their social situation but rather a rationale for continued social engagement;" Ibid., 128.

Elliott has argued strongly that a metaphorical understanding of the 'exiles and strangers' words "has resulted in a serious misconception of the letter as a whole." (*Homeless*, 129) He says, "The failure to see that the letter is encouraging its readers *to remain* aliens rather than suggesting that they *have become* aliens in a metaphorical religious sense has resulted in serious misconceptions of the letter as a whole." The original recipients of 1 Peter are actually resident aliens in Asia Minor, people living on the fringes of society, he argues, and to make of 'aliens and exiles' a metaphor for Christian believers as 'exiles' on earth—their true home and citizenship in heaven—is to misconstrue the message. The latter thesis is advanced by, for example, Peter Davids, (in the 1980s) that a metaphorical reading of the 'exiles' language in 1 Peter was erroneous; his concern is the potential loss of the social-ethical impact of 1 Peter, and this is a valid concern.

But 1 Peter fills the home- or native-country slot in at least two ways, and there is a prime exemplar, a prototype, of an exile, a stranger, who manages to live in view of both home countries—Jesus Christ. First, consider the slot filler options. Sometimes the (authorial audience) readers' native earthly country is the old home country; by joining the Christian movement, they in effect leave the native old country and take up 'diapsora' identity.[11] Now they are 'strangers' in their

---

The First Epistle of Peter (New International Commentary on the New Testament; Grand Rapids: Eerdmans, 1990), 95.

In a 1990 Yale dissertation, Troy W. Martin asserts that Elliott's assumption that 'strangers and aliens' must be taken in their literal, socio-political meaning is a major fallacy, marring his entire thesis. Martin argues that the *only* way 'strangers' or 'exiles' can be understood in the context of the letter is metaphorically and suggests, contra Elliott, that "paraenetic texts may not be the desultory musings of an impetuous author, but the skillful construction of a cogent rhetorician." Troy W. Martin, *Metaphor and Composition in 1 Peter* (Atlanta, GA: Scholars Press, 1990), 142, 275.

A cognitivist analysis of this dispute notes that alternative construals of the source domain (ways of filling the 'home country' slot) yield different blends and entailments, inferences. The either/or of these interlocutors (Elliott and Martin; socio-historical vs. literary-metaphorical) is not entirely necessary. The 'aliens and exiles' are actually aliens in some socio-politically definable manner, but Elliott has misconstrued what their status is. Martin's 'only metaphorical' verdict is flawed; this error is due, in part, to his misunderstanding of the role (conceptual) metaphor plays in the discourse.

[11] Troy Martin argues that the diaspora motif is the 'controlling' metaphor of the letter as a whole (*Metaphor and Composition in 1 Peter*, 144). Martin's analysis is limited by the (traditional, "category mistake") working definition of metaphor he borrows from David R. Olson: "the simplest characteristic of a metaphor is a discrepancy between what you say and what you mean" (Ibid., 141, n. 24). Further, Martin uses this traditional understanding of metaphor (as a mere literary device) with an odd twist, in that he claims a connection between metaphor and ontology. "The ontological statements and their admonitions provide the compositional markers for the sections of 1 Peter ... These ontological statements in 1 Peter are almost exclusively expressed by similes and metaphors" (Ibid., 141). "Since metaphors and similes are used to express the ontological status of the recipients, they become important compositional indicators .... *Only* those metaphors that describe or relate directly to the readers and provide the basis for an exhortation determine the compositional structure. These metaphors not only describe the readers but also determine the exhortations addressed to them. Moreover, metaphor clusters, a series of metaphors connected in ancient thought, become the primary indicators of the major sections of the letter" (Ibid., 143, emphasis mine). Metaphors and metaphor clusters, Martin thinks, are the "is" component that grounds or funds the ensuing paraenetic "ought"—and these same metaphors are the structural markers that provide 1 Peter's literary coherence. While I agree that metaphors contribute to the letter's literary coherence, I argue that the mechanisms by which this happens are better accounted for via cognitive linguistic methods for

own native countries. That is, a blended space emerges when 'People of God/New Israel' combines with language of 'exile' and 'sojourner.' Where the land of sojourn slot is filled with an actual land or country, the new identity tags given to Peter's addressees, 'The People of God' and 'The New Israel,' and so on, become markers of their new primary identity, replacing these Roman provincial (perhaps mostly) non-Jews' original identity. They become, in effect, exiles or resident aliens in their own original home region. Since they now belong to the metaphorical 'Israel', their families of origin, their native peoples, have become 'Gentiles' to them. 'Your' belonging, says Peter, is no longer bound to the people from whom you are biologically descended.[12] Here is how the Exile Frame can be mapped onto a target frame, the Christians in Asia Minor as a Social Entity:

Christians in Asia Minor Are Exiles from their Native Lands

Exile: Source Domain	→ *Christians in Asia Minor: Target Domain*
SLOTS	SLOTS
displaced person or group of people	Christian believers as individuals and as a group
home country	Native land [Or 'in Christ' / the church / heaven]
sending-out or banishing force, usually a ruler	former affiliates: familial, societal, religious
reason for banishment (offense; condition)	belief in Jesus as Christ; renunciation of 'pagan' ways
host country	former (actual) country of origin, citizenship
boundaries	living by new ways OR by former 'futile' ways
journey	life together as believers; pilgrimage; sojourn (+ below)
length of stay in host country	life 'in Christ' on earth, then in 'resurrection'?

---

analyzing conceptual metaphors and mental space blends that underlie the rhetorical devices to which Martin points. Rhetoric works via conceptual metaphor and mental space blending. Martin, *Metaphor and Composition in 1 Peter*, 144.

[12] With Achtemeier, I disagree with the either/or thinking implied in Elliott's earlier treatment of these issues.

RELATIONS	RELATIONS
ruling force causes exiles to leave home	belief in Christ is a force moving people to shift allegiances
exiles are or are not welcomed by hosts	Christians are no longer welcomed by their own families, societies
exiles do not belong in the host land	Christians do not belong in their former homes, social circles
exiles do or do not assimilate	Christians choose to assimilate to 'pagan' culture or not
exiles belong with each other	Christians' primary belonging is among other Christians
rulers have power over exiles	societal & cosmic rulers have power over Christians (Great Chain)
in a host country, exiles are not full citizens	Christians are no longer mere citizens in their actual countries
exiles usually have lower status than full citizens	mapped? notion of voluntary low status?

Notice that since in this mapping the second slot is filled with 'native land,' several subsequent slots are filled in such a way as to be consistent with that second slot choice. Slot-filling influences inferential entailments.

Now consider how a different metaphor cluster results when the 'home country' slot is filled with 'heaven' in the target frame:

Christians in Asia Minor Are Exiles from Heaven

Exile: Source Domain → *Christians in Asia Minor: Target Domain*

SLOTS	SLOTS
displaced person or group of people	Christian believers as individuals and as a group
home country	heaven [Or Native land / 'in Christ' / the church]
sending-out or banishing force, usually a ruler	being born? evil? Devil?
reason for banishment (offense; condition)	Offensive condition: being born fallen?
host country	biological lifetime on earth; social-political cultural context 'world'

boundaries	biological life (outside); heavenly-cosmic sphere (inside)
journey	lifetime as sojourn 'below'
length of stay in host country	relatively short, temporary nature of mortal life in comparison with heavenly, eternal life
RELATIONS	RELATIONS
ruling force causes exiles to leave home	Evil causes banishment of human family from heaven?
exiles are or are not welcomed by hosts	Mapped?
exiles do not belong in the host land	Christians do not yet belong in heaven
exiles do or do not assimilate	Christians choose to assimilate to earthly 'pagan' ways or not
exiles belong with each other (within their own group)	Christians' primary belonging is among other Christians
rulers have power over exiles	cosmic rulers have power over Christians (Great Chain)
in a host country, exiles are not full citizens	Christians are no longer mere citizens in their actual countries
exiles usually have lower status than full citizens	mapped? notion of voluntary low status?

This is a different metaphor, with quite different inference patterns than those the first option yielded. As the diagram indicates, it is possible to find places in the text where Peter fills the 'home country' slot with 'in Christ,' or with 'in the gathering of believers.' Each mapping yields distinctive entailments. Moreover, other schematic variations are possible. Source concepts can be drawn from framings akin to—but distinctive from—exile: Expatriate, sojourner, resident alien, and so on. Similarly detailed mapping of the slots, relations, properties and knowledge belonging to each of these respective framings onto the target domain would have to include considerations of how exilic suffering (a important property in the source domain's conceptual pool) is redefined.[13]

---

[13] Target domain shifts are also possible.

Jesus Christ as Prototypical Stranger

In 1 Peter, it is Jesus Christ who demonstrates how to negotiate the confusing waters at the confluence of multiple options for belonging. He came from heaven, belongs there, (1.20, 3.22) traveled to the 'lower regions,' (3.19) but also lived so fully, so deeply rooted on earth, such an earthy life, that he suffered (3.17–18, 4.1, 5.1)—even to the point of death by execution on a Roman cross. As Peter's moral exemplar, Jesus is the one who gives himself for the sake of others, so that they might be free from oppressive identity claims and their concomitant 'futile' behaviors. (1.18) If a reader of 1 Peter does have heaven as home in mind, keeping the Jesus prototype in mind constrains the range of coherent readings. If the Jesus Peter points to is one of the input spaces, then the entailments of the blended space could not take people—individuals or the collectivity—out of earthy suffering or engagement with others. Even with heaven as one's 'native land,' action on behalf of others' healing and freedom is appropriate exile behavior in this schema. Moreover, if Jesus is the prototypical exile or stranger, then the disposition of his would-be followers towards strangers takes on a certain poignancy. They are to be, says Peter, 'stranger-lovers' among themselves (φιλόξενοι 4.9).

Heaven as home does qualify the picture in the complex blended space Peter evokes. Heaven opens up a higher, vaster, 'world' space; lifts the lid, extending the significance and arena of human moral action and thought far beyond the immediate, out into the heavens (time and space).

Ἐν τοῖς ἔθνεσιν As Site of Moral Interplay; Court of Moral Judgment

With this understanding of Peter's usage of 'people' or 'nation' language and the way it is (metaphorically) connected to the 'resident alien and exile' concepts explored above, notice how ἔθνος works in moral logic of this discourse:

2.11 Ἀγαπητοί, παρακαλῶ ὡς παροίκους καὶ παρεπιδήμους
Loved ones, I encourage as transients and exiles

ἀπέχεσθαι τῶν σαρκικῶν ἐπιθυμιῶν αἵτινες στρατεύονται
to hold off yourself of the fleshly desires which soldier

κατὰ τῆς ψυχῆς
against the soul / self

2.12 τὴν ἀναστροφὴν ὑμῶν ἐν τοῖς ἔθνεσιν ἔχοντες καλήν, ἵνα, ἐν ᾧ
the behavior of you in the [nations] having good, so that in what

καταλαλοῦσιν ὑμῶν ὡς κακοποιῶν ἐκ τῶν καλῶν ἔργων
they talk against you as bad doers from the good works

ἐποπτεύοντες δοξάσωσιν τὸν θεὸν ἐν ἡμέρᾳ ἐπισκοπῆς
observing they might give glory the God in day of oversight

> NRSV: Beloved, I urge you as aliens and exiles to abstain from the desires of the flesh that wage war against the soul. Conduct yourselves honorably among the Gentiles, so that, though they malign you as evildoers, they may see your honorable deeds and glorify God when he comes to judge.

> BH paraphrase: 11) Loved Ones, I instruct all of you, thinking of yourselves as though you were resident aliens and foreign visitors, to abstain from the desires that belong to the unbelieving world, [desires] that wage war against your very lives. (12) [Do this] *by maintaining honorable behavior among the 'Gentiles,'* so that when they call you evildoers, they may, because they observe your good deeds, praise God on Judgment Day—the Day of Visitation.

The phrase ἐν τοῖς ἔθνεσιν—'in' or 'among' the 'Gentiles'—evokes a range or sphere, a metaphorical bounded space and landscape, in which Christians (those who are 'in Christ') live and move and have their being. As with 'in Christ,' the dative ἐν Peter uses here evokes a container metaphor, this specific kind of spatial image schema. For some readers, the words will evoke a specific kind of container, a landscape or geo-political territory, in which the Christian 'exiles' and 'resident aliens' are located. The Christians, remember, are the New Israel. Like the Israelite people, they live among other peoples, Gentiles. They actually live in Gentile territory (and strictly, literally speaking, most of them are Gentiles in the usual sense of the word). But now that they are the Chosen People, they are to live accordingly—and their mission is like that which Israel's prophets articulated: To live such just and holy lives among the Gentiles, that God is honored and all peoples are gathered into the one people.[14]

In 1 Peter, this 'behavior' or 'conduct among the Gentiles' is the behavior upon which the Christians will be judged in the interim by their non-Christian neighbors, husbands, and governmental functionaries—the basis of their Moral Accounting (as a people). The shape of their lives together is to be distinctive, not conforming to

---

[14] See, e.g., Isa 52.10, 66.19–21.

'Gentile' mores, which happen to be the values and behavior patterns of the Christians' own native culture. Bad moral behavior and low moral standing belong to the ἔθνη, whose characteristic behaviors are outlined in the vice lists. But καλῶν ἔργων—'good works, good deeds, good living'—are to characterize the Christians' behavior as 'exiles' so completely that they do not deserve the reputation of κακοποιῶν—'evil doers.'

Summary: Moral Conduct & Moral Accounting ἐν τοῖς ἔθνεσιν

Moral accounting and judgment in 1 Peter occur at more than one level. First, there are the kinds of moral evaluations that people make of each others' behavior—husbands notice their wives' attitudes and behavior; masters and overseers watch how slaves comport themselves; governmental functionaries are charged with judging and punishing certain kinds of wrongs. But all of those judgments amount to a kind of interim phase, foregrounded for a time—and taken seriously in 1 Peter—but still carrying the flavor of mere foretaste of the level of judgment to be expected in the Age to Come. All of these intermediate or interim phase judgments play out on the temporal, human stage, but the backdrop of ultimate Judgment looms large. Peter's vision of this judgment contains key features—that God himself is the Judge; that all the peoples of the earth are included; that the basis of judgment is the moral tenor of each people's character; that this reckoning begins with God's Chosen People.

Peter is steeped in his Jewish heritage, a heritage that trusts God's special care and unique concern for a Chosen People, and includes their relationship to 'the nations' or Gentiles. This concern is expressed in specific texts delineating God's desires for human wholeness in the form of behavioral standards and boundaries, as well as in the wider sweep of the Story of the People embodied in the Israel's memory and told in the traditional Israelite scriptures. These values and standards Peter passes on to the new, (mostly non-Jewish) Christian converts in Asia Minor. He does so by way of giving them the language of that history and heritage, the language of the Chosen (elect) and Holy People among the nations or Gentiles (ἐν τοῖς ἔθνεσιν). This good behavior ἐν τοῖς ἔθνεσιν is one set of ways the particular scope of the Moral Accounting Schema is constrained and defined in this discourse.

Οἶκου τοῦ Θεοῦ—Living In God's Household

πάντας τιμήσατε, τὴν ἀδελφότητα ἀγαπᾶτε
honor everyone; love the brotherhood (2.17a)

The scope of Peter's moral discourse is indeed wide. It encompasses people groups and nations (ἔθνος) and reaches to the heavens (οὐρανός). But Peter also very quickly moves to discuss behavior in everyday, ordinary households. Some of the ways a household frame figures into Moral Accounting and is linked to the Great Chain of Being have been considered in previous sections of this study; it was not possible to talk about moral consequences and the structure of moral authority in 1 Peter without mentioning input from familial concepts. This section will build on the household-morality connections established in earlier parts of the analysis, adding additional features to the picture.

On one level, the household is a literal locus of behavior, and much of Peter's exhortation is directed towards shaping the conduct of wives and husbands, slaves and (by implication) masters. But more interesting are the ways he uses everyday experiences of primary social relationships in households to ground the more abstract aspects of the discourse, providing framing that constrains the range of meaningful inferences. This section will demonstrate that when households are approached in this manner, the *conceptual* connections between the household and some key moral concepts can be highlighted. Many core moral concepts rely on οἶκος framing, among them: Morality Is Honor (τιμή), Morality Is Obedience (ὑποτάσσω), Goodness Is Self-Giving and Brotherly Love (ἀγάπη; φιλάδελφος); Good Moral Standing Is Inheriting the Family Fortune.[15] To understand the moral and ethical implications of these household-grounded metaphors, and to trace their action in the discourse, it is helpful to delineate the contours of the frame itself.

---

[15] Regarding honor-shame culture, see J.G. Peristiany, ed., *Honour and Shame: The Values of Mediterranean Society*, The Nature of Human Society Series (Chicago: University of Chicago Press, 1966; London: Weidenfeld and Nicolson, Midway Reprint, 1974); and David D. Gilmore, ed., *Honor and Shame and the Unity of the Mediterranean*, A Special Publication of the American Anthropological Association, 22 (Washington: American Anthropological Association, 1987).

Household Frame

First, consider some elements of a 1st-century Greco-Roman household frame. Admitting that there were considerable variations on the theme, a basic frame can be outlined with reasonable accuracy. The following chart summarizes some of the slots, relations, properties, and knowledge pertaining to such a frame. On the left side, some of the specific Greek vocabulary that evokes familial, household concepts is listed. The right-hand column lists places where this vocabulary is found in 1 Peter; potential or likely metaphorical usage is indicated in bold type.

1st-century ΟΙΚΟΣ Frame

SLOTS

Potential Greek Triggers	English	*1 Peter instantiation*
Physical, material household		
οἰκία	house, home, property, family	
οἶκος	house; household	2.5, 4.17
οἰκητήριον	house	
οἰκοδομέω	build, erect a house	2.5, 2.7
οἰκέω	dwell, live in	
Extended Family		
γένος	family, race, ancestry	2.9
γενεά	generation, contemporaries	
γένεσις	birth, ancestry	
σάρξ, σαρκός	biological descent	1.24; 3.18, 21; 4.1, 4. 2, 6
σπορά	procreation	1.23
σπέρμα	descendants, children	
ῥίζα	scion, offspring	
οἰκεῖος	family member	
οἰκιακός	household member	
πανοικί (adv)	with one's household	
συνοικέω	living together, to dwell with	3.7
πατριά	family; clan	
πατρίς	homeland, home town	
πατριάρχης	patriarch	
προπάτωρ	forefather	

πατροπαραδότος	handed down	1.18
συγγενής	kin, countrymen	
γεννάω	being born	(2.23)

Household Member Slots

πατήρ	father, ancestor	1.2, 1.3, 1.17
ἀνήρ, ἀνδρός	husband	3.1, 5, 7
πρεσβύτερος	elder	5.1, 5.5
γυνή	wife, married woman	3.1, 5
σκεῦος	own body; own wife	3.7
χήρα	widow	
υἱός	son, offspring	5.13
κληρονόμος	heir	3.7, 3.9 vb
ἀδελφός	brother	5.12
ἀδελφότης	brotherhood	2.17, 5.9
φιλαδελφία	brotherly love	3.8
θυγάτηρ	daughter	3.6
ἀδελφή	sister	
τέκνον	child	1.14; 3.6
ἀρτιγέννητος	newborn	2.2
βρέφος	infant	2.2
παιδίον	young child	
δεσπότης	master, supervisor	2.18
οἰκοδεσπότης	household, master	
οἰκονόμος	treasurer, steward	4.10
ἐπίσκοπος	over-seer	2.25, 4.15
ἐποπτεύω	vb. oversee	3.12
κύριος	master	1.3, 1.25; 2.3, 2.13; 3.6, 3.12, 3.15
κατακυριεύω	vb. master	5.3
(ἐλεύθερος)	free man	2.16
δοῦλος	slave	2.16
δουλεύω	vb. serve	
διακονέω	vb. serve	1.12, 4.10, 4.11
οἰκέτης	house servant	2.18

Shame

αἰσχύνη	shame	4.16 (vb)
ἀφόβως	shameless	
ἀναίδεια	insolence	
καταλαλιά	slander	2.1, 2.2

Honor

ὄνομα	name	4.16
τιμή	honor	1.7, 2.7. 3.7

τίμιος	respected	1.19
τιμάω	to honor	2.17 (x2)
ἔντιμος	respected	2.5
δόξα	glory, honor	1.7, 11, 21, 24; 4.11, 13, 14; 5.1, 4, 10
δοξάζω	to honor	1.8; 2.12; 4.11, 16
δοκιμή	approved	1.7
καλός	noble, morally good	2.12 (x2), 4.10
καλός	fittingly, rightly	1.19
ὑπέρ	above (status)	2.21, 3.18
φόβος	reverent, respectful	1.17, 2.18, 3.2, 14, 16

RELATIONS

Each household member must know his or her place and behave accordingly. The head of the household has authority over everyone else. Some of this authority can be delegated, as when a son or servant represents him in a business transaction.

PROPERTIES

Father: Potent, strong, strict, honorable, nurturing, generous, powerful, high status, wise, responsible, kind (and the opposites of these qualities)

Mother: Fertile or barren, chaste or not, beautiful or not, submissive, obedient, nurturing

Children: obedient, needy, growing

Sons: 1st has highest status, primary heir; strong

Daughters: lower status, needing protection, marriage-able? chaste? beautiful?

Slaves: Obedient, loyal, hard-working, honest, strong. There are sub-rankings among slaves [lowest status = little girl slave]

Manager-Slaves: All of the above, plus resourceful, shrewd in business dealings, able to manage other slaves

Friends: Parallel in status w/ Head; loyal, honorable, honest, generous. They would typically be free, not enslaved. [But note that certain kinds of slaves might have higher status in a sense, more responsibility and honor and protection than certain freemen—by virtue of their relationship to their masters and belonging in the household.]

KNOWLEDGE

One who disobeys the father can be punished or even banished and disinherited. The father rules (but note cultural nuances). Children and wives should submit to, honor, and obey the father. To do so is to uphold and guard the honor of the family name. The father has a right and responsibility to be strong and honorable. Servants have lower status but are vital to the smooth operation of the household. Some servants—managers—have decent status and lots of responsibility. Knowing one's place is key. There is protection, belonging, and honor here.[16]

Notice that not all of the Household frame slots are filled in 1 Peter, but many are. Not all of the relational properties listed are in evidence in 1 Peter, but again, many are. Notice, above all, that the bold type is plentiful; the household figures into 1 Peter mostly metaphorically, rather than literally. And, while the specific moral advice directed to certain household members is significant, it is this wealth of *metaphorical* connections that contributes most powerfully to the moral discourse.

What Is and Is Not Metaphorical

Methodologically, a first task, once the basic frame is outlined, is to ask which of the slots and relations and so on in the Household frame show up *literally* in 1 Peter.[17] Notice that Peter addresses wives (3.1–6) and husbands (3.7). He also addresses actual slaves (2.18–25), and in the course of giving this advice, mentions masters (2.18–20).

But, significantly, before he gives advice to slaves (obey and submit, even to unkind, crooked masters), he has urged his readers ὡς θεοῦ δοῦλοι, 'as slaves of God' to live ὡς ἐλεύθεροι, 'as free people, freemen'. (2.16) That is a *metaphorical* move. Actually, it is several metaphorical moves at once, a blend. Three slots in the Household frame are

---

[16] Social anthropological sources for household data include: Peristiany, *Honour and Shame;* Gilmore, *Honor and Shame and the Unity of the Mediterranean;* David D. Gilmore, "Anthropology of the Mediterranean Area," *Annual Review of Anthropology* 11 (1982): 175–205; Jane Schneider, "Of Vigilance and Virgins: Honor, Shame and Access to Resources in Mediterranean Societies," *Ethnology* 10 (1971): 1–24; Paul Veyne, "The Roman Empire," in *A History of Private Life: I. From Pagan Rome to Byzantium,* tr. Arthur Goldhammer, ed. Philips Aries and George Duby, no. 1. (Cambridge, Mass.: Harvard University Press, Belknap Press, 1987); Stephen Benko, *Pagan Rome and the Early Christians* (Bloomington and Indianapolis: Indiana University Press, 1984).

[17] Regarding the cognitive linguistic connotation of the term 'literal,' see Chapter 2, above.

John H. Elliott's more recent work on 1 Peter indicates that he is aware of some ways *images* of honor and the *idiom* of honor and shame are vehicles for the conceptualization of the relationship between the social and the sacred in this letter. J.H. Elliott, "Disgraced Yet Graced. The Gospel according to 1 Peter in the Key of Honor and Shame," *Biblical Theology Bulletin* 25 (Winter 1996), 166–178.

filled: Christians Are *Slaves* but also *Freemen*; God Is the Household *Master* or *Paterfamilias*. Moreover, some of the Slaves of God are literally, in real life, slaves of some other actual masters, but probably the majority of the Slaves of God are *not* literally slaves. They are being asked to live by the metaphor Christians Are God's Slaves, to use it to shape how they think about their relationship to God and to other people, allowing it to constrain their everyday experience and actions, their thoughts and choices. At the same time (a double-scope blend) they are to understand their status and identity by another metaphor, Christians Are Freemen—even if they actually are, in everyday life, slaves in someone's household.[18] There are literal slaves and metaphorical Slaves in 1 Peter, and the moral exhortation pertains to them all.

The House For Household Metonymy

A key conceptual feature of the household language in this discourse is more metonymic than strictly metaphorical. That is, the οἶκος itself, the house (physical domain) stands for the household, the relationships within the extended family (συνοικέω—relational domain). The metonymy could be named

Οἶκος For Συνοικέω τίνι

or

House For Household / Family

One can see this happening in 2.4–8, where Peter presents the picture of a 'spiritual house' (οἶκος πνευματικὸς 2.5) in which the Christians (who have just been referred to as 'newborn infants' 2.2) are to think of themselves *as* 'living stones,' (ὡς λίθοι ζῶντες), part of a 'living' house. The metonymic dynamic allows the solidity, structure, and foundation of a house to be evoked along with the 'living' and 'spiritual' relational qualities belonging to the household. Via metonymy, in this expression the building (house) stands for the solid human and spiritual relationships being built among and through the people.

---

[18] Additionally, each time Peter uses 'Lord' (Κύριος) in conjunction with Jesus, a Slave/Master Frame is potentially evoked; the conceptual metaphor is Christians Are Slaves of Christ. About double-scope blends, see G. Fauconnier and M. Turner, *The Way We Think*, 131–135.

The image then shifts slightly and 'you' (plural, αὐτοί) are put in a different slot, one belonging to a novel extension of the typical household frame.

> καὶ   αὐτοὶ   ὡς λίθοι ζῶντες οἰκοδομεῖσθε οἶκος πνευματικὸς εἰς
> and yourselves as stones living are being built house spiritual into
>
> ἱεράτευμα ἅγιον ἀνενέγκαι πνευματικὰς θυσίας εὐπροσδέκτους ...
> priesthood holy to bring up spiritual   sacrifices well-accepted ...
>
> NRSV: like living stones, let yourselves be built into a spiritual house, to be a holy priesthood, to offer spiritual sacrifices acceptable ... (2.5)

Now the (authorial audience) readers are priests ('holy priesthood' ἱεράτευμα ἅγιον) ministering in this 'house,' which has (apparently) become the (metaphorical) Temple, God's 'house' (οἶκος).

The core metonymy (Οἶκος For Συνοικέω τίνι—House For Household) and the metaphors just discussed, together with many of those in the ensuing section of the discourse, create a complex megablend that is in turn networked with other metaphors and blends in the discourse to create a dazzling display of conceptual connections. Various mappings from the Household Frame to a basic Church As Household of God metaphor are evident in other parts of the discourse. To locate those metaphors, one needs to notice expressions with household connections, words and phrases that potentially serve as triggers evoking household domain concepts, but one then needs to consider what specific properties from the source domain concepts are mapped onto a target domain, and to locate the correct target domain. The following sections demonstrate how that set of methods can be deployed.

The Church Is God's Household

One way to check whether the analysis is truly locating source concepts belonging to the Greco-Roman context, rather than importing them from American English, is to see if the conceptual metaphor could be given a *Greek* name. Just now, we were able to give a Greek name to a core metonymy located in the discourse. This challenge can be taken up with regard to the metaphors, as well. Consider, for example, these options:

Target		Source
Χριστιανός	←	Οἶκος
Christian[s]	Are	a Household

Or

Χριστιανός ← Οἶκος Θεοῦ
Christian[s] Are The House of God

The first option relies, further, on the metonymy named in the previous section (Οἶκος For Συνοικέω τίνι). As the analysis proceeds, we will want to keep these proposals in mind, and continue to test them, to see if they remain coherent as the nuances of the mappings, the details, proliferate.

The details of the mappings of these major metaphors and metonymies significantly shape the inferential patterns evoked. To see how that happens, one needs to notice how various frame slots are filled by input from the target domain. For example, when Christian believers as a group constitute the target domain, they are fitted into selected slots in the Household Frame. As we have seen, Peter's readers are not always being asked to use the Christians Are God's Slaves metaphor. 'Christians' also are fitted into the Child slot: they are 'little children, infants' whose desire to grow 'into salvation' is expressed as a 'longing for the pure, spiritual milk.' (2.2) Peter specifies the kinds of entailments he has in mind: infantile longing for milk is mapped onto adult desire to 'grow' into salvation. The metaphor "A Christian Believer Is a Child [or Infant] of God" also shows up in other expressions from 1 Peter:

> he has given us a new *birth* ... (1.3)
> like *obedient children* (1.14)
> You have been *born anew*, not of perishable but of imperishable seed. (1.23)

In the 1.14 example, the *moral* concept of duty, of obedience, is being understood (and potentially, then, experienced) in terms of children's obedience towards their parents and elders. The general conceptual metaphor can be named Morality Is Childlike Obedience, but the specific entailments of that metaphor as it is used in 1 Peter are keyed to a child's relationship with the father in the socio-cultural model with which the text works. Moreover, the other metaphors with which this one blends put pressure on this one, qualifying it in certain ways.

'Infants' (2.2) receive care and enjoy the safety and love of the household, but they cannot literally obey. For the obedience metaphor to work, the babies have to become children (τέκνα 1.14); the metaphors shift as the words that prompt them change.[19] Sometimes in this text the

---

[19] In the text, the 'children' metaphor comes before the 'newborn infant' one.

'children' have grown up; they become *heirs* (1.4; 3.7, 3.9) and *brothers* (1.22, 2.17, 3.8, 5.12) and even *elders* (5.1, 5.5).

The Brotherhood

When Christians are 'brothers' in the metaphorical Household that is the church, a filial quality is given to the bonds forged in this association. This shows up clearly in expressions that use the word 'brother':

> Τὰς ψυχὰς ὑμῶν ἡγνικότες ἐν τῇ ὑπακοῇ τῆς ἀληθείας εἰς
> The souls your having purified in the obedience of the truth *for*
>
> φιλαδελφίαν ἀνυπόκριτον, ἐκ καθαρᾶς καρδίας ἀλλήλους
> *brotherly love* unhypocritical from clean heart one another
>
> ἀγαπήσατε ἐκτενῶς
> love intensely
>
> NRSV: Now that you have purified your souls by your obedience to the truth so that you have genuine mutual love, love one another deeply from the heart. (1.22)

Certain translation issues arise for English Bible readers at this point. How should φιλαδελφίαν be rendered, by 'brotherly love' or 'familial love' or in some other manner? 'Genuine mutual love' is more palatable to many modern readers because it is not so patriarchal, so male. But the 1st-century, Greco-Roman conceptual framework is grounded in 1st-century social experience. Given that experience, it is the power in *brotherhood* that is worth evoking. It is the 'beloved' (ἀγαπητοί—2.11), the 'brothers' who once were 'strangers' to one another and now together are 'exiles, sojourners' who have the power (and, now Peter argues, the responsibility) to extend their love, express their hospitality, towards other 'strangers.' They are to do this so often, so habitually, that they are known not only as 'brother-lovers' (φιλάδελφοι, 3.8), but also 'as stranger-lovers' (φιλόξενοι 4.9, mentioned above).

In this discourse the Brotherhood stands For Church Family, metonymically:

Ἀδελφότης	For	Οἶκος Χριστιανοῦ
Brotherhood	For	Christian Household
	and	
Ἀδελφότης	For	Οἶκος Θεοῦ
Brotherhood	For	God's Household

The name or title, 'Stranger-lovers' also functions metonymically; one aspect of the relational pattern within the Christian social group stands for the group identity:

φιλόξενοι For [relational patterns among] Οἶκος Χριστιανοῦ

Stranger-lovers For Christian Household [relational character]

Brothers (and Daughters) Are Heirs

Remember that honor, in this system, is inherited most directly by the male children. When that familial concept is mapped onto the moral domain, the metaphor is something like Good Moral Standing Is Heirship or Honor Is Inheritance; Good Moral Standing Is Inheriting the Family Fortune. One of the conventional entailments of the source concept, *heir*, is male gender. But look at the expressions from 1 Peter that use the *heir* slot, and notice the specific entailments in these mappings:

1) into an *inheritance* ... (1.4)
εἰς κληρονομίαν

2) paying honor to the woman ... since they too are also *heirs* of the gracious gift of life. (3.7b)
ἀπονέμοντες τιμὴν ὡς καὶ συγκληρονόμοις χάριτος ζωῆς

3) so that you might *inherit* a *blessing* (3.9b)
ἵνα εὐλογίαν κληρονομήσητε

Peter has declared his readers members of the Family of God, and he now makes it clear that in his thinking, the new (Gentile) converts to the Christ-way, Χριστιανός (4.16, here even taking that 'name') belong to the prototypical Family of God, the family of Abraham. So members of the (Christian, now) Family of God are also Children of Abraham. Women in the church Family (likely mostly Gentiles) are now to think of themselves *as daughters* of Sarah, especially in connection to their moral conduct (3.6): "You have become her *daughters* as long as you *do what is good* and never let fears alarm you." They are invited, then, to leave one family system ('the futile ways inherited from your ancestors' 1.18) and join another—this new Israelite-style household. (Good Christian Wives Are Daughters of Sarah). Moreover, in the Household of God, women, too are 'heirs' (3.7) and deserve honor from their husbands. Good Is Honor. The injunction for husbands to 'pay honor' to their wives '*as* heirs of the gracious gift of life' coheres with Peter's direction to 'honor everyone' (πάντας τιμήσατε 2.17a).

God as Paterfamilias: Honor and Holiness

Why is Peter calling these wives 'daughters' of Sarah? In the cultural model with which Peter works, the father's honor protects and is projected onto the entire household; conversely, the father's honor must be protected and defended. A family member's primary duty is to serve that honor, to act honorably, so as not to bring shame upon the household. The Petrine discourse's adoption and adaptation of this model is evident at several points. Notice that the injunction to behave like obedient children (1.14) is immediately followed by a declaration of God the Father's honor:

ἀλλὰ κατὰ τὸν καλέσαντα ὑμᾶς ἅγιον καὶ αὐτοὶ ἅγιοι ἐν
but by the one having called you holy and themselves holy ones in

πάσῃ ἀναστροφῇ γενήθητε, διότι γέγραπται [ὅτι] Ἅγιοι
all behavior become because it has been written [that] holy ones

ἔσεσθε, ὅτι ἐγὼ ἅγιος [εἰμι].
you will be because I holy [I am]

As he who called you is holy, be holy yourselves in all your conduct; for it is written, "You shall be holy, for I am holy." (1.15–16)

This Father's honor is displayed in his character, and that character is holiness itself. His Children, the intimate members of his Family, are to reflect that character as well: be like he is, holy. In fact, the household is to be so permeated by this Father's character, that another way to express what it is like to live there is to say, "live in holiness."

ἐν ἁγιασμῷ πνεύματος εἰς ὑπακοὴν
in holiness of spirit for obedience

NRSV: sanctified by the Spirit to be obedient (1.2b)

The bounded space opened by 'in' (ἐν) and qualified by 'holiness' (ἁγιασμῷ) is, more concretely, the Father's Οἶκος, the sphere of living wholly in honorable, harmonious relation to this Father and to the other members of his household. Moreover, within that household the Father's power to protect and support is assured:

πᾶσαν τὴν μέριμναν ὑμῶν ἐπιρίψαντες ἐπ' αὐτόν, ὅτι αὐτῷ
all the anxiety of you having thrown on him because to him

μέλει περὶ ὑμῶν ...
it is a care about you (pl)

Ὁ δὲ θεὸς πάσης χάριτος ... αὐτὸς καταρτίσει, στηρίξει,
the But God of all favor-grace himself will order will strengthen

σθενώσει   θεμελιώσει.
will invigorate will found, establish

NRSV: Cast all your anxiety on him, because he cares for you ... the God of all grace ... will himself restore, support, strengthen, and establish you. (5.7, 10a,c)

If the injunctions demanding obedience sounded hard and the warnings of judgment frightening, Peter's finishing touches soften and round out the picture; this is a strong but nurturing, deeply caring *paterfamilias*.

Traditional Israelite Household: Blessing and Honor

The Household Frame used here cannot be a standard 1st c. Greco-Roman one. Peter's Israelite heritage comes through loud and clear, not only because he mentions Sarah, but because his father God is strong but also nurturing and supportive. One can hear this source material from within Peter's Jewish heritage again when Peter injects into the discourse the notion of fatherly blessing (3.9).

Familial blessing and honor are essentially inherited, bestowed on the basis of belonging and the will of the *paterfamilias*. They are not, strictly speaking, earned. This is one way in which Moral Accounting is subverted or altered, qualified, in this discourse. The picture is not that the Father's blessing and the family honor are given because of, as rewards for, obedience. Rather, since the children in this family have inherited such a great name, honor is bestowed upon them; it accrues to them since they belong to this household. But then, as heirs, they are to live up to the household name, maintain the family honor. They did not earn their way into the household by their behavior. Instead, by virtue of their having been 'called' by Jesus Christ, who suffered and died, they were 'born' into this family. Think dative of sphere, rather than dative of instrument.

Ἐν ὀνόματι Χριστοῦ—The Family Name

Peter's teaching concerning household honor comes to its clear climax in chapter four. Here, The New Family of God bears the name of Christ and lives—and suffers—ἐν ὀνόματι Χριστοῦ (4.14), *as* Christians—ὡς Χριστιανός ... ἐν τῷ ὀνόματι τούτῳ (4.16). Behavior which upholds and guards the honor of this family name is expected—as is the suffering this will bring (4.14–16). This *name* is the pivot point, the crux, of the whole matter—it expresses the central Christian moral motivation and identity, and discloses the cost of so living.

How might a cognitivist analyze the function of ἐν τῷ here? One question would be, what *rudimentary image schema* might ἐν τῷ activate or evoke? The traditional grammatical label 'instrumental dative' is not inaccurate, it simply is not self-explanatory. Does ἐν τῷ evoke a sphere of power, almost an honorable-name force-field? Then by this name, because you bear this name, because you live in this sphere of honor, you will behave thusly, and you may well suffer accordingly.

The Cognitive *Power of Household Conventions*

Metaphors and metonymies using conventional Household framing, blended and networked, adapted and extended, shape Christian moral teaching. They lend structure to the Christians' identity, bestowing a family name, honor, and suggesting a specific locus in which a particular ethos can thrive. The House of God is a safe, bounded space in which honorable behavior makes sense, is 'good.' The implied constraints define a powerful and effective range of motion. Being a slave is not inherently good, but being a slave in God's household gives one such honor and status that one is free indeed. And by virtue of that freedom, one is free to serve others in everyday life—to not be defined by (ordinary, cultural) notions of status and honor according to caste or skill level, etc. Identity as a Child of God, an heir in that family, allows one to transcend ordinary (apparent, earthly) identities based on gender, social status, biological heritage, and so on. To belong in this household is to not be held down or back. It means to not have to wait for or strive for honor and power—or for the right to be a full moral agent. The message is clear: Christians do not have to wait until the second coming, until they enter heaven, to live in God's presence. They can do so now, in this world of broken social systems, dysfunctional families and households, and countries with pagan rulers. Christians do not have to wait for heaven to come down, nor do they get to wait until the Apocalypse sets everything straight—balances the moral books—to live good lives, to reflect the Father's honor.

Nested Houses or Spheres

This discourse weaves exhortation concerning behavior in ordinary houses and households into a discussion of cosmic proportions. It is as though the regular households are nested inside the 'spiritual' house (Church As Temple), which in turn is nested inside the ethnos (Church As People of God), which then is but a part of the heavenly domain or household, the cosmic sphere of God's dwelling. All are 'houses' of God; none is outside the scope of this father's power and concern. His honor, his essential moral character, which is holiness, permeates the whole House, at all levels. Honorable behavior in the microcosm—in ordinary households—reflects the character of the macrocosm, and displays moral status.

The Household is not, however, the smallest sphere, the most micro-level, Peter's moral discourse addresses and evokes. The human body itself is a site of moral struggle and strength, and it is to a consideration of the conceptual power of metaphors rooted in bodily experience that we now turn.

Ἐν τῷ σώματι, ἐν σαρκὶ βιῶσαι: Good Living In the Body

Ἀγαπητοί, παρακαλῶ ὡς παροίκους καὶ παρεπιδήμους
Loved Ones, I encourage as transients and resident aliens

ἀπέχεσθαι τῶν σαρκικῶν ἐπιθυμιῶν αἵτινες στρατεύονται
to hold off yourself of the fleshly desires that soldier

κατὰ τῆς ψυχῆς
against the (soul)

NRSV: Beloved, I urge you as aliens and exiles to abstain from the desires of the flesh that wage war against the soul. (2.11)

BH paraphrase: Loved Ones, hear my instruction. Listen to me! Think of yourselves as resident aliens—foreigners, visitors—in your present (native) cultural setting. You no longer belong here, at least not in the way you once did. Accordingly, you need to change the way you think about the relationship between your bodies and your psyches and your souls. Abstain from the kinds of bodily desires that belong to the unbelieving (non-Christ-honoring) world-culture, because now you know that those kinds of uncontrolled drives wage war against your very lives!

ὃς τὰς ἁμαρτίας ἡμῶν αὐτὸς ἀνήνεγκεν ἐν τῷ σώματι αὐτοῦ ἐπὶ τὸ
who the sins of us himself brought up ιν the body of him on the

ξύλον,   ἵνα   ταῖς ἁμαρτίαις   ἀπογενόμενοι   τῇ δικαιοσύνῃ
wood so that   in the sins   having become off   in the rightness

ζήσωμεν,   οὗ   τῷ μώλωπι   ἰάθητε
we might live   whose   the wound   you were healed

NRSV: He himself bore our sins in his body on the cross so that, free from sins, we might live for righteousness; by his wounds you have been healed. (2.24)

We have now surveyed metaphors for morality grounded in four very large domains—in Christ, in Time, in a Nation or People Group, and in the Household. But a survey of the metaphorical dynamics in 1 Peter would not be complete without a consideration of the role of a fifth domain, the arena of everyday bodily existence. Physical suffering and raw bodily desire are directly addressed in 1 Peter. But again, even more interesting than Peter's specific moral advice in this arena is the way in which bodily existence—with all of its messiness and its drive, verve, and force—serves as a complex source domain for thinking and talking about other equally real aspects of human existence: psychic suffering, hunger for spiritual growth, and the drive to find paths to transcendent value or goodness. Cognitive metaphor methodology encourages us to notice how language evokes those connections. Some Greek vocabulary directly evokes the bodily domain (σάρξ: flesh, the body itself; σῶμα: body, living body, mortal life, human existence), and this study will focus on how such words operate in Peter's moral discourse.[20] But the bodily domain figures into the moral discourse in other kinds of expressions as well, places where the Greek words we translate into English 'body' or 'flesh' do not appear, and we will attend to that dynamic, not only in the interest of thoroughness, but to demonstrate a point. The metaphorical work is *cognitive*; it does not happen just at the verbal level. Accordingly, this is not a 'word study' in the sense in which that has been carried out in (inexpert) biblical studies. I will argue that the deeper significance of Peter's use of the σάρξ and σῶμα vocabulary is concep-

---

[20] It is important not to conflate σάρξ and σῶμα. Achtemeier notes that in 1 Peter ἐν σαρκὶ ('in the flesh') often means 'human existence,' and not "the sinful nature of humanity. That is," says Achtemeier, "Christians must live in accordance with God's will, despite the suffering that may entail, for as long as human existence in its present condition continues." Achtemeier, *1 Peter*, 281, n. 66. Davids and Selwyn concur with Achtemeier's translation of ἐν σαρκὶ here as the sphere of mortal life or human existence. Davids, *The First Epistle of Peter*, 150; Ernest G. Selwyn, *The First Epistle of St. Peter* (2d ed.; London: Macmillan, 1955), 210.

tual. These 'body' and 'flesh' words can stand for not just the body, but for mortal life, or for the sphere of mortal life.[21] And these verbal expressions have the potential to evoke deep moral concepts—the notion that the body is a site of moral struggle and that bodily desire is a strong force connected to the cosmic struggle between good and evil.

Methodology and Reading Process Issues

First World, 21st-century readers cannot help but bring certain understandings and questions to the reading of this text. We have legitimate questions to raise about the connections between body and mind, psyche and neuron, and we are ready to sniff out (and eschew) body/mind splits, Neoplatonic or otherwise. We suspect the ancients of denigrating the body, deeming it dirty and defiling; our suspicions therefore find some corroborating evidence in this text. Further, we bring deep theodicy questions to 1 Peter: What does suffering mean? What does it indicate about a person's—or a people's—moral status? Is suffering a sign of sin and impending or present judgment? Is it a sign of abandonment by God—or even of God's absence or non-existence? If suffering is in 1 Peter a sign of solidarity with Jesus Christ, and therefore a good sign—a mark of election and blessing—then has Christianity indeed begun with the seeds of the legitimation of acquiescence in the face of unjust suffering that we tend to think so obviously ought to be rejected? We are wary readers. But in our wariness we might be aware that we bring our own conceptual baggage to the text, to the reading. (Thus my own moral exhortation).

Body, Ψυχή and Βίος: Sites for Display of Good and Evil

This section begins to unpack the role of the Body domain in Peter's moral discourse. Looking now over the letter as a whole, it is evident that the 'bodily desires' (σαρκικῶν ἐπιθυμιῶν 2.11) Peter tags are key to the behavioral changes and altered moral framework Peter is urging Christians to adopt and live by. They are to so live in and with their

---

[21] See, in this regard, Achtemeier's note regarding *sarki* and Calvin's interpretation of 1 Peter 4.1; *1 Peter*, 277, n. 17, n. 18.

bodies that they do not deserve the reputation of 'evil doers' (κακοποιῶν 2.12). This kind of language is most clearly seen later in the letter, at the beginning of the fourth chapter:

Χριστοῦ οὖ παθόντος σαρκὶ καὶ ὑμεῖς τὴν αὐτὴν ἔννοιαν
Of Christ then having suffered *in body* also you the same insight

ὁπλίσασθε, ὅτι ὁ παθὼν σαρκὶ πέπαυται
arm yourself because the one having suffered *in body* has stopped

ἁμαρτίας, εἰς τὸ μηκέτι ἀνθρώπων ἐπιθυμίαις ἀλλὰ θελήματι θεοῦ
sin for the no longer of people desires but want of God

τὸν ἐπίλοιπον ἐν σαρκὶ βιῶσαι χρόνον.
the remaining *in body* to live time

NRSV: Since, therefore Christ suffered in the flesh, arm yourselves also with the same intention (for whoever has suffered in the flesh has finished with sin), so as to live for the rest of your earthly life no longer by human desires but by the will of God. (4.1–2)

BH paraphrase: Here is the point: You know that Jesus Christ suffered *in his body*, both literally—when he was crucified—and in the sense that he suffered throughout his bodily, earthly life, the way all people do. Knowing that, you ought to fortify yourselves [arm yourselves in the war against evil] with the same kinds of desires, motivation and intention that Jesus had. (Because anyone who has suffered the way he did—in the body, in his earthly life—is finished with sin, is done with "missing the target"). Live this way—like Jesus—so completely that for the rest of your earthly life you are not guided and driven by human desires and drives but by God's will and desires.

Notice that God Is a Person, with human-like will and desires. Multiple metaphors and metonymies grounded in the physical domain blend and cluster in this section of Peter's discussion of everyday morality, and in a moment we will discuss desire and will, but first notice how yet another zone is opened up with 'in' (ἐν) and other dative markers. 'In bodily life' (ἐν σαρκὶ βιῶσαι) may metonymically stand for life as a whole, serving as a tag for human earthly, mortal existence as opposed to heavenly or spiritual existence.

Ἐν Σαρκὶ βιῶσαι For Mortal Existence

Bodily Life For Mortal Existence (in its totality)

But the dative form—σαρκὶ—also opens up a spatial zone, where The Body Is a Container, a site or bounded region, and Christ's body is a site of suffering. Consider how that concept operates in 2.24, where σάρξ does not appear:

ὃς   τὰς ἁμαρτίας ἡμῶν αὐτὸς ἀνήνεγκεν ἐν τῷ σώματι αὐτοῦ ἐπὶ τὸ
who the   sins   of us himself brought up   *in the body* of him on the

ξύλον, ἵνα ταῖς ἁμαρτίαις ἀπογενόμενοι τῇ δικαιοσύνῃ
wood, so that in the sins   having become off in the rightness

ζήσωμεν,   οὗ τῷ μώλωπι   ἰάθητε   (2.24)
we might live whose the wounds you were healed

> NRSV: He himself bore our sins in his body on the cross, so that, free from sins, we might live for righteousness; by his wounds you have been healed.

Here the words ἐν τῷ σώματι evoke the conceptual metaphor The Body Is a Container. The words are different but the concept is congruent with that in 2.11 and 4.1. Consider, further, a place where the Body As Container conceptual metaphor is operating without the use of either of the explicit body words—no σάρξ or σῶμα language:

ὧν   ἔστω οὐχ ὁ   ἔξωθεν ἐμπλοκῆς τριχῶν καὶ περιθέσεως
Of whom let be not the *from outside* braiding of hair and setting around

χρυσίων ἢ ἐνδύσεως ἱματίων κόσμος ἀλλ' ὁ κρυπτὸς τῆς καρδίας
of gold or dressing of clothes adorned but the *hidden*   *of the heart*

ἄνθρωπος ἐν τῷ   ἀφθάρτῳ τοῦ πραέως καὶ ἡσυχίου πνεύματος,
human being in the incorruptible of the gentle and quiet   spirit

ὅ ἐστιν ἐνώπιον τοῦ θεοῦ   πολυτελές.
which is before   the God very costly / valuable

> NRSV: Do not adorn yourselves *outwardly* by braiding your hair, and by wearing gold ornaments or fine clothing; rather, let your adornment be the *inner self* with the lasting beauty of a gentle and quiet spirit, which is very precious in God's sight (3.3–4).

Human bodies—here, wives' bodies—have outsides and insides. By cultural conventional belief, the inside of the container holds a person's true moral essence.[22] The tacit questions addressed here are about value, both aesthetic and ethical, but also tactical: How is authentic beauty and goodness to be displayed in a Christian wife's life, so that God (the legitimate and ultimate Moral Authority) is pleased and her husband is drawn into the Christian household? Peter's position is that a wife's *inner* moral qualities—her Moral Essence—is of much

---

[22] Regarding moral essence, see Lakoff and Johnson, *Philosophy in the Flesh*, 306–308, and Lakoff, *Moral Politics*, 250. Lakoff observes that in contemporary Western culture, "The heart is the metaphorical locus of moral essence." 250. Also see the discussion of Moral Essence and its place in Moral Accounting in Chapter 5, above.

more importance than her *outward* beauty.[23] In this moral system, the prized moral dispositions, character traits issuing from someone with good moral essence, are indeed gender-qualified, if not entirely gender-specific. So Peter lists the character preferences in Christian wives: a general purity and reverence of life (3.2 Morality Is Purity), a gentle and quiet spirit (3.4); whereas he exhorts husbands (these would be Christian husbands, not the non-Christian husbands of the wives addressed above) to 'show consideration' and 'honor' their wives (3.7). But Peter may be bucking convention, or at least pushing it, when in his address to wives he uses the phrase ὁ κρυπτὸς τῆς καρδίας ἄνθρωπος, 'hidden in the *human* heart' (3.4).[24] What Peter says to wives he bases on an argument about what is *human*. Peter goes on to urge husbands to honor wives as full 'heirs of the gracious gift of life.' Presumably, men who acted that way would be gentle and have quiet spirits as well. Indeed, a little later in the letter Peter urges all of his readers, κύριον δὲ τὸν Χριστὸν ἁγιάσατε ἐν ταῖς καρδίαις ὑμῶν. A wooden translation is: 'make holy in your hearts, Christ as Master'. (3.15)[25] The holiness of everyone's 'heart'—not just of women's moral essence—is of concern to Peter.

The human body, then, is conceptualized as a primary site or container for inner moral essence, a container which becomes a vehicle for display of that essence. Some cautions are in order, however. Container metaphors inherently entail boundaries; separation between an 'inside' and an 'outside' is a key conceptual inference such image schemas carry.[26] Modern readers may too easily inject ancient Platonic or modern Cartesian mind—body splits into the picture. One way of reading and interpreting Peter's point here is to see him drawing a distinction between what happens 'in the body' over against mental or spiritual life. But this author's cultural roots are in tradi-

---

[23] The thought here coheres with the teaching of Jesus, directed to male Pharisees, regarding the primacy of *inner* moral essence over *outer* or outward displays or apparent goodness. See, e.g., Mark 7:14–23.
[24] Note that the metonymy Heart For Core or Important, and the metaphor Central Is Important are in play.
[25] NRSV has: "but in your hearts, sanctify Christ as Lord."
[26] Cognitive linguistic analysis lends support to the conclusions reached by Achtemeier, et al. (n. 21, above), who use the notion of dative of sphere to interpret ἐν σαρκὶ as "human existence." From a cognitive linguistic perspective, 'dative of sphere' works via cognitive processes such that *en* evokes a container schema. In addition, ἐν σαρκὶ may metonymically stand for human existence. An English shorthand name for this metonymy would be "Body For Human Life."

tional Jewish understandings of the wholeness of the human person. Accordingly, his construal of the Body As Container image schema does not entail a separation between body and mind; there is no separation between the physical container and its contents. Peter is emphasizing embodiment over against a lack of concern with 'life in this world' among his audience.[27] 'Life in the body' would include the container plus *all* of its contents—mind and ψυχή. Peter insists that even for those anticipating Christ's return and their own (bodily) resurrection, life in the body matters. The Body As Container concept here, then, is more about the whole person being embodied than 'inbodied.'[28]

To see how this container becomes a zone or site of *struggle* between good and evil, we must consider another key component of these complex blends, the conceptual notion of effective force.

The FORCE of Bodily Desire

Moral Force Is Physical Force turns up in various guises. First, consider how the concept of the *moral* force of bodily desire is grounded in our human experience and observation of ordinary cause and effect. Joseph Grady outlines how the primary metaphor [Psychological] COMPULSION IS A COMPELLING FORCE is motivated, and gives a few English examples:

> Motivation: The correlation between deliberate action and motion through space
>
> (corollary of ACTION IS SELF-PROPELLED MOTION).

---

[27] This suggestion comes from Joel B. Green, personal correspondence, March 18, 2003.

[28] The range of usages—of evocative potential—in Greek 'body' vocabulary, including σάρξ and σῶμα, bears out this 'embodied' interpretation. Louw and Nida, for example, find it necessary to list σάρξ in six different domains: Body, Body Parts (8.4, 8.63), People (9.11, 12, 14, 15); Kinship Terms (10.1); Trouble, Hardship (22.20); Physiological Processes and States (23.90); Attitudes and Emotions (25.29); Psychological Faculties (26.7, 8). The primary bodily experiential concepts associated with σάρξ are ready source material for figurative, metaphorical appropriation; Body Is Life. Similarly, but *not* in identical fashion, σῶμα potentially evokes a range of concepts, from the very concrete ("human body"; Louw and Nida 8.1) to the more abstract, "physical being" (9.8). It then is available to stand for the church (11.34), for a slave (87.78) or, most abstractly, for an "archetype or foreshadowing" (58.66). Louw and Nida, *Greek-English Lexicon of the New Testament Based on Semantic Domains*, 2d ed. (New York and London: United Bible Societies, 1988, 1989).

Examples: Vanity finally *drove* me to have the operation.
My friends *pushed* me into volunteering.²⁹

We use our experience of physical cause and effect to understand and express the feeling that motivation is sometimes coming to us from outside, from some outer force. Now consider the following expressions from 1 Peter, where Bodily Desire Is a Strong Force:

1) Ἀγαπητοί, παρακαλῶ ὡς παροίκους καὶ παρεπιδήμους
Loved ones, I encourage as transients and   strangers

   ἀπέχεσθαι   τῶν σαρκικῶν ἐπιθυμιῶν αἵτινες   στρατεύονται
   to hold off yourself of the bodily   desires   which soldier/make war

   κατὰ   τῆς ψυχῆς (2.11)
   against the   soul

Here the verb ἀπέχω evokes the (physically grounded) concept of *holding off from oneself, controlling physical* desires, as though desire itself were a force-wielding object. One primary metaphor operating here is DIFFICULTIES ARE OPPONENTS, which Grady suggests is motivated by "the correlation between feelings of strain and discomfort and physical struggle."³⁰ When the mappings are constructed, in some cases the force of evil or good is an *inner* force, and the struggle between good and evil seems to play out entirely inside the container of the human person. But in other cases, Evil Is an External Force and Evil Is an Opponent, where the force encountered is conceptualized as coming *from outside*.

Accordingly, Grady's style of analysis fits with another part of the expression in 2.11, the verb στρατεύομαι κατὰ—'soldiering against, warring against'. It fills out an image schema, elaborating the kind of force and struggle that goes on in the moral domain—it feels like war! (Inner Moral Struggle Is War) In this case, the *war* is between aspects of the person. Ἐπιθυμιῶν ("desires") and τῆς ψυχῆς ('inner self, essence; life'; or 'person') are *at war* with one another.³¹ This coheres with the way

---

²⁹ Grady, "Foundations of Meaning," 287.
³⁰ Ibid., 291.
³¹ The word ψυχή is capable of evoking many concepts, all related to dynamics of human personal existence. Louw and Nida locate it in at least three major domains: Psychological Faculties (26.4, "inner self," "the essence of life in terms of thinking, willing, and feeling"); Physiological Processes and States (23.88; "to be alive, to live, life"); and People (9.20; "person, people."). The latter is, they say, "a figurative extension of [the] meaning of ψυχή 'inner self, mind,' 26.4." Louw and Nida, *Greek-English Lexicon*

Peter uses a very different set of words in 4.1 (cited above) from the war/battle domain:

> 2) Χριστοῦ οὖν παθόντος σαρκὶ καὶ ὑμεῖς τὴν αὐτὴν ἔννοιαν
> Of Christ then having suffered *in body* also you the same insight
>
> ὁπλίσασθε,
> *arm* yourself (4.1)

Arm yourself for this war. This is a struggle one can prepare for, an idea Peter gets across with (1.13) another very bodily expression, but one in which physical preparation is used to talk about mental preparation:

> 3) Διὸ ἀναζωσάμενοι τὰς ὀσφύας τῆς διανοίας ὑμῶν νήφοντες
> So that *having bound up the hips of the intelligence your being well-balanced*
>
> τελείως ἐλπίσατε ἐπὶ τὴν φερομένην ὑμῖν χάριν ἐν ἀποκαλύψει
> completely you hoped on the being carried to you favor in uncovering
>
> Ἰησοῦ Χριστοῦ
> of Jesus Christ (1.13)
>
> NRSV: Therefore prepare your minds for action; discipline yourselves; set all your hope on the grace that Jesus Christ will bring you when he is revealed.

The metaphors are not in the words; they are conceptual and conventional. What we have here is a series of evocations of a conventionalized view of the make-up of the human person. Within the Human Person Container, separate competing faculties vie for control, and are ideally kept in balance. But that schema is intertwined with another schema in which a cosmic battle between the forces of good and evil is waged. A basic War Frame, then, gets filled in differently, depending on whether the battle site—the Container—is the individual, the church (or another social group), or the cosmos. Macrocosm and microcosm mirror one another in Peter's universe, and at every level good and evil are strong forces impossible to avoid.

As Peter winds up his letter, his picture of that good versus evil struggle turns vivid:

> 4) Νήψατε, γρηγορήσατε. ὁ ἀντίδικος ὑμῶν διάβολος ὡς λέων
> Be well-balanced, keep awake. The opponent of you s landerer as lion

---

of the New Testament Based on Semantic Domains, §9.20; 23.88; 26.4. Here ψυχή seems to evoke the concept of 'essence' or personal inner self which struggles against 'desires' that would destabilize or taint that core.

ὠρυόμενος περιπατεῖ ζητῶν [τινα] καταπιεῖν. ᾧ ἀντίστητε
roaring walks around seeking whom to swallow. whom stand against

στερεοὶ τῇ πίστει ...
solid in the faith

NRSV: Discipline yourselves, keep alert. Like a roaring lion your adversary the devil prowls around, looking for someone to devour. Resist him, steadfast in your faith ... (5.8–9a).

Evil is personified in the form of a roaring lion. Evil Is a Wild Animal (Lion)—or Lion For Wild Animal+Evil Is an External Force. Evil is ὁ ἀντίδικος, 'the opponent,' certainly. And this opponent metaphor is blended with the lion metaphor to evoke a rich picture full of entailments: evil is a predatory, dangerous, strong, and cunning external force. Peter's moral advice is νήψατε, γρηγορήσατε, ἀντίστητε στερεοὶ ('keep your balance, stay sober; watch out and stand firm') against evil. That is, Peter borrows understandings and experience from the domain of human bodily experience to explain how he understands moral struggle.

The moral struggle is not merely individual struggle to maintain personal piety. It is not mere bodily desire regarding which Peter is suggesting his readers must 'keep your heads clear; maintain balance.' For readers familiar with the traditional Jewish scriptures, especially with particular Psalms, the prowling lion words could (would?) evoke associations with economic and social injustice. Here is part of Psalm 10, for example:

> Why do you stand so far off O Lord:
>   and hide your face in time of need and trouble?
> The wicked in their pride *hunt down the poor*:
>   let them be snared by their own devices.
> ...
> They *lie in ambush* in the villages:
>   and in secret they murder the innocent,
>   *stealthily* they watch for the helpless.
> They *lie in hiding, as a lion lurks in its den*:
>   they *lie waiting to seize their prey*.
> They seize the poor: and drag them off in their net.
>   the innocent are cursed,
>   and sink down before them:
>   the weak cannot stand against their might.
> They say in their heart, 'God has forgotten:
>   God has looked away and will never see it.'
> Arise O lord God, and lift up your hand:

> do not forget the poor in their need.
> Why should the wicked make light of God:
> and say in their heart,
> 'God will not call us to account'?[32]

Notice that Moral Accounting is in play in this Psalm, and that the innocent and poor call on God to 'see' (and therefore to know—Knowing Is Seeing) what economic oppressors are doing. The psalmist calls on God to come to the aid of the 'weak' and to come near—not to 'stand far off.' For readers who know this Psalm and others like it, Peter's prowling lion words potentially evoke this whole scenario. In addition to a societally (not individually)—keyed version of the Moral Accounting Schema, other stock metaphors for morality are evoked, both in the Psalm and in the 1 Peter passage, by the Evil Is a Prowling Lion words:

> MORALITY IS STRENGTH (κραταιός, κράτος 5.6, 5.11; στηρίζω—strengthen 5.10; σθενόω—invigorate 5.10)
> MORALITY IS BALANCE (νήφω 1.13; 4.7; 4.8) and, by extension, the same verb connotes sobriety, so that
> MORALITY IS CLEAR-HEADEDNESS/ SOBRIETY (1.13; 4.7; 4.8)

The more abstract conceptual metaphors for morality like Evil Is a Force and Good Is a Force are often found alongside this sort of more tangible, generic level metaphor. They work together to create coherent, persuasive moral discourse.

Good Desire / Bodily Goodness

Bodily Desire is not always evil or malignant in 1 Peter. Consider the following positive uses of desire as force:

> 1.12c εἰς ἃ   ἐπιθυμοῦσιν   ἄγγελοι   παρακύψαι
>   for which desire   messengers / angels to stoop down
>
> NRSV: things into which angels long to look!

Here human desire for understanding is projected onto how angelic beings might feel. The overall thrust is emphatic; a rhetorician would call it *pathos*. What do the angels long to look into? They 'desire' hidden things that are contained in the message declared, what was

---

[32] Ps 10. 1–2, 8–14. And see Chapter 2.

'uncovered' and made clear to the prophets who testified 'in the spirit' about Christ's sufferings. The desire is positive, not a sign of evil.

And consider the following example of desire that is good:

2.2–3 ὡς ἀρτιγέννητα βρέφη τὸ λογικὸν ἄδολον γάλα ἐπιποθήσατε, ἵνα
as newborn infants the reasonable unguile milk *desire longingly* so that

ἐν αὐτῷ αὐξηθῆτε εἰς σωτηρίαν, εἰ ἐγεύσασθε ὅτι χρηστὸς
in it you might grow into deliverance if you taste that kind

ὁ κύριος
the master

NRSV: Like newborn infants, long for the pure, spiritual milk, so that by it you may grow into salvation—if indeed you have tasted that the Lord is good.

The verb here is an aorist imperative form of επιποθέω ('desire, long for'). It would be hard to find a clearer example of good desire than an infant longing for milk. The picture is very physical: we know what it is for newborns to want milk, and we have seen the desperation that they can display, the determination with which they usually get what they want. This desire is based on real need. Not only for growth, but for life itself, infants have to get this milk and take it in. A number of primary metaphors are at work here:

DESIRE /NEED IS HUNGER
THE NECESSARY MATERIAL FOR A PROCESS IS FOOD (e.g. spiritual milk)
APPEALING IS TASTY.

Transferred to the moral domain, they fund some basic blends: Desire For Moral and Spiritual Growth Is Hunger; The Necessary Material For Moral Growth Is Food, Appealing Moral/Spiritual Input Is Tasty Food; Moral Development Is Physical Growth. Again some stock metaphors for morality are in play: Morality Is Health; Morality Is Strength.

Some of these same stock metaphors are displayed again, a little later in the letter:

3.10 ὁ γὰρ θέλων ζωὴν ἀγαπᾶν καὶ ἰδεῖν ἡμέρας ἀγαθὰς παυσάτω τὴν
the one for wanting life to love and to see days good let stop the

γλῶσσαν ἀπὸ κακοῦ καὶ χείλη τοῦ μὴ λαλῆσαι δόλον ...
tongue from bad and lips the not to speak guile

NRSV: For Those who desire life and desire to see good days, let them keep their tongues from evil and their lips from speaking deceit.

Desire, rooted in physical experience, is a vehicle for understanding longing for more abstract goods—good days in general, long life. The (OT) author Peter quotes uses commonplace human desire for these good ends to motivate specific moral behavior, self-control and honesty. Notice again that Evil Is a Force one should 'stop' (Moral Conviction Is Strength; Moral Action Is Resisting A Strong Force).[33] Here, Evil Is a Force that attempts to control a part of one's body. The tongue and lips metonymically stand for the faculty of speech (Tongue/Lips For Speech), and speech may stand for self-expression. Morality Is Self-control, specifically, control of what one says. Honesty, congruence in one's speech with what one knows to be true, is clearly a value. This value is conceptually tied—via these metaphors and metonymies—to a kind of desire that is good, to moral motivation. Peter says, in effect, if you want to live well and prosper, then live by these metaphors for morality.

Misreading Desire

That bodily desire is *not* always evil or malignant in 1 Peter is very important, because this letter has been misread—and misused in preaching, moral teaching and ethical thinking—at this very point. While it is true that in 4.2 the passions or desires of people are opposed to the will or desire of God, in other places Peter displays an understanding of positive, good human desire. Here is one way of understanding the nature of the misunderstanding: There is a set of conventions regarding struggle and another set of conventions regarding struggle between body and soul. These sets of conventions interact in the text and as the reader interprets it. Peter both adopts and adapts certain cultural and conceptual conventions regarding struggle, the body, and inner life; his adaptations and re-definitions rely on the reader's understandings of the conventions.

Struggle is conventionally framed in terms of sport or other difficult physical effort. But 1 Peter also uses a War Frame, with given (unconsciously presupposed) slots, relations, properties, and relying on specific knowledge of war (socio-culturally specific, that is—based on

---

[33] Lakoff and Johnson discuss self-control as the forced movement of an object. Self Control Is Object Control is then combined with Action is Movement and Causes are Forces to get Self Control Is the Forced Movement of An Object; *Philosophy in the Flesh*, 271–272.

experience and stories particular to the author's culture). That frame is applied in more than one way in 1 Peter. Sometimes the contestants or warring factions slot is filled by ψυχή and σάρξ; but in other places those slots are filled by ἀγαθός and κακός, good and evil. Especially when these multiple slot-fillings are closely juxtaposed, the reader—seemingly naturally, effortlessly—blends the two uses of the same frame. The two are conflated, so that a conceptual coordination arises: ψυχή is to good as σάρξ or σῶμα is to evil.[34]

But modern readers also are apt to insert conventions from later developments in Western culture. The problem is not just one of juxtaposition in the text. One set of Western conventions regarding the relationships between body and soul could be summarized:

BODY: MORTAL: BAD: WEAK: WOMAN
SOUL: IMMORTAL: GOOD: RATIONAL: MAN.

This is the modern upshot of Neoplatonic assumptions, and the crux of the mind/body split with which we've struggled in the Christian West for lo these many centuries. But as I have shown, in 1 Peter sometimes bodily desire is used to understand and experience *good* desire (even good physical desire) and moral motivation. Modern Western traditional conflations and conventions can be misleading, and a reader who held onto them would not fully be able to enter the authorial audience.

When Peter refers to wives as 'weaker vessels' (3.7b ἀσθενεστέρῳ σκεύει), for example, he may seem to be endorsing this entire set of (Neoplatonic and genderized body/mind split) conventions. But, as I have argued, when he names women "heirs" and directs husbands to accord wives honor Peter makes it clear that he does not accept the entire convention (expressed in the linked concepts above). Peter also is not endorsing the linkage between Body and Bad implied in this conventional schema. He has a different way of construing the struggle with desire, and he uses yet another set of conventions to get his ideas across.

What Peter does say, however, certainly opens up questions about the relationships between body and soul, ψυχή and mind, and the roles they play—their interplay—in the moral life. We would like to understand better the nuanced differences between desire and will, and between

---

[34] Σάρξ and σῶμα are not identical; see n. 28, above. See also Achtemeier's discussion of σάρξ in *1 Peter*, 276–279.

kinds of desire—appetite or thirst as opposed to lust, for example. The bodily grounding of desire seems clear, and one would expect desire for basic human needs—food, water, sex—to be central cases. People get what they want by grasping and holding, eating, drinking—and these are indeed used to conceptualize and express how other, non-physical, desires are met. But human social needs for relationship and belonging are also basic—perhaps just as basic as the physical needs—and so are the drives to knowledge, power, status.

Body, Desire and Holiness: What Does Peter Teach?

Peter's ethical ideal and moral stance in the face of suffering is expressed in the concepts of balance, sobriety, trust, and the perseverance and honor of soldierly battle. Suffering in this world does not come as a surprise nor as an insult. Peter's counsel is against denial or avoidance. He also forbids retaliation or revenge—the customary violent underbelly of conventional Moral Accounting. But neither does he begin to make kingdom-on-earth social-political plans; he does not seem zealous to reform broken social structures (patriarchal marriage; slavery)—except … Except by way of calling all Roman (human) hierarchies, social structures, into question with the ways in which he adapts and customizes those structures. Putting the Roman Empire under question is no small move.

The moral world of 1 Peter is fully physical while being aware of the power of the human ψυχή (granting that the construal there differs from our post-Freudian one). But reductionistic materialism would never fly in Peter's context. For his is a reality stretching into transcendence—or rather, the transcendent reaches into the ordinary at every point. Peter believes that heaven is real. He believes that Jesus is Christ and that he has been raised from the dead. He believes that this Christ has transcendent power but that he is identical with the Jesus who suffered. He believes, then, that physical suffering does not negate meaning or transcendence. But he does not recommend suffering in and of itself as a means to attaining transcendence or as payment for moral debt. He lets the suffering life and the death by crucifixion of Jesus frame the believers' present reality of suffering. In Christ, bodily and heavenly actuality are united. Peter's practical moral advice makes sense within the cultural context in which it is conceptually framed. It is easy to misread. If 21st c. readers imagine that in χρόνος Peter has created cocooned Christians who will fly only in some heavenly butterfly zone (καιρός), this is a sign that we have failed to enter the authorial audience. For Peter, the risen Christ brings καιρός right into χρόνος, creating an earthy transcendent meaning space in the body. And it is a space in which he urges his readers to live, in their here and now. Καιρός and kingdom impinge on present reality, messy and distorted though those present arrangements may be. In Peter's opinion, Christians do not have to wait—for the apocalypse, for the Day of Reckoning and its rewarding aftermath—to be good. They do not *have to* wait, and they do not *get to* wait. This message comes through, loud and clear, across the centuries, across the cultural divide.

Conclusion: Metaphors Christians Live In and By

How are moral issues defined and addressed in this letter? Peter's moral landscape is wide and detailed; the discourse addresses moral issues in the social-political realm, in households and economic structures, in church relationships and structures. He manages to focus, as well, on individual moral development, character, and disposition. Some tough issues are considered: How should Christians who are slaves respond to abusive treatment by their masters? How should Christians who are slaves deal with the condition of servitude in general? How should women who have become Christians behave towards their non-Christian husbands? How should Christians respond to verbal abuse and slander, and to other kinds of persecution? Peter is concerned about some general topics: 1) The Christians' stance vis-à-vis the state, governmental authorities. 2) Church leaders' understanding of (and use of) their power and authority within the group. 3) Personal sexual morality; personal integrity (in financial matters, for example—no stealing). Along the way, Peter manages to bring into consideration some metamoral issues: The nature of moral responsibility and agency; moral consequences, both immediate and long-term; the structure of legitimate moral authority; the notion of justice and fairness; and, again, the significance of moral character and the necessity—and the possibility—of moral development, of change.

This moral discourse is constructed with and communicates via a number of metamoral metaphors Peter uses to open up moral-behavioral spaces. Some of the more distinctive features of Peter's moral discourse consist in the overarching schematizations that provide structure and grounding for his specific moral advice—especially the image schemas ἐν Χριστῷ, and ἐν καιρῷ, and the notion that both holiness (*like* that which is central to God's essential character) and suffering (*as* Jesus did) are expected to permeate Christian living in all spheres—in the social-political realm, in household and economic relationships, and in personal daily existence in the body.

The letter is fully immersed in its 1st-century cultural context, yet manages to be translatable and understandable. Its rootedness in primary metaphor and its employment of metamoral metaphorical schematization facilitates that understandability, while working out the details of source domain mappings onto specific target concepts highlights its unique and foreign characteristics. But the work of reading and interpreting 1 Peter as exemplar of Christian moral discourse is not complete. Reading such a document evokes various responses. In Chapter 9, we consider how 21st-century Christians readers might engage this early exemplar of Christian moral discourse.

CHAPTER NINE

AFTER READING 1 PETER

> *Let the Torah never be for you an antiquated decree, but rather like a decree freshly issued, no more than two or three days old ... But Ben Azzai said: Not even as old as a decree issued two or three days ago, but as a decree issued this very day.*
>
> —*Pesikta* of Rab Kahana[1]

This investigation, the 'reading,' has identified seven major fields of metamoral metaphors in 1 Peter. The letter's moral message coheres within these complex, blended spaces that provide the setting, the moral context, for Christian living. Peter's readers are enjoined to live holy lives: 1) in view of immediate and ultimate consequences (Moral Accounting) and 2) legitimate moral authority (the Chain of Being); 3) in Christ, 4) in time (καιρός and χρόνος), 5) in social-political reality (ἔθνος), 6) in an extended family and economy (οἶκος θεοῦ), and 7) in the human body (σαρκός, σῶμα), bodily life. But to read 1 Peter as exemplar of Christian moral discourse is to enter a process and a conversation. The process does not end when investigation and descriptive work ends.

The conversation—or conversations, plural, since a given reader may belong to multiple discourse communities—is ongoing and ancient. I, for example, belong to several reading communities: the Christian community, which for centuries has held 1 Peter as canonical Scripture; the community of Christian ethicists, which recognizes 1 Peter as a source of authority,[2] my NT scholarly community, for which 1 Peter is an object of study; my linguistics community, for which this text is

---

[1] This version of the *pesikta* is quoted from David Hartman, *A Heart of Many Rooms: Celebrating the Many Voices Within Judaism*, piska 12:12 (Woodstock, Vt.: Jewish Lights Publishing, 1999), 53. Another translation is available in *Pesikta de-Rav Kahana: R. Kahana's Compilation of Discourses for Sabbaths and Festal Days*, tr. William G. Braude and Israel J. Kapstein (Philadelphia: Jewish Publication Society of America, 1975).

[2] Scripture is not just one source among many; it is the *norma normans non normata*—"norming norm not normed by something else." That which grounds the Christian ethical discussion.

an example of the 1st-century *koine* Greek epistle and of interest for its conceptual metaphorical features; my local faith community, for which 1 Peter is a devotional and liturgical source, and sometimes an object of study, even sometimes—hallelujah—a voice to which we listen and allow to shape our life together. If the reader has at all entered the authorial audience, the conversation has been joined long before the reading—or a first reading—was completed. If the reader belongs to a reading community, in some ways the conversation is only now beginning; the moral discourse 1 Peter prompts can begin in earnest, now that a 'reading' has been undertaken.

Now, then, the task is to ask how 1 Peter construes Christian morality and to respond to that construal. What kinds of moral ideas and ideals are in evidence? How are moral problems defined and understood? What experiences are construed as *moral* conflicts, as morally weighted? What kinds of difficulties are recognized to be moral difficulties or to have moral verve, charge, and consequences? Moreover, since in 1 Peter so much of the metaphorical work happens at the *metamoral* level, the question is, do the *metamoral* metaphors in 1 Peter mesh with our own, or not? Where they differ, can we yet understand the 1st-century concepts well enough to respond to them?

But let me clarify the approach taken here by saying what it is *not*, taking the *via negativa:* Response to 1 Peter as exemplar would not be about choosing which points of moral advice we find relevant, nor is it about accepting or rejecting the 'worldview' of 1 Peter. It is not about finding or selecting certain moral lessons to apply to our own situation, and thereby de-selecting what strikes us as irrelevant or even absurd. Again, the task will not be to bring a current moral problem to this text and ask it to resolve our problem.

Instead, after reading we get to talk back, to enter into the discourse as dialog partners. This phase of the conversation is about continued reflection, in light of what 1 Peter has said, on the moral issues highlighted. But even more than attention to the particular 'issues' raised, the interest here is in how the *ethos*, the approach to morality, 1 Peter has demonstrated strikes us. Where do we resonate and receive it readily? Where do we resist, and why? Can readers in the Christian faith community give Peter *Christian moral* reasons for resisting particular points? When we resist points of advice (as, for example, that given to slaves with harsh masters) or particular facets of this construal of faithful Christian living, can we become aware of the conceptual metaphors at work in our own thinking? That is, we now have the task of reflecting on our own moral *ethos* and moral struggles in the light of what we have experienced as we attempted to become members of 1 Peter's authorial audience.

In the sections that follow, I sketch findings in each of the seven metamoral metaphor arenas and respond to those findings, indicating some of the ways in which I find myself being 'read' by this text. To be 'read' by the text means that as I read 1 Peter, input from my own experience and understanding is evoked, input that I inevitably blend with what I pick up as I engage the text. Sometimes this reading and being read by the text prompts associations with current social-ethical issues and memories of my own experiences. Reading 1 Peter raises questions for me, questions that I ponder on my own, but also issues I want to discuss with my (various) reading communities. Accordingly, each section below also includes questions that I would address to my reading communities, in the wake of reading 1 Peter, in the hope that together we will be moved to enter the discourse.

Moral Accounting and Authority in 1 Peter

1 Peter's ethic is expressed in view of immediate and ultimate consequences, and these are addressed in conjunction with questions about how Christians identify legitimate moral authority. Cognitive metaphor study points to the shaping significance in the moral discourse of 1 Peter of a general Moral Accounting metaphor and of specific schematic and framing variations on that theme. Complex social constructs of honor and shame and of the patron-client relationships through which honor and shame were experienced in everyday life contribute distinctive flavor to the version of Moral Accounting encountered in the letter. 'Balancing' the moral books turns out to be a social, collective concern here, rather than a merely personal matter. Moral responsibility is, accordingly, keyed to the moral balance—honor—of the group to which one belongs, to the societal ties that define identity. It is not that individual responsibility is erased, but personal moral accountability is inextricably linked to one's social identity and belonging. Moral agency and responsibility, then, are indeed expressed in terms of Moral Accounting in 1 Peter.

Accounting for moral status in 1 Peter is expressed via blends of Moral Accounting metaphors with framing from the legal domain. Moral Accounting becomes 'judgment,' at more than one level, keyed to more than one time frame. In the ongoing present, there is interim judgment delegated to legitimate moral authorities (governmental officials, heads of families and churches). But the Moral Accounting picture in 1 Peter cannot be completed or understood absent the notion of ultimate judgment, the Day of Oversight, in which the accounts will all be reviewed by the ultimate accountant/judge: God himself. Moral behavior—good and bad, individual and societal—has both incremental and cumulative consequences. Moral Accounting metaphors provide a framework in which people have moral obligations as individuals and as churches and as nations, and in which there are both immediate and ultimate consequences for failure to meet those obligations. But there is another twist in the 1 Peter version: Deliverance, redemption is offered, and that makes all the difference. While in some expressions, the text seems to evoke a simple *quid pro quo* accounting, this is blended with the expectation of release (λύτρωσις, 'deliverance') from the moral debt accrued.

Response: Reading 1 Peter makes me acutely aware of my own location as a 21st-century North American, middle class, white woman, with training in Christian ethics and NT scholarship. I am also a member of the faith community that holds this text as canonical Scripture. The challenges and questions Peter's perspectives present for me are many.

Individual and Collective Accountability

Some of the language in 1 Peter challenges me to think in terms of group accountability, and that makes me uncomfortable. I wonder what it would mean to understand my belonging in my faith community as being so tight, so deep, that my own moral accountability is tied in with our collective accountability. A lot would need to change in the way I think about myself and my identity—and my relationship to these others—if I were to try on the notion of group honor. Radical individualism is not so good (as Bellah, et al., have shown), but what happens to moral agency if group responsibility is taken to its extreme? As an American, I tend to think of moral accountability as a matter of accepting personal responsibility and consequences, thinking in terms of personal moral agency. Peter challenges me to consider a different version of accountability, of social-communal accountability. The central question for me seems to be, How does belonging to the household of God gathered in

Jesus' name alter one's personal, communal and social moral responsibilities? My own nation is so vast; even the city in which I live is overwhelmingly large. To have my own personal moral responsibility tied to these collectivities seems unfair and unwieldy. But perhaps the local church is a locus of belonging on human scale. Hold that thought.

Moral Accounting and Deontology

Is Moral Accounting inextricably tied to moral *duty* in 1 Peter? When he speaks of judgment 'according to each deed' he speaks the language of deontology. But Peter is also addressing, as we said above, collectivities, people groups—not just individuals. You, plural, are being called to be a people of a certain moral character: live in holiness. That is a call to deeper moral development, to the cultivation of habits and virtues of (social) character. Simple, lock-step obedience would not suffice. Moreover, deontology does not have to be about lock-step obedience. If we let the advisory and judgment 'according to each deed' parts of Peter's letter be a portrait of a deontological mode of living, we get a dynamic picture in which people respond in freedom and gratitude to the God who delivers them from futile behavioral and relational patterns. Peter can open up our understanding of deontology, and help us see that at its best, it is wedded to concerns for human character development and fits into a large picture of the shape of a people's life together.

Justice Models: Blame and Guilt Versus Shame and Honor

In my first readings of 1 Peter, I noticed the Judge 'accounting for each deed' and thought I was looking at conventional Moral Accounting. That was disappointing, because it seems not to fit the grace that characterizes the central canonical message. But as I re-read, I began to notice the ways the judge and the father and Jesus the Christ, the Lord, figure into the Accounting picture here. That the Accounting frame blended with the Legal frame was not so surprising, but the variations injected when the Household frame is blended in seemed major: A Father who sincerely desires to guard the honor of the household and each member in it modifies the picture.

In *Moral Politics*, George Lakoff draws caricatures of the two major brands of (North American) Christianity—Strict Father-based Christianity, and Nurturing Father-based Christianity. Keeping in mind that his model concerns modern American culture, I wondered if one would find precursors or traces of such a split, of alternative family models, in 1 Peter. If 1 Peter licenses one sort of family model over the another, what would be the impact on Moral Accounting frames? Peter's honor-shame cultural model precludes simple identification or parallel with these modern family models, but my own reading (admittedly biased) is that in the end, Peter opts for a version of *paterfamilias* who is nurturing. The Father God in 1 Peter judges in a caring, 'watching over,' manner and is actively engaged in supporting, helping, sustaining. Moreover, that model fits what Peter would have remembered about how Jesus talked about and related to the Father. A 'nurturing' accountant-father-judge blend also coheres with the 'deliverance' theme.

Questions: How faithful to Peter's vision is my understanding of God as Judge? How am I blending that image with my notion of God as Father? Am I picturing a strict or nurturing father? Does the blend I run tend toward expectation of mercy and grace or towards assuming God will condemn and punish? Am I injecting inputs from my own native justice frame, which is about assigning individual blame, experiencing guilt, and meting out punishment to pay (individual) moral debt?

Deliverance or Release and Suffering as Payment of Moral Debt

If deliverance makes all the difference in Peter's version of Moral Accounting, what difference does it make? Lakoff has observed that many American Christians talk and act as if the promised moral debt-erasure were a one-time-only transaction. If a personal 'salvation' event clears the (personal) account once and then it starts up again, the 'freedom' does not last. In my first readings of 1 Peter, the language of debt payment and of 'release,' combined with certain language from the sacrificial cult domain (the 'sprinkled blood,' for example), prompted me to input modern atonement doctrine concepts (penal substitutionary atonement, to be exact) and create a certain kind of blend. But re-reading and working out the specific potential source domain inputs for 'release,' (λύτρωσις), as well as the composite picture of God the Father in 1 Peter led me to question the adequacy of that reading. If there is 'payment' via Jesus' suffering in 1 Peter, the payment certainly is not being made to an angry, remote, Strict Father

God. That construal does not cohere with the message of the letter; it clashes too severely with the rest of the conceptual metaphor pool.

Well-Being, 1st-Century Style

The notion of well-being is modified in 1 Peter; it deviates from the standard modern Western list of well-being indicators. Honor, in the 1st-century, is a well-being indicator, for example, as is status. And in 1 Peter, financial wealth may not be the prototypical well-being indicator that it is in my context. Wealth is good—or at least indebtedness is bad. This much is similar in both contexts. But it is the notion of familial inheritance, inheritance of honor and blessing, that is central to the well-being category Peter works with. I find that concept refreshing, potentially freeing. Moreover, suffering as Jesus did is sometimes tied to well-being, at least in the sense of being acceptable in the short run, and a possible path to ultimate well-being, in the long run. I find this concept challenging.

Questions: As a member of the Christian faith community—What 'counts' as suffering like or with Jesus? When is suffering a consequence of personal or societal evil? Am I (are we) thinking of suffering as meaningless? Are we understanding certain sorts of suffering as 'payment' for wrongs done? When (and how) would suffering 'in Christ' become a sign of solidarity with Christ and a path to glory? When are we habitually thinking of others' suffering (for example, suffering of the poor or of non-Christians) as being 'payment,' a sign or consequence of bad behavior or being cursed? How is Peter re-framing or challenging that kind of thinking? Can suffering really work as a sign of wellbeing? What do I make of the alternative ways financial and material well-being figures into the moral discourse of 1 Peter?

Rejection of Retaliation and Retribution

Peter's injunction to 'pay back with a blessing' is radical and challenging for me personally. I cannot hear this in my post-9/11, context without noticing the stark contrast with some of the language that certain Christian leaders are using to support the U.S. federal administration's war against Iraq and other states. One evangelical pastor wove an argument that wed OT holy war events with Trinitarian doctrine to conclude that Jesus would wage (literal) war on terrorists and bomb Iraq!

Peter was addressing Christians of low social status and limited political power, a largely disenfranchised minority group. Is his non-retaliation advice, then, merely a survival tactic for the disempowered? Is it an 'interim ethic'? I wonder how he would counsel North American Christians to comport ourselves as we potentially wield enormous power, both personally and collectively. Christians' moral stances—and our empowerment to act—depend to some extent on how we see ourselves as individuals and as a collectivity in relation to the governmental and economic forces that plan and execute war. Many of us probably hear Peter's exhortation as a nice rubric for interpersonal relations, but one that has little practical value in international relations. Peter could not possibly have foreseen a situation in which Christians themselves would be in a position to exercise imperial power. But even if his likely intended meaning does not fit how we frame our own context, his advice is not irrelevant.

Some of us act (and think) as though our nation were a family (A Nation Is a Family) whose honor was insulted and security breached by the 9/11 events. Given that framing, American Christians may feel more than justified in retaliating. But that thinking flies in the face of the message of 1 Peter. In Peter's view, Christians' identity and belonging is keyed to their belonging 'in Christ,' and in God's household, not their (secular) national or ethnic identity. The honor of the Christian family is secure in Christ and in the Father God whose name is holiness. This *paterfamilias*' honor is, admittedly, challenged constantly. He promises to deal mercifully and justly with those challenges. The Christian household is secure in that Father's honor; the Christians themselves are not enjoined to protect and defend that honor—especially not offensively—except by way of behaving peaceably and honorably themselves.

My reading of 1 Peter encouraged me to support the consensus view expressed by the leadership of the major Christian denominations and of the Roman Catholic Church hierarchy, which counseled against preemptive military strikes and urged the U.S. government to pursue diplomatic solutions to the problems and threats it faced.[3] It is from the spirit of such texts as 1 Peter 3.9 that the anti-revenge counsel arises.

---

[3] Laurie Goodstein, "Diverse Denominations Oppose the Call to Arms," *New York Times* (March 6, 2003), A12. Goodstein reports that "Jewish organizations are split," and that "some Muslim groups have voiced their opposition" [to war], "as have small

Questions: How literally can we take Peter's advice? That is, what kinds of debts are we prepared to repay with blessings? What would that kind of repayment look like? When we move from the interpersonal, or even the level of the extended household, to the macro-societal level of the modern state and of geopolitics, what would eschewing revenge, retaliation, and retribution entail? What would have to change in the American churches' stance(s) vis-a-vis the state and the international geopolitical context, were we to live by this rubric?

Moral Authority Structures

Peter assigns moral authority to governmental functionaries, to leaders within the church, and to husbands. But by addressing slaves and wives directly, he also implies that individuals have the responsibility and the agency to choose how they will behave, even in difficult household situations where they have low status. Slaves who are being mistreated and wives whose husbands do not yet share their belief and trust in Jesus can and must choose how they will respond. Some readers hear Peter legitimating social structures that by modern standards are unjust. Some expert readers (Balch, Furnish) hear Peter counseling Christians to acculturate, to accommodate to societal (non-Christian) mores, to blend in. But this study has demonstrated that Peter's strategy is to finesse the situation. He declares that Christians should obey the imperial authorities as God's delegates and view governmentally-imposed penalties as divinely sanctioned. But then he says Christians ought to 'honor *everyone*.'

Response: As an American, I experience strong culture clash when I encounter Peter's position toward governmental authority. Moreover, I am not only an American, I live in a town where I often see a bumper sticker that reads, "Question Authority." I naturally (given my status) assume that I have a right—even a responsibility—to question authority. When Peter writes, 'honor *everyone*,' proclaims Jesus κύριος, and reminds me that God is above even the Roman emperor in the hierarchy, I hear both a hard-to-implement challenge and an opening to demote imperial claims to ultimate authority.

Buddhist organizations." But "There is support for a war among some leaders of large ministries, and of conservative evangelical and Pentecostal churches." She names the Ethics and Public Policy Commission of the Southern Baptist Convention as among the administration's staunchest supporters.

I also belong to reading communities that embrace this text as canonical Scripture. The canonical message challenges me to consider carefully who and what has a legitimate claim to exercise moral authority over me and my community. Within the NT canon, several voices propose alternative approaches to Roman authority. In Acts, Luke has Peter (!) observing that sometimes "we ought to obey God, rather than men." John, in the Revelation, casts Rome as the enemy which ought to be resisted and whose ultimate demise is the work of the God who raised Jesus from the dead. There is, then, an intra-canonical conversation concerning these issues of authority. The churches have a long and on-going conversation on these matters, and I will reflect further on that conversation below, as I consider Peter's specific approaches to authority structures in the household and the socio-political realm.

Questions: When Peter uses social authority structures to understand and discuss moral authority and responsibility, is he legitimating and baptizing those structures? How are conventional hierarchies altered or amended in 1 Peter? What is the scope of legitimacy governmental and social sanctions? That is, how does a Christian revision of the Great Chain revise the structure of moral authority?

How do differences in Great Chain models affect the socio-political and ethical conclusions we reach? How do we display our belief that behavior in the microcosm accrues and displays moral essence—and 'counts' at the macro-level? When is it more Christian—morally advisable—to buck traditional chains of command? How do we decide together when the church and we as individual Christians ought to stand against societal or governmental authority structures? That is, when is morality *not* submission and obedience? Is there a higher morality than lock-step obedience? Or, as Dorothee Sölle puts it, how can Christians after WW II ever talk about "obedience" as if the word were morally neutral?[4]

What properties and knowledge about judges and accountants, governors and slave masters, do we habitually transfer to the moral domain? How are we using these concepts to reason about moral authority and the nature of moral accountability?

---

[4] Dorothee Sölle, *Creative Disobedience*, tr. Lawrence W. Denef (Cleveland, Ohio: Pilgrim Press, 1968, 1995).

Conclusion: Exemplary Response to Moral Accounting in 1 Peter

Readers have choices to make in response to the moral authority structures and moral accounting schemas embedded in 1 Peter. As outside readers, we are in a position to notice and evaluate some of the assumptions displayed in 1 Peter. So, although the reading strategy advocated in this study encourages readers to find ways to *enter* the authorial audience, and one stage of the reading strategy demands imaginative entry into a 1st-century version of the Great Chain and of Moral Accounting, 21st-century readers cannot play 1st-century forever. 21st-century readers at some point have to decide how to critically engage this authority and accounting structure.

It is inappropriate to use this 1st-century document to legitimate current unjust power and authority structures. How can I say that? With conceptual metaphor methods it can be demonstrated that certain readings, certain construals of meaning, fit the constraints of the discourse better than others.

Timely Good Behavior 'in Christ'

When Peter urges his readers to live 'in' Christ he creates a coherent, large picture of Christian moral life that is nevertheless immediately brought down to human scale. His positive behavioral advice ('live here, this way') is located in juxtaposition to certain negative zones ('in the futile ways'). Peter declares his readers delivered out of those futile ways and urges them to live 'in Christ.' By the logic of the schema, behavior may or may *not* be 'in' Christ. Readers are tacitly exhorted to choose between living spaces, to choose to leave one zone and move into another. Peter grounds Christian, 'in Christ' morality *in* time. He connects historical time and events with moral action and its consequences. That is, time frames, moral accounting, and behavioral exhortation are connected in a coherent manner in this discourse. Ultimate moral consequences—*future* judgment—are contingent upon behavior *in the present time*. In view of the *events* of Jesus' life, death, and resurrection, Peter urges readers to change their *present* behavior, to eschew certain behaviors patterns of the *past*. In 1 Peter, moreover, Jesus Christ traverses all of these times zones and then becomes (metonymically) a space in which Christians can live. The complex blends by which the writer constructs this space lend narrative coherence to the letter. They also do something much more profound: they allow Peter to offer a meta-narrative to readers, inviting them to join their own stories with this one, urging them to allow their own lives to be read by this story.

Response: The strict delineation of boundaries, of 'in Christ' as opposed to 'not in Christ,' of outdated 'futile ways of living inherited from your ancestors' versus new standards of behavior—these boundaries are both good news and hard news. Petrine temporal topography both coheres and clashes with typical 21st-century assumptions about time and events and history and their moral significance. Particular points of challenge for modern readers include the following:

Exclusive Christianity

For many readers, the way Peter blends 'good people,' and 'God's chosen' with an insider-group (In Christ) will be offensive. Though I sense that his aim is to invite as many as will accept the invitation to join this 'in group,' the clear message here is that there is an 'in' and there is an 'out.' 'Out' is down, dark, and literally damned. Behavior patterns are markers of moral status in this letter, and of belonging (or acting appropriately) in the in group (or not). Whether he means that Christians have now become The Chosen People (and that the Jews are now 'Gentiles') is not clear to me. I rather think that he means to graft the Christians into the category of the Chosen.

Χρόνος and Καιρός: Time and Time Again

For modern readers, the χρόνος kind of time is relatively easy to understand; we connect it with 'clock time' (though we ought to remember that while sundials might have been used in Peter's day, clocks as we know them had not been invented). But harder to grasp is Peter's καιρός time, via which godly time-space is interwoven with χρόνος, so that there is no purely secular time. Some Christian devotional writers have picked up the notion of καιρός and attempted to display how 'καιρός moments' can and do still occur. I appreciate the way in the *Prayer Book of the Anglican Church in New Zealand*, certain liturgical settings adapt the 1 Peter text for current use, and manage to locate the present moment in the larger time picture.

If we suffer, let it not be for murder, theft or sorcery,
Nor for infringing the rights of others;
But if we suffer as Christians
We should feel no disgrace,
But confess that name to the honour of God.
It gives us a share in Christ's sufferings.
That is cause for joy!
...

Giver of the present, hope for the future:
Save us from the time of trial.
When prophets warn us of doom,
Of catastrophe and of suffering beyond belief,
Then, God, free us from our helplessness,
And deliver us from evil.
Save us from our arrogance and folly,
For you are God who created the world;
You have redeemed us and you are our salvation.
...

God of opportunity and change,
Praise to you for giving us life at this critical time.
As our horizons extend, keep us loyal to our past;
As our dangers increase, help us to prepare the future;
keep us trusting and hopeful,
Ready to recognize your kingdom as it comes.[5]

This liturgy lets present suffering and danger be seen in the context of a much larger narrative. It echoes 1 Peter's exhortation against becoming known as thieves and murderers and adds a modern concept: infringing others' rights. In addition, the adaptation includes 'sorcery,' a set of behaviors that has caused much pain and suffering among the peoples of this land. What is a Christian response to legitimate and real suffering? It is to pray for deliverance from 'helplessness' and from evil, from arrogance and folly. But it is also to live in gratitude, not in abject fear, looking to God for protection and hope. This is an exemplary response to 1 Peter's message. It takes from Peter (and, presumably, from the canonical literature) the sense of identity keyed to Christ. In keeping with the role Peter assigns the people he tags Χριστιανός in the larger geopolitical frame, it declines any imperial, triumphalis-

---

[5] *A New Zealand Prayer Book* (San Francisco: HarperCollins, 1997), 134–135. The liturgy juxtaposes text and concepts from 1 Peter to input from the particular situation of the church in modern New Zealand, so that not infringing the *rights* of others is included, creating a dynamic blend.

tic role. Perhaps reading from the New Zealand context, it is easier to hear and accept Peter's framing than it is for Christians in North America.

Apocalyptic Now?

Peter's moral discourse cannot be understood absent the concept that there will come a Day, a day for ultimate Moral Accounting, that the judgment for evildoers will be harsh, and that the Day is coming soon. I do not like the attempt to motivate via fear of judgment. But I also hear Peter saying there is a bigger picture, a longer, larger story, than what is happening in the present. As I read, I wonder how dependent on an apocalyptic world-view Peter's moral exhortation is. There is an urgency to his message, but some of that urgency may be attributed to the imminent persecution rather than to fear of eschatological judgment. I also have negative reactions to the black-and-white (literally light versus dark) caricature of the good people versus the bad ones. But I wonder if my own culture's shades of gray have distorted the moral picture for me, or prevented me from seeing clear distinctions. Peter's teachings regarding reprisal and vindication for the righteous also seem potentially mean-spirited and self-righteous. (Them versus Us, and they'll get what's coming to them). But read within the broad scope of the canonical (OT and NT) narrative, I hear an invitation to trust that justice is indeed going to be done, and that God will enact this ultimate justice.

Lifespans (Individual, National) and History are Morally Meaningful

Peter is neither a pessimist nor an historical cynic; in Peter's mind, even in view of the Apocalypse, there is room, there is time, for good living in this world. But historical time-space is both adequate and limited, and human beings have choices to make about how their time will be marked. As with individuals, so in a people's lifespan they can work together for good or evil.

Moral Development

People become known by their behavior over time, in the long run, and are judged by the shape of that life. Patterns are developed; a people develops moral character by which it is known and whose consequences affect their descendents.

Questions: How might Peter address the pervasive cynicism of our time? How can we in the 21st-century take seriously, as urgent, Peter's moral message when clearly his sense of historical timing (the immanence of the end) was off? Or was it? To what extent, and in what ways, do Christians create apocalyptic framings now—and with what consequences, to what ends? What have been the positive and negative effects on the church's moral teaching of apocalyptic framing?

Christ as Paradigm

That Jesus is the moral model in 1 Peter is clear; it softens, qualifies, the rest of the message. That is, the insider/outsider language is stark, but since the man Jesus traverses those boundaries, and since his version of holy living is so friendly towards 'strangers' and people in moral debt trouble, the overall picture of life 'in Christ' is inviting.

Questions: How does Jesus function as the moral paradigm in 1 Peter? How does Peter think Christians could live 'in Christ' as ordinary citizens (and non-citizens) vis-a-vis non-Christian society? Given the particular moral stances Peter advises Christians to take in their families, their church, and in their society, how do these cohere with the character of Christ—with the life, the suffering, the death, and the resurrection of Jesus Christ?

In what ways can we alter our culturally received conceptual metaphorical time structures? How do our habitual ways of thinking about Christian moral living display assumptions that there are separate secular and sacred time spheres? How does that affect our construal of the moral life in comparison with the way Peter connects time and behavior?

Christian Living In Social-Political Reality

The moral discourse of 1 Peter makes sense only in light of the reframed identity by which he addresses his readers. They are διασπορά, actually spread throughout the Roman provinces of Asia Minor, perhaps small cell groups meeting here and there. But as διασπορά, they must think of themselves as a distinctive People, even a 'nation' located in an imaginary geo-political region. When Peter attributes διασπορά peoplehood to his readers, it is *the* nation, the people of Israel that he calls to mind. A certain moral logic follows: Now that they are the Chosen People, they are to live accordingly. Their mission: To live such just and holy lives among the 'Gentiles,' that God is honored and all peoples are gathered into the one people. As a διασπορά People, they are also παρεπιδήμους and πάροικοι, exiles, strangers. They are not to merely conform to conventional 'Gentile' mores, the ethos of (their own native) surrounding culture.

Response: My NT scholarly reading community's ongoing conversation about this letter prompts me to consider to what extent the moral values Peter propounds are acculturated or nonconformist (in 1st-century Asia Minor). Before reading, I wondered if I could detect places where he was going against the grain. Certainly, his injunction to 'honor *everyone*,' is striking. Moreover, if the God whom Jesus taught his followers to call 'Father' is indeed above the Roman emperor on the Great Chain (and he is), then even the Roman emperor's power is put in question, is it not? That is, if behavior 'below' must conform to the honor of the beings above in order to be honorable, then a Nero or a Caligula ought himself to be held accountable to this higher, holier authority—and found wanting. Read that way, Peter's message is potentially subversive of the social-political structure within which he and his original readers were embedded.

Exiles

Equally provocative, however, are the potential questions raised by the exile / sojourner / stranger / διασπορά cluster of metaphors for the church. Peter foregrounds this set of identity tags when he puts them in the salutation. They are a People, a chosen and special, set-apart People, who are then to be 'strangers' in their own land. They are People, then, who belong (in the church, to each other) but do not belong (to their former families and in the ordinary associations of the dominant culture). Is this a 'sectarian' model? Certain points of exhortation weigh in against such a conclusion, or at least against reading here a strong version of sectarianism. Participation in, acceptance of, given social-political structures is recommended—at least at the level of basic judicial procedure and sanction. As much as I dislike the idea, Peter does say, 'Honor the emperor.' But then he immediately qualifies that, or potentially qualifies it, with 'honor everyone.' He does *not* say, *Become* the emperor. The thrust of the letter is to invite Christians to claim a new identity and to land so deeply in that new belonging that they become, in effect, 'strangers' in their own home country. Working out the Exile framing was instructive for me, as I considered how this picture could be coherent—how a people group could embrace both identities: emperor-honorers and 'strangers' in the land. Is this not the survival mechanism that exiles do often take? But is it not (again) qualified, modified, if Israel's experience of exile is evoked, is blended into the picture? That is, a moderated, considered respect for the socio-political reality in which exiles find themselves is in order, while at the same time their hope is invested in a higher reality, their allegiance ultimately vested in a higher, worthier power.

Let me bring this reflection to my own home country. I wonder how distinctively Christian the American churches' identity actually is. Where do we speak and act against the grain? Have, as some claim and many assume, Christian moral standards and values so permeated American culture that there is a seamless identification, such that American = Christian? Or has the Christian church been so co-opted by the secular culture, that there is hardly any distinctive Christian ethic at all? Probably the truth is somewhere between those extremes, but examples of both extreme cases can be found. It would be impossible, in any case, for someone to enter Peter's authorial audience without taking on 'exile' and 'resident alien' and 'stranger' identity. I wonder, then, to what extent it is possible for North American Christians to hear and respond fully to Peter's message.

My own tradition of origin has a mixed history in this regard. The conservative wing of the American evangelical church accuses the rest of the churches of being co-opted and secularized ('worldly'). But it seems unable to extricate itself from—let alone critique—ordinary American consumerism and lust for dominance (via military power, for example). At its worst, the evangelical church not only refuses 'stranger' status, but demonstrates that it has forgotten it ever had such status when it neglects or effectively excludes the poor and lowly. If one looks at the conservative churches' habitual stances towards actual strangers in our land (immigrants—legal or not, the profoundly disabled, people whose family configurations or sexual orientations are 'other'), one is more likely to encounter xenophobia rather than the xenophilia Peter had in mind. I commend the churches who are changing these habits, who are working with and for immigrants and migrants, who are allowing their images of 'America' and of the church to be recreated.[6]

But perhaps the forces of secularization and globalization increasingly evoke in middle class Americans the sense of being strangers in their own home country. Then Peter's message takes on a different role; the warnings and the hope, the reminders of core, grounded identity, could be taken to heart.

Questions

When Peter argues that governmental authorities and sanctions are valid for Christians, he implicitly raises questions that—down through history—became classic Church/state questions. Admitting that we do still live by versions of the Chain of Being (either consciously or—more often—unconsciously), in what ways are the hierarchies we live with like and not like those Peter had to contend with? How does a church embedded in (theoretically) modern democratic social and governmental systems hear 1 Peter? Even ordinary, middle-class American Christians enjoy a level of power and freedom unimaginable to Peter and his contemporaries. How might Peter's vision of a holy 'people of God' be enacted, given such power?

In the 'globalized' 21st-century, governmental forces unite (or are subsumed by) economic and business powers, which the governments protect, defend, and extend via military force. How is this powerful, even hegemonic, complex like and not like the Roman Empire which held geopolitical sway over Asia Minor in the 1st-century? How would 1 Peter's message challenge us to modify our dispositions and our actions in our own geo-political context? In whom or what do we trust?

---

[6] See Dana W. Wilbanks, *Re-Creating America: The Ethics of U.S. Immigration and Refugee Policy in a Christian Perspective* (Nashville: Abingdon, 1996).

Good Living 'in the Household'

With the language of οἶκος and συνοικέω, of God as father, Christians as heirs and brothers and as household slaves, and above all, as 'beloved,' Peter evokes multiple mappings of metaphors using a Household frame. He thus gives distinctive shape to Christian identity and moral expectations. Peter's readers are enjoined to leave behind the old ways of their actual ancestors, and in so doing they are invited to join a new family, belong in a new, alternative 'household.' 'Christian' and 'in Christ' then become a family name, and the honor of the head of that household is transferred to the family. But what is most interesting is the way the framing, the coordinated metaphors, lend unique conceptual constraints to the scope of Christians' ethical thinking and create clear boundaries for behavioral morality.

Unique conceptual constraints are evident especially in the ways conventional Moral Accounting is qualified and revised in this discourse. Because familial blessing and honor are inherited, bestowed by the *paterfamilias*, they are not earned, not even in reward for obedience or exemplary moral behavior. Instead, the heirs in this most honorable of all households (God's household) are to live up to the given household name—to be who they are 'in Christ' in daily life *because they bear this name*. By virtue of their having been "called" into this household by Jesus Christ, they were 'born' into this family.

Moreover, the 'family' or 'household' is both the local gathering, the church, and the larger movement, the Church. If churches are modeled on households, the Church is modeled on the notion that the People group, Israel, is one big, extended Family. So for Peter, the Church Is the New Israel blends with Church as Family and Israel as Family to entail that Christians must (by their very nature) display the moral character distinctive to this Household.

Response: In mapping The Church Is the Family/Household of God metaphors, I noticed that the entailments varied significantly, depending on the family model plugged into the source domain slots. The notion of honor, of the individual's responsibility for maintaining family honor, is a powerful constraining factor in these mappings. I wondered if Peter's version of Christian morality was inherently, intrinsically hierarchical and obedience-driven, and if it was possible to detect any chinks in that edifice. The injunction to 'honor everyone,' his demonstration of how that kind of honoring would look as he addresses slaves and wives directly, respectfully requesting their consideration of his argument, altered my initial impression that this was mere conventional wisdom.

Household Code

Peter's modifications to the customary 1st-century household code are significant. They signal that from the outset, Christians were expected to have to thoughtfully consider how any given cultural conventions did and did not fit 'in Christ' values and goals. Particular circumstances, social locations, statuses and access to power are taken into account in Peter's construal. In this case, the Christians constitute a relatively powerless minority group; it would have been inappropriate at that time for Peter to urge all the slaves to stage an uprising. Slaves are not, however, simply told to do their duty and take abuse without considering its meaning, without placing their trust in God for ultimate honor and eventual liberation.

I do *not* read the code here as Christian legislation for all times and places. For modern readers to do so would be unfaithful, since it would require denying the gifts of freedom and status given (and won) over many centuries of struggle.

Slavery

The injunction to slaves to obey harsh masters is hard to hear. It has to be qualified by the tacit declaration in the text that Jesus is Lord (master), and by canonical context: Exodus. The canonical context insists that we remember when *we* were slaves, that God's stated and demonstrated purpose is liberation of those in servitude, and to act accordingly. Peter's words must be read in this context or they will be misread.

The challenge is to notice where there is slavery now, in our own society, and to move out of the denial that assumes we are above and beyond it. We are not above and beyond it. Within recent memory, a man and his son were arrested in my town for having bought young girls in India, brought them here, and used them as sex slaves. Also in recent memory in my home state, California, there have been prosecutions of traffickers in human beings—slaves being imported from China, from Mexico, and elsewhere. Slavery is illegal—not sanctioned by the state—and yet the prosecutions are few and far between.

I would argue, moreover, that certain work in my society is essentially slave-status work. It may even be more difficult and demeaning than slavery, since the farm and factory workers I have in mind do not have the kind of protection (household belonging, a guaranteed basic sustenance) afforded slaves in (good) masters' households. The US has a long history of migration back and forth across our southern border. This migration is essentially economically driven: the growers are dependent on cheap labor; the laborers need work. Many, if not most, of the laborers are Roman Catholic Christians; they are (metaphorical) brothers and sisters, *tias* and *tios*, in the larger Christian family. The good news is that the backbone and much of the energy behind the movement to better their plight has been faith-based. But how much more quickly would the injustices (substandard housing, exposure to pesticides and herbicides, substandard wages, etc.) be remedied if the wider Christian community actively pursued their brothers' and sisters' liberation? Many of us have resources and power that is lordly, and collectively we have a potentially strong voice.

Would Peter counsel *these* slaves to just take the beating? I think not. While these pockets of slavery can be found, they are not the norm in our society, as they were in his. The God who says, "Let my people go!" has indeed worked literal liberation for many—and the people of the Land of the Free are then called to remember their liberation, to be in solidarity with those not yet free, to work actively for that freedom on their behalf.

Instead of facing literal slavery, and working for the liberation of those who suffer oppressive living and working conditions, most of us desire to be masters. Not, I grant, literal slave masters. But we expect to hold considerable sway over our own destinies, to be fed and housed and entertained in a fashion that (by 1st-century standards, by 3rd-World 21st-century standards) is lordly. How shall we then live, if we allow ourselves to be read by 1 Peter? The Master master in 1 Peter is Jesus, the suffering one, the liberator. It is his example which would-be masters must follow. So then, they will be ever found among the lowly, always suffering with the lowly, always working to free the lowly and despised. This is the portrait of the Christian master, how that slot is (by the logic of the discourse) filled.

Wives

The advice to wives is tempered, softened somewhat, by the promise of inheritance (heir status), the 'human' language, and the injunction to husbands to *honor* wives. Peter's 'daughters of Sarah' suggestion, his invocation of the Hebrew matriarchs' submission to husbandly authority, is strained. He is addressing Christian converts with non-Christian husbands; how, then, do these husbands fit the 'Abraham's sons-in-law' slot? They do not. Clearly, only a small portion of the potential in the source domain is mapped. The notion that inward moral essence ('purity') is of supreme importance and that temporary discomfort can be borne in view of the longer-term, in light of the larger story, and that having a place in that larger picture is honor—all of this is consistent with Peter's overall message. Wives are not being singled out for especially hard duty.

The general household structure Peter outlines is the given one of his day; it fits the 'natural' order (Great Chain, macrocosm in microcosm). He does not, however, simply accept the cultural givens without comment or critique. His insistence that a wife does have the freedom to belong among the Χριστιανοί even when the husband does not bucks the conventional expectation that a man's entire household will follow his lead, when it comes to religion and cult practice. Peter does the women the honor of arguing, of persuading them to choose to behave in certain ways for the sake of evangelism and in line with the roles faithful women have taken in salvation history.

Obedience

The prevalence of the ὑποτάσσω ('submit, obey') vocabulary in the letter is unmistakable: One (one!) metaphor for morality in 1 Peter is Morality Is Obedience. It is always an obedience referenced above all to the God who holds each one and the people together in his care.

I recall again Dorothee Sölle's articulation of the challenge for modern Christians, when she reminds us that after World War II, after the churches' complicity with much that was evil, the word 'obedience' cannot be used "as if nothing had happened."[7] As an American Chris-

---

[7] Sölle, *Creative Disobedience*, x.

tian, and as a woman, I would add that we also must use that word, 'obedience,' in view of our history of subjugation and abuse of women and of literal slaves. We must not read 1 Peter as if nothing had happened in the meantime, as if certain actual slave masters who named the name of Christ had not abused other human beings and used even these texts in their own sordid defense. Refusal to speak these truths, to speak our repentance, and to give thanks for our brothers' and sisters' liberation, would be unfaithful reading and response to 1 Peter. 'Obedience' in the 21st-century spells 'responsibility,' the church's responsibility for what it has done (for the ethical responsibility it has failed to take) in the name of duty.

Questions: What role can the notion of familial 'honor' play for modern Christians for whom this is a cross-cultural concept? How are we to think of moral responsibility and authority in the church—in light of the 'shepherding' metaphors Peter uses and Peter's repeated use of the title 'master' for Jesus? Which of our church conflicts can be traced to alternative understandings of these structures of moral authority and responsibility?

If Peter and the authorial audience simply assumed the legitimacy of certain social structures and practices—the debt slavery system, patron-client relationships, and household hierarchy—what do we, as seasoned Christians, knowing what we do about world and Christian history, say back to them about those structures' fit (and lack of fit) with the core of the Gospel? On the other hand, what social structures are we simply assuming are morally superior that need to be altered?

'In the Body': Body as Site for Moral Struggle

The moral world of 1 Peter is fully physical while affirming the essential transcendence and potential holiness of human persons. In 1 Peter, human bodily existence, with all of its drive, verve, and force, serves as a complex source domain for thinking and talking about other equally real aspects of human existence: psychic suffering, hunger for spiritual growth, and the drive to find transcendent value and ultimate goodness. The body is a site of moral struggle and bodily desire is a strong force connected to the cosmic struggle between good and evil. But the connections are not drawn in simple primary colors; it is not as though the body and physical desires were necessarily evil.

When 'in the body' (ἐν σαρκὶ βιῶσαι χρόνον—4.2) metonymically stands for life as a whole in 1 Peter, it is a tag for human earthly, mortal existence as opposed to heavenly or spiritual existence. But the dative form, ἐν σαρκὶ βιῶσαι, also opens up a spatial zone, a site or bounded region containing a person's moral essence and providing a site for experience, including the experience of suffering.

Because he knows Jesus, knows the shape of the man's life and the manner of his death, Peter cannot interpret suffering as intrinsically a sign of shame and dishonor. But neither does suffering simply serve as payment for moral debt in this discourse. Human suffering 'in Christ' certainly does not negate meaning or transcendence, but neither does Peter advocate that readers therefore seek it out. For Peter, the life of the suffering servant, Jesus, and his death by crucifixion grounds Jesus' followers' present suffering, providing deep motivation for perseverance.

Peter does not stop at counseling perseverance, however. His ethical ideals and moral stance in the face of suffering are expressed in the (physical) metaphorical concepts of balance and sobriety. The perseverance and trust he envisions, the honor in suffering, are framed in terms of battle and preparation for actual war. In Peter's construal of suffering, denial or avoidance is eschewed, but he also forbids retaliation or revenge. To live 'in Christ' and 'in the body' is sometimes to suffer; suffering in this world does not come as a surprise nor necessarily as an insult.

Desire, rooted in physical experience, is a vehicle for understanding longing for more abstract goods—good days in general, long life, more holy life. Bodily desire is not always evil or malignant in 1 Peter, though of course it can be. Desire for basic human needs—an infant's longing for milk—is good. Peter uses conceptual metaphors grounded in the human experience of desire, of struggling to get what we need and want—by grasping and holding, eating, drinking and so on—to conceptualize and express how other, non-physical, desires are met.

Response: Peter opens up questions for me about the relationships between body and soul, psyche and mind, and the roles they play—and their interplay—in the moral life. I am encouraged to find that desire is not inherently evil, for Peter. This surprises me, and shatters a caricature (that in the New Testament, the body is always or mostly associated with evil). Peter writes *before* Descartes' error was reiterated in Christian doctrine, and his holistic approach to the body is worth deeper consideration.

Again, the re-framing of suffering, even physical suffering, challenges me. On one hand, I hear Peter giving advice, offering survival tactics for the lowly, for people with very few resources facing dire circumstances. It seems like bad advice for the long term. But what do I, located in such a privileged position, know of such suffering, of suffering in such a powerless position?

Questions: What are the differences between desire and will (what is 'will')? What are the conventional conceptual metaphors for non-physical human desires—our drives for knowledge, power, and status? We would like to understand better how desire to obtain or attain those social and other abstract goods is conceptualized via physical, bodily desire.

Some parts of the American church have focused (almost exclusively) on the evil potential of the body and bodily desire. Peter's take on the nature of the human moral struggle does not endorse such an exclusive focus. In other regions of the church, there is a move to embrace the goodness of the body and of bodily desire, even to the extent of endorsing seemingly any and every imaginable bodily practice. Peter's perspective calls that attitude into question as well.

What counts as 'suffering'? Is the concept not cheapened when it is reduced to personal inconvenience? How ready are North American Christians for intense suffering, even martyrdom? Are we staying alert, maintaining moral balance? Where does our national drive for retribution and retaliation clash with Peter's counsel?

Ethics Review

1 Peter is not a formal ethical treatise, it is an epistle whose author engages in moral discourse and dispenses some ethical advice. It is appropriate, then, to ask how the metaphors for morality in Peter's discourse might point to answers to the kinds of questions modern ethicists ask when we analyze ethical arguments.

Starting Point

Peter's letter begins with reminders and assertions about the readers' identity and location. Their 'location' is multi-layered: they are geographically located in Asia Minor; they are temporally located in χρόνος but also in the wider, loftier time-space of καιρός; and, finally, they are located in a situation. They face persecution, and are suffering at many points. The identity tags Peter offers them are key: Exiles and strangers, diaspora, elect (chosen) and destined, newborn members of a new family, inheritors of a permanent place and honor 'in Christ.' His message: Seeing who you are, live accordingly. Hard circumstances and hard choices can be faced, given your new identity in Christ.

NT scholars discuss the significance of Peter's 'data': whether the intense suffering, the 'fiery ordeal' Peter alludes to has already come or is imminent. Few doubt that at least the verbal abuse, the slander, has begun. The household situations discussed (slaves dealing with mistreatment; Christian wives negotiating life in non-Christian households) root the argument in the concrete. Nothing in this scenario feels farfetched; Peter is facing what is before him (and them, the potential readers) head-on, and proposing behavioral and dispositional strategies.

Loyalties

On whose behalf ought we to make moral decisions? Peter frames his implicit answers to this question in terms of the Family or Household of God. In all the situations he addresses, he urges his readers to remember their new identity 'in Christ' as 'brothers' in this new household. They are to live honorably ὡς Χριστιανός—to bring honor, not shame, upon that family name.

Values

Peter does not present a *theory* of value, but he displays his core values throughout his letter. His key values:

– holiness—ἅγιος, ἁγιοσύνη *like* God's core character
– honor—τιμή
– goodness
    Goodness Is Strength—ἀγαθός
    Goodness Is Beauty—καλός, ἄκακος
    Goodness Is Virtue—ἀρετή
    Goodness Is Purity—καθαρισμός, ἁγνός
    Goodness Is Making/Doing Good—ἀγαθοποιός
    Goodness Is Kindness, Favor—χάρις, χάριτος

Goodness Is Humility—ταπείνωσις, ταπεινός
Goodness Is Righteousness/Justice—δικαιοσύνη, δίκαιος, δικαιόω
Goodness Is Mercy—ἔλεος, ἐλεέω
- love
　Goodness Is Self-Giving Love—ἀγάπη, ἀγαπάω
　Goodness Is Brotherly Love—φιλαδελφία, φιλάδελφος
　Goodness Is Love of Strangers—φιλόξενος
- conscience—συνείδησις
- freedom—ἐλεύθερος
- perseverance, endurance—ὑπομονή
- obedience—ὑποταγή, ὑποτάσσω

It is important, above all, to know one's place in the scheme of things, and act accordingly. But the Christians' placement in the scheme of things has been radically revised 'in Christ.' To honor *everyone* shifts hierarchies in the Chain of Being and, therefore, in the chain of command.

Normative Modes: Duty vs. Teleology vs. Character

Does the metamoral tenor of the Moral Accounting in 1 Peter sound more like the ethics of duty and obedience (deontology) or of consequences (utilitarianism and consequentialism), of good ends, human well-being and flourishing (teleology), or of character and virtue? This is a huge and difficult question. One can cite expressions and list metaphors for morality in 1 Peter that fit into each of these standard ethical analytical categories. Peter mixes ethical modes, then, but he leans heavily toward giving deontological advice in view of teleological hope. The duty / obedience mode is strong, but it is qualified. The deontological-sounding advice is cast in an almost-narrative tone, when, for example, he asks women to think about their present situation in light of a larger, longer story. Moreover, the heavenly, cosmic scope within which one's duty is to be done precludes petty, lock-step drudgery, and the clear thrust towards character development (growth) lends depth to the composite picture. Character (and virtue, ἀρετή) does matter to Peter; he even uses the classical Greek language of virtue and of honor and of the good (ἀρετή, τιμή, ἀγαθός). Overall, I find this text presenting a nuanced and sophisticated blend, with regard to normative mode.

Authorities

What are the sources Peter uses to justify his moral claims? Peter's moral claims are rooted in certain traditions and in Jesus. He quotes (and spins metaphorical extensions of metaphors) from the Hebrew Scriptures—from the Psalms, the prophets. In doing so, however, he does not lay down the law in a "Thou shalt not" fashion, but reminds readers of (or introduces them to) Judaic tradition and history. The historical experience of the Chosen People is instructive, is relevant, to the situation at hand, he argues. Readers are invited to think about how Sarah's experience is like their own, and to consider how Jesus' unjust suffering—in his death, but also in life—is their your own. He prompts them to remember the (newly minted) Christian traditions, the eyewitness stories about Jesus, the tradition as Christians ὡς Χριστιανός, and behave accordingly. The appeal to the Jesus traditions, then, is also an appeal to lived experience and to the model of a moral exemplar, the character of Jesus himself. Moral authority is also asserted when the salutation claims apostolic status for (at least one) of the authors: Πέτρος ἀπόστολος Ἰησοῦ Χριστοῦ—'Peter, Apostle of Jesus Christ.'

Autonomy and Agency

Peter addresses both individual moral agents and groups in his moral discourse. Individual agency is implied, since individuals are urged to change behavior, to adopt new metamoral metaphors, to make alternative choices. But group mores and character are also in view. Peter's cultural grounding, his understanding of identity, is likely to have been less individualistic and more strongly group-oriented than 20th-and 21st-century North American models of human identity. His ethic, therefore, includes a construal of group agency, and his advice is focused accordingly.

Motivation

Why follow moral norms? Peter appeals to impending judgment, both in the short term—via governmental and societal sanction—and in the end, in the Final Judgment. Rewards are in store for those who do good and avoid evil. But he also motivates by encouraging readers to realize that they are newly empowered and freed to choose a different course.

Evangelism is a third, and not unrelated, motivational factor: Live pure and holy lives, so that others will be attracted to the way of Jesus, and will want to join us. He draws on traditional wisdom regarding the connection between well-being, long life, and good moral living, as well. God is watching over you and will bless as you live in holiness. But the over-riding motivation is maintenance of family honor: *because you bear this name* (4.16).

The flip side of these positive motivational factors is, of course, the warnings Peter issues about the negative consequences of failing to do good. Bad behavior on the part of the Christians will result in further persecution and suffering, and will bring shame upon the name, upon the Household of God. Inattention to moral discipline and growth makes you vulnerable to slander and attack from the 'Gentiles' but also, ultimately, from the evil force personified as ἀντίδικος, διάβολος. Evil Is a Strong Force in 1st Peter, and ought to be feared and avoided.

Model of Justice

Justice ultimately is in God's hands, in Peter's construal. The One who sees all, watches over and sustains the good, will work justice in the end. Meanwhile, God delegates to human leaders, authorities, the responsibility to reward good and punish evil. Peter sees human justice structures in the microcosm expressing macrocosmic order. He does, however, qualify that model when he urges his readers to 'honor everyone.'

Human behavior does count; its consequences are significant and lasting. Both individual and group behavior and character are being evaluated. Key conceptual metaphors: Justice Is Balance; Judging Is Auditing Books; Justice Is Setting Straight.

Freedom

Peter believes that 'in Christ' people are free to make moral choices. Even in circumstances that are less than optimal, this freedom persists. Slaves, wives in non-Christian households, Christian converts who encounter ostracism and slander, all are addressed as free moral agents expected to take the responsibility to choose how they will face these difficult circumstances, how they will find ways to live honorably. Actual enslavement and actual political disenfranchisement cannot erase moral agency and freedom to choose: live as free people (2.16).

Virtue and Character

Peter's letter is premised on the notion that behavior change is possible, and he is keen to encourage his readers towards moral growth and character development. To desire this kind of growth is good (2.2). Virtuous models are offered: Sarah and the Hebrew women ancestors (3.5–6), but preeminently, Jesus Christ.

Some Implications for NT hermeneutics

Changing minds: Translating versus understanding

The many primary metaphors and conceptual metaphors 21st-century English speakers share with *koine* Greek mean that much of 1 Peter can be readily translated; a significant core of the human experience grounding this moral discourse is effectively transcultural.

Moreover, much of what cannot be directly or easily translated can still be understood, given sufficient socio-cultural (source domain) data. Given information about 1st-century household schemas, Moral Accounting variations (patron-client, honor-shame), understanding of the text opens up and entry into the authorial audience becomes more likely, more complete. At the same time, modern readers using conceptual metaphor study methods can become aware of nodes of cultural clash; the ensuing cross-cultural dialog can be interesting and fruitful.

Framing the Moral Discourse: Epistle, Exhortation, Exemplar

Engagement with 1 Peter as exemplar entails coming to the reading with awareness of our own social, cultural, philosophical, theological locations. It also means being ready to notice what questions and issues arise within the text, or within us as we read the text and after reading. The moral significance of 1 Peter cannot (ought not to be) reduced to an object—a set of paraenetic passages, exhortations, moral principles or even a single 'controlling metaphor.' 1 Peter is not merely a (dated) set of moral advice that modern readers then judge to be helpful (or not, mostly not). Engagement with this exemplar entails noticing how moral issues are framed and identified via particular expressions. Readers can use cognitive metaphor analysis to ask of the text questions like the following:

How does 1 Peter …
  Locate moral issues?
  Discuss moral options?
  Understand the impact of living 'in Christ' on social, political, familial, and ecclesial ethics?
  Frame and constrain the scope of moral discussion?
  Connect with earlier moral discussions and decisions?
What moral dispositions, skills, and attitudes does it prize and aim to cultivate?

Reading Communities

Modern readers can take up the challenge to enter the authorial audience, but to do so, they must join a linguistic, cultural, reading community. Christian ethicists, biblical scholars, or historians might read the letter *as* moral discourse or ethical treatise, *as* an artifact, or *as* primary source material. The point is that the wise reader becomes aware of reading *as*, and the critical reader will want to think about how the meaning construed is thus affected.

Blended Spaces

Each way of *reading as* opens up a particular kind of blended space. Some disagreements about how 1 Peter ought to be read—and even about its status as source of authority for contemporary ethics—are disagreements about (or uncertainty about) the status of these blend(s). Underneath these disagreements are varying beliefs about the social authority that gives shaping authority to a writer or speaker ("Peter, apostle of Jesus Christ") or to a text (is it Scripture or Bible or 1st-century artifact?). When 1 Peter is read as a letter and as Scripture (and as an artifact from another culture) we combine conventional knowledge and inference patterns from more than one domain to yield a new category, to create a new space. This is a matter of linguistic community. When church parishioners read 1 Peter as if it were a letter to them (and if they believe it is Scripture for them) the metaphors hide. The reader no longer feels the 'as if.' The text gains enormous power in such a community, since performativity is dependent on the status of the speaker (or text).

Conclusion: Responsive Reading of 1 Peter

Peter's practical moral advice makes sense for the (original) situation it addressed, but its meaning and significance is not confined to that 'world.' For Peter, the risen Christ brings καιρός right into χρόνος, creating an earthy, transcendent meaning space in the body, in ordinary households, and in broader geopolitical landscapes. Although the conceptual framework with which Peter constructs his discourse is inherently embedded in 1st-century cultural models, and these must be taken into account as reading and interpretation proceed, many of the core metamoral concepts with which Peter works are effectively transcultural, and much is cross-culturally accessible, given adequate sociocultural information.

CONCLUSION

BECAUSE YOU BEAR THIS NAME

> *Conceptual metaphor grounded in basic embodied human experience recognizes a shared moral language and discourse between the NT writers and readers of the NT today. In the reading and interpretive process, moral dispositions are generated and moral imagination is shaped via conceptual metaphor and blended mental spaces. This theory of metaphor provide links between the fields of NT studies and Christian ethics and offers more productive ways to look at the relationship between Scripture and constructive ethics.*

Metaphor is not "mere" and imagination is not magic. Metaphor is neither a category mistake nor a mysterious (or intrinsically divine), magical catalyst or connecting spark. On one level, reading a text like 1 Peter imaginatively is both ordinary and simple. Scripture is, like every other written text, a human language product, and reading it requires only ordinary actions of our human minds. Scripture is not more— nor is it less—metaphorical or imaginative than any other body of human writing. But that is not to deny the complexity of the cognitive, imaginative work required in ordinary reading and reflection. Just let us not consign Scriptural texts to some "odd duck" category, as though the language were particularly difficult to decipher, intrinsically 'other' because 'religious' or 'classic,' or opaque to linguistic analysis because it is accorded divine authority. Conceptual metaphors shape Scriptural moral discourse in powerful, evocative, ubiquitous, mentally charged, bodily grounded ways—just as they shape all discourse.

To draw this study to a conclusion, let us return to some of the questions that engendered it. Is it possible to have a shared moral language and discourse between the NT writers and readers of the NT today? Can we find a more productive way to look at the relationship between Scripture and Christian ethics? Can the impasse between the fields of NT studies and Christian ethics be broken; can reliable links between the fields be forged? What roles does metaphor play in the moral meaning of 1 Peter? Does noticing the metaphorical dynamics help us understand 1 Peter? The methods and insights of cognitive metaphor analysis point to new ways to address these questions. Our 1 Peter study has some implications for the field of cognitive linguistics, too. Since it is written that "the last shall be first," let us take these issues in reverse order, beginning with the contribution to linguistics.

Implications for Cognitive Linguistics

A survey of metaphors for morality in 1 Peter produces plentiful evidence that the *koine* Greek of the NT employs many conceptual metaphors and frames familiar to those of us working on compiling lists of stock moral metaphors. Good Is Up (and Light, and Clean) and Evil Is Down (and Dark, and Dirty) in Greek, as in English.[1] 1 Peter also offers some new candidates for inclusion in cognitive linguists' comprehensive lists of metaphors for morality, and certain culturally nuanced spins on the stock metaphors. 1st-century social structures and practices—among them the slavery system, patron-client relationships, a justice model whose concern is restoration of honor and social balance, and remedies for debt centered on 'release' and 'deliverance'—are key to understanding Moral Accounting in 1 Peter. The way the text blends financial accounting domain concepts with legal justice and household management frames to create a coherent, composite Moral Accounting scenario is unexpectedly complex (and interesting). In addition, I Peter works with interesting variations on the conventional Great Chain of Being metaphor, and certain culturally grounded time concepts (καιρός, χρόνος) lend unique flavor to the discourse. Primary social relationships and experiences in households prove to be an especially rich source domain for metaphors for morality in 1 Peter, and these are also culturally constrained and nuanced.

Metaphor analysis methods are useful in other aspects of NT study, as well—not just in discourse analysis. Mental space blending theory contributes incisive tools for locating the metaphorical functions evoked by the Two Worlds model. The ability to identify the compression at work in that model is crucial to the analysis of the 'problem' scholars face in the Scripture and ethics field. These methods also allow a deeper and more accurate assessment and critique of the ways anal-

---

[1] Comprehensive lists of metaphors located in the text are compiled in the Appendices.

ogy has been construed in Christian ethics and scriptural hermeneutics. Blend theory shows a way out of the analogy versus metaphor impasse. Perhaps even more significant, however, is the cognitive paradigm's critique of the essentialism underlying earlier understandings of analogy and its provision of a workable, empirically justifiable, alternative model. In the biblical hermeneutics and Christian ethics fields, analogy historically has been called upon to finesse the blends between human, finite words and divine, transcendent Word. Cognitive linguistic insight into the status and function of analogical blending is potentially a major contribution to these fields.

Deploying current cognitive linguistic analytical tools on 1st-century texts requires certain methodological refinements and adjustments. When the object of study is an ancient text like 1 Peter (and therefore belongs to another cultural and linguistic context), it is important to name the metaphors in the language studied, and not to give them (only) English labels. Especially when working from the set of metaphors for morality researchers have identified in modern English, this practice of finding Greek names for the metaphors and metonymies is helpful, even crucial. It can prevent one from simply "finding" what one is looking for.

Since accuracy of mappings and of entailment deductions depends on reliability of source domain information, it is necessary in analyzing ancient texts like 1 Peter to rely on socio-cultural and anthropological data and analyses. The reliability of such secondary data is at least questionable; the mappings and conclusions drawn on the basis of that questionable information are, accordingly, qualified.

Basic conceptual metaphor mapping methods provide key methodological tools for discourse analysis, but thorough treatment requires an array of additional cognitive linguistic and cognitive scientific theories and methods. Use of such an array yields a more complete picture of conceptual coordination and systematicity than otherwise would be the case. Grady's primary metaphor theory and analytical methods provide deeper grounding for metaphor study. Analysis of textual (rather than spoken) data requires that the reading process be considered. Turner and Fauconnier offer (in *The Way We Think*) refined and dynamic methods for locating and describing mental space blending and other conceptual interactions. Blend analysis helps explain why (and some of how) any text has potential to evoke multiple meanings in the complex process we call 'reading'. Without those methods, the results of metaphor study are unsatisfactorily rudimentary.

Interdisciplinarity Required and Revised

Does conceptual metaphor study generate a link between the fields of NT studies and Christian ethics? Cognitive approaches provide ways to discern links between fields of study that have been separated and whose interaction has been problematized. At the nexus between biblical studies and constructive Christian ethics, conceptual methods highlight shared conceptual structures and conventions, while the points of clash and areas of contention are also illuminated. Cognitive approaches provide new ways to talk about how Scripture study and ethics are related, while preserving disciplinary integrity for each field of study. But preservation of disciplinary integrity does not mean acceptance of the status quo; cognitive approaches entail revisions in each discipline. These revisions include both methodological additions and theoretical corrections that challenge the traditional boundaries of the fields as they have been defined.

Cognitive approaches suggest a new model of interdisciplinarity for the Scripture and ethics field. This new model relies on the theory of blended mental spaces. It allows us to notice that before we work in blended, interdisciplinary space there is a generic space in which there is a field of study with theories, methods, and warrants, and some notion of an object (or array of objects and issues) that is studied. But the generic space does not suffice for, nor does it describe, interdisciplinary space. In this case, there are three input spaces, the fields of biblical studies, cognitive linguistics, and Christian ethics. Each of these fields has its own theories, methods, warrants, and objects of study. The fields have a history of interaction. In fact, in the beginning, biblical studies and Christian ethics were not separate fields, and modern biblical studies has roots in philology. Currently, there is some cross-talk between these input spaces, even absent cognitivist input. Biblical scholars borrow linguistic theories and methods, and Christian ethicists borrow methods and theories from biblical studies. Certain rudimentary blends, then, have been run between these input spaces.

The ways in which the input spaces are construed affect what happens when we run the blend. Specifying that the input from the linguistic field is from *cognitive* linguistics alters the blend. And if, in the biblical studies space, the methods and theories are constrained by a (19th-century) historical critical paradigm, these constraints will determine what can and cannot be blended with input from the linguistics and ethical spaces. If biblical scholars assume that constructive ethics is outside their area of concern, their work will be shaped accordingly. On the other hand, when Christian ethicists assume that the biblical texts are so historically and culturally alien as to be of little or no use for modern constructive ethics, The Two Worlds model derived from Lessing's Ditch metaphor is being allowed to constrain the range of possible plausible interactions between the 'world' of the text and its author and the 'world' of the modern reader. This, in turn, shapes the way Scripture is (both intentionally and unconsciously) allowed to interact with modern morality and contemporary ethics. By the same kind of logic, when the field of ethics confines itself to the tasks of problem solving and metaethical theorizing, the potential contribution of Scripture in the blended space is tightly restricted. Scripture's diversity (or diversities: linguistic, literary, theological, and so on) and historical-cultural distance loom large. The range of biblical materials that seems to have bearing on constructive ethics is narrow, when the blend is run this way.

Scholars in these fields have choices to make about how they run the biblical studies and ethics blend. Ogletree, Hays, and Spohn (and Gustafson, before them) have called for greater awareness of the presuppositions and expectations we bring to our work. Cognitive scientific descriptive and analytical methods can aid us in that project.

Scripture and Ethics

Does conceptual metaphor study offer a more productive way to look at the relationship between Scripture and Christian ethics? This is a slightly different question than the previous one. Here we are asking not so much about the disciplinary interaction (biblical study field / ethics field) as about the biblical text-Christian ethics interaction. Cognitive metaphor study is one way to do what David Tracy and William Spohn counsel we need to do—to get at the particulars, the rich variety of concrete images and metaphors of the text. But it does more than add descriptive detail to fund ethical 'use' of Scripture as 'source.' Conceptual approaches' explanatory powers can give us a better understanding of how reading exemplary texts functions to engender dispositions and shape moral character as readers engage and are engaged by the discourse. Cognitive analytical methods also shed new light on the old 'problem' of Scripture and ethics.

The 'Problem(s)'

When we listen with cognitive linguistically-trained ears to the scholarly discussion of the 'problem' of Scripture and ethics, we can hear the metaphors that have been used to frame the debate. Scripture itself has been problematized on two major counts: Diversity and Distance. The biblical materials, so the argument goes, are too diverse to be of much use for contemporary constructive ethics. There is no unified, clearly articulated ethic of the sort that is pragmatically effective for work on modern problems. Then there is the distance problem, the temporal-cultural Gap between the Worlds. Conceptual blending analysis allows us to notice that in this schema, all of the features belonging to the cultures and literary genres of the biblical contexts are compressed into one space evoked by the word 'World.' Then a similarly wide array of features of modern contexts (cultural, philosophical, social-political, and so on) is compressed into another 'World.' When these compressed Worlds are juxtaposed, their differences, not their similarities, are highlighted.

Conceptual methods and theory allow us to query the appropriateness of this scenario and challenge the accuracy of its account of reader-text-context interactions. Recognizing that the Two Worlds scenario is a human construct, we are free to ask whether the stated 'problem,' (the 'gap') is in fact the main issue facing contemporary readers and would-be performers of Scripture. The Two Worlds model does have some positive explanatory power. There are undeniable differences between 1st-century Greco-Roman Palestinian (and Asia Minor) cultural-historical settings and those in which any 21st-century readers live. There is no use denying the differences. But the biblical texts—and even some aspects of their 'world'—are part of our 'world.' The Bible As Scripture is an integral component of the context of the present Christian community. Moreover, even the context of modern secular society in the West is permeated by the stories and concepts, the core narrative, of the Judeo-Christian Scriptural tradition. Like it or not, the 'worlds' are not entirely separate.

Conceptual analysis provides a clearer understanding of how the Two Worlds model works. With that in hand, then, the hegemony of a historicism that has distorted our view of the dynamic interplay of Scripture and constructive Christian ethics can be challenged. A too-rigid, overstated social constructivism (wedded to radical historicism) has been allowed to obscure and deny what actually can and does happen in moral discourse when modern, even 21st-century, readers interact with the NT texts as Scripture. How have we ever been able to understand and translate and act on these texts, save that there is much that is cross- or transculturally human?

Conceptual metaphor and mental space study offers new ways to represent and investigate the cultural interplay that is entailed as modern readers encounter ancient texts. Core conceptual metaphors and image schemas modern readers share with the texts enable understanding and response. In both contexts, Good Is Light and Evil Is Dark, and both good and evil are Forces one wields or resists—and these are only a few of the key conceptual metaphors that allow cross- and transcultural understanding to flow. There are nodes of cultural clash, and these, too, can be identified via conceptual metaphor analysis. The contexts do not have to be identical—between the reader and the text—in order for meaning to be created and a workable understanding to be achieved. Given adequate source domain input we can still make decent translations, and given those connections, we can (and will) act on what we have perceived.

Exemplar, not Source

The conceptual model is compatible with the observation that in some reading communities, NT texts like 1 Peter serve as more than 'sources' for Christian ethics. 1 Peter is itself an exemplar of faithful approaches to Christian ethics, of moral discourse in progress. Changing the basic hermeneutical metaphor from Scripture As Source for Christian Ethics to Scripture As Exemplar of Christian Moral Discourse changes the questions, though. Instead of presenting modern problems to Scripture (under the Source Model), the Exemplar Model requires us to observe how the NT texts themselves define moral issues and problems and then to ask what our response will be.

The Source Model can prompt playacting. It has Christian ethicists going through all sorts of maneuvers to transpose thorny, modern biotechnological issues (for example) into the key of 1st-century Roman Palestine. In the face of the difficulty of that kind of charade, it has others of us dismissing Scripture as irrelevant when it cannot resolve to our satisfaction the dilemmas we pose.

Scripture as Exemplar allows us to grow beyond dissociation, on the one hand, and withdrawal and dismissal, on the other. An Exemplar can be approached with curiosity about the kinds of experiences that will be construed as moral conflicts and challenges. To honor the texts as exemplars does not entail a denial of our temporal-cultural differences, but rather seeks to uncover in the reading process cultural and conceptual clashes and blends, congruencies and divergences, in the interest of discerning what the Spirit might be saying to the churches today. It requires us to back off of our insistence, however, that Scripture conform to modern models of what an adequate ethical source will look like and do. It challenges us to open up (and reclaim) the scope of the Christian ethics field beyond dilemma-solving to include the deep matters of moral character and disposition, of moral development and formation. It pushes us to consider these matters in the context of social dynamics and groups, and not to confine our concern to the difficulties faced by individual moral agents. It invites us to allow even our core metaethical concepts—justice, goodness, freedom—to be reframed or recast.

Metaphorical Moral Imagination versus Analogical Imagination

The status and role of analogy in theological and ethical discourse remains a significant and potentially problematical issue. The essentialism that problematized religious language and any talk of the transcendent forced theologians into reliance on analogy in the first place. If essentialism is rejected, perhaps we do not need to have recourse to analogy to explain how authentic God-talk can happen. That is, if the divine and human worlds, the infinite and the finite are not such essentially distinct worlds, then the elaborate maneuvers that an Aquinas undertook are no longer necessary.

Still, it seems prudent (even necessary) to discern the distinctive roles analogy and metaphor play in the discursive dynamic, in reading and hermeneutics. At the very least, a certain clarification or sanitizing of terminological boundaries is in order. The sense people have that there is some qualitative difference between analogy and (traditionally defined) metaphors needs to be noticed and honored.

Fauconnier and Turner's work is crucial. Blended mental space theory allows us to describe how conceptual blending—via various kinds of mental space interactions—operates in the reading and interpretive process. Biblical interpreters are better advised to expend energy learning how to navigate in and run the blends, rather than in holding the 'Worlds' of the text and of the reader-interpreter apart.

Paradigm Shift

Cognitive methods are not, however, available as a simple, add-on toolkit. A theoretical paradigm shift is required in order to fully access the methods. It is the paradigm shift that allows us to admit that the Gap has been overstated. Language—including metaphor and analogy—works *conceptually*, and human concepts are rooted in human experience. The conceptual model invites us to read texts with greater awareness of our own core metaphors for morality, looking for what is *trans*cultural, noticing interesting *cross*-cultural variations.

Universal Foundations

Does the cognitivist paradigm pull the rug out from under ethicists' attempts to find a universal foundation for moral concepts and norms? Under the cognitivist paradigm, the search for 'universal' foundations for ethics is redirected.[2] Cognitivism calls into question (and denies) the Cartesian theory that thought is always conscious and is essentially disembodied. It queries and critiques Kant's (metaphorical) construal of Universal Reason, via which he attempted to ground universal moral laws. It does this with empirical evidence; Cartesian and Kantian-style 'universals' are at odds with the findings emerging from second generation cognitive science.[3]

But does the cognitive critique, then, open the door to radical relativism? Does it remove any hope of finding cross-cultural foundations for moral norms and ethical concepts? No. The cognitive paradigm locates specific constraints on moral reasoning, and these are grounded in logical structures and inferential patterns from a broad range of dimensions of human experience. Cognitive-style 'universals,' then, arise from empirical evidence of certain core human conditions and

---

[2] A more accurate, and more humble term would be 'global.'
[3] Lakoff and Johnson, *Philosophy in the Flesh: The Embodied Mind and its Challenge to Western Thought* (New York: Basic Books, 1999), 391–439, 548.

experiences; its philosophical basis is in experiential realism, not objectivist foundationalism.[4]

Embodied primary metaphors, image-schematic structures, and metamoral conceptual metaphors are key to the cognitive approach to universals. Primary metaphors are part of the human cognitive unconscious.[5] Lakoff and Johnson summarize:

> We acquire them automatically and unconsciously via the normal process of neural learning and may be unaware that we have them. We have no choice in this process. When the embodied experiences in the world are universal, then the corresponding primary metaphors are universally acquired.[6]

Some primary metaphors are shared transculturally; some are culturally nuanced. Given appropriate cross-cultural sensitivity and adequate socio-cultural (source domain) information, even conceptual metaphors grounded in different cultural experiences and structures are understandable to outsiders. Basic understandings and experiences of human well-being found our understanding and experiences of morality, our notions of the good, and ground our ethical logics.

Grounding Cross-cultural Ethical Critique

We cannot escape the cultural, contextual components of moral and ethical concepts, not even of Scriptural moral and ethical concepts. Metaphors for morality are keyed to collective human wisdom, based on our observation and experience, about what dispositions and behaviors promote human flourishing, well-being. In virtually every culture, Morality Is Strength, Morality Is Uprightness, Morality Is Health, Morality Is Wealth; Good Is Light and Evil Is Dark. These are the kinds of core concepts with which our formal, abstract ethical reasoning works and within which it coheres. Ethical critique, then, must be founded on and argued from within this contingent reality.

The dismissal of Scripture as source (or its demotion to third or fourth place among the 'sources') for contemporary Christian ethics on account of its cultural contingency can also be critiqued from this

---

[4] Ibid., 328–329.
[5] Ibid., 56.
[6] Ibid. Significantly, Lakoff and Johnson point out that some of these conceptual metaphors are manifested in grammar, art, and ritual and *not* in language. Ibid., 57.

perspective. There is no supra-cultural 'objective' ground on which to build a firmer, more reliable foundation. All attempts at finding such ground and building such edifices have failed and will fail, for the simple reason that human reason is embodied and inextricably culturally contingent. We will do better, however, to treat Scriptural moral exhortation as exemplary, and to stop consigning it to a 'sources' framework. The conceptual metaphors—primary, generic, and metamoral—along with the image schemas, frames, analogies, and other kinds of blended mental spaces with which Scripture communicates make its moral and ethical views cross- and transculturally accessible and subject to evaluation. By the same token, ethical constructions and proposals coming from outside the Scriptural tradition are subject to comparison and evaluation from Scriptural perspectives. Discourse is possible, the discussion can be opened, along these lines.

Within communities that hold the biblical texts as Scripture, the collective wisdom of those texts and of the tradition and history of the communities that belong to the texts is held to be qualitatively other, 'sacred,' privileged. We have a cultural belief, based on our collective experience, that these words can speak Words to us from outside, from a God not of our own making, and from people who struggled in ancient times to live according to those Words and in relation to the One who speaks them. We have a history of interaction with these texts, of discussion and debate about their significance and meaning as we face new challenges in different contexts. We then choose to privilege these Scriptural voices when they speak about the ways that lead to wholeness, to holiness, to goodness for the human community, and when they display the consequences of refusal or failure to respond to the voice that calls us 'beloved.' The God revealed in these Scriptures is not a disembodied god; this is an incarnational God who desires to engage humanity fully, to be known and to know. It is time for the Christian community to leave behind the god of disembodied reason whose 'absolutely authoritative' lies turned out to be such poor substitutes for the richly imaginative, diverse, lively, and true Word. We did not find enlightenment in that god's house, the house of Objective Reason. But neither will it do to erase the nuances of the many distinctive voices that speak in and through Scripture. Guidance and critique of our own culturally embedded confusion, then, can now be received and acted on—if we will enter the Scriptural authorial audience(s) and allow our imaginations to be revived and retooled.

Lively Moral Discourse

Does conceptual metaphor make possible a shared moral language and discourse between the NT writers and readers of the NT today? Via conceptual metaphor analysis, a shared moral language and discourse can be *recognized*. It is not that metaphor study creates that language and discourse, but that this methodology can foreground what has potentially been there all along. The cognitive approaches to metaphor, then, make these features of the discourse—within the text and in the reading and interpretive process—available for further analysis and reflection. The methods do not so much provide a link between the text and modern readers as they reveal some of the ways that texts and readers have always been connecting (or missing each other). It is not the method or theory of conceptual metaphor and blended mental spaces that is the connecting link; rather, the conceptual spaces and metaphors themselves constitute the connecting fabric and lines of communication. They do not perform all the transcultural communicative functions between texts and authors and readers, but they are indispensable components of that discourse.

Primary metaphors that ground more complex image schemas and metaphors people use in multiple contexts (the biblical contexts and modern readers' contexts) make discourse possible. Imagine how much more difficult it would be to understand texts from a cultural context in which Good Is Light and Evil Is Dark were not givens. Or again, imagine attempting to communicate with beings from a context with radically different image-schematic structures—where thought and expressions did not and could not rely on core concepts like part-whole, center-periphery, link, cycle, iteration, contact, adjacency, forced motion, support, balance, straight-curved, and near-far.[7] *That* would be cross-world communication, and it would be very difficult, indeed. We share so many core metaphors with the biblical cultural contexts—and we are linguistic heirs of the Hellenized Greek conceptual system—that although the discourse is strained at points, we yet can navigate with remarkable ease through their context. Conceptual metaphors allow cross-and transcultural understanding to flow. There are nodes of cultural clash, to be sure. But these, too, can be identified and parsed in

---

[7] This partial list of basic image schemas is from Lakoff and Johnson, *Philosophy in the Flesh*, 35.

more detail via conceptual metaphor analysis. Both understanding and misunderstanding can be partly accounted for via conceptual metaphor and blended space theories and methods. All of this is possible because human languages and expressions arise from basic embodied human experience and primary social relationships.

Required Reading

The Scripture As Exemplar model requires that Scripture be read, and read in community. Cognitive conceptual analysis can help explain how vague allusions to half-remembered verses or parables, and conflated reconstructions of a mega story or a narrative function in our moral formation and reasoning. But the Scripture As Exemplar approach to Scripture and ethics is rooted in engagement with the texts themselves. The level of engagement exemplary reading calls for requires work and collaboration.

All readers are interpreters and all reading requires us to run mental space blends. Expert readers in the biblical studies and ethics fields bring their own stock of conceptual knowledge and expectations to the reading. Scholars who become exemplary readers will become aware of the content of their conceptual stocks and grow adept at recognizing how conceptual mappings and blends proliferate in the reading process. We will begin to notice inference patterns and start to query specific entailments. We will want to think about how the formative Christian communities and early Christian theologians and scholars ran the blends as they interpreted these texts. We will want to think about the implications for social ethics of reading these texts, of construing its metaphors and running the blends in certain ways. Work on the biblical texts using this set of methods has just begun; we have much to learn. Confronting—as far as possible on their own terms—these diverse texts from these varied cultural and belief contexts will be extremely difficult. We need to collaborate; even identifying and cataloging the metaphors for morality (let alone other kinds of metaphors) in the NT is an enormous task. But it can and should be done. The data gathered from such conceptual metaphor study could give us a thicker description and more finely tuned and coherent reading of the moral discourse within the NT (and of the canon as a whole). And it could open up our discourse with the texts, closing that old 'gap' that once seemed so wide.

But the aim of faithful biblical scholarship is to give the Bible back to ordinary readers in a more readable and understandable form; it is not to take the book out of their hands and proclaim them incompetent to touch it. Scholars do not own these texts. In fact, while scholars have been busy problematizing the texts, many ordinary readers have been making the kinds of connections we are proposing and pointing to. Study of the conceptual dynamics of the reading process reveals some of the complexity and contingency of even ordinary reading. We ought to honor ordinary readers and notice the amazing connections they are able to make when they encounter an ancient text like 1 Peter.

But both 'expert' and ordinary readers run blends and, in the process, run the risk of running the wrong blend. We run the wrong blend when we let the modern scenario dominate in the blend. When that happens, we effectively rename our own modern moral system as "1 Peter". In this shell game, authentic moral discourse between the modern reader and the ancient text is lost is the shuffle. Such reading requires little or no adjustment on the reader's part, causes little or no discomfort, and likely yields no change of mind (and heart?). The strangeness of the text's context is erased or subsumed; we hardly enter the authorial audience at all. Both ordinary and expert readers run the risk of projecting into the text their own conceptual structures and assumptions. Conceptual metaphor and mental space blending analysis can help readers become aware of the text's conceptual structures, but unless we also become aware of our own expectations and assumptions, we will misread. We cannot help it.

Hard Reading

Does a reader have to know Greek in order to read 1 Peter and the rest of the New Testament? Yes. And no. The New Testament is in Greek; its conceptual structure is expressed in Greek and its inference patterns are rooted in Hellenized Judaic and Greco-Roman cultural models and social structures. The primary text in NT study is the Greek New Testament, and translations are simply someone else's (or more likely, a committee's collective) take on how to map the metaphors and parse the grammar and run the blends. Readers who like to think for themselves will do what it takes to work with the Greek New Testament. But English Bible readers can still use conceptual metaphor study methods. The best results will be obtained when several translations are consulted, and such results are to be viewed as provisional, as educated guesses.

The higher hurdle that must be leapt, the greater challenge for both lay and expert readers who wish read 1 Peter with understanding and respond appropriately, is not the linguistic barrier, the Greek-English difference. I suspect that, at least for Euro-American (churched, "Christian," middle- and upper-middle class) readers, harder than learning adequate Greek is the challenge entailed in setting aside our customary framing of the church in relation to society and government—and world. The metaphors many American Christians live by are going to clash with those with which Peter grounds his moral appeal in this letter. How can those of us dedicated to the Church Triumphant and who sincerely believe that the (actual) nation in which we live is the Promised Land, God's country, hear a word to exiles, strangers, resident aliens? How can those of us who equate divine blessing with comfort, plenty, and safety hear Peter's call into suffering among the lowly, like Jesus? We tend to like the 'royal priesthood,' 'holy nation,' 'people belonging to God,' metaphors. We tend to skip over the harder passages, the calls to be 'slaves' of God who are 'stranger-lovers' (the opposite of xenophobia). We like the title, 'Christian,' but do we embrace the suffering Peter promises will be entailed if we dare to live ὡς Χριστιανός ... ἐν ὀνόματι τούτῳ 'as Christians ... because you bear this name'? In order to truly enter this authorial audience, these kinds of challenges to our customary framing of Christianity must be engaged and accepted, at least at an imaginative level. The hope here is that that engagement will be transformative and will allow us to enter more deeply into the kind of honorable and responsible moral behavior Peter envisions for followers of Jesus Christ.

Coda: Why go to all this trouble?

For we all of us, grave or light, get our thoughts entangled in metaphors, and act fatally on the strength of them.
——George Eliot[8]

Conceptual metaphor study is worth the trouble because George Eliot is right: We do all of us, grave or light, scholar or lay reader, get our

---

[8] George Eliot, *Middlemarch* (London: Penguin Classics, 1994 [1871–1872]), 85.

thoughts entangled in metaphor. We do not just speak in metaphors when we are waxing poetic. We do not encounter metaphors only or mostly when politicians and preachers are framing their appeals to us in metaphor. We think metaphorically. And when we are thinking about what is good and what is evil, when we are considering moral choices or evaluating others' behavior, we think metaphorically. We cannot help it. To think about such abstract things as good and evil, justice and honor, we need to use our understanding and experiences of concrete things like bookkeeping and dirt, sickness and health, the inside of a container versus the outside, and even relationships in households. Our choices and actions are rooted in the inferences we make based on the understandings and experiences metaphors evoke and express. We *inevitably* act on the strength—or the weakness—of those understandings, of those metaphors. Responsive reading of 1 Peter entails noticing the metaphors Peter suggests Christians ought to live by, and it means taking responsibility for our choices as we accept or reject his message, as we do or do not faithfully bear this name.

APPENDICES

Appendix to Chapter Two
Variations of the Literal Truth Theory

[Compiled from Lakoff and Turner, *More than Cool Reason*. Each variation is marked by a title in italics. Lakoffian objections to the traditional theory follow each description.]

The Paraphrase Position. "On this view, a metaphorical expression can be meaningful only if it can be paraphrased in language that is non-metaphorical, that is, 'literal language.'"
—This position "fails to account for both the inferential and conceptualizing capacity of metaphor."

The Decoding Position. A variation of the Paraphrase Position, here it is claimed that a metaphor is part of a code that must be broken in order that an author's meaning can be revealed.
—Source domains do not merely give a set of words that work as a kind of symbolic code for concepts in the target domain that are understood independently of the metaphor.

The Similarity Position. Seeing a metaphor is to notice that two concepts share some 'literal,' nonmetaphoric properties. If that is the case, then "the sole conceptual power metaphor might have is to highlight similarities that are already there."
—Some kind of similarity is involved in metaphor, but it is not a matter of similar objective properties. "Metaphor always results in a similarity of image schemata structure between the source and target domains."

The Reason-versus-Imagination Position. This is the assumption that reason and imagination are mutually exclusive. "Reason is taken to be the rational linking up of concepts, which are nonmetaphoric, so as to lead from true premises to true conclusions."

—Many of our inferences are metaphoric. "Indeed so much of our reason is metaphoric that if we view metaphor as part of the faculty of the imagination, then reason is mostly if not entirely imaginative in character."

The Naming Position. In their 'proper' use, words designate literal concepts; a metaphor is the use of a word to mean something it does not 'properly' mean.
—"This position has the false consequence that metaphor has no conceptual role; ... it cannot be used in reasoning, conceptualizing, and understanding."

The Deviance Position. "All concepts and conventional language are non-metaphoric, and we make metaphors only by deviating from normal conventional usage."
—"Ordinary everyday language is ineradicably metaphoric ... Conventional metaphorical thought and language are normal, not deviant."

The Fallback Position. Since the normal, ordinary use of language is literal, we first look for a literal meaning of any sentence, and "seek a metaphorical meaning (that is, a paraphrase) only as a fallback, if we are not content with the literal meaning."
—"Our concepts in certain domains are often *primarily metaphorical,* as when we understand death as departure, loss, sleep, and so on."

The Pragmatics Position. Since metaphor is not normal, conventional language, the study of it belongs in the field of "pragmatics", not "semantics." Under this rubric, "no conventional metaphor is considered metaphor at all; only novel metaphorical expressions count."
—The traditional semantics-pragmatics distinction is false. Pragmatic principles of conversation do often combine with conceptual metaphors (especially in the understanding of poetry), but metaphor cannot be reduced to or relegated entirely to the sphere of pragmatics.

The No Concepts Position. The meaning of expressions in a language are independent of human cognition. Language is not based on any conceptual system, so there is no distinction between the meanings of words and the meanings of concepts.

—Lakoff says this position "has all the drawbacks" of the Literal Meaning Theory and the Deviance Position, and incorporates the (erroneous) Dead Metaphor Theory, as well.

Appendix to Chapter Five
The Moral Bookkeeping Schema
Instantiation in 1 Peter

Chart 1. Slots

SOURCE: Financial Accounting Domain	→	TARGET: Moral Domain	EXAMPLES
Ledger/ account book γράμμα	→	Moral Record of good or bad deeds or people	γράμμα Here is the list of what you owe (Luke 16.6). (Lit)
χειρόγραφον			χειρόγραφον erasing the record that stood against us with its legal demands (Col 2.13b–14a)
λόγος			ἀπολόγος Always be ready to make your defense (ἀπολογίαν) to anyone who demands from you an accounting (λόγον) for the hope that is in you (3.15)
To keep financial records ἐλλογέω λογίζομαι To settle or check accounts συναίρω	→	To keep track of behavior	ἐλλογέω ... but where there is no law, no account is kept of sins (Rom 5.13) συνᾶραι λόγον Mt 18.23–24
Debit ὀφειλή ὀφείλημα	→	Bad Deed; result of wrong-doing	If you endure when you are beaten for doing wrong (ἁμαρτάνοντες), what credit (κλέος) is that? (**2.20**)
To have financial debt; to owe ὀφείλω To owe something to someone in return προσοφείλω	→	To have moral obligation	Lit. Mt 18.28; Fig. Mt 6.12 Philemon 19

Debtor ὀφειλέτης	→	Wrongdoer, sg./pl.	Do not repay evil for evil or abuse for abuse; but, on the contrary, repay with a blessing. (3.9)
Credit χάρις	→	Result of good deeds OR debt cancellation	Lit. Romans 4.4 Fig. For it is a credit (χάρις) to you if, being aware of God, you endure pain while suffering unjustly. (2.19) But if you endure when you do right and suffer for it, you have God's approval (χάρις παρὰ θεῷ, 2.20).
Payment ἐπικαλύπτω Lit. "to cover" [different metaphor?] ἀποδίδωμι Lit. "give back"	→	Good deed that cancels bad To reciprocate (morally)	Love covers (καλύπτει) a multitude of sins (4.8; see list of actions that fill out the meaning of "love" here; and see Romans 4.7). Do not repay (μὴ ἀποδιδόντες) evil for evil or abuse for abuse; but, ... repay with a blessing (δὲ εὐλογοῦντες 3.9).
Accountant 1st c.: οἰκονόμος household manager; city manager/treasurer [Blend with Household Frame]	→	Moral Authority Figure; administers consequences, God's judgment and mercy	Like good stewards (οἰκονόμοι) of the manifold grace (ποικίλης χάριτος θεοῦ) of God, serve (διακονοῦντες) one another. (4.10) Who is the οἰκονόμος of the house of God (οἴκου τοῦ θεοῦ, 4.17)?
Judge in a property or monetary dispute [Blend with Legal Frame]	→	Moral Authority Figure A. God (+Father) B. Human Ruler or Judge C. Individual Agent	A. If you invoke as Father the one who judges (κρίνοντα) [all people] impartially according to their deeds (τὸ ἑκάστου ἔργον 1.17). But if you suffer for it, you have God's approval (χάρις παρὰ θεῷ 2.20; also 2.12, 3.10–12,4.5). B. Governors (ἡγεμόσιν), as sent by [God] to punish those who do wrong and to praise those who do right (ἐκδίκησιν κακοποιῶν ἔπαινον δὲ ἀγαθοποιῶν 2.14). C. Can we find the notion of moral self-evaluation or of the individual as moral authority operating in 1 Peter?
To Audit Books συναίρω To settle or check accounts cf. To judge κρίνω and ἐποπτεύω To oversee, observe	→	To review, analyze, observe behavior; to make moral judgment	But they will have to give an accounting to him who stands ready to judge (ἔχοντι κρῖναι) the living and the dead (4.5; and see 4.6, 4.17, 1.17, 2.23). ἐπίσκοπος 2.25; ἐποπτεύω 2.12, 3.2

To Submit to an Audit	→	Submit to moral evaluation	Always be ready to make your defense (ἀπολογίαν) to anyone who demands from you an accounting (λόγον) for the hope that is in you. (3.15) But they will have to give an accounting (ἀποδώσουσιν λόγον) to him who stands ready to judge (ἔχοντι κρίναι) the living and the dead. (4.5)
Total / Balance	→	Evidence of moral status	For the time has come for judgment (τὸ κρίμα) to begin with the household of God; if it begins with us, what will be the end (τὸ τέλος τῶν ἀπειθούντων) for those who do not obey the gospel of God? (4.17)
Penalties	→	Negative consequences of bad behavior or warped character	… what will be the end (τὸ τέλος τῶν ἀπειθούντων) for those who do not obey the gospel of God? (4.17)
Rewards, Dividends	→	Positive consequences of good behavior or character	And when the chief shepherd appears you will win the crown (κομεῖσθε … στέφανον) of glory that never fades away (5.4).
To cancel debt ἀφίημι let go χαρίζομαι give freely; pay a debt ἐξαλείφω blot out or erase a written record ἀπολύω release, let go	→	To forgive moral failure	ἀφίημι Mt 6.12, 18.32 χαρίζομαι Colossians 2.13, Luke 7.42; 2 Cor 12.13 ἐξαλείφω Colossians 2.14 ἀπολύω Luke 6.37
Cancellation of debt A. Mercy: Release from financial/property debt ἔλεος B. Ransom λύτρωσις vb. λυτρόω (esp. from debt slavery) Redeemer: λυτρωτής [Blend with debt slavery and ransom frames]	→	A. Mercy: Release from moral debt B. Release from consequences of bad behavior	A. Once you had not received mercy (οὐκ ἠλεημένοι), but now you have received mercy (νῦν δὲ ἐλεηθέντες 2.10; also 1.3). B. You were ransomed (ἐλυτρώθητε) … with the precious blood of Christ, like that of a lamb without spot or blemish (1.18–19).

| Final Audit / Reckoning of Account | → | Ultimate Moral Judgment: Day of Reckoning | But they will have to give an accounting (ἀποδώσουσιν λόγον) to him who stands ready to judge (ἔχοντι κρῖναι) the living and the dead. (4.5; and see 2.12) |

Chart 2. Relations

SOURCE: Financial Accounting Domain		TARGET: Moral Domain	EXAMPLES
Account holder to credits	→	Agent to good deeds: responsibility for good deeds	They may see your *good deeds* and glorify God when he comes to judge. (2.12)
Debtor to Debts	→	Agent to bad deeds: Responsibility for bad deeds	4.18 Proverbs 11.31 If the righteous are *repaid* on earth, how much more the wicked and the sinner?
Debtor to Lender or Creditor 1st-c. variations: Client to patron Debt slave to owner/ master	→	Responsibility of agent to moral authority Moral authority variations: God, ruler, household master, church elder.	… governors, as sent by him to *punish* those who *do wrong* and to *praise* those who *do right*. (2.14)
Debtor or account holder to Judge	→	Ultimate moral accountability of agent before moral authority: God, ruler, master, elder	God opposes the proud, but gives grace to the humble. Humble yourselves therefore under the mighty hand of God, so that [God] may exalt you in due time. (5.6)
Redeemer to debt holder / debt slave	→	Relationship of one who brings or effects release or forgiveness to moral agent(s)	Christ suffered for sins once for all, the righteous for the unrighteous, in order to bring you to God. (3.18)

Chart 3. Properties

SOURCE: Financial Accounting Domain	TARGET: Moral Domain	EXAMPLES
Ledgers are incremental	→ Moral consequences accumulate by increments	4.2–6
Accounts accumulate value over time	→ Over time, moral deeds shape character	4.2–3, and see 2.12, 19, 4.8f
Auditors have authority both to audit and to prescribe consequences: rewards and punishments	→ God (and lesser moral authorities delegated by God) has legitimate moral authority and the right to punish and reward behavior.	If you invoke as Father the one who judges all people impartially according to their deeds … (1.17) … governors, as sent by him to punish those who do wrong and to praise those who do right. (2.14) But they will have to give an accounting to him who stands ready to judge the living and the dead. (4.5)
Financial auditing is impartial	→ Moral judgment by legitimate authority is fair, impartial	If you invoke as Father the one who judges all people impartially according to their deeds … (1.17)

Chart 4. Knowledge

SOURCE: Financial Accounting Domain	TARGET: Moral Domain	EXAMPLES
Debts accumulate and become overwhelming; in 1st-c. Palestine and Asia Minor, this could lead to debt slavery. [Blend with debt slavery frame]	→ Moral failures and their consequences accumulate and can become overwhelming.	If it is hard for the righteous to be saved, what will become of the ungodly and the sinners? (4.18; and see 1.17–18, 2.5; cf. Col. 2.13–14)

Debtors suffer, but sometimes the suffering is a direct consequence of unwise or improper financial decisions	→ Moral failure is connected with suffering, sometimes "deserved."	If you endure pain when you are beaten for doing wrong, what credit is that? (2.20; and see 3.17a, 4.15, 4.1, 4.12–13)
Social status is tied to financial well-being	→ Social status / honor can be tied to moral capital, moral standing.	3.7, 5.1b-3
Shame and dishonor accompany debt; honor accompanies wealth and debt-free status	→ Shame and dishonor accompany bad deeds or character; honor accompanies good deeds, character.	1.18a, 2.12; 2.15, 3.16, 4.16
Indebtedness can be a temporary condition. Debt slavery was expected to be temporary.	→ Moral failure, laxity, or even bad character can be a temporary condition.	2.1, 10; 3.9–15
1st-c. debt slaves worked off their debt. It could take several years, but when the debt was paid, honor was restored and freedom was given.	→ Good works can cancel bad deeds. Doing good works forms good character. Restitution and rehabilitation are possible	(4.8) (2.6)
Debt can be too large to work off: need for a Kinsman-redeemer, ransom-payer	→ Moral guilt and its consequences can be too great for the individual (or collective) agent to deal with; intervention is needed.	(1.18–19, 2.10, 2.24, 3.18)

Appendix to Chapter Six
"Living in Christ"

Metaphors

    ἐν Χριστῷ Image Schema: Christ Is a Container
    ἐν ἁγιασμῷ πνεύματος Image Schema: Holy Spirit Is a Container
    States Are Locations
    Social Groups Are Containers
    The Church Is a Container
    Coordinated Spatial Metaphors: In and Out, Into and Out of
    Behavior Is Moving Back and Forth (ἀναστρέφω)
    Behavior Is Work / Behavior Is Making an Object (ποιέω)
    Good Behavior Is Good Work / Good Behavior Is Making a Fine
       Object
    Bad Behavior Is Bad Work / Bad Behavior Is Making a Bad Object
       (κακοποιέω)
    Morality Is Strength (ἀγαθός)
    Good Is Bright / Good Is Light
    Evil Is Dark (σκότος)
    Dangerous Is Dark
    Taking on Christian Identity Is Going from Dark into Light
    A Path Is a Bounded Space
    A Footprint Is a Container
    Blend: Doing Evil Is Traveling in a Dark Place
       Life Is a Journey
    Christ's Life Is a Journey
    The Life Journey (or Path) of Christ Is a Moral Pattern
    Morality Is Purity
    Immorality Is Impurity
    Immorality Is Lawlessness

Metonymies

    Christ For Church
    ἐν Χριστῷ ← [Ἐκκλεσία]

Appendix to Chapter Eight
Time and Events: Structured Spaces for Moral Living

Metaphors

    Time Is a Space
    Time Is Motion
    Time Is a Path; Time Is Motion Along a Path
    Spatial Time Containers (image schemas)
        clock time spatial time zone—[ἐν] χρόνος
        divine spatial time zone—ἐν οὐρανοῖς
        "in due time / the right season"—ἐν καιρῷ
        An Era Is a (Living) Space/ Container
        Exile Is a Spatial Time Container—πάροικος
        Awe Is a Container < EMOTIONAL STATES ARE CONTAINERS
    Moments In Time Are Objects in Motion
    The End /Time of Completion [τὸ τέλος] Is an Object in Motion
    Time Is a Substance

SD: Substance	→	*TD: Time*
Amount of Substance	→	Duration of Time
The Size of the Amount	→	The Extent of the Duration
Motion of Substance	→	The "Passage" of Time[1]
Past the Observer		

Metonymies

    Event For Time
    Name of Day For Event
    Event For Process
    'The Day' For Process of Rendering Ultimate Moral Consequences
    Days For Era
    Days For Lifespan
    State For Time; Exile As Time (παροικίας)

---

[1] Adapted from Lakoff and Johnson, *Philosophy in the Flesh*, 145.

Appendix to Chapter Nine

Nation Section Metaphors

    Ἔθνος Container Schema / Gentile Nation Image Schema.
    Christians Are the People of God
        Χριστιανος' ⟵ Λαὸς θεοῦ Christians Are a Nation
    Christians Are a People Group
    The Church Is a Chosen Nation/ Chosen People
    The Church Is Israel or The Church Is the New Israel
    The Church (People) Is The (Jerusalem) Temple
    Christians Are a Royal (or Temple) Priesthood
    Christians Are a Holy Nation
    (The Chosen) People Are Possessions of God
    God Is a Person
    The Church Is an Object
    The Church Is a Possession of God (where God Is a Person)
    Christians Are The People
    The Church Is the (Jewish) Diaspora
        Hebraic prototypes of Diaspora and Exile
    Exile Is The Church in Society
        Strangers / Resident Aliens / Transients
        Παροῖκοι *resident aliens, sojourners*
    Native Land Is Home
    Heaven Is Home
    Jesus Is the (protypical Stranger / Exile)

Metonymies

    Diaspora For Israel/ Chosen People
    'Priest' For Essence of a People
    Building For Institution
    LOCATION FOR PEOPLE THERE
    STATE FOR DURATION
    EVENT FOR DURATION

Ὄικος Section

    Well-Being Is Honor
        Εὐδαιμονία ⟵ Τιμή
    Honor Is Obedience
        Τιμή ⟶ Ὑποτάσσω
    Status Is Up
    Honor Is Up
    Morality Is Purity
    Goodness Is Self-Giving: ἀγάπη *self-giving love*
    Good Moral Standing Is Inheriting the Family Fortune or Blessing

Good Relationship Is Brotherly Love
Household Frame
Christians Are Members of God's Household or God's Family
Christians Are Brothers in the Same Family
A Christian Believer Is a Child [or Infant] of God
Morality Is Childlike Obedience
Good Christian Wives Are Daughters of Sarah
Christians Are Slaves (in God's Household)
Christians Are Freemen
God Is the Paterfamilias
Jesus Is the Master
Jesus Is the Chief Shepherd
The Church Is a Flock Of Sheep
The Church Is a Building
God's People Are God's House
    Οἶκος Θεοῦ → Συνοικοδομέω Θεοῦ
Christians Are Living Building Stones
Christians Are Housebuilders
Church Leaders Are Elderly Household Members

Metonymies

    Οἶκος For Συγγένεια:
        House For Household / Family
    Ἀδελφότης For Οἶκος Χριστιανόν
        Brotherhood For Christian Household
    Ἀδελφότης For Οἶκος Χριστοῦ
        Brotherhood For House of Christ
    Ἀδελφότης For Οἶκος Θεοῦ
        Brotherhood For Household of God

Body Section Metaphors

    Doctrine of Moral Essence: Characteristic Behavior Is Moral Essence
    The Human Person Is a Container
    The Human Body Is a Container
        Human Faculties Are Smaller Containers (Inside the Larger Container)
    Good Is Up / Evil Is Down
    Morality Is Upright Posture
    Morality Is Straightness
    Immorality Is Crookedness
    Justice Is Straightness
    Injustice Is Crookedness
    Morality Is Purity
    Morality Is Health
    Morality Is Strength κράτος, ἀγαθός

Good Is Balance / Evil Is Imbalance
Morality Is Sobriety
Morality Is Clear-headedness
Conduct Is Movement Along a Path
    Good Conduct Is Movement On the Correct Path
Conduct Is Movement Inside a Container
    Good Conduct Is Movement Inside the Correct Container
Human Volition Is a Force / AGENCY IS FORCE
Moral Force Is Physical Force

War Frame

Evil Is a Strong Force
Evil Is a Wild Animal
    Evil Is a Lion
Evil Is an Adversary
    Legal Adversary
    Military Foe
Good Is a Strong Force
The Interaction of Good and Evil Is War
The Human Body Is a War Zone
The Human Person Is a War Zone
Inner Moral Struggle Is War
Moral Education Is Physical Training
Resisting Evil Is Holding Off a Strong Contender
Moral Conviction Is Strength
Moral Action Is Resisting A Strong Force
Moral Assistance Is Support
Psychic Suffering Is Physical Suffering
Desire For Moral and Spiritual Growth Is Hunger
The Necessary Material For Moral Growth Is Food
Appealing Moral/Spiritual Input Is Tasty Food
Moral Development Is Physical Growth
The Heart Is a Container (of Moral Essence)

Metonymies

Tongue/Lips For Speech
Ἐν σαρκὶ For Human Existence
Body For Human Life

Primary Metaphors

AGENCY IS FORCE
CENTRAL IS IMPORTANT
ESSENTIAL IS INTERNAL
FUNCTIONALITY / VIABILITY IS ERECTNESS

ASSISTANCE IS SUPPORT
ACTION IS SELF-PROPELLED MOTION
COMPULSION IS A COMPELLING FORCE
DESIRE / NEED IS HUNGER
THE NECESSARY MATERIAL FOR A PROCESS IS FOOD (e.g. spiritual milk)
APPEALING IS TASTY
DIFFICULTIES ARE OPPONENTS
IMPERFECTION IS DIRT
MORALLY GOOD IS CLEAN
MORALLY GOOD IS HEALTHY
NORMAL IS STRAIGHT
MORALLY GOOD IS STRAIGHT (e.g. σκολιός masters; δίκαιος judges)
BEING AWARE IS BEING AWAKE
A BELIEF IS A PHYSICAL POSITION / ORIENTATION (e.g., in which you *stand*).

BIBLIOGRAPHY

Primary Sources

Aquinas, Thomas. *Summa Theologiae*. Great Books of the Western World Edition. Translated by Fathers of the English Dominican Province, revised by Daniel J. Sullivan. Chicago and London: Encyclopedia Britannica, 1952.
Aristotle. *Poetics*. Ann Arbor Paperbacks Edition. Translated by Gerald F. Else. Ann Arbor: University of Michigan Press, 1967, 1970.
———. *Rhetoric*. Great Books of the Western World Edition. Chicago and London: Encyclopedia Britannica, Inc., 1952.
Augustine. *Concerning the City of God against the Pagans*. Penguin Classics Edition. Translated by Henry Bettenson. London: Penguin Books, 1972, 1984.
———. *Confessions*. Great Books of the Western World Edition. Translated by Edward B. Pusey. Chicago and London: Encyclopedia Britannica, 1952.
———. *On Christian Doctrine*. Great Books of the Western World Edition. Translated by J.F. Shaw. Chicago and London: Encyclopedia Britannica, 1952.
———. *The Works of Saint Augustine: A Translation for the 21st Century*. Edited by John E. Rotelle, translated by Edmund Hill. Brooklyn, N.Y.: New City Press, 1990.
Cicero. *Cicero on Oratory and Orator*. Translated and edited by J.S. Watson. Carbondale, Ill.: Southern Illinois University Press, 1970.
Dogmatic Constitution on Divine Revelation, Vatican II, *Dei Verbum* (November 18, 1965), 24–25.
Hegel, George Wilhelm Friedrich. *The Philosophy of Fine Art*. Translated by William M. Bryant. New York: Appelton, 1879.
Hobbes, Thomas. *Leviathan*. Cambridge Texts in the History of Political Thought Edition. Cambridge: Cambridge University Press, 1991, 1994.
Kant, Immanuel. *Critique of Practical Reason*. Translated by Werner S. Pluhar. Indianapolis: Hackett Publishing Co., 2002.
Mill, John Stuart. *A System of Logic: Ratiocinative and Inductive*. Edited by J.M. Robson. Toronto: University of Toronto Press, 1974.
Nietzsche, Friedrich. "On Truth and Falsity in Their Ultramoral Sense." In *The Complete Works of Friedrich Nietzsche, Vol. 2*, edited by Oscar Levy, translated by Maximilian A. Mügge, 173–192. New York: Russell and Russell, Inc., 1964.
Plato. *Ion*. Great Books of the Western World Edition. Chicago and London: Encyclopedia Britannica, Inc., 1952.
———. *The Republic*. Vintage Classics Edition. Translated by Benjamin Jowett. New York: Random House, 1991.

———. *Symposium*. Great Books of the Western World Edition. Chicago and London: Encyclopedia Britannica, 1952.
Pliny, *Letters and Panegyricus*. 2 vols. The Loeb Classical Library. Cambridge Mass: Harvard University Press, 1969; London: William Heinemann, 1969.
Plutarch, *Plutarch's Lives*. Translated by Bernadotte Perrin. 10 vols. The Loeb Classical Library. Cambridge, Mass.: Harvard University Press, 1914–1926; London: William Heinemann, 1914–1926.
Quintilian. *The Institutio Oratoria Libri Duodecim*. Translated by H.E. Butler. 4 vols. The Loeb Classical Library. Cambridge, Mass: Harvard University Press, 1953; London: William Heinemann, 1953.
Suetonius, Gaius Tranquillus. *Lives of the Twelve Caesars (De vita Caesarum)*. Translated by Robert Graves. New York: Welcome Rain Pub., 2001.

History of Metaphor and Hermeneutics; Traditional Approaches to Metaphor

Ashworth, E. Jennifer. "Medieval Theories of Analogy." In *The Stanford Encyclopedia of Philosophy* (Winter 1999 Edition). Edited by Edward N. Zalta. URL = http://plato.stanford.edu/archives/win1999/entries/analogy-medieval/.
Brown, Peter. *Augustine of Hippo*. Berkeley: University of California Press, 1967.
Copeland, Rita. "Medieval Theory and Criticism." In *Johns Hopkins Guide to Literary Theory and Criticism*. Baltimore: Johns Hopkins University Press, 1994: 500–507.
Copi, Irving M. *Introduction to Logic*. New York: Macmillan, 1968.
Emmet, Dorothy. *The Nature of Metaphysical Thinking*. New York: St. Martin's, 1945.
Grant, Robert M. and David Tracy. *A Short History of the Interpretation of the Bible*, 2d ed. Philadelphia: Fortress, 1984.
James, William. *The Principles of Psychology*. Cambridge, Mass.: Harvard University Press, 1983.
Johnson, Mark, editor. *Philosophical Perspectives on Metaphor*. Minneapolis, Minn.: University of Minnesota Press, 1981.
Lakoff, George and Mark Johnson. *Philosophy in the Flesh*. New York: Basic Books, 1999.
MacIntyre, Alasdair. *A Short History of Ethics*. New York: Macmillan, 1966.
Meeks, Wayne A. *The Origins of Christian Morality: The First Two Centuries*. New Haven: Yale University Press, 1993.
Ricoeur, Paul. *The Rule of Metaphor: Multi-disciplinary Studies of the Creation of Meaning in Language*. Translated by Robert Czerny. Toronto: University of Toronto Press, 1977.
Thistleton, Anthony C. *New Horizons in Hermeneutics*. Grand Rapids, Mich.: Zondervan, 1992.

Conceptual Metaphor Theory and Method

Coulson, Seana. *Semantic Leaps: Frame-shifting and Conceptual Blending in Meaning Construction.* Cambridge and New York: Cambridge University Press, 2001.
Damasio, Antonio R. *Descartes' Error: Emotion, Reason, and the Human Brain.* New York: G.P. Putnam's Sons, 1994; San Francisco: HarperCollins, 2000.
Fauconnier, Gilles and Mark Turner. "Conceptual Projection and Middle Spaces." *UCSD Cognitive Science Technical Report* (1994).
Fauconnier, Gilles. *Mappings in Thought and Language.* Cambridge: Cambridge University Press, 1997.
Fauconnier, Gilles and Mark Turner. *The Way We Think: Conceptual Blending and the Mind's Hidden Complexities.* New York: Basic Books, 2002.
Fauconnier, Gilles and Eve Sweetser, editors. *Spaces, Worlds, and Grammar.* Chicago: University of Chicago Press, 1996.
Fillmore, Charles. "Frames and the Semantics of Understanding." *Quaderni di Semantica* 6, no. 2 (1985): 222–253.
Gardner, Howard. *The Mind's New Science.* New York: Basic Books, 1985.
Goffman, E. *Frame Analysis.* New York: Harper and Row, 1974.
Goldberg, Adele E., editor. *Conceptual Structure, Discourse, and Language.* Stanford, Cal.: CSLI Publications, 1996.
Grady, Joseph E. "Foundations of Meaning: Primary Metaphors and Primary Scenes." Ph.D. dissertation, University of California, 1997.
Held, Virginia. "Whose Agenda? Ethics versus Cognitive Science." In *Mind and Morals: Essays on Ethics and Cognitive Science,* edited by Larry May, Marilyn Friedman, and Andy Clark, 69–88. Cambridge, Mass.: MIT Press, 1996.
Johnson, Mark. *The Body in the Mind: The Bodily Basis of Meaning, Imagination, and Reason.* Chicago: University of Chicago Press, 1987.
———. *Moral Imagination: Implications of Cognitive Science for Ethics.* Chicago and London: University of Chicago Press, 1993.
Klingebiel, Chris. "Moral Arithmetic." UC Berkeley, unpublished ms., 1990.
Kosslyn, Stephen M. *Image and Mind.* Cambridge, Mass.: Harvard University Press, 1980.
Lakoff, George. "The Contemporary Theory of Metaphor." In *Metaphor and Thought,* edited by Andrew Ortony, 202–251. Cambridge: Cambridge University Press, 1993.
Lakoff, George and Mark Johnson. *Metaphors We Live By.* Chicago: University of Chicago Press, 1980.
Lakoff, George. *Moral Politics: What Conservatives Know that Liberals Don't.* Chicago: Chicago University Press, 1996.
Lakoff, George and Mark Turner, *More than Cool Reason.* Chicago and London: University of Chicago Press, 1989.
Lakoff, George and Mark Johnson. *Philosophy in the Flesh: The Embodied Mind and its Challenge to Western Thought.* New York: Basic Books, 1999.
Lakoff, George. "The Metaphor System for Morality." In *Conceptual Structure, Discourse, and Language,* edited by Adele E. Goldberg, 249–266. Stanford, Cal.: CSLI Publications, 1996.

Lakoff, George. *Women, Fire, and Dangerous Things: What Categories Reveal about the Mind.* Chicago and London: University of Chicago Press, 1987.

Moore, Kevin E. "Spatial Experience and Temporal Metaphors in Wolof: Point of View, Conceptual Mapping, and Linguistic Practice." Ph.D. dissertation, University of California at Berkeley, 2000.

Narayanan, Srinivas Sankara. "Embodiment in Language Understanding: Sensory-Motor Representations for Metaphoric Reasoning About Event Description." Ph.D. dissertation, Department of Computer Science, University of California, Berkeley, 1997.

Oakley, Todd. "Presence: The Conceptual Basis of Rhetorical Effect." Ph.D. dissertation, University of Maryland, 1995.

Regier, T. "A Model of the Human Capacity for Categorizing Spatial Relations." *Cognitive Linguistics* 6–1 (1995): 63–88.

Ross, Robert N. "Ellipsis and the Structure of Expectation." *San Jose State Occasional Papers in Linguistics* 1 (1975).

Sandel, Margaret Anne. "Understanding Religious Language: An Integrated Approach to Meaning." Ph.D. dissertation, Graduate Theological Union, 2002.

Shepard, Roger N. and L.A. Cooper. *Mental Images and Their Transformations.* Cambridge, Mass.: MIT Press, 1982.

Sweetser, Eve. "Blended Spaces and Performativity." *Cognitive Linguistics* 11–3/4. Special issue on blended spaces. Edited by Seana Coulson and Todd Oakley. (2000): 305–333.

———. *From Etymology to Pragmatics: Metaphorical and Cultural Aspects of Semantic Structure.* Cambridge: Cambridge University Press, 1990.

———. "'The suburbs of your good pleasure': Cognition, culture and the bases of metaphoric structure." In *The Shakespearean International Yearbook, vol. 4: Shakespeare Studies Today*, edited by G. Bradshaw, T. Bishop and M. Turner, 24–55. Aldershot, England: Ashgate Publishing, 2004.

Talmy, Leonard. "How Language Structures Space." In *Spatial Orientation: Theory, Research, and Application*, edited by H.L. Pick and L.P. Acredolo, 225–282. New York: Plenum Press, 1983.

Tannen, Deborah, editor. *Framing in Discourse.* Oxford: Oxford University Press, 1993.

Taub, Sarah. "Language in the Body: Iconicity and Metaphor in American Sign Language." Ph.D. dissertation, University of California at Berkeley, 1997.

———. "Moral Accounting." UC Berkeley, unpublished ms., 1990.

Reading Theory

Holland, Norman. *5 Readers Reading.* New Haven: Yale University Press, 1975.

LeGuin, Ursula K. *The Telling.* New York: Harcourt, 2000.

Rabinowitz, Peter J. *Before Reading: Narrative Conventions and the Politics of Interpretation.* Columbus, Ohio: Ohio State University Press, 1987.

Stembrouck, Stef. "What Is Meant by Discourse Analysis?" Available at

http://bank.rug.ac.be/da/da.htm; Internet. Accessed April 2001.
Stubbs, Michael. *Discourse Analysis: The Sociolinguistic Analysis of Natural Language.* Oxford: Basil Blackwell, 1983.
Thomas, Francis-Noel. *The Writer, Writing.* Princeton: Princeton University Press, 1992.
Turner, Mark. *Reading Minds: The Study of English in an Age of Cognitive Science.* Princeton, N.J.: Princeton University Press, 1991.

Biblical Hermeneutics and Theological Approaches to the Figurative

Betz, Hans Dieter. *Galatians.* Hermeneia Commentary. Philadelphia: Fortress, 1979.
Chilcote, John Wesley, editor. *The Wesleyan Tradition: A Paradigm for Renewal.* Nashville: Abingdon, 2002.
Dibelius, Martin. *A Fresh Approach to the New Testament and Early Christian Literature.* The International Library of Christian Knowledge. London: Ivor Nicholson and Watson, 1936 [1926].
Fish, Stanley. *Is There a Text in This Class? The Authority of Interpretive Communities.* Cambridge, Mass.: Harvard University Press, 1980.
Green, Joel B., and Max Turner, editors. *Between Two Horizons: Spanning New Testament Studies and Systematic Theology.* Grand Rapids, Mich.: Eerdmans, 2000.
Green, Joel B. and Mark Baker. *Recovering the Scandal of the Cross: Atonement in New Testament and Contemporary Contexts.* Downers Grove, Ill.: InterVarsity Press, 2000.
Green, Joel B. "Scripture and Theology: Failed Experiments, Fresh Perspectives." *Interpretation* 56, no. 1 (January 2002): 5–20.
———. "Scripture and Theology: Uniting the Two So Long Divided." In *Between Two Horizons: Spanning New Testament Studies and Systematic Theology*, edited by Joel B. Green and Max Turner, 23–43. Grand Rapids, Mich.: Eerdmans, 2000.
———. "Scripture in the Church: Reconstructing the Authority of Scripture for Christian Formation and Mission." In *The Wesleyan Tradition: A Paradigm for Renewal*, edited by Paul W. Chilcote, 38–51. Nashville: Abingdon, 2002.
Gustafson, James M. "The Place of Scripture in Christian Ethics." *Interpretation* 24 (1970): 430–455.
Hays, Richard B. *The Moral Vision of the New Testament: Community, Cross, New Creation; A Contemporary Introduction to New Testament Ethics.* San Francisco: HarperSanFrancisco, 1996.
Hirsch, E.D. "Current Issues in Theory of Interpretation." *Journal of Religion* 55 (1975): 298–312.
———. "Three Dimensions of Hermeneutics." *New Literary History* 3 (1972): 245–261.
———. *Validity in Interpretation.* New Haven: Yale University Press, 1967.
Holland, Norman. "Literary Interpretation and Three Phases of Psychoanalysis." *Critical Inquiry* 3 (1976): 221–233.

Houlden, J.L. *Ethics and the New Testament*. New York: Oxford University Press, 1973.

Kelsey, David H. *The Uses of Scripture in Recent Theology*. Philadelphia: Fortress, 1975.

Lessing, Gotthold E. "On the Proof of the Spirit and of Power." In *Lessing's Theological Writings*, translated and edited by Henry Chadwick. Stanford, California: Stanford University Press, 1967[1957].

Lynch, William F. *Christ and Apollo: The Dimensions of the Literary Imagination*. New York: New Modern Library, 1963.

McClendon, James. *Doctrine: Systematic Theology, Volume 2*. Nashville: Abingdon, 1994.

———. *Ethics: Systematic Theology, Volume 1*. Nashville: Abingdon, 1986.

McDonald, J.I.H. *Biblical Interpretation and Christian Ethics*. Cambridge: Cambridge University Press, 1993.

Ogletree, Thomas W. *The Use of the Bible in Christian Ethics: A Constructive Essay*. Philadelphia: Fortress Press, 1983.

Phillips, Gary A. and Danna Nolan Fewell. "Ethics, Bible, Reading As If." *Semeia* 77 (1997): 1–22.

Ricoeur, Paul. *Figuring the Sacred: Religion, Narrative, and Imagination*. Minneapolis, Minn.: Fortress Press, 1995.

Schrage, Wolfgang. *The Ethics of the New Testament*. Translated by David E. Green. Philadelphia: Fortress, 1988 [1982].

Spohn, William C. *Go and Do Likewise: Jesus and Ethics*. New York: Continuum, 1999.

———. *What Are They Saying about Scripture and Ethics?* Revised and expanded edition. Mahwah, N.J.: Paulist Press. 1995.

Tracy, David. *Analogical Imagination: Christian Theology and the Culture of Pluralism*. New York: Crossroad, 1981.

———. *Blessed Rage for Order: The New Pluralism in Theology*. Chicago and London: University of Chicago Press, 1975, 1996.

Turner, Max and Joel B. Green. "New Testament Commentary and Systematic Theology: Strangers or Friends?" In *Between Two Horizons: Spanning New Testament Studies and Systematic Theology*, 1–22. Grand Rapids, Mich.: Eerdmans, 2000.

Verhey, Allen. *The Great Reversal: Ethics and the New Testament*. Grand Rapids, Mich.: Eerdmans, 1984.

Wilder, Amos. *Early Christian Rhetoric: The Language of the Gospel*. Rev. ed. Cambridge, Mass.: Harvard University Press, 1971.

Wright, N.T. "The Letter to the Galatians: Exegesis and Theology." In *Between Two Horizons: Spanning New Testament Studies and Systematic Theology*, edited by Joel B. Green and Max Turner, 205–236. Grand Rapids, Mich.: Eerdmans, 2000.

1 Peter

Achtemeier, Paul J. *1 Peter: A Commentary on First Peter*. Hermeneia Series. Minneapolis, Minn.: Augsburg Fortress, 1996.
———. "Newborn Babes and Living Stones: Literal and Figurative in 1 Peter." In *To Touch the Text: Biblical and Related Studies in Honor of Joseph H. Fitzmyer, S.J.*, edited by M.P. Horgan and P.J. Kobelski, 207–236. New York: Crossroad/ Continuum, 1988.
Balch, David L. "Early Christian Criticism of Patriarchal Authority: 1 Peter 2:11–3:12." *Union Seminary Quarterly Review* 39 (1984): 161–173.
———. "Hellenization / Acculturation in 1 Peter." In *Perspectives on 1 Peter*, edited by Charles H. Talbert, 79–102. NABPR Special Series 9. Macon, Georgia: Mercer University Press, 1986.
———. *Let Wives Be Submissive: The Domestic Code in 1 Peter*. Society of Biblical Literature Monograph Series, 26. Atlanta: Scholars Press, 1981.
Beare, Francis W. *The First Epistle of Peter: The Greek Text with Introduction and Notes*. 3d ed. Oxford: Blackwell, 1970.
Boring, M. Eugene. "Interpreting 1 Peter as a Letter [not] Written to Us." *Quarterly Review* 13 (Spring 1993): 89–111.
Brox, Norbert. *Der erste Petrus Brief*. Evangelish-Katholischer Kommentar zum Neuen Testament, 21. Zurich: Benziger Verlag; Neukirchen-Vluyn: Neukirchener Verlag, 1979.
Davids, Peter. *The First Epistle of Peter*. New International Commentary on the New Testament; Grand Rapids, Mich.: Eerdmans, 1990.
Elliott, John Hall. *The Elect and the Holy: An Exegetical Examination of 1 Peter 2:4–10 and the Phrase βασίλειον ἱεράτευμα*. Supplements to *Novum Testamentum* 12. Leiden: E.J. Brill, 1966.
———. *A Home for the Homeless: A Social-Scientific Criticism of 1 Peter, Its Situation and Strategy*. Philadelphia: Fortress Press, 1981, 1990.
———. *1 Peter: A New Translation with Introduction and Commentary*. The Anchor Bible. New York: Anchor Doubleday, 2000.
Furnish, Victor P. "Elect Sojourners in Christ: An Approach to the Theology of 1 Peter." *Perkins Journal* 28 (1975): 1–11.
Goppelt, Leonnard. *A Commentary on 1 Peter*. Edited by Ferdinand Hahn, translated by John E. Alsup. Grand Rapids, Mich.: Eerdmans, 1978, 1993.
Green, Joel B. "Faithful Witness in the Diaspora: The Holy Spirit and the Exiled People of God according to 1 Peter." In *The Holy Spirit and Christian Origins*, edited by Graham Stanton, Stephen Barton, and Bruce Longenecker. Grand Rapids, Mich.: Eerdmans; Edinburgh: T. & T. Clark, forthcoming.
Horrell, David G. "The Product of a Petrine Circle? A Reassessment of the Origin and Character of 1 Peter." *Journal for the Study of the New Testament*, 86 (2002): 29–60.
Martin, Troy. W. *Metaphor and Composition in 1 Peter*. Society of Biblical Literature Dissertation Series, 131. Atlanta: Scholars Press, 1991.
Selwyn, Ernest G. *The First Epistle of St. Peter*. 2d ed. London: Macmillan, 1955.

Talbert, Charles H. *Perspectives on 1 Peter*. NABPR Special Studies Series, 9. Macon, Georgia: Mercer University Press, 1986.
Unnik, W.C. van. *Sparsa Collecta: The Collected Essays of W.C. van Unnik*. 2, Supplements to *Novum Testamentum* 29. Leiden: E.J. Brill, 1980: 3–82.

New Testament—Cultural Background

Bartchy, Scott S. "Slave, Slavery." In *Dictionary of the Later New Testament and Its Developments*, ed. Ralph P. Martin and Peter H. Davids. Downers Grove, Ill.: InterVarsity, 1997: 1098–102.
Barcley, William B. *Christ in You: A Study in Paul's Theology and Ethics*. Lanham, N.Y.: Oxford University Press of America, 1999.
Benko, Stephen. *Pagan Rome and the Early Christians*. Bloomington and Indianapolis: Indiana University Press, 1984.
Dandamayev, M.A. "Slavery (Ancient Near East) (Old Testament)." In *The Anchor Bible Dictionary*, 6. Edited by David Noel Freedman, et al. New York: Doubleday, 1992: 58–65.
Ferguson, Everett. *Backgrounds of Early Christianity*, 2d ed. Grand Rapids, Mich.: Eerdmans, 1993.
Finley, Moses I. *Ancient Slavery and Modern Ideology*. New York: Viking, 1980.
Gilmore, David D. "Anthropology of the Mediterranean Area." *Annual Review of Anthropology* 11 (1982): 175–205.
Gilmore, David D., editor. *Honor and Shame and the Unity of the Mediterranean*. A Special Publication of the American Anthropological Association, 22. Washington: American Anthropological Association, 1987.
Griffiths, J. Gwyn. *The Divine Verdict: A Study of Divine Judgement in the Ancient Religions*. Leiden and New York: E.J. Brill, 1991.
Harris, William V. *Ancient Literacy*. Cambridge: Harvard University Press, 1989.
Hopkins, Keith. *Conquerors and Slaves*. New York: Cambridge University Press, 1978.
Peristiany, J.G., editor. *Honour and Shame: The Values of Mediterranean Society*. The Nature of Human Society Series. Chicago: University of Chicago Press, 1966; London: Weidenfeld and Nicolson, Midway Reprint, 1974.
Sakenfeld, Katharine D. "Love (OT)." In *Anchor Bible Dictionary*, 4. Edited by David Noel Freedman, et al. New York: Doubleday, 1992: 377–380.
Saller, Richard P. *Personal Patronage Under the Early Empire*. Cambridge; New York: Cambridge University Press, 2002.
Schneider, Jane. "Of Vigilance and Virgins: Honor, Shame and Access to Resources in Mediterranean Societies." *Ethnology* 10 (1971): 1–24.
Veyne, Paul. "The Roman Empire." In *A History of Private Life: I. From Pagan Rome to Byzantium*, translated by Arthur Goldhammer, edited by Philips Aries and George Duby, no. 1. Cambridge, Mass.: Harvard University Press, Belknap Press, 1987.
Wallace-Hadrill, Andrew, editor. *Patronage in Ancient Society*. London; New York: Routledge, 1989.

Biblical Reference Works

Bauer, Walter. *A Greek-English Lexicon of the New Testament and other Early Christian Literature.* 2d ed. Translated and edited by William F. Arndt, F. Wilbur Gingrich, and Frederick W. Danker. Chicago: Chicago University Press, 1979.

Blass, F. and A. Debrunner. *A Greek Grammar of the New Testament and Other Early Christian Literature.* Translated and revised by Robert W. Funk. Chicago and London: University of Chicago Press, 1961.

Liddell, Henry G. *A Greek-English Lexicon.* Compiled by H.G. Liddell and Robert Scott. Rev. ed. Oxford: Clarendon Press; New York: Oxford University Press, 1996.

Louw, Johannes P. and Eugene A. Nida, editors. *Greek-English Lexicon of the New Testament Based on Semantic Domains,* 2d. ed. New York: United Bible Societies, 1988, 1989.

Zerwick, Max, S.J. *A Grammatical Analysis of the Greek New Testament,* 4th ed. Rome: Editrice Pontificio Instituto Biblio, 1993.

Miscellaneous Works

A New Zealand Prayer Book: He Karakia Mihinare o Aotearoa. The Anglican Church in Aotearoa, New Zealand, and Polynesia. San Francisco: HarperSanFrancisco / HarperCollins: 1989, 1997.

Eliot, George [Mary Ann Evans]. *Middlemarch.* London: Penguin Classics, 1994 (1871–1872).

Hartman, David. *A Heart of Many Rooms: Celebrating the Many Voices Within Judaism.* Woodstock, Vermont: Jewish Lights Publishing, 1999.

Pesikta de-Rav Kahana: R. Kahana's Compilation of Discourses for Sabbaths and Festal Days. Translated by William G. Braude and Israel J. Kapstein. Philadelphia: Jewish Publication Society of America, 1975.

Sölle, Dorothee. *Creative Disobedience.* Translated by Lawrence W. Denef. Cleveland, Ohio: Pilgrim Press, 1968, 1995.

Wilbanks, Dana W. *Re-Creating America: The Ethics of U.S. Immigration and Refugee Policy in a Christian Perspective.* Nashville: Abingdon, 1996.

AUTHOR INDEX
NRSV

Achtemeier, Paul, 88n66, 183n38, 225n45, 234n3, 242, 242n15, 267, 268n4, 273n12, 293n20, 297n26
Ashworth, Jennifer, 39n63

Balch, David, 183nn36, 37; 317
Barcley, William B., 235
Bauer, Walter, 247n19, 268n6
Beare, Francis, 242n15
Betz, Hans Dieter, 133n69
Boring, M. Eugene, 179n28, 180
Brown, Peter, 36n57
Brox, Norbert, 235n3

Damasio, Antonio, 55n92; 66n17; 74n35; 82n56; 170nn8, 9
Davids, Peter, 271n10, 293n20
Dibelius, Martin, 133, 133n69; 134, 134n72, 135

Eliot, George [Mary Ann Evans], 1, 4, 4n5, 185, 355
Elliott, John Hall, 183nn38, 39; 234n3; 267; 267n2; 268nn4, 7; 271; 271n10; 273n12; 283n17

Fauconnier, Gilles, 65n16; 66; 66n17; 85, 85n61; 86; 92–93; 93nn74, 75; 100–104; 100n89; 101n94; 102; 103n102; 104n107; 112n7; 167; 169n7; 171n12; 172; 187n6; 196n21; 213; 239; 242n16; 268n5; 284n18; 343; 348
Fish, Stanley, 172
Furnish, Victor, 183n39, 271n10, 317

Goppelt, Leonhard, 77n43, 235n3
Grady, Joseph, 61n8, 69n26, 82n54, 84n59, 100, 189n9, 191n16, 250n1, 299, 343
Grant, Robert M., 45n75
Green, Joel B., xvii–xix, 122n44, 152n111, 160, 177n22, 180, 240n12
Gustafson, James M., 109, 150n105, 345

Hays, Richard B., 5, 127–158, 345
Held, Virginia, 59n2
Holland, Norman, 172
Houlden, James L., 133–134, 134nn70, 72

James, William, 123
Johnson, Mark, 4; 14n2; 15n4; 18; 19nn13, 14, 16; 24, 24n27; 49–51; 51n87; 52n88; 59; 60, 60n6; 66; 69n27; 72, 72n32; 75; 77n42; 78n44; 80n47; 81; 82, 82n55; 83; 84; 88, 88n64; 89; 90; 91n71; 96; 119; 123; 124; 170; 186n4; 190n13; 196n22; 197n23; 201; 237nn9, 10; 242n15; 251; 257nn9, 11; 259nn15, 16; 296n22; 304n33; 350, 350n6

Kelsey, David H., 109, 141–142, 141n84, 142n87, 153–154
Klingebiel, Chris, 201

Lakoff, George, 4; 15n4; 24nn27, 28; 59–107; 59n2; 60n5; 62n10; 63n12; 65n15; 69n27; 72nn31, 32; 74n36; 77n42; 78n44; 79n46; 80n47; 82n55; 88n64; 91nn68, 71; 97n80; 123; 165; 170; 182; 186; 186nn3, 4; 188; 189; 189nn9, 10; 193; 196, 196nn21, 22; 197; 201; 214; 228n52; 229, 229n55; 237nn9,

10; 251; 257nn9, 11; 259nn15, 16; 296n22; 304n33; 313; 314; 350, 350n6; 357–359
LeGuin, Ursula, 167, 173
Lessing, Gotthold E., 103, 121n43, 345
Louw, Johannes P., 61n7, 67, 67n22, 68, 68n24, 83, 83n58, 207, 298n28, 299n31
Lynch, William F., 118, 118n31, 123

MacIntyre, Alasdair, 26n30, 247n18
Martin, Troy, 272nn10, 11
McClendon, James, 178n25, 180n32
McDonald, James I.H., 3n4
Meeks, Wayne, 109, 132n66
Moore, Kevin E., 80, 80nn49, 51

Narayanan, S.S., 80n47
Nida, Eugene, 61n7, 67, 67n22, 68, 68n24, 83, 83n58, 207, 298n28, 299n31
Nietzsche, Friedrich, 48, 50–54

Ogletree, Thomas W., 113n13, 125n52, 151, 345

Phelan, James, 165, 173, 173n16, 175, 175n19

Rabinowitz, Peter, 165, 171, 173, 173n16, 175, 177, 179n29, 182
Ricoeur, Paul, 38n62; 40n64; 41n65; 42n66; 43; 89n67; 96; 131n64
Ross, Robert, 178

Sakenfeld, Katharine, 201n30
Sandel, Margaret, 28n31, 45n74

Schrage, Wolfgang, 134n72
Selwyn, Ernest, 293n20
Sölle, Dorothee, 318, 330
Spohn, William, 2n2; 3n4; 5; 110–128; 110n2; 113n13; 115nn18, 20; 116n24; 119n38; 125n52; 127nn57, 58; 149; 156–158; 254n7; 263n21; 345
Stembrouck, Stef, 168n4
Stubbs, Michael, 168
Sweetser, Eve, 59n3, 66n17, 84n59, 153n112, 165, 171, 181n33, 196n21, 246n17

Tannen, Deborah, 178
Taub, Sarah, 201
Thistleton, Anthony, 29n32, 53
Thomas, Francis-Noel, 172n13
Tracy, David, 3n3, 42n65, 45n75, 48n78, 100n88, 109, 115n20, 118, 123, 159, 159n118, 345
Turner, Mark, 66, 66n17; 72, 72n31; 74n34; 85, 85n61; 86; 91–107; 91n68; 93nn74, 75; 97n80; 100n89; 101n94; 102n95; 103nn102, 104; 104nn106, 107; 106n111; 112n7; 125n51; 165; 169–177; 169n7; 170n9; 171n12; 173n17; 177n24; 186n4; 196n21; 213–214; 228nn50, 51, 52; 229; 239; 242n16; 268n5; 284n18; 343; 348

Unnik, W.C. van, 206n38

Wilder, Amos, 109, 155
Wright, N.T., 121n43, 158

Zerwick, Max, S.J., 236n8

SUBJECT INDEX

Accounting
  See 1 Peter, judgment; Moral accounting
Actual reader
  See Reading
Allegory, 20, 29, 29n32, 32–33, 36–37, 36n57, 45–46. 46n76, 47
Analogical imagination, 3n3, 106, 109–161, 348
  critique of, 110, 112, 121–127, 156–161, 348–349
  distinguished from metaphor, 112, 119–120, 119n38, 125
  driven by conceptual metaphor, 112
  and moral imagination, 115, 115n20, 116, 348
  Richard Hays and, 130–132, 156
  and Scripture, 110, 112, 117–118, 120
  William Spohn and, 110–127, 119n38
  and transcendent meaning, 118
  See also Hays, Richard; Spohn, William; Tracy, David
Analogy
  analogy of being, 25–26, 38n62, 41
  Aristotelian, 21, 22, 25, 26, 41, 100
  associated with metaphor, 100, 100n88, 101, 101n94, 102, 106n111, 124–125, 125n51, 130–131, 137–140, 149, 155
  Augustinian, 29
  and category structures, 100–106, 100n89, 101n94, 103n104, 104nn106, 109, 125
  cognitive definitions, 124–125

  compared to metaphor, 3, 21, 24–26, 38, 43–44, 100–102, 104–106, 106n111, 119, 124–125, 130–131, 137, 139, 149, 343, 348
  and compression, 102–103; 103n102
  as conceptual space blending, 87, 100, 102–104, 112, 124–125, 349, 351
  constraints on, 124–125
  and conventions, 103–104
  defined, 100, 124–125
  and entrenchment, 102, 104, 104n107, 124–125
  and essence, 38–40, 42, 47, 57–58, 343
  and frames, 102–103, 105
  and God-talk, 26, 30–31, 37–48, 109–110, 156, 343, 348, 351
  hermeneutics of, 5, 116, 159
  "it's all analogy" position, 100, 105, 119, 124
  and logic, 101–102, 106, 117
  mapping, 100, 102, 104, 131
  medieval theories, 29, 39n63, 41–43
  modern theories, 100nn88, 89, 101, 101nn93, 94
  and moral reasoning, 109–112, 115–126, 150n105, 156, 160, 343, 348–349
  and Plato, 14n2
  proportional, 41–43, 43n67, 44, 49, 101, 104, 116–117, 116n24, 123–124
  Thomistic, 29, 41–43, 41n65, 42n66, 47, 100n88, 106, 116, 116n24
  Two Worlds, *See* Two Worlds Model

See also Analogical imagination; Aquinas; Aristotle; Hays; Spohn
Aquinas, Thomas, 37–48
  analogy and essence, 38, 48
  analogy and logic, 41–42, 44
  analogy and metaphor, 38, 43–45, 48n78
  analogy and word meanings, 41, 44
  analogy of being, 38, 41
  analogy of participation, 41–42, 41n65, 42n66
  analogy of proportion, 41–44, 116, 116n24
  and Aristotelian thought, 38, 43–45, 47
  essences and God-language, 38–39, 48
  four senses of Scripture, 46–47
  imagination and Scripture, 47–48
  language theory, 39–44
  and metaphor, 38, 41n65, 43–45, 45n73, 47–48
  metaphor and theology, 38, 47–48
Aristotle, 13, 21–27, 56
  and analogy, 21, 22, 25–26, 41–42, 106
  and Being, 25–26
  category model, 22, 24–26, 39, 53–54, 62–63
  compared to Plato on metaphor, 27–29, 38
  definition of metaphor, 21–24, 26, 101, 106
  empiricism, 25, 27, 28n31, 38, 43
  essences, 24–26
  and the "fitting" in metaphor, 21, 23, 26, 43–44, 49, 106, 117
  imagination and practical reason, 26–27, 54
  influence on Western metaphor models, 13, 24, 27, 29, 38–44, 49, 53, 54, 56, 62–63, 101, 106
  intuitive perception, 21, 23–24, 62, 106
  linguistic metaphor theory, 13, 22, 24, 26, 40, 56
  metaphor and analogy, 21, 25–26
  metaphor as deviance from the ordinary, 22–23, 26, 106
  metaphor and ethics, 26–27, 54
  metaphor as transfer of names, 22, 26, 106
  similarity in dissimilars theory, 21, 22, 26, 62, 101, 106
  worldview and metaphor, 24–28, 28n31
Augustine, 30–37
  ethics and figurative language, 34–37
  on literal-figurative split, 32–33
  on metaphor and interpretation of Scripture, 30–37
  words as signs, 31, 31n37, 33–34, 35n57, 37
Authorial audience
  See First Peter, authorial audience; Reading
Authority, 145, 222–232, 234, 307, 309, 311, 317–319, 324, 331, 339–341, 360, 362, 363
  and exemplary reading, 184, 317–319, 324
  in first century, 68n24, 180, 183n37, 222–232, 254, 282, 317, 324, 330, 336, 360–363
  Scripture as, 2–3, 5, 29, 35, 113, 122n44, 129n61, 132n66, 147, 158, 176, 180n32, 181, 311
  sources in Christian ethics, 2–3, 29, 113, 122n44, 129n61, 132n66, 158, 176, 181, 309, 339–341
  See also Moral authority; Scripture and ethics, Scripture As Source model

Bi-directionality (in metaphors), 56, 57, 70, 71, 95, 99, 130, 131n64
  See also Mapping
Blend diagram, 85–86, 87, 94, 212, 213, 214

See also Megablend
Blending
  blended mental spaces, 65n17, 84–86, 112n6, 172, 178n25, 213, 301, 303, 305, 309, 311–314, 317, 319, 339, 341, 342–346, 348–349, 351–354
  and complex metaphors, 84–87, 192, 207, 213, 225, 243, 247, 255, 267, 276, 298, 319, 327, 365
  conceptual / cognitive, 59n3, 65n17, 85n61, 87, 93, 93nn74, 75, 112n6, 172, 178n25, 225, 247, 339, 343, 344–346, 348–349, 351–354
  and culture, 92, 93, 93nn74, 75, 94, 95, 210, 311–314, 317, 320, 321n5, 325, 327, 342, 360–361, 362
  defined, 85n61
  double-scope, 93n74, 284, 284n18
  and frames, 86, 94, 102, 305, 311–314, 342, 351, 360–362
  generic space in, 85, 86, 87, 213, 344
  input spaces in, 66n19, 85–87, 95, 102, 209, 213, 276, 344, 345
  integration networks, 87, 93n74
  megablends, 213–214, 285
  metaphorical blending, 84–86, 192, 301, 303, 360–365
  negative space blends, 268n5
  running the blend, 87, 92, 93, 94, 95, 206n38, 209, 212, 213, 267, 314, 344, 345, 349, 353, 354
  See also Reading

Categories
  and analogy, 100–106, 101n94, 125
  Aristotelian, 21–26, 24n28, 39, 41, 47, 53, 54, 62–63
  Augustinian, 33
  category structures, 26, 28, 58, 62–68, 100–106, 125, 216, 315
  cognitive models of, 62–68, 100–106, 125, 216, 315, 339
  conventional, 63–64, 84, 103–104
  entrenchment, 84, 98, 100n89, 102, 104, 104n107, 105
  and logic, 101–102
  Platonic, 15, 17
  and prototypes, 15, 62–63, 62n10, 63n12, 65n15, 124, 136, 138, 207, 218, 226, 231, 268, 272, 276, 288, 315
  radial, 63, 63n12, 64, 138, 226, 231, 268, 306
  Thomistic, 39–41, 47
  See also Blending, Conventions, Metaphor
Causation
  and Aquinas, 39
  and Aristotle, 24, 24n28, 25
  cause-and-effect compression, 112n7
  and essence, 17, 39
  and Kant, 51
  in 1 Peter, 192–193, 213, 229, 236, 237, 241, 243, 244, 298–299
  informal theory, 229, 298–299
  medieval models, 29
  and metaphor, 79, 79n46, 192–193, 213, 298–299, 304n33
  and Platonic essence, 17, 39, 44
Chain of Being
  See Great Chain of Being
Cognitive linguistics, 4, 12–13, 59–107, 342–344
  and category structure, 62–68
  and discourse analysis, 168–172, 187n6
  evidence for conceptual metaphor, 60n5, 66n17
  and frames, 64–65, 196n21
  implications of this study for, 220–221, 342–344
  and linguistic universals, 84
  and mental space theory, 66, 66n17
  and metonymy, 72n30, 90–91
  need for, 55–58, 95, 159
  and pragmatics, 168–169
  and primary metaphor, 81–84

and reading theory, 165–184
study of moral discourse, 182, 186, 186n4, 188–193
theorists, 4, 59, 59n3
view of language, xvii, 168–169, 169n7
view of metaphor, 55–58, 59, 61, 66, 68–90
See also Metaphor
Cognitive science, xvii, 75n38, 82n56, 169, 169n7, 349
See also Neuroscience
Cognitive unconscious, 82, 82n55, 350
Community
linguistic, 89, 93–94, 104, 104n107, 121, 173–176, 179–183, 250, 309–310, 339–340
and linguistic convention, 89, 89n67, 93–94, 104, 179–180, 221, 250
and moral discourse, 110–111, 121, 147, 221, 309–310, 312, 318, 339
moral values expressed in metaphor, 4, 21, 147–149
multiple, 7, 173–175, 309–310, 318, 324
reading, 94, 152–155, 152n111, 173–184, 177n22, 221, 309–310, 315, 318, 324, 339, 346, 351, 353
Scripture reading, 7, 110–111, 113, 116–117, 121, 124, 126, 128, 135–136, 139–149, 152–155, 173, 176–178, 177n22, 180–184, 221, 309–310, 312, 315, 318, 324, 329, 339, 346, 351, 353
See also Hays, "new community"; Reading

Complex blend, 84–87, 183n38, 192, 207, 213, 225, 228, 243, 247–248, 255, 267, 276, 285, 298, 309, 319
See also Blending
Complex metaphor
See Metaphor, complex

Compression
in analogy, 102–103
in cultural models, 93
in mental space blending, 93, 102–103, 103n102, 112n7, 342, 346
in ritual, 112, 112n7
Concepts
Begriffe, 141n84, 154
blending, *See* Blending; Mental Spaces
and conceptual frameworks, 13, 26n30, 40, 62–64, 66, 97, 113, 125, 133, 173, 175, 278–280, 287, 294, 312, 340
conceptual operation versus conceptual product, 93n75
and constraints, 25, 46, 78, 79, 80n51, 85, 88, 92–93, 124–125, 142, 153, 156, 177, 178, 181, 188, 215–216, 229, 232, 233, 238, 262, 276, 278–279, 291, 319, 327, 339, 342, 345, 349
and conventions, 6, 55–56, 60n5, 61, 63, 64, 65, 72, 74, 75, 77, 80, 89, 92–96, 104–105, 104n107, 107, 115, 130, 169, 174–175, 185–186, 193, 224, 228, 232, 245, 259, 288, 300, 304–305, 327, 333, 344, 353
disembodied, 39, 50, 51, 96–97, 97n80, 99, 118, 159, 332–333
and the divine, 39, 40, 159–160
embodied, 5, 7, 55, 55n92, 60–62, 60n6, 68, 80, 80n51, 83, 106–107, 159–160, 173, 298, 306, 332–333
emergent, 85n61, 86–87, 237
and experiential grounding, 5, 7, 60–61, 60n6, 64, 68, 79–80, 80n51, 84, 91, 107, 160, 173, 189, 222, 236–237, 298n28, 332, 349
literal, 50, 79n46, 95–97, 99, 357, 358

mentally constructed, 39, 55, 55n92, 60–62, 66, 66n17, 80, 83, 105, 148, 169–170, 172, 300, 349
metamoral, 6, 185, 307–308, 310–311, 335, 340, 348, 350, 351
moral, 4, 7, 11, 17, 20, 54–55, 79–83, 92–93, 95, 109, 113, 133, 165, 169, 182, 189, 190–192, 197, 214, 220–222, 229, 233, 234, 239, 242–243, 249, 263–264, 279, 285–286, 295, 298, 302, 304, 306, 318, 332–333, 340, 342, 344, 349, 352
non-linguistic, 55, 55n92, 60–61, 72, 83, 95, 99, 107
objective, 39–40, 50, 56, 96–97, 97n80, 159
philosophical, 11, 14n2, 17, 20, 26n30, 28, 39–40, 51, 54, 60, 62, 79, 159
prototypes, *See* Categories
source and target, 70–71, 74, 77, 78, 92, 99, 140, 187, 191, 199, 207, 214, 220–221, 258, 266, 275, 357
systematic, 6, 60–62, 68, 75, 79–80, 84, 88n64, 91, 96–97, 107, 137, 143, 182, 189, 222, 233, 228, 248, 305, 343, 354, 358
time and events, 80n49, 249–264
See also Blending, Categories, Conceptual space, Domain, Metaphor, conceptual, Universal
Conceptual blend, *See* Blending
Conceptual mapping, *See* Mapping
Conceptual metaphor, *See* Metaphor
Conceptual space, 66, 66n17, 76, 77, 79, 85–87, 92–94, 100, 102, 104n106, 105, 107, 123, 171–172, 181, 212–213, 233, 235n5, 237, 239, 242–248, 249–264, 339, 352–354
and landmarks, 239, 242, 242n16, 247
and logic, 100, 102, 104n106, 123, 172
See also Blending; Mental space
Constraint, *See* Meaning, constraint
Container schemas
and biblical hermeneutics, 122, 147, 356
and body metaphors, 295–298, 297n26
church as, 239, 300
coordinated spatial metaphors, 246–248
and emotion, 261n18
and ethnic boundaries, 268, 277
in 1 Peter, 78, 237–248, 254–255, 259–261, 277, 295–298
human person as, 298–300
and image schemas, 75, 78–79, 235n5, 237
"in Christ" container metaphor, 237–247, 255, 277
and invariance principle, 78–79
and schematic logic, 78–79, 237–238, 237n10
social groups as, 239, 268
and spatial time, 254–255, 259–261
Controlling metaphor, *See* Metaphor, controlling
Conventions
cultural, 6, 64–65, 80, 84, 88–90, 93, 96–97, 175, 183–184, 202, 215–217, 221–222, 224–225, 229–232, 259n16, 288, 291, 296–297, 300, 304–306, 313, 318, 324, 327–328, 330, 339, 342, 344
reading, 63, 90, 94–95, 153–154, 165, 173–183, 173n16, 177n22, 221, 245, 247, 304–305, 309–310, 318, 324, 339, 346, 351, 353–354
See also Community; Frames; Metaphor, conventional; Reading; Scenario
Cross-domain mapping, *See* Mapping

SUBJECT INDEX

Cultural knowledge
  and reading process, 64–65, 88–90, 93n74, 103, 124, 130, 178, 181, 196n21, 204–205, 208, 211, 213, 215–216, 222–223, 226n46, 227, 231, 232, 234n2, 265, 270, 286, 289, 305, 318, 325–338, 343, 350, 353
  See also Cultural models; Frames
Cultural models, 64–65, 84, 92–94, 207, 208, 211, 216, 225, 226n46, 227–232, 234n2, 265, 286, 289, 305, 313–314, 318, 325–338, 340, 342, 343, 345–346, 348, 354

Dead metaphor theory, 56, 88, 88n64, 90, 95, 98, 102n95, 359
Deontological ethics, *See* Ethics
Directionality, 56, 57, 70, 71, 95, 99, 130
  See also Mapping, Metaphor
Discourse, 4–7, 11–14, 17–18, 20, 21, 23, 25–26, 28, 30, 32, 34, 37, 40n64, 43, 50, 53, 66n16, 88, 90, 94, 107, 124–127, 141–142, 146–147, 150–152, 158, 165–169, 182, 187–193, 196, 212–213, 233–234, 247, 250, 254, 255, 259, 261–264, 265, 271, 307, 309–311, 322, 327, 332–333, 336, 338, 341, 345, 347, 351–354
  analogy in, 100, 105–106, 124–125
  and cultural values, 182, 205, 211, 220, 222, 229, 231, 233–234, 292–293, 307, 322, 338, 340, 352
  defined, 4n7; 168; 187n6
  experiential basis, 188
  inferential patterns, 88, 100, 186n3, 219, 271, 276, 302, 329
  and imagination, 5, 13, 18, 20, 32, 50, 57, 66n16, 106–107, 147
  marker, 77
  and mental spaces, 66n16, 285
  and metaphorical structure, 57, 66n16, 190–193, 196, 198–199, 232, 271, 272nn10, 11, 279, 285, 289–290, 302, 307, 319, 342
  moral discourse, xviii–xix, 1, 4–7, 4n7, 11–13, 21, 34, 37, 43, 76, 94, 105–107, 119n38, 124–125, 127, 132, 139, 141–142, 146–147, 150–152, 154, 158, 165–169, 181, 182, 187–188, 190–193, 198–199, 204–205, 212–213, 219–220, 222, 229, 231, 233–234, 247–248, 250, 254, 255, 259, 261–264, 265, 271, 272nn10, 11, 276, 279, 285, 289–290, 292–293, 302, 307, 309–311, 322, 327, 332–333, 336, 338, 341, 345, 347, 351–354
  and reading, xviii, 5, 7, 12, 32, 90, 94, 105, 139, 150, 150n105, 151, 152, 158, 165–167, 168–170, 175, 181, 208, 212–213, 219–223, 229, 231, 233, 248–249, 261, 264, 309–311, 319, 322, 324, 339, 341, 347, 353–354, *See also* Discourse analysis
Discourse Analysis, 168–175, 187n6, 342–343, 347
Ditch, *See* Gap; Lessing's Ditch; Two Worlds Model
Domain, 66–69
  and analogy, 104
  and blending, 85, 85n61, 94, 213–214, 339, 342
  cognitive or conceptual, xvii, 64, 66–67, 70, 72, 78–79, 80n47, 85n61, 93, 97, 99, 189, 251, 263, 275, 293
  concrete and abstract, 57, 61n8, 69, 73, 74, 77, 79, 189n9, 191, 196, 245
  coordinated, 246, 248
  defined, 66–68
  and mental spaces, 66, 72, 85, 85n61
  and metaphor, xvii, 56–57, 66n19, 68–71, 81–83, 95, 97–99, 130
  metaphor as cross-domain

SUBJECT INDEX   389

mapping, 56–57, 68–69, 70–71, 73, 78, 80n47, 81, 97, 130, 140, 189n9, 190, 227, 231
and metonymy, 90, 284
semantic domain, 61n7, 63, 64, 66–67
sensorimotor, 81, 83
socio-culturally specific, 63–64, 67n22, 92–94, 140, 182, 187, 191–193, 195, 200, 202–205, 208–211, 218, 221–222, 231, 250–251, 256–257, 265, 285–286, 311, 327, 338, 342–343, 350
source and target domains, xvii, 66n19, 69–71, 73, 74, 77–78, 81, 85, 98–99, 189–190, 199, 213–219, 245, 266, 293–308, 298n28, 299n31, 308
structure preserved, 78–79, 97, 189–190, 196–197, 204, 246, 258, 263, 288, 292
subdomain, 61n7, 63, 67, 68, 207
words as prompts or triggers, 66, 78, 85, 203, 206, 209–210, 218, 221n44, 280, 285, 314
See also Blending
Double-scope blend, *See* Blending
Duty, *See* 1 Peter, duty in; *See also* Ethics, deontology

Embodiment
embodied experience as grounding for metaphor, 5; 60n6; 82nn54, 55; 83; 107; 251; 298; 298n28; 341; 349; 350; 353
embodied mind, xvii, 83, 170–171, 170nn8, 9
embodied reason, 106; 107; 170–171, 170nn8, 9; 349; 351
See also Experience, embodied
Emergent concept *See* Concept, emergent
Emotions
and analogy, 104

and ethics or morality, 16n7, 27, 83, 116, 299, 316
and metaphor, 27, 79n46, 83, 83n58, 125, 236–237, 244, 261n18, 299, 299n31, 302, 366
versus reason, 15–16, 15n5, 16n7, 19
Enlightenment
views of metaphor, 2, 48–54, 96, 351
See also Hobbes, Kant, Nietzsche
Entailments
concept explained, 71–72, 74, 85, 186, 343, 353
examples, 78, 85–86, 122, 137, 197, 210–211, 225, 238, 255, 262, 272n10, 274–276, 286, 288, 297, 301, 327
See also Inference
Entrenchment
in analogy, 102, 104–105
of blends, 104n107
of category structures, 102, 104
of conventional metaphors and frames, 84, 104
of "dead" metaphors, 98
of idiomatic metaphors, 88n66
in metaphor, 84, 105
in metonymy, 88n66
See also Categories; Metaphor
Essence
essentialism, 14–15, 15n4, 17, 19, 19n13, 22, 24n28, 24–26, 38–40, 42, 47, 48, 57, 228, 228n52, 229, 343, 348
moral essence, 17, 89, 228, 228n52, 239, 242, 267, 292, 296–297, 296n22, 297n23, 299, 299n31, 308, 318, 330, 331, 332, 367, 368, 369
See also Aquinas, Aristotle, Plato
Ethics
deontology or duty, 11, 139, 151, 153–154, 198, 242, 286, 289, 313, 327–328, 331, 335–336
experiential grounding for, 153n112, 189, 189n10

in 1 Peter, 198, 212–215, 242,
    286, 289, 313, 327–328, 331,
    335–336
in Hays, 138–139, 151, 154
metaphors and, xviii, xix, 1–4,
    7, 11, 123, 138–139, 153n112,
    189, 189n10, 198, 286, 289,
    313, 331
metaphoricity of ethical concepts,
    1–2, 4, 11–12, 17–18, 20, 26–27,
    54–55, 79, 83, 92, 106–107,
    123, 125–126, 154, 229, 229n55,
    246–247, 278–279, 311, 348,
    350
teleology, 139, 151, 153, 335
virtue and character ethics, 11–13;
    15–17; 15n5; 16nn6, 7; 26–27;
    54; 61; 110; 113; 116; 139; 158;
    189; 212; 213; 215; 219; 225;
    228–229; 232–233; 239; 242;
    246–247; 247n20; 248; 253;
    260; 263–264; 269; 278; 289;
    293; 297; 307–308; 313; 323;
    327; 334–338; 345; 348; 361;
    363–364; 368
See also Scripture and ethics
Events metaphors *See* Time and
    Events
Event-structure concepts, *See* Time
    and Events
    Exemplar 1 Peter as, xix, 5, 93,
        160, 165, 167, 184, 234, 308–
        310, 338–339, 347–348, 351
    Jesus Christ as, 126–127, 138, 272,
        276, 336
    Scripture as, xix, 5, 93, 158–161,
        184, 234, 345, 347–348, 351,
        353
    See also Reading, exemplary
Experience
    cultural, 61, 63–64, 65, 80, 83,
        84, 160, 178, 187–192, 201–202,
        205, 210, 215–222, 224, 225,
        226n46, 231, 265, 279, 284,
        286–287, 305, 311, 317, 338,
        342, 349
    embodied, 5–7, 60, 60n6, 61,
        62n10, 81–84, 81n51, 99–100,
        107, 170, 170n9, 173, 210, 224,
        236–238, 252, 265, 298–299,
        301, 304, 332, 349–350, 353,
        356
    as grounding for metaphor, 5–7;
        43; 59–62; 62n10; 63–68; 79–
        84; 79n46; 80n51; 82nn54, 55;
        84; 96; 99–100; 107; 119; 123;
        160; 165; 170n9; 173; 178; 187–
        192; 189nn9, 10; 199n28; 201–
        202; 205; 210; 215–218; 220–
        222; 224–226; 226n46; 231;
        236–238; 251–252; 254n7; 265;
        279; 284; 286–287; 292; 298;
        298n28; 299; 301; 304–305;
        311; 314; 325; 332; 336; 338;
        341–342; 349–351; 353; 356
    metaphor and conceptualization
        of, 28, 39, 51, 64, 67–68, 80–
        81, 80n51, 82, 96, 123, 224
    as source of meaning, 28, 62n10,
        80, 80n51, 84, 96, 123, 160,
        170n9, 173, 201, 216, 220, 222,
        224, 231
    universal human, 80, 82–83,
        82n55, 188–189, 349–350
Experiential realism, 350
Expert reader, *See* Reading

Facts-values dichotomy, 132, 158
Faculty psychology, 15, 19, 19n14, 57,
    106
Family frames, 64–65, 91, 210–211,
    225–226, 279–291, 309, 313–316,
    327–329, 334, 337, 367, 368
    See also Household frames
Figurative language, 4, 5, 19n16,
    20, 23, 31–37, 43, 45, 47–52,
    77, 83n58, 84, 88, 101, 101n94,
    102n95, 105, 114, 125, 125n51,
    199n28, 298n28, 299n31, **357**
    See also Literal-figurative split;
        Metaphor
First Peter (1 Peter)
    and apocalyptic, 2, 88, 177, 217,
        322–323

authorial audience, 92, 94–95, 173, 175, 175n19, 176–177, 179–180, 181, 187, 205, 218, 226n46, 227, 240, 240n12, 247, 272, 285, 298, 305, 307, 310–311, 319, 325, 331, 338, 339, 351, 354–355
authorship, 179, 179n30
body, 292–308, 331–333, 340, 368–369
brotherhood, 91, 225, 279, 281, 287–288, 327, 329, 331, 334, 335, 368
"Christians"—χριστιανός, 204, 226, 234, 234n3, 265–267, 269, 286, 290–291, 316, 327, 336, 355, 367
container metaphors, 75–76, 78–79, 237–248, 247n20, 254–255, 259–261, 261n18, 268, 277, 295–300, 297n26, 356, 365–369
coordinated spatial metaphors, 246–248, 246n17, 365
desire, 71–72, 72n30, 243–245, 253, 276–278, 286, 292–295, 298–306, 299n31, 331–333, 338, 369–370
duty, 198, 286, 289, 313, 328, 331, 335–336
evil, 77–78, 78n44, 85, 186, 189, 194–195, 197, 203, 205, 211–213, 216, 221, 225, 260, 263, 274–275, 277–278, 294–295, 298–305, 315, 321–322, 331–333, 336–337, 342, 347, 350, 352, 356, 360, 365, 368–369
exiles, 182–183; 185; 195; 208; 218; 224; 241; 261–262; 261nn19, 20; 265–266; 269–275; 271n10; 276–278; 287; 324–325; 334; 355; 366–367
exile as source domain, 98, 270–275, 271n10
family, *See* Family frames; Household conventions and roles

Gentiles, 88, 219, 227, 245, 265, 268, 268n6, 273, 277–278, 288, 320, 324, 337, 367
Great Chain of Being, 176, 222–231, 274–275, 279, 309, 318–319, 324, 326, 330, 335, 342
holiness, 77, 228–229, 230n57, 241–243, 242n15, 266–269, 271, 277–278, 285, 289, 292, 297, 306, 308, 309, 313, 316, 323–324, 326, 331–332, 334, 337, 351, 355, 365, 367
homelessness, 98; 271; 271nn9, 10
honor, 12, 86, 88n65, 92, 187, 198–199, 201–202, 210–211, 213, 218–220, 223–224, 230–231, 234n2, 269–270, 277, 279, 281–283, 283n17, 288–292, 297, 305–306, 311–317, 324–325, 327–328, 330–332, 334–338, 342, 355–356, 364, 367
household conventions and roles, 63–64; 183; 183nn36, 37, 38; 206; 208–213; 216–217; 219; 222–228; 230–232; 269; 279–297; 307–308; 312–313; 316–318; 327–331; 334; 337–338; 340; 342; 356; 359–362; 367–368
household of God, 198; 208–213; 216–217; 219; 222–227; 230–232; 269; 279–292; 307–308; 312–313; 316–318; 327–331; 334; 337–338; 360–362; 368
human person container metaphor, 297–298, 300
"in Christ" image schema, 221, 233–248, 255, 264, 265, 273–275, 277, 306, 315–316, 319–320, 323, 327–328, 332, 334–335, 337, 339, 365
Jesus Christ as moral paradigm, 203–204, 203n37, 207, 224–226, 227, 231, 233–234, 248,

272, 276, 308, 314–315, 319, 323, 329, 332, 336–338, 367
judgment, 88–90, 208–213, 217–220, 222, 234, 242, 249–250, 252, 256, 259n16, 261–262, 276–278, 290, 294, 311–314, 318–319, 322–323, 336–337, 360–363
justice, 77n43, 88, 187, 190n13, 197, 203–206, 208–211, 218, 229, 269, 271, 277, 301, 307, 313–314, 316, 322, 335, 337, 342, 348, 356, 368
καιρός, *See* Time and events
"living spaces", 233, 248, 249, 253, 255, 260, 262, 319, 366
λυτρόωμαι, 194, 203n35, 205–208, 206n38, 244, 312, 314, 335, 361
metamoral metaphors, 185–232, 229, 229n55, 264, 307–308, 309–311, 335, 336, 340, 350, 351
Morality Is Balance metaphors, 187, 197, 197n23, 198, 201, 211–212, 230, 256–257, 291, 300–302, 306, 311, 332–333, 337, 342, 352, 361, 369
Morality Is Clear-headedness metaphor, 256–257, 300–302, 306, 369
Morality Is Strength metaphor, 302–303, 350, 365, 368
and moral politics, 6, 165, 182–184, 271
moral values in, 182–183; 183nn36, 37; 218; 221; 224; 233; 278; 296; 304; 324–325; 328; 334–335
Moving Time metaphor, 257–258, 260
οἶκος Θεοῦ, *See* Household of God
obedience; Morality Is Obedience, 76–77, 185–186, 230, 241, 279, 282, 286, 289–290, 313, 318, 327, 330–331, 335, 367, 368

παρεπίδημος, 178, 240, 269–277, 292, 299, 324, 334
πάροικος, 208; 244; 261–262; 261n19; 266n1; 269–278; 271nn9, 10; 292; 299; 324; 366; 367
people of God, 180, 183n38, 207, 263–267, 273, 292, 326, 367
psyche—ψυχή, 243, 292, 294, 298–299, 299n31, 305–306, 331–332
reading as a letter, 76; 169; 174; 176–184; 179nn28, 30; 191; 212; 219; 239–241; 240n12; 248; 249; 257; 262–263; 265–266; 271n10; 272n11; 294–295; 304; 307–308; 309; 319; 325; 333; 339–340
resident aliens, 12, 178, 224, 240, 269–273, 271n10, 275–277, 292, 325, 355, 367
reward and punishment, 196n22, 197, 200, 219, 224–225, 290, 307, 327, 336–337, 361–363
σάρξ, 71, 71n28, 253, 271n9, 280, 292–298, 293n20, 294n21, 297n26, 298n28, 299–300, 305, 305n34, 331–332
shame, 92, 198, 210–211, 218–219, 230–231, 234, 234n2, 279–281, 283n17, 289, 311–314, 332, 334, 337–338, 364
slave, slavery, 60–61;63; 182; 187; 201–208; 202nn32, 34; 203nn36, 37; 216–217; 220; 222–224; 226; 231; 278–279; 281–284; 284n18; 286; 291; 298n28; 306–307; 310; 317–318; 327–329; 331; 334; 337; 342; 355; 361–364; 368
stranger, 12, 91, 183, 239, 241n13, 262, 268n6, 269, 271n10, 272, 276, 287–288, 299, 323–326, 334–335, 355, 367
σῶμα, 292–298, 293n20, 298n28, 305, 305n34

SUBJECT INDEX   393

time and events, 80n49, 88, 217,
  219, 249–264, 274–276, 309,
  312, 319–323, 334, 342, 363,
  366
virtues, 12, 189, 246, 266, 269,
  313, 334–335, 338
wives, 160, 223–224, 231, 242,
  253–254, 278–279, 282–283,
  288–289, 296–297, 305, 307,
  317, 327, 330–331, 334, 337,
  368
women, 223–224, 231, 242,
  253–254, 263, 278, 281–282,
  288–289, 296–297, 305, 307,
  317, 330–331, 334–335, 338,
  368
the "Fitting"
  in Aristotelian metaphor model,
    See Aristotle and "the fitting"
    in metaphor
  in ethics, 120, 229
Four Senses of Scripture, 45–47
  See also Aquinas; Medieval
    semantics
Frames
  and analogy versus metaphor,
    102–105, 112
  and conventions, 65, 90, 102, 104,
    202, 204, 221, 304–305, 338,
    342, 355
  conceptual and semantic,
    defined, 64–65, 196n21
  examples, 64–65, 86–87, 103, 201,
    211–212, 225, 241–243, 280–
    286, 300, 360–361, 362–363,
    368–369
  knowledge, 65, 103, 270–275,
    280–284, 363–364
  and mental spaces, 66, 86, 94,
    102, 104, 104n107
  properties in, 65, 103, 270–275,
    280–284, 363
  relations, 65, 103, 270–275, 280–
    284, 362
  and schema semantics, 64–65,
    65n16
  slots, 65, 103, 203, 211, 270–271,

    273–275, 280–286, 305, 359–
    362
  social-cultural factors, 63–65,
    202–204, 225–226, 228, 241–
    242, 273–274, 280–284, 286,
    290–291, 305, 306, 312–314,
    338–340, 342
  words as triggers for, 65, 184, 190,
    203n35, 241
  See also Blending

Gap, xviii, 2, 3, 5, 30, 37, 39–41, 103,
  121–127, 140, 148–150, 155–160,
  167, 346, 349, 353
  See also Lessing's Ditch; Two
    Worlds Model
Generic space, See Blending
Gestalt structures, 76, 237
God
  doctrine of essences and language
    for, 19n16, 28, 30–31, 38–44,
    48, 308, 348
  and human imagination, 11, 16,
    19n16, 30–31, 33, 34, 36, 40,
    43, 348, 351
  metaphors for, 44, 61, 88, 92,
    195, 198, 200, 203, 212, 215,
    219, 220, 222, 226–229, 231,
    262, 269, 278, 284–286, 289–
    294, 295, 302, 312–317, 324,
    327–329, 337
Great Chain of Being, 222–231, 279,
  341
  in 1 Peter, 176, 222–231, 274–275,
    279, 309, 318–319, 324, 326,
    330, 335, 341–342
  and macrocosm and microcosm,
    176, 230
  and moral authority, 222–231, 279
  reading process, 176, 227, 279
  in 21st century, 176, 227–228,
    228n50

Hays, Richard, 127–158
  analogical imagination, 129, 131,
    156
  analogy versus metaphor, 130–132

analytical model and methods, 128, 132–133, 139–142, 144, 146, 150, 152, 153
definitions of metaphor, 129–132, 138, 148
focal images, 136–137, 140, 142–146, 142n86, 151n107, 152
hermeneutics as "metaphor-making" process, 131, 147, 148
"key" metaphors, 136, 141–142, 145, 149, 153
Lessing's Ditch, 127, 133–135, 140, 146–150, 155, 156–158
modes of ethical appeal to Scripture, 150–151
morality as obedience, 136, 138–139, 144, 151, 153–154
"new community", 139, 144, 144n93
"read and apply" method, 153
"ruling" metaphors, 138
"single synoptic" model, 141–148, 152, 153
See also Analogical imagination
Hesed, 200–201, 201n30, 208
Historicism, 110, 114, 126–129, 156–159, 177, 320, 346
Hobbes, Thomas, 48–50, 52, 54
Aristotelian definition of metaphor, 49
and the literal-truth paradigm, 49–50, 54
on metaphor and reason, 49, 52
Household, *See* 1 Peter, household

Idiomatic metaphors, 88–90; 88nn64, 66; 283n17
Image
cognitive definitions of, 62n10, 72–75, 72n31
conventional, 72, 74, 88–90
evoked in reading, 89–90
inference structure of, 78, 79
neural, 55n92, 74n35, 75n38, 170n8

See also Image metaphor; Image schema
Image metaphor, 72–75, 72n31, 137
conventional, 74–75, 90
distinguished from conceptual metaphor, 72, 74, 231
examples in 1 Peter, 73–76, 285
See also Image; Image schema
Image schema, 75–77; 235n5
examples in 1 Peter, 76–77, 231, 235, 237, 241, 242n14, 243, 277, 291, 297–298, 299, 308, 365–367
inference structure of, 78, 79, 347, 350–352, 357
See also Container schemas; Image; Image metaphor; Metaphor; Two Worlds
"In" Christ Schema, *See* 1 Peter, "In Christ" image schema
Inference
and analogy, 101–102, 123
body-based, 79, 81, 258
in conceptual blending, 93, 213, 233
constraints on, 279, 297, 353
inconsistent, 57, 297
metaphorical mapping, 57, 60n5, 69, 78, 80n47, 81, 97, 102, 155, 186, 186n3, 193, 196–197, 205, 211, 221, 258, 272n10, 275, 297, 356, 358
mistakes in, 208, 272n10, 297
neural mechanisms, 80n47
patterns, 57, 60n5, 69, 81, 95, 97, 102, 123, 155, 181, 186, 186n3, 193, 196–197, 211, 221, 258, 275, 339, 353, 354, 356
in reading, 181, 208, 213, 266, 297, 339, 353, 356
structure, 79–81, 258
See also Entailments
Input space, *See* Blending, Input space; Generic space
Interaction theory, 99; 131n64
See also Bi-directionality; Metaphor, directionality

SUBJECT INDEX   395

Interdisciplinarity
  in Scripture and ethics
    approaches, 3n4, 12, 158–161,
    344–345
Invariance principle, 78–79, 106n111
"It's all analogy" theory, 100, 105,
  119, 124
"It's all metaphor" position, 54, 99

Judgment, *See* 1 Peter, judgment in

Kant, Immanuel, 50–52, 112, 349
  on metaphor and imagination
    in moral deliberation, 1, 48,
    50–51
Kelsey, David, 109
  "single synoptic" model, 141–142,
    141n84, 153–154

Landmark
  characters as, 239, 242n16, 247
  in conceptual space, 239, 242–
    243, 242n16, 247
Lessing's Ditch, 103, 121, 121n43,
  133, 345
  See also Gap; Two Worlds Model
Literal-figurative split
  Aquinas, 43–48
  Aristotle, 23, 24, 26, 43
  Augustine, 31–37, 33nn43, 46
  and biblical hermeneutics, 6, 12,
    32, 33–36, 33n43, 45–48, 114,
    202–205, 208, 217, 223–224,
    240n12, 272n10, 283–284,
    317
  cognitive views on, 50; 50nn84,
    85; 52; 79; 79n46; 95; 96–97;
    101, 101n94; 102n95; 105;
    125n51; 199n28; 234; 251
  Enlightenment versions, 49–52
  Hobbes, 49–50, 54
  Kant, 50–52
  Nietzsche, 52
  Spohn on, 114, 125
Literal meaning theory, *See* Literal
  truth paradigm; Literal-figurative
  split

Literal truth paradigm, 49–51;
  50nn84, 85; 52; 54; 79n46; 95;
  96–97; 101–102; 199n28; 357–358
  See also Literal-figurative split

Mapping
  alternative, 77, 85–86, 89, 92,
    149, 187, 190n13, 197n25,
    217–218, 233, 275, 285, 299
  analogy, 100, 102, 104, 131
  blends, 85–87, 92
  conceptual, xvii, 68, 72, 74, 78,
    80, 87, 91, 118, 232, 258, 343,
    353
  constraints on, 215, 217, 232, 327
  conventional, 80, 89–91, 102, 104,
    130, 215, 217, 232, 286, 327
  co-orientation, 246n17
  cross-domain, 68–71, 80n47, 81,
    130–131, 149–150, 210–211, 215,
    218, 273, 285, 299
  directionality, 70, 71, 95, 98–99,
    130
  as hermeneutical model, 149
  image metaphors, 72–75, 74n36,
    78, 89
  image schema, 74n36, 75–76, 299
  inferential, 81, 155, 233, 274, 353
  metaphors, xvii, 68–76, 78, 80,
    81, 89–90, 102, 118–120, 130–
    131, 136–137, 139, 145, 149,
    155, 190n13, 210–211, 215, 217,
    218, 232, 233, 246n17, 258, 273,
    286, 299, 327, 343, 353
  metonymy, 91, 286
  mistakes in, 218, 343
  multiple, 85, 119, 327
  and naming metaphors, 70, 150
  neural image, 74n35, 80n47
  primary metaphors, 81, 299
  in reading process, 155, 308, 327,
    343, 353
  schema, 65, 74n36
  See also Entailments
Meaning
  constraints on, 26, 46, 64, 77–78,
    80n51, 85, 88, 92–93, 125, 157–

159, 181, 188, 215–216, 229, 232, 233, 238, 262, 276, 279, 319, 327, 339, 340, 343, 345, 347, 349
  disembodied, 349
  emergent, 85n61, 86–87, 237
  range of, 205, 207, 221n44, 276, 279, 298n28, 345
  See also Literal meaning theory
Medieval semantics, 13, 28–29, 37–43, 39n63, 45–48
  See also Four Senses of Scripture
Megablends, See Blending
Mental spaces, 66
  and analogy, 100, 102, 105, 112
  cultural, 92–93
  defined, 66, 66n17
  and frames, 102
  and image schemas, 235n5
  input and generic spaces, 85–86
  and metaphor, 107, 112, 123
  and reading, 94–95, 172, 213, 343, 347–348, 351–354
  and rhetoric, 272n11
  and ritual, 112n7
  unconscious, 123
  See also Blending
Metamoral
  concepts, 6, 185, 307–308, 309–311, 335, 340, 348, 350, 351
  defined, 193, 229n55
  metaphors, 185–232, 229, 229n55, 264, 307–308, 309–311, 335, 336, 350, 351
Metaphor, xvii, 59–61, 68, 72n31
  asymmetric, 56; 66n19, 69n27 See also Metaphor, similarity in
  bi-directionality, See Mapping, directionality
  for church, 91; 135; 139; 142; 144; 149; 216–217; 225–227; 239; 248; 266–269; 268nn4, 6; 273–274; 285–288; 292; 298n28; 300; 318; 324–325; 327; 331; 355; 365; 367–368
  clusters, 6, 55, 130, 136, 138, 139–140, 142, 143, 144, 226, 232,

233, 248, 269, 272n11, 274, 295, 324
complex metaphors, 78n44, 82n54, 84–87, 183n38, 192, 207, 208, 213, 225, 228, 243, 247, 249, 255, 262, 267, 276, 285, 298, 309, 319, 352; See also Blending
conceptual, xvii, 5–7, 14n2, 20, 42n66, 51n87, 55, 60, 68–70, 72–75, 80, 83–84, 89, 106–107, 112
container, See Container
metaphor 'controlling', 12, 98, 153, 183n38, 268n4, 272n11, 338
conventional, 34, 52, 55–56, 60n5, 61, 63–64, 65, 71, 72, 74–75, 77, 80, 84, 88–91, 93, 95–99, 102, 102n95, 107, 112, 119n38, 121, 123, 129–130, 138, 148–149, 169, 184, 193, 216, 224, -225, 245, 247, 291, 300, 304–306, 327, 333, 339, 342, 358
coordinated, 246–248, 246n17, 263, 327, 365
cross-domain mapping, See Mapping, cross-domain
dead-metaphor hypothesis, 56, 88, 88n64, 90, 95, 98, 102n95, 359
defined, xvii, 59–61, 68, 72n31
directionality, See Mapping, directionality
entailments, See Entailments
entrenchment, See Entrenchment
everyday, 4, 12, 22–23, 52, 56, 60, 81, 84, 96, 98, 190, 197, 358
evidence for systematic conceptual, 60n5
experiential grounding, See Experience
expression, See Metaphorical expression
figurative "feel", 104, 125, 125n51, 179n30, 181, 339

SUBJECT INDEX 397

"fitting" 120, 229, 282; *See also* Aristotle, "the fitting"
grounding, *See* Experience
idiomatic metaphor, 88–90; 88nn64, 66; 283n17
image metaphor, 72–76, 72n31, 90, 137, 231, 285
inferences, *See* Inference
mapping, *See* Mapping
names of, 70
notation, 70
novel extensions, 56, 60n5, 77–78, 77n42, 88n64, 89, 102n95, 104–105, 104n107, 125, 190, 213, 285, 358
one-sided, 66n19
ontological correspondences, 28, 38–41, 47, 57, 69, 96, 272n11
ordinary, 4, 12, 22–23, 34, 52, 56, 60, 81, 84, 96, 98, 190, 193, 197, 358
poetic metaphor, xvii, 2, 14–23, 15n4, 27, 36, 44, 52–54, 56, 73, 97, 356, 358
  primary, *See* Primary metaphor
  root metaphor, 140, 268n4
ruling metaphor, 138
semantic change, 57, 60n5
similarity in, xvii, 21–26, 33–34, 33n46, 37, 41, 44, 48, 56–57, 62, 65, 69, 69n27, 80n51, 99, 106, 129, 138, 148, 357
social grounding, *See* Experience
source domain, *See* Domain
spatial, 246–248, 246n17, 252–257, 256n8, 264, 277, 295, 332, 365–366
stock, 56, 77, 89–90, 104, 121, 193, 239, 302–303, 342
structured, xvii; 6; 57; 60–64; 65n16; 66; 66n19; 68–69; 72; 72n32; 74–76; 78–81; 85n61; 86–87; 92; 95; 97; 99; 104n107; 105–107; 125; 148; 154; 169; 170n8; 178; 182; 189–191; 191nn21, 22; 197; 204; 214; 222; 226; 229; 231; 233; 237; 249; 253; 258; 259n16; 261–264; 272n11; 291; 308; 323; 349–350; 352; 354; 357; 366
systematic, xvii, 2, 6, 60, 60n5, 61, 68, 69, 79–80, 92, 96–98, 107, 119n38, 130, 137, 154–155, 169, 182, 186, 188, 191–192, 195, 199, 202, 205, 214, 222, 229, 233
target domain, *See* Domain
ubiquitous, 4, 23, 34, 52, 56, 60, 61, 62, 84, 96, 98, 130, 190, 341
unconscious, xvii, 55n92, 62, 63, 80, 82–83, 82n55, 98, 123, 171, 196n21, 227, 229, 304, 326, 345, 350
unidirectional, *See* Mapping, directionality
Metaphorical expression, 12, 32–33, 52, 55, 56, 57, 60, 66, 68–69, 71, 77, 79, 82, 84, 88–90, 95, 99, 107, 125, 125n51, 130, 136, 137, 139, 170, 186, 189–191
  distinguished from metaphorical concept, 60, 66, 68, 77, 79, 82, 89, 99, 107, 130, 140, 143–144, 151, 186, 189–193, 197
  See also Literal-figurative split
Metonymy
  blended with metaphors, 261, 291, 295
  compared to metaphor, 90–91
  conceptual, 62n10, 66, 91, 91n71, 251, 286, 304
  definition of, 90–91, 251
  examples, 72n30; 78n44; 88n66; 91; 136–138; 149; 226; 239; 251; 259nn15, 16; 260; 284–287; 297nn24, 26; 319; 332; 365–369
  experiential grounding, 91
  naming, 259, 284, 285–286, 288, 297n26, 343
  systematic, 91
Mind
  and Aquinas, 40, 45n73
  and Aristotle, 23–25
  and Augustine, 31, 34–35, 36n57

cognitive models of, xvii; 62; 97; 100; 123; 165; 169–171; 170nn8, 9; 173; 173n17; 294; 332
embodied, xvii, 170n9, 173, 297–298, 305, 332
and Platonic models, 15; 19nn13, 14, 16; 305
and *psyche*—ψυχή, 298, 299n31, 305, 332
and reading, 169–171, 227, 294, 297–298, 338, 341, 354
and traditional metaphor models, 57, 97, 97n80, 123
Misreading, 156, 165, 187, 206, 208, 304, 306, 328, 354
and Hays, 127, 144
and Spohn, 117
See also Reading
Moral accounting system, 185–232, 278, 311–313, 319, 359–364
and altruism, 196, 196n22, 199–201, 208, 220
and balance, 197–198, 197n23, 210–212, 230, 291, 311, 337, 342, 361, 369
and bookkeeping, 196–197; 197nn23, 25; 208–209; 211–212; 215–217; 291; 311; 337; 356; 359–364
and collective moral responsibility, 190, 198, 204, 211–212, 216–220, 268, 278–279, 290, 302, 307, 311–313, 336–337, 348
and debt slavery, 201–208, 203n35, 216–217; 220; 222; 331; 342; 361–364
and deliverance, 187, 203n35, 203–208, 256, 256n8, 312–314, 319, 342
and economic justice, 77n43, 88, 190n13, 301–302, 308, 329, 337
and financial accounting, 65, 190, 190n13, 192, 192n18, 193, 195, 197, 206–213, 217, 220, 222, 231, 313, 342, 359–364
and honor, 198–199, 201–202, 210–211, 213, 218–220, 224, 230–231, 234n2, 278–279, 289–291, 311–315, 324, 338, 342, 356, 364
and household frames, 198, 206, 210–214, 216–217, 219, 222, 225–227, 232, 279, 282, 290, 313–314, 327, 338, 342, 359–364
and judgment, 208–213, 217–220, 222, 234, 242, 250, 252, 259, 259n16, 263, 278, 311–314, 319, 322, 337, 359–364
and legal frames, 190n13, 208–213, 216–218, 232, 311, 313, 342, 359–364
as metamoral metaphor, 229, 335
and moral agency, 192, 205, 212, 215, 224, 307, 311–312, 336–337, 348, 360, 362, 364
and moral authority, 211–212, 222–223, 225–228, 231–232, 234, 279, 311–314, 317–319, 360, 362–363
and moral credit and moral debt, 185, 187, 189–190, 194–195, 197n25, 197–218, 220, 222, 231, 306, 312, 314–315, 317, 323, 331–332, 338, 342, 359–364
and moral duty, 198, 230, 313, 335
and moral guilt versus shame, 205, 211, 218, 313–314, 364
and moral logic, 65, 189, 196–198, 211, 221–222, 229n55, 335
primary metaphors in, 191n17
and ransom, 195, 200–208, 203n35, 222, 244, 246, 312, 314, 361, 364
and shame, 218, 311–314, 338
significance of, 185–187, 219–220, 311, 319, 342
and time concepts, 250, 252, 259, 259n16, 263, 319, 322, 342
and well-being, 188–189, 189n10, 191–192, 202, 202n32, 220–221,

221n44, 228, 230, 315, 335, 337, 350, 364, 367
  and well-being as wealth, 191–192, 220–221, 221n44, 315, 350, 364
Moral authority, 225–233
  in 1st century churches, 226–227, 336
  in 1st century households, 211–212, 226–227, 279
  in 1 Peter, 211, 212, 225–232, 317, 336
  and the Great Chain of Being, 222–223, 227–232
  legitimate, 234, 296, 307, 318
  literal and metaphorical authority, 212, 223–232, 296, 311, 318, 360–363
  of Scripture, 2–3, 5, 29, 35, 113, 122n44, 129n61, 132n66, 147, 158, 177, 180n32, 181, 311, 319, 331
  structures of, 217, 223, 307, 309, 311, 317, 331
  See also Authority
Moral bookkeeping schema, *See* Moral accounting
Moral debt, *See* Moral accounting
Moral discourse, xviii–xix, 1, 4–7, 4n7, 11–13, 21, 34, 37, 43, 76, 91, 94, 105–107, 119n38, 124–125, 127, 132, 139, 146–147, 150–152, 154, 158, 165–169, 181–182, 187–193, 198–199, 205, 219–223, 228–229, 231–232, 233, 247–248, 252, 254, 265–266, 279, 283, 292–294, 307, 309–311, 315, 322, 324, 332–333, 336, 338–339, 341, 347, 351–354
  defined, 4n7, 165–166, 169
  as dynamic event, 5, 7, 94, 158, 165–167, 170, 254, 309–310, 339, 347, 352–354
  and metaphor, 1, 4–5, 7, 11–12, 21, 32, 34, 76, 88, 90, 107, 119n38, 124, 132, 132n66, 139, 146–147, 152, 154, 166–167, 182, 187–188, 190–193, 198–199,

205, 213, 219, 221–222, 225, 229, 231–232, 234, 247–249, 261, 265–266, 272n10, 276, 279, 283, 292–294, 307, 309–311, 322, 324, 327, 332–333, 336, 338–339, 341, 347, 348, 351–354
  of New Testament, 5, 6, 11–12, 76, 77, 91, 132n66, 139, 146–147, 165–167, 169, 181, 187, 190–193, 198–199, 205, 211, 219, 221–223, 229, 231–232, 223–234, 247–249, 254, 265–266, 279, 283, 292–294, 307, 309–311, 315, 322, 324, 332–333, 338–339, 347, 353–354
  See also Discourse analysis; Reading
Moral essence, 17, 39, 42, 89, 228, 239, 242, 267, 296–297, 296n22, 297n23, 299, 299n31, 318, 330, 332, 367–369
Moral freedom metaphors, 145, 145n99, 202–205, 207, 270, 291, 314, 335, 337
Moral health metaphors, 79, 188, 303, 350, 356, 368, 370
Moral schemas, 71–72, 72n30; 196;196nn21, 22; 215; 222; 228; 307–308; 311; 319; 359

Neoplatonism, 14, 17–20, 29–31, 37–38, 42n66, 45, 53–54, 294, 305
  and Augustine, 17, 20, 29–31, 37–38, 53–54
  influence on Christian hermeneutics, 18, 29, 31, 45, 53–54, 305
  metaphor in, 18–20, 29, 31, 37, 42n66, 45, 54
  See also Augustine, Philo
Neuroscience, xvii, 75n38, 82n56, 170nn8, 9
  neurobiology, xvii, 170nn8, 9
Nietzsche, Friedrich, 48, 50–54
  metaphor as perceptive process, 52

400   SUBJECT INDEX

on truth and objectivism, 50n85,
    52–53, 52n89
Norms and normativity (ethical),
    1–2, 16, 35, 109, 113–114, 115n18,
    117, 124–128, 132, 132n66, 152,
    152n111, 154–158, 188, 309n2,
    335–337, 349

Objectivism
    and analogical imagination, 113,
        114
    cognitive views of, 56, 96–97,
        97n80, 105–106, 110, 159,
        350–351, 357
    in traditional metaphor models,
        39, 52, 56, 96–97, 102
    See also Embodiment; Experience

Paradigm
    Christ as, 111, 126–127, 323
    conceptual—cognitive, 97, 105,
        107, 156–157, 160, 343–344,
        349
    literal truth, 49–50, 50n85, 54, 97
    objectivist, 97, 105
    Two Worlds, 154, 156–157
    See also Hays, Richard;
        Objectivism; Spohn, William;
        Two Worlds Model
1 Peter, See First Peter
Plato, 14–21, 25–27, 26n30
    and analogy, 14n2
    and categories, 15, 17, 297
    and essence, 15, 17, 19, 19n13
    metaphor of the Divided Line,
        18, 19n13
    on politics and poetry, 16–17,
        16n6, 20–21
Platonism, See Neoplatonism
    Primary metaphor cloaked, 84,
        350
    and cultural models, 84, 224, 350
    defined, 77, 81–83, 82n55,
        189n9
    in 1 Peter, 191n17, 224, 230n57,
        245, 298, 299, 303, 369
    grounding in bodily experience,
        81–83, 82n54, 84, 99, 165,
        189n9, 298n28, 299, 303
    implications for hermeneutics,
        308, 338, 342–343, 350–352
    and metaphors for morality,
        82n56, 83, 189n9, 224, 303,
        342, 350
    and primary scenes, 59n3, 82,
        82n54, 99–100
    and social experience, 99, 165,
        224, 342
Prime analogate, See Analogy;
    Aquinas; Spohn
Prompts, See Words
Prototypes, See Categories

Reading
    actual reader, 171–173
    authorial audience, See First Peter,
        authorial audience
    cognitive models of, 92–94, 159,
        167–184
    communities and conventions,
        92–95, 152–154, 173–183,
        177n22, 221, 309–310, 315, 318,
        324, 339, 346, 351–353
    exemplary, 160, 165, 184, 321,
        345, 347, 353
    expert reader, 317, 353, 354, 355
    as mental space blending, 92–
        95, 169n7, 172, 181, 213, 339,
        347–348, 352, 353, 354
    misreading, 1–2, 156, 165, 187,
        206, 208, 304, 306, 328, 354
    NT reading as "reading other
        people's mail", 146–148, 157,
        179, 180
    ordinary reader, 224, 338, 341,
        354–355
    reader response theories, 172–173
    role of belief in, 4, 93–95, 176–178
    structures of expectation, 178
    See also Community
Reciprocation, See Moral Account-
    ing
Resident alien, See 1 Peter, resident
    alien

Retribution, *See* Moral Accounting
Root metaphor, 140, 268n4, *See also* Metaphor

Scenario
  and inferences, 93, 204, 233, 346, 354
  stock, 65, 71, 72n30, 88, 93, 202, 204–206, 211, 217, 219, 229, 257, 302, 334, 342, 346
Schema
  cultural elaboration and variation, 64–65, 205, 215, 266–267, 270, 275–276, 305, 311, 338, 346
  defined, 64–65, 196n21
  examples, 72n30; 196; 196nn21, 22; 222; 228; 257; 266–267; 269–271; 274–276; 302–305; 346; 359
  and frame semantics, 64–65, 65n16, 196, 196n21
  image schema, *See* Image schema
  logic and inferences, 65, 79, 196, 222, 270, 275, 279, 311, 346
  mapping, 65n16, 215
  as mental spaces, 66
  and reading, 205, 228, 311, 319, 338
  stock, 65, 257, 304
  See also Image schema; Moral schema; Two Worlds Model
Scripture and ethics
  as "problem", xviii, 1–3, 3n4, 109–110, 116, 121, 123, 126–128, 132–133, 146–149, 151, 152n111, 155–160, 310, 342, 344–348, 354
  "Read and apply" method, 117, 153, 156–157, 166
  Scripture as Exemplar model, xix, 5, 93, 126–127, 138, 158–161, 165–166, 167–168, 184, 234, 308, 309–310, 319, 321, 336, 338, 345, 347–348, 351, 353

Scripture As Source model, 1–3, 2n2, 29, 113, 122, 124, 126–127, 129n61, 132n66, 147, 154, 157–160, 177–178, 181, 309n2, 339, 345, 347–348, 350–351
  See also Exemplar; Lessing's Ditch; Two Worlds model
Semantic domain, *See* Domain
Source domain, *See* Domain, source and target
  See also Metaphor, Metonymy, Primary metaphor
Spatial metaphors, *See* Metaphor, spatial
Spohn, William, 110–127
  and analogical imagination, 115–118, 115n20, 119n38, 120–123, 126–127, 156–157
  and analogy, 115n20, 116–120, 122–125
  and approach to New Testament, 114–115, 156–157
  and Christian community as locus of discernment, 111, 113, 116–117, 121, 124, 126
  and "concrete universal", 111, 126
  and cultural-historical gap, 114, 121–122, 123–124, 156–159
  and ethics "of" Scripture versus role of Scripture "in" ethics, 110, 124, 126, 157
  and historical meaning as "prime analogate", 116–118, 124, 159
  and Jesus as paradigm, 111–112, 115, 120, 126–127
  and metaphor, 112, 115, 119–126, 119n38
  and "read and apply" method, 117, 156
  and Scripture as source of authority, 113, 122, 124, 126
  and Two Worlds model, 114, 116–117, 121–122, 156–157
Stranger, *See* 1 Peter, stranger

Target domain, *See* Domain, source and target
  See also Metaphor, Metonymy, Primary metaphor
Time and events, 217, 249–264, 312, 319–323, 333–334, 342, 361, 363, 366
  conceptual grounding, 80n49, 249–264, 342
  Greek time vocabulary, 250, 253–256, 256n8
  metaphors and schemas, 88, 217, 251–258, 274–275, 319–323, 363, 366
  metonymy, 250–251; 259–261; 259nn15, 16; 262; 366
Trigger, *See* Words
Two Worlds Model or Schema, 5; 102–103; 103n102; 114; 116–117; 121–122; 140; 147; 149; 154–158; 160; 342; 345–346
  See also Analogy; Compression; Gap; Lessing's Ditch

Universals, 16, 80, 82–84, 82n55, 123, 127, 150, 171, 349–350
  'concrete universal', 111, 126

ethical, 1, 3, 35, 51, 83–84, 150, 349–350
foundations, 349–350

Virtues
  classical, 11–13; 15; 16; 16nn6, 7; 54; 246, 269, 335
  in 1 Peter, 12, 246, 266, 269, 313, 334–335, 338
  and metaphor, 11–13, 15n5, 16n7, 54, 189, 246, 266, 269, 334–335
  in Scripture, 139, 158, 313, 334

Well-being and morality, 188–189, 189n10, 191–192, 202, 202n32, 220–221, 221n44, 228, 230, 315, 335, 337, 350, 364, 367
Words
  medieval semantic model of, 28, 31–37, 31n37, 39–47
  as prompts or triggers for conceptual mapping, 63–65; 72; 74; 74n35; 76; 78; 85–86; 88; 137; 167; 169n7; 170nn7, 8; 203; 206; 209–210; 218; 221n44; 231; 235–236; 239–241; 243; 247; 256; 271n9; 277; 280; 285; 286; 293–294; 301–302; 314; 346

www.ingramcontent.com/pod-product-compliance
Lightning Source LLC
Chambersburg PA
CBHW021351290426
44108CB00010B/192